A MATTER OF OBSCENITY

A Matter of Obscenity

THE POLITICS OF CENSORSHIP IN MODERN ENGLAND

Christopher Hilliard

PRINCETON UNIVERSITY PRESS

PRINCETON & OXFORD

Published by Princeton University Press
41 William Street, Princeton, New Jersey 08540
6 Oxford Street, Woodstock, Oxfordshire OX20 1TR

press.princeton.edu

All Rights Reserved
ISBN 978-0-691-19798-2
ISBN (e-book) 978-0-691-22611-8
Library of Congress Control Number: 2021934950

British Library Cataloging-in-Publication Data is available

Editorial: Ben Tate and Josh Drake
Production Editorial: Kathleen Cioffi
Jacket Design: Lauren Smith
Production: Danielle Amatucci
Publicity: Alyssa Sanford and Amy Stewart

This book has been composed in Miller

Printed on acid-free paper. ∞

Printed in the United Kingdom

10 9 8 7 6 5 4 3 2 1

CONTENTS

A MATTER OF OBSCENITY

Introduction

MERVYN GRIFFITH-JONES'S QUESTION in the *Lady Chatterley's Lover* trial is the most famous self-inflicted wound in English legal history. Prosecuting Penguin Books for publishing D. H. Lawrence's novel three decades after the author's death, Griffith-Jones asked the jury how they would feel having the novel lying around at home: "Is it a book that you would even wish your wife or your servants to read?" Griffith-Jones was used to cutting an intimidating figure in court. He had prosecuted Nazis at Nuremburg. But when he asked this question jurors laughed.[1] Griffith-Jones had talked past the three women in the jury box, and by 1960 very few British families employed live-in servants—certainly not the retail and manual workers on the jury.[2] It was a moment whose significance was clear to those who had secured one of the sought-after places in the gallery.[3] An American writer turned to the English novelist next to him and said: "This is going to be the upper-middle-class English version of our Tennessee Monkey Trial."[4]

Griffith-Jones certainly was out of touch, but his argument would have been familiar to anyone who followed obscenity trials. Griffith-Jones repeatedly drew the court's attention to the low price of the paperback edition of *Lady Chatterley's Lover*. He made it clear that a paperback that working-class people could afford was an altogether different proposition from an expensive hardcover for scholars or collectors.[5] This distinction—"O.K. in vellum and not O.K. in paper," as one contemporary summarized it before the trial—had a long pedigree.[6] Publishers knew the score. In the late nineteenth century daring French novels appeared in deluxe editions to show that the publishers were not actively courting working-class readers. This is an instance of what Ian Hunter, David Saunders, and Dugald

Williamson have called "variable obscenity," the idea that a book's acceptability depends on who is reading it as well as the book itself.[7]

English obscenity law bore the imprint of Victorian debates about literacy and citizenship. The leading case on obscenity dated from 1868, months after the Second Reform Act extended the franchise to working-class men who met certain conditions. When Victorian intellectuals considered the implications of mass literacy their thoughts often strayed to the issue of suffrage. The question of how wisely working men used their literacy intertwined with the question of how responsible they would be as voters. One observer called literacy "the literary franchise," playing with the idea that the ability to read and write was itself part of being a full citizen.[8] Successive attempts to widen the electoral franchise wrestled with the question of what level of rent or income tax liability could serve as a proxy for the self-mastery required for the vote. Judges and prosecutors dealing with offensive books made analogous calculations. Obscenity law took income or wealth as an indicator of the responsibility a reader would need in order to avoid being corrupted by sexually frank books. Titles that might be tolerated in expensive limited editions risked confiscation if they were published in mass-market formats easily available to readers supposed to have weaker defenses than middle-class men. Officials, all of them men, worried about female readers too, but while price could divide readers on class lines, there was no equivalent device for keeping a book out of the hands of women while leaving it available to men. Keeping bad books away from women could only be the responsibility of the steady male head of a household. That patriarchal duty carried over from private life to jury service. Jurors' wives and teenage daughters were often invoked in obscenity proceedings as people the law was supposed to protect. While the democratizing currents of the 1920s and 1930s made it dangerous for politicians to utter bald class judgments, and while slurs on women's mental and moral capacity later became risky too, the law remained a safe space for these attitudes for much longer. Griffith-Jones was not simply a throwback; his question was a glaring example of the way the timeframes of cultural change are not always in sync.

The prosecutor's misjudgment created an opportunity to challenge these assumptions and the defense seized it. "The whole attitude is one which Penguin Books was formed to fight against," the defense counsel, Gerald Gardiner, declared, continuing, "This attitude that it is all right to publish a special edition at five or ten guineas, so that people who are less well off cannot read what other people do. Is not everybody, whether they are in effect earning £10 a week or £20 a week, equally interested in the society in which we live?"[9] The jury acquitted the publishers, whose case was helped greatly by the Obscene Publications Act passed the previous year. The new law enabled defendants to argue that, though it was explicit or offensive, a book had literary merit and publication was for the public good. Gardiner called a procession of literary critics and other eminences to testify about the value of Lawrence's novel. At the same time as he asked the jury to endorse freedom of expression he asked them to defer to experts. The Obscene Publications Act of 1959 was the result of years of lobbying by authors to carve out a protected space for literature. Erotica from Paris and comic books from across the Atlantic were entitled to no such protection. Freedom for what was deemed literature was premised on restrictions on porn and pulp.[10]

The *Lady Chatterley's Lover* trial's synthesis of democratization and deference unwound within a decade. By the end of the sixties, the law was under attack from a new cohort of morals campaigners. And the anticensorship forces were now less likely to accept the distinction between art that deserved protection and trash that didn't. There was a shift from anticensorship arguments based on the special status of literature, or the need to test opinions in a marketplace of ideas, to seeing the freedom to read and write as an end rather than a means. This change was part of a more general move away from deference and conformity—the elaboration, as the historians Deborah Cohen and Jon Lawrence have shown, of traditional norms of privacy into an expansive ethos of personal autonomy and choice.[11] The philosopher Bernard Williams, chairing a committee that reviewed censorship in the seventies, spoke of a society capable of supporting pluralism rather than consensus.[12]

People who wrote to the Williams Committee explaining how they felt about censorship extrapolated from conventions of neighborly conduct—if you "kept yourself to yourself," other people would let you be—to arrive at a homespun version of the liberal principle that consenting adults could do as they wished in private, as long as immorality was not on public display. Others cited John Stuart Mill's precept that people should be free provided their exercise of their freedom did not harm others. Many of those campaigning for personal freedoms in the sixties and seventies saw themselves as engaged in a struggle against the vestiges of Victorian morality, but this was also a struggle that pitted Victorian liberalism against supposedly Victorian morals. The gay-rights campaigners and porn magnates who quoted Mill to the Williams Committee were not necessarily Victorian liberals at heart: rather, the takeaway version of *On Liberty* was supple enough to articulate rights claims in a time of rapidly changing personal and cultural expectations.[13] If you wanted to engage with authority on its own terms, that is. Feminists tended not to invoke Mill; punks did not make submissions to official inquiries.[14]

Censorship has been an arena where ordinary people and officials alike wrestled with social change—from the growth of literacy and democracy to second-wave feminism and gay rights, multiculturalism, and the impact of the internet. For a long time English obscenity law reflected uncertainties about what could be said—and, crucially, how and to whom—in a changing society. This is as true of the 1860s as the 1960s. The law evolved—and didn't evolve—as modern literature and popular culture took shape. The subjects of cases and controversies included penny dreadfuls, unexpurgated classics, "sex-problem" novels, risqué postcards sold in seaside resorts, modernist fiction, comic books, gangster novels, handwritten erotica, pornographic playing cards, avant-garde plays, television documentaries, pornographic magazines, the underground press, 8 mm films, horror movies, sex education, videocassettes, and online pornography. Many of these cultural forms were imports, the products of an increasingly international culture industry. Obscenity law was, among other things, a membrane through which foreign influences were filtered.

⁂

Obscenity was the younger sibling of blasphemy and sedition. To understand these crimes we need to reach back briefly to the seventeenth and eighteenth centuries. During the Restoration, the Court of King's Bench hatched new crimes, "seditious libel" and "blasphemous libel," out of the old crime of libel in the familiar sense, defaming another person in writing.[15] In a country with an established church, blasphemy easily became sedition. A modern judge put it like this: "In the post-Restoration politics of 17th and 18th century England, Church and State were thought to stand or fall together. To cast doubt on the doctrines of the established church or to deny the truth of the Christian faith upon which it was founded was to attack the fabric of society itself; so blasphemous and seditious libel were criminal offences that went hand in hand."[16] In 1727, the Court of King's Bench recognized another kind of dangerous publication. In a sign of things to come, the case that invented the common law of obscenity, *R v. Curll*, involved nuns. A lot of libertine writing in the seventeenth and eighteenth centuries dealt with the imagined secrets of the convent. In an age when religious and political power intertwined, bawdy tended to be irreligious and tracts against religion often took the form of pornography.[17] Publishers such as Edmund Curll exploited the overlap. Curll was brought before the court for distributing an imagined dialogue between two nuns on sexual topics, translated from the French by one of his employees. He protested that *Venus in the Cloister, or, The Nun in her Smock* was "written in Imitation of the Style and Manner made use of by ERASMUS in his COL-LOQUIA, and with the same Design, to lay open the Abuses and Corruptions of the Church of Rome," though at the time as he was selling *Venus in the Cloister* Curll was also stocking *A Treatise on the Use of Flogging in Physical and Venereal Affairs*.[18]

The difficulty of separating the religious from the temporal cut both ways. Curll's counsel argued that morals were a matter for the ecclesiastical courts. The attorney general disagreed. "What I insist upon," declared Sir Philip Yorke, "is, that this is an offence at common law, as it tends to corrupt the morals of the King's subjects, and is against the peace of the King. Peace includes good order and government, and that peace may be broken in many instances without . . . actual force." He elaborated: "As to morality. Destroying that is destroying the peace of the Government, for government is no more than publick order, which is morality." "The peace," which the authorities were tasked with maintaining, was an almost mystical concept. If Yorke was unusually syllogistic, he was not alone in thinking that the peace could be breached without disorder in the streets. The Chief Justice, Lord Raymond, agreed, but his fellow judges were not so sure. Mr. Justice Fortescue stated: "I own this is a great offence, but I know of no law by which we can punish it." Another judge thought immoral writings were punishable only if they led directly to an actual breach of the peace, and the fourth member of the bench thought that Curll's actions should be "punishable at common law, as an offence against the peace, in tending to weaken the bonds of civil society, virtue, and morality," but said consideration of the question should be put off to another day.[19] Curll remained in prison for a time, was released, and then brought back before the court after publishing another book, whereupon the charge relating to *Venus in the Cloister* was revisited. In the meantime, King George II had removed Fortescue from the Court of King's Bench and replaced him with Sir Francis Page, whose reputation as a hanging judge may not have been deserved but was rendered indelible by Pope, Fielding, and Dr Johnson.[20] This time the court "gave it as their unanimous opinion, that this was a temporal offence."[21] Curll was put in the pillory.

The Court of King's Bench thus recognized obscene books as a species of publication that could disturb the peace. The connection with public order, however abstruse, had a special ideological significance: as long as the offense of obscene libel was based on a publication's tendency to disturb public order, the judges claimed, "there was no occasion to talk of the Court's being censor morum [censor of morals] of the King's sub-jects."[22] Since the end of formal pre-publication censorship in the wake of the Glorious Revolution in 1688, lawyers and statesmen had congratulated themselves on the freedom of the press that flourished in Britain while kings and bishops on the Continent kept their censorship apparatuses. To reconcile the idea of a free press with the reality of imprisonment and fines for convicted blasphemers and pornographers, jurists had to argue that the various kinds of libel were offenses against public order: words and beliefs in themselves were not being punished. As Sir William Blackstone wrote in his *Commentaries on the Laws of England* (1765–1770):

> The liberty of the press . . . consists in laying no *previous* restraints upon publications, and not in freedom from censure for criminal matter when published. Every freeman has an undoubted right to lay what sentiments he pleases before the public: to forbid this, is to destroy the freedom of the press: but if he publishes what is improper, mischievous, or illegal, he must take the consequence of his own temer-ity. To subject the press to the restrictive power of a licenser, as was formerly done, both before and since the revolution, is to subject all freedom of sentiment to the prejudices of one man, and make him the arbitrary and infallible judge of all controverted points in learning, reli-gion, and government. But to punish (as the law does at present) any dangerous or offensive writings, which, when published, shall on a fair and impartial trial be adjudged of a pernicious tendency, is necessary for the preservation of peace and good order, of government and reli-gion, the only solid foundations of civil liberty.[23]

Allowing for changes in diction, this passage would have been at home in many pronouncements on censorship made in the first half of the twen-tieth century. "You are not sitting as a board of censors," judges would intone to juries before they decided whether to send a publisher to prison. Censorship connoted an institution more than a practice. Britons spoke of "a censorship" or "the censorship"; not until after World War II did it become common to use the word as an abstract noun without an article. The claim that only "prior restraint" counted as real censorship was also common in the United States before the thirties. No less a figure than Oli-ver Wendell Holmes, Jr., endorsed the idea that freedom of expression—and the First Amendment's protection of it—ruled out prior restraint but permitted post-publication sanctions. So did at least one civil liberties organization.[24] It was different elsewhere in the common-law world. Set-tler colonies such as Australia and New Zealand, with their enthusiasm for state intervention, set up censorship boards.[25] British reformers periodically considered Australian and New Zealand solutions as models, but always rejected them.

From the middle of the nineteenth century, the common-law crime of obscene libel was complemented by legislation. The Obscene Publications Act of 1857 gave courts the power to order offensive publications destroyed. The legislation was introduced in response to lobbying by anti-vice campaigners, who wanted the authorities to be able to clear offensive matter off the market without having to go through a costly and time-consuming jury trial first. It is often said that this person or that person was charged under the 1857 act, but no one ever was. If someone was tried for obscenity, they were tried for common-law obscene libel. Court proceedings under the 1857 act were applications for destruction orders, which publishers and retailers, but not authors, could contest. If they failed to persuade the court to keep the books from the incinerator, they did not incur a fine or go to prison: they just lost their wares. Given how many careful scholars get this wrong, it is worth repeating: no one was ever charged under the Obscene Publications Act of 1857.

The fact that a magistrate in one town found a book obscene and ordered it destroyed did not oblige a court in another town to follow suit. The Paris edition of Vladimir Nabokov's *Lolita* lived a dangerous itinerant existence in Britain for several years in the fifties, condemned by benches in some towns and circulating unchallenged elsewhere. Nevertheless, for an established British publisher with capital to lose and directors to answer to, a court order usually meant the withdrawal of the book. It was never strictly true to say that a book was "banned" in Britain. Customs and Excise could ban the import of a book or film: James Joyce's *Ulysses* was the subject of an import ban, and so, fifty years later, was the pornographic movie *Deep Throat*. Customs' writ stopped at the dock or the airport, however. It was not illegal to own a copy of *Ulysses* or *Deep Throat*. If you tried to sell your copy, though, it could be confiscated, and if you tried to send it through the mail you might be charged under the Post Office Act. But again, there was some truth to assertions that Britain did not have "a censorship" in the sense that ancien régime France or modern Australia did.

At least not for print. Play scripts had to be approved by the lord chamberlain before a performance could be licensed. Movies were subject to cuts or outright bans by the British Board of Film Censors (BBFC), an industry body to which municipal governments in effect delegated their cinema-licensing powers.[26] Both theater and film censorship were the subjects of persistent grumbling but roused no seismic controversy until the second half of the twentieth century. The revolution in British drama in the fifties and sixties led to a renewed push for the abolition of the lord chamberlain's powers, which was achieved in 1968; violent movies, avant-garde films from Italy and France, and changes in cinema-going habits put tremendous pressure on the British Board of Film Censors in the seventies. Concerns about horror and pornography invading the home by video-cassette in the following decade unexpectedly shored up its position, with the board assuming responsibility for a new classification system.

The theater censors vetted scripts, so they were able to demand changes to scenes instead of rejecting a play entirely. With British-made films, the censors negotiated with the filmmakers over the script; John Trevelyan, secretary of the BBFC in the fifties and sixties, liked to see himself as a partner in the artistic enterprise.[27] In recent years historians and literary critics have written extraordinary books tracking the thinking of censors in communist East Germany and apartheid South Africa as they worked to shape a literature consonant with the ideal society they were trying to create and defend.[28] There can be no direct equivalent for Britain, as print censorship was post-publication. Nevertheless, officials and lawyers read and thought about and discussed books with each other. They read texts trying to gauge how other people, jurors included, would read them; they considered how words and images affected people. In obscenity trials, the text itself was usually the only evidence the prosecution submitted, so counsel had to model a type of reading that would lead to a conviction. Their way of reading was reminiscent of the "plain man" style that literary journalists used against Joyce, Virginia Woolf, and T. S. Eliot.[29] Rather than take censors seriously as readers and thinkers, most accounts of censorship in Britain treat them as amusingly preposterous monsters. It has to be said that prosecuting counsel, civil servants, and politicians provide plenty of material for that approach. But it badly underestimates the censors. It makes it impossible to see why they were able to wield the power they did. We also should not let the follies of Mervyn Griffith-Jones and other double-barreled bullies obscure the self-deceptions of those on the other side.

{⸻◦W◦⸻}

All through the nineteenth and twentieth centuries, state action on public morals had no obvious center, and the most powerful politicians and officials were seldom able or eager to take charge. (The main exception was the 1920s, when the Home Office and the director of public prosecutions made a concerted assault on modernism and the culture the First World War had unleashed.) There were few unambiguous worldly rewards for either liberalizing the law *or* enforcing it: where public morals were concerned it was impossible to please all of the people all of the time.[30] Multiple government agencies had a stake in obscenity regulation—the Home Office, the director of public prosecutions, Customs and Excise, the Post Office, the Metropolitan Police, the attorney general, occasionally the lord chancellor, later on the minister for the arts too. Provincial police forces and magistrates' benches could diverge from those in London. Because the system had so many moving parts, changing the law proved difficult, and the authorities often found themselves backed into legal proceedings by other officials or by vigilantes.

Activists played an outsized part in the politics of censorship. In the early twentieth century antivice groups embraced the opportunities for cooperation across borders provided by international accords on the traffic in obscene publications. Large numbers of women took part. In contrast, the anticensorship cause was male-dominated, and made efforts to change this only in the late sixties and seventies as it tried to compete with Mary Whitehouse's National Viewers' and Listeners' Association. Britain's most influential morals campaigner, Whitehouse had learned a lot from the new consumer rights activists.[31] She and her allies also began to practice another kind of political action appropriate to the new regulatory age: litigation against public bodies such as the commercial television regulator and the London County Council. In the process morals campaigners gave new life to laws that had been dormant or marginal. Whitehouse's prosecution of *Gay News* for eroticizing the Crucifixion revived the old crime of blasphemous libel, which lawyers had for decades thought was a dead letter. At multiple points over the nineteenth and twentieth centuries, English obscenity law was transformed when lawyers and litigants manipulated the rules of the game to turn the system in on itself and when legal reforms changed the relationship between censorship and other processes. Changes in procedure implemented before the *Lady Chatterley's Lover* trial, permitting expert witness testimony, allowed Penguin Books to bring the rhetorical energy of evolving ideas about culture and democracy into a system that had been sufficiently self-contained to to exclude them.

This is a book about how ideas twist across time—beneath the clear-cut date ranges in the chapter titles run longer and overlapping temporal arcs—and through different spheres of human activity. It shows how offensive publications crystallized questions of culture, freedom, and order for censors and their opponents, jurists, artists, and ordinary people. To do that we need to reconstruct the unostentatious thinking going on in the routines of policing and activism as well as the spectacular cases and set-piece debates.[32] That involves mixing archival research with the kinds of reading characteristic of literary criticism and intellectual history. Reading for patterns of argument and reference across a wide range of material makes it possible to see how the meaning of a maxim or a metaphor changed as it moved between a literary review and a courtroom or from a conversation in the street to a submission to the Home Office.[33] In this history the routine matters as well as the reflective, the lay as well as the learned.

Accordingly, the book draws extensively on a wide range of archives. Saying everything really is the secret of being boring, though, and for detail about some books (like *Fanny Hill*) and some genres (such as birth control literature), the reader will have to go elsewhere.[34] The book looks sideways at broadcasting and the theater, not at all at music, and pays more detailed attention to film censorship at key points (the 1910s and 1920s and the 1970s and 1980s). It ventures into the history of sedition and blasphemy as well as obscenity.[35] It does not deal with political censorship and government secrecy, which raise quite different questions.[36] It merely glances at the two world wars, which were boom times for political (and postal) censorship but much less eventful in the history of obscenity law than the two postwar periods were.[37] And while the larger questions concern the United Kingdom as a whole, and although the coverage of the postwar period touches on the Edinburgh scene and some Scottish cases, the variations in legal systems across the union mean that this book is largely about England.[38]

The eight chapters span the period from 1857 to 1979, from the first Obscene Publications Act to the Williams Report; the Conclusion surveys developments since 1979. The first four chapters trace the persistence of the Victorian twinning of censorship and citizenship through the democratic and artistic experiments of the first half of the twentieth century, and on to the challenge to the culture of conformism, paternalism, and deference mounted in the *Lady Chatterley's Lover* trial. The second half of the book traces the shift towards a more pluralist culture from the sixties onwards. Censorship controversies did more than simply register these changes. Penguin Books called its trial "probably the most thorough and expensive seminar on Lawrence's work ever given."[39] Subsequent obscenity trials likewise turned into public "seminars" interrogating cultural change; and the Williams Committee's call for submissions prompted people to express their feelings about freedom and license or work out what they thought by scribbling essays at their kitchen tables. In modern Britain censorship has both inhibited speech and made people talk.

CHAPTER ONE

Obscenity, Literacy, and the Franchise

1857–1918

FOR THE VICTORIANS, censorship talk blurred into citizenship talk. Obscenity law took shape as Britain debated the extension of the franchise and as mass literacy changed expectations about politics and culture. That said, the proliferation of cheap periodicals that spurred Parliament to enact a new law against obscene publications was not so much a function of an upsurge in popular literacy—which had been increasing steadily over the course of the nineteenth century—so much as changes in urban life and commerce.[1] By the time of the 1851 census, half the British population lived in towns and cities. The concentration of people in towns and cities made it hard to ignore displays of immorality, and it made plebeian cultural life more visible to middle-class observers.[2] Urbanization created a hitherto unknown public of working-class readers, and it made their reading more conspicuous.

"The unknown public" was Wilkie Collins's phrase. Writing in 1858 in Charles Dickens's weekly *Household Words*, Collins described his rambles through "the second and third rate neighbourhoods" of London and the penny fiction papers he started to notice everywhere, "in fruit-shops, in oyster-shops, in lolly-pop shops." These crudely written publications catered to a massive, unfathomable readership. Collins was conjuring with the idea of Britain as divided into two nations, the rich and the poor—or, in this case, "the customers at the eminent publishing-houses, the members of book-clubs and circulating libraries, and the purchasers and borrowers of newspapers and reviews" and the people who read romance and adventure stories in penny journals bought from confectioners.[3] Collins wrote as a curious and worldly author, anticipating a time when the unknown public would become a known market for novelists like himself. In the decades to come, other commentators would repeat his gambit, buying a selection of penny papers and using their contents to generalize about popular sensibilities. These critics asked different questions from Collins. Did the appetite for sports news prevent working-class readers becoming informed citizens? Did high-society romances seduce them into an unconscious conservatism? Did the achievement of mass literacy open the way to moral corruption?[4]

Lord Campbell's Act

For the better part of a century the twin pillars of English obscenity law were the Obscene Publications Act of 1857 and the judgment in the case of *R v. Hicklin* a decade later. The 1857 act was largely the work of Lord Campbell and delivered a solution that antivice campaigners had been calling for.

Prosecutions for obscene libel were uncommon for a long time after the 1727 *Curll* decision. Most of the few trials were the result of private prosecutions, as gentlemen took it upon themselves to enforce the king's peace. As the evangelical movement grew in strength towards the end of the eighteenth century, however, prosecutions for obscene libel increased.[5] Some of these proceedings were instituted by the Proclamation Society, which was founded by the most famous evangelical of all, William Wilberforce.[6] By the beginning of the nineteenth century, the Proclamation Society's mission passed to the larger Society for the Suppression of Vice. Reflecting its origins during the Revolutionary and Napoleonic Wars, the Vice Society (as it became known) was a patriotic conservative movement, exercised by vice as a force of social disorder, and not simply an evangelical body.[7] In its first decade, the society concerned itself with a full suite of vices, including gambling, animal cruelty, and the use of false weights and measures, but after a crisis in its internal organization—and after the end of the Napoleonic Wars—the society regrouped and narrowed its focus to blasphemy and obscenity.[8] The Vice Society pressed charges against an average of three traders in obscene publications each year and nearly always managed to secure convictions. Even if the society had had the money to prosecute every pornographer it identified, it still could not have taken all their stock off the market. When a dealer in erotica was convicted of obscene libel, the publications described in the indictment were forfeited, but the rest of the trader's stock was safe.[9] Some operators were willing to treat imprisonment a cost of doing business. The secretary of the society, Henry Prichard, explained in 1837: "When a person is convicted, he hands over, perhaps, an immense stock of books and prints, and snuff-boxes, and things of that description; he hands them over to others engaged in the trade, or else some person continues his trade at his shop for him. In some cases it has been known that the wife and a shopman have continued the trade the whole time that the dealer has been in prison under the sentence of the Court of King's Bench."[10] What was needed, Prichard suggested, was the power to seize indecent publications independent of a conviction for obscene libel or an offense against the Vagrancy Act, which regulated "public displays," including shop windows.[11] Prichard got his way in 1857, when Lord Campbell abruptly took up the cause.

Campbell was a Whig politician and the Lord Chief Justice. He juggled court hearings with parliamentary debates. He had a good record as a law reformer. Both the Libel Act of 1843, which made truth a defense in criminal libel cases, and the Fatal Accidents Act of 1846, which authorized wrongful-death suits by relatives, were known as "Lord Campbell's Act."[12] By the end of 1857, there would be a third piece of legislation so nicknamed: the Obscene Publications Act. On a Saturday in May that year, Campbell presided over the trials of two men prosecuted by the Vice Society for publishing or "uttering" obscene libels.[13] William Dugdale and William Strange were serial defendants. Both were also veterans of the "radical underworld" in the aftermath of the Napoleonic Wars. A spy's report in 1818 described Dugdale as "a very active incendiary of Profligate and Deistical principles."[14] Strange had been one of the leaders of the "unstamped press" of the 1830s (so called because it evaded the stamp duty, one of the "taxes on knowledge" the state imposed to inhibit radical and working-class newspapers).[15] The two men were part of a cohort of London bookseller-publishers who evolved from radicals and infidels into more straightforward pornographers.[16] Strange's case alerted Campbell to the true scale of the traffic in pornography.[17]

Unlike Dugdale, who dealt in pricey books, Strange was selling weekly papers such as *Paul Pry* for a penny. Paul Pry was one of British culture's personifications of intrusive curiosity, like Peeping Tom, or, later, Nosey Parker. Beginning as a stage character in the 1820s, he lent his name to many Victorian papers.[18] The Paul Pry of the paper Strange sold was on a mission to investigate vice in London. The paper carried notes on brothels and the women who worked in them, together with gossip and reports on scandals—titillation posing not very convincingly as moral exposé. The item that the Vice Society chose as the object of the indictment described the Right Honourable Filthy Lucre's drunken seduction of one of his female servants.[19] As Lynda Nead observes, what is striking about *Paul Pry* and other targets of obscenity policing at this time is their "low-level smuttiness." Nead writes: "These are not the most explicit sexual representations from the period, but are examples drawn from the borderline of Victorian commercial culture; where sensation shades into sex and where the distinction between acceptability and unacceptability must be made most emphatically."[20]

Two days after the trial, Campbell took to his feet in the House of Lords to announce that as a result of the trial "he had learned with horror and alarm that a sale of poison more deadly than prussic acid, strichnine, or arsenic—the sale of obscene publications and indecent books—was openly going on." This melodramatic flourish did not come out of nowhere: the government was preparing to introduce a bill regulating the sale of actual poisons, and Campbell used that as a pretext for raising the subject of obscene publications. Alluding to the difference between Dugdale's case and Strange's, Campbell went on: "It was not alone indecent books of a high price, which was a sort of check, that were sold, but periodical papers of the most licentious and disgusting description were coming out week by week, and sold to any person who asked for them, and in any numbers."[21] No prominent author expressed concern that the bill might apply to publications other than penny papers. Many of those following the debate on the Obscene Publications Bill accepted Campbell's assurances that serious literature, including the sexually frank classical texts that were part of the cultural patrimony of educated men, would not be caught in the new law's net.[22] But the legislation outlasted its author, and in time the Obscene Publications Act would be deployed against bawdy classics and avant-garde literature.

The act empowered magistrates to issue warrants enabling the police to search premises, breaking in if necessary, for "any Obscene Books, Papers, Writings, Prints, Pictures, Drawings, or other Representations" after hearing a complaint made under oath.[23] The magistrate or justices had to be satisfied that the material in the complaint was comparable to the kinds of books or prints that would support an indictment for obscene libel. Once the search was executed, the police would bring the confiscated material before the magistrate, who would issue a summons calling the owner of the house or shop that had been searched to come before the bench and argue why the papers or pictures should not be destroyed. If, after hearing the owner's arguments, the magistrate was satisfied that the material was obscene *and* that the owner was selling it for commercial gain, the magistrate would issue a destruction order. These provisions were modeled on the Betting Act of 1853, which authorized the police to search suspected betting offices and seize racing lists and cards.[24]

The new legislation thus delivered the powers that the Vice Society had long sought; Campbell had worked with its leaders in drafting it.[25] It is important to emphasize what the act did *not* do. It did not establish any new offenses. Statutes seldom did. In the nineteenth century, it was accepted that the criminal law was largely the responsibility of the judges, not of Parliament.[26] Codification projects went nowhere near as far in England as they did in other common-law jurisdictions, including Britain's colonies.[27] The Obscene Publications Act's "destruction orders" were proceedings *in rem*—that is, they involved the objects rather than their owners or handlers.[28] A hawker whose stock of pornographic postcards was seized and destroyed was not personally charged with a criminal offense. In order to punish the hawker with a fine or imprisonment, a prosecutor still needed to bring an indictment for obscene libel. To justify a destruction order, the material was supposed to be bad enough to justify an indictment for obscene libel, but destruction orders were conceived as a quicker, cheaper, and more effective alternative to obscene libel prosecutions. Lord Campbell's decision to hitch the legislation to the common-law offense in this way meant that the Obscene Publications Act did not have to define obscenity: Parliament left that to the judges and the evolving common law. English law arrived at a lasting definition of obscenity in an appeal against a destruction order a decade later.

The Hicklin *Case*

The destruction order in *R v. Hicklin* concerned a pamphlet entitled *The Confessional Unmasked*—a reunion of anti-Catholic propaganda and obscenity. The pamphlet consisted of extracts from writings by Catholic authorities, in Latin with facing English translations, advising priests how to handle challenging issues that came up in confession. Half-way through, the advice turned from casuistry to questions about sex—for instance, whether it was a mortal or a venial sin for a married couple to have intercourse in "an unnatural position . . . viz., sitting, standing, lying on the side, or from behind, after the manner of cattle," and so on.[29] *The Confessional Unmasked* fitted into recognizable genres of pornographic prose—the exposé of the sexual secrets of Catholic life, the moralizing tract providing immoral entertainment. It had been circulating for decades; the first publisher of *The Confessional Unmasked* was none other than William Strange.[30] Yet the distributors of the edition that was the subject of *Hicklin* were not simply using antipopery as a pretext for publishing pornography. The Protestant Electoral Union was an organization dedicated to protesting against Catholic heresies and campaigning for the election of MPs who would resist the spending of public money "for Romish purposes."[31] Its edition of *The Confessional Unmasked* was peppered with extraneous footnotes criticizing Saint Patrick's College, Maynooth, a seminary which had, controversially, been the recipient of a government grant since 1845.[32] The Protestant Electoral Union printed 25,000 copies of *The Confessional Unmasked* in 1865 and another 15,000 in 1867.[33]

The sale of *The Confessional Unmasked* in Wolverhampton in 1867 led to the *Hicklin* case. Wolverhampton in the 1860s was fertile ground for antipopery. The Catholic Church was opening more schools for the children of the town's growing Irish population, and in the following decade Conservative candidates' support for state subsidies to church schools, Catholic as well as Anglican, helped drive a wedge between working-class voters and the Liberal Party.[34] In February of 1867 the town erupted into rioting incited by a lecture tour by William Murphy, a former Catholic turned anti-Catholic firebrand. Special constables proved insufficient to contain the violence the night of the first lecture, and the remaining lectures went ahead only after the mayor of Wolverhampton succeeded in summoning reinforcements from the county police and two cavalry troops from Birmingham and Coventry. Murphy's fifth and final lecture was entitled: "Maynooth and Its Teaching and The Confessional Unmasked. Shewing the depravity of the PRIESTHOOD and the Immorality of the CONFESSIONAL."[35] Shortly after Murphy left for the Potteries and Birmingham, the site of even greater mayhem, the Wolverhampton watch committee sought an order under the Obscene Publications Act against Henry Scott, a metal broker and a member of the Protestant Electoral Union who was selling copies of *The Confessional Unmasked*. Two Wolverhampton justices of the peace granted a warrant and Scott's house was searched. The police took away 252 copies of *The Confessional Unmasked*. A meeting of the ratepayers censured the watch committee for taking action against Scott (which the borough would have to pay for). The sentiment of the meeting was that Scott was seeking to educate rather than make a profit, and that it was inconsistent for the borough to protect Murphy at great expense while punishing Scott for selling the text that was the subject of Murphy's last lecture. The watch committee pressed on regardless, and the justices of the peace ordered the confiscated copies of *The Confessional Unmasked* to be destroyed.[36]

Scott appealed. His case was heard at the May 1867 quarter sessions presided over by the recorder of Wolverhampton, a part-time judge. The recorder, John Powell, evidently accepted that the second half of the pamphlet was obscene, but found—like the ratepayers who assembled at Wolverhampton's Agricultural Hall—that Scott's object was political, not commercial.[37] For the Obscene Publications Act's machinery to be set in train, the offending items had to be distributed "for Purposes of Gain."[38] And British thinking about freedom of the press placed a special premium on political expression. In *On Liberty* (1859), John Stuart Mill argued that the press had to be free so that opinions could be tested and majority positions confronted by minority ones.[39] As the political theorist Gregory Conti has shown, there were other arguments in favor of free expression that were not canonized in *On Liberty*. What Conti calls the "pacific theory" held that the open exchange of views was more conducive to social peace than suppressing them to the point where they boiled over.[40] It is impossible to know what thinkers, if any, guided Powell, but he clearly thought that an indecent book with a political purpose called for special treatment. The recorder decided that the destruction order against *The Confessional Unmasked* should be quashed, but he referred the matter to the Court of Queen's Bench for confirmation of the point of law.

That court heard the case in the Easter term of 1868.[41] Benjamin Hicklin was one of the Wolverhampton justices of the peace. *R v. Hicklin* bears his name, and not that of Henry Scott, the person who had most at stake, because the case was an appeal against a destruction order, not a conviction.[42] Scott was represented in court by Samuel Kydd, who was advancing a cause in tune with his own history. Before he was called to the bar in his late forties, Kydd had been a Chartist, much in demand as a lecturer and secretary of the radical democratic movement's executive during the drama of 1849. He then mutated into a "Tory radical" like his new mentor, Richard Oastler.[43] Presenting Scott's case, Kydd invoked John Milton, a hero in the free speech pantheon. Kydd quoted a judge in an earlier cause to the effect that while *Paradise Lost* had many doubtful bits, "the clear object and effect was . . . to promote the reverence . . . of our religion."[44] Kydd tried to make a comparable argument for Scott and *The Confessional Unmasked*: the obscenities in it needed to be seen in the context of Scott's larger, earnest purpose. Skeptical, the judges interrupted Kydd repeatedly.[45] Representing the Wolverhampton justices of the peace was a local barrister with a more orthodox background. Alexander Staveley Hill read law at Oxford and within a year of the case he would be Conservative MP for Coventry, beginning a thirty-two-year career in the House of Commons.[46] Hill quickly drew a distinction between motive and intention: "If intention is necessary, it must be inferred that the appellant intended the natural consequences of his act, which the recorder finds are to prejudice good morals, and the motive of such a publication cannot justify it."[47]

English law held that to be criminally responsible, a defendant had to have had criminal intentions or culpable recklessness—*mens rea* (a guilty mind). But English law also assumed that intentions could be inferred from actions. (This was one of the reasons it was deemed unnecessary for defendants to be able to testify on their own behalf, a right established as late as 1898.)[48] Lord Ellenborough, in a case heard in 1814, went so far as to call it a "universal principle" that people intend the natural consequences of their actions.[49] Mr. Justice Blackburn quoted Ellenborough in his opinion in *Hicklin*.[50] Chief Justice Cockburn, who delivered the lead judgment, remarked: "I think that if there be an infraction of the law the intention to break the law must be inferred, and the criminal character of the publication is not affected or qualified by there being some ulterior object in view (which is the immediate and primary object of the parties) of a different and of an honest character."[51] This perfectly orthodox understanding of the legal position made it irrelevant to weigh the claims of freedom against the claims of order. Cockburn went on to make his influential pronouncement on obscenity: "I think the test of obscenity is this, whether the tendency of the matter charged as obscenity is to deprave and corrupt those whose minds are open to such immoral influences, and into whose hands a publication of this sort may fall."[52] Poised on the edge of meaninglessness, Cockburn's dictum nevertheless had the cadences of authority. It rapidly became the leading statement on obscenity in courts throughout the British Empire.[53]

Its longevity can seem surprising, for this is a definition that does not do much defining. A spiral of disputes ensued about what the verbs "deprave" and "corrupt meant. The jurist Fitzjames Stephen, always searching for ways to sharpen the rational edge of English law, thought it would be better to define obscenity in terms of social standards rather than raise issues about morality and causation.[54] (Answering the question "Does this engraving offend respectable sensibilities?" involved fewer contortions of reasoning than "Is someone likely to be depraved by the sight of this engraving?") The less striking terms in Cockburn's definition were actually the crucial ones. The unassuming word tendency, which was used in the law of seditious libel too, had a particular legal meaning.[55] To decide whether a pamphlet was obscene or seditious, a court was not obliged to refer to anything other than the pamphlet itself. A prosecutor did not need to show that any reader had been moved to insurrection by a seditious pamphlet, or had their morals compromised by a salacious story. And the requisite criminal intention could, following Lord Ellenborough's "universal principle," be reliably inferred from the words or images at issue. The *Hicklin* judgment thus set a low bar for a destruction order or an obscene libel indictment.[56] By disposing of matters of intention and consequences, Cockburn in effect made the criterion for obscenity whether justices, magistrates, and jurors thought that a publication before them was the kind of thing that could affect the morals of impressionable people.

Not every mind was equally susceptible to moral corruption. Whether a publication was marketed to those whose minds were open to immoral influences—whether it was likely to fall into their hands—had a bearing on whether it would be condemned under the Obscene Publications Act. This is what Mr. Justice Lush was getting at when he interrupted Kydd as the barrister rattled through a list of literary, scholarly, and artistic works that had not been suppressed under English obscenity law. Lush said the Dulwich Picture Gallery might display its *Sleeping Venus* (initially believed to be by Titian), but it did not follow "that photographs of it might be sold in the streets with impunity."[57] A gallery's clientele was middle-class; street vendors were down-market. Cockburn's judgment took what was implicit in Lush's interjection and pushed it further.

Indeed, Cockburn made his famous pronouncement about obscenity in the midst of his own rebuttal of Kydd's argument. It helps to retrace his reasoning:

> It is perfectly true, as has been pointed out by Mr. Kydd, that there are a great many publications of high repute in the literary productions of this country the tendency of which is immodest, and, if you please, immoral, and possibly there might have been subject-matter for indictment in many of the works which have been referred to. But it is not to be said, because there are in many standard and established works objectionable passages, that therefore the law is not as alleged on the part of this prosecution, namely, that obscene works are the subject-matter of indictment; and I think the test of obscenity is this, whether the tendency of the matter charged as obscenity is to deprave and corrupt those whose minds are open to such immoral influences, and into whose hands a publication of this sort may fall. Now, with regard to this

work, it is quite certain that it would suggest to the minds of the young of either sex, or even to persons of more advanced years, thoughts of a most impure and libidinous character.[58]

Yes, Cockburn is saying, there were obscenities in Chaucer and Byron that the law did not bother with: that doesn't matter: the test for obscenity is whether the material tends to deprave and corrupt those liable to be depraved and corrupted and who might get their hands on this. The semi-colon before the famous maxim about obscenity signals a tack in Cock-burn's logic. The low probability of vulnerable readers getting their hands on obscene material was what made Chaucer and Byron irrelevant to the fate of *The Confessional Unmasked*—just as the threat posed by a paint-ing in a gallery was less than the threat posed by an engraving of it for sale to anyone on the streets of London. Cockburn had heard that *The Confessional Unmasked* was being "sold at the corners of streets, and in all directions, and of course it falls into the hands of persons of all classes, young and old."[59]

Cockburn's chief concern was the moral safety of the young. But the idea that the context of publication and distribution was decisive, that a book's permissibility depended on whose hands it could fall into, would be routinely coupled to the assumptions about the limitations of working-class people's judgment and self-control.[60] *Hicklin* worked its way through the courts in the months either side of the Second Reform Act, which extended the franchise to nearly one million working-class men, doubling the electorate in England and Wales, and three years before the Education Act made elementary schooling practically compulsory. In the ensuing decades, Cockburn's test of obscenity became a vehicle for a com-plex of questions about popular literacy and the franchise as Victorian Britain wrestled with the advent of mass politics.

"The Literary Franchise"

When judges based decisions about a borderline book's acceptability on matters of price and distribution—how likely it was to fall into the hands of the masses, rather than circulating discreetly among gentlemen who could be trusted—they were engaging in the same kind of thinking that became commonplace in the debates surrounding the Second Reform Act (1867). As Britain debated the extension of the suffrage in the middle decades of the nineteenth century (and with periodic intensity thereafter up to the enfranchisement of young women in 1928), discussions of the franchise and other entitlements were marked by contrasts and exclusions: men weighed against women, financially secure workers contrasted with the improvident, metropolitan Britons compared with subject peoples in the colonies.[61] In the 1860s, the challenge for Parliament was how to enfranchise the working class without "swamping" the middle and upper classes in the House of Commons and hampering the constitution's capacity to balance the nation's several interests, which meant "a due and proper balance of the representation of the land, trade, commerce, and industry," as well as social classes.[62] The idea that "every class and every interest should have a voice in parliament" was by this time generally accepted, by Conservatives and Liberals alike.[63] Extending the vote to a selection of working-class men to represent their whole class required MPs to draw a line somewhere, and all the proposed ways of drawing that line took an economic variable relating to income or property as a serviceable index of character and responsibility.[64]

With the unsuccessful reform bills they brought forward in 1860 and 1866, the Liberals took pains to spell out exactly how much the electorate would expand if working men paying such and such an annual rent on their homes were granted the vote.[65] Gladstone, the party's leader in the Commons in 1866, told the house: "A 6*l.* rental, calculated upon the most careful investigation, and making every allowance and deduction that ought to be made, would give 242,000 voters, whom I should take as all belonging to the working class, making a gross total of 428,000 persons, which would . . . give over the majority of town constituencies into the hands of the working class. We propose, therefore, to take the figure next above that—namely, 7*l.* clear annual value."[66] Clearly, this was a judgment about the consequences of reform rather than the character of potential voters. Most MPs were concerned chiefly with these consequences—with the size of the new electorate—but they needed the numbers to align with some rough social and moral perception about the men who would be enfranchised.[67] There was no argument for a £7 franchise that would not also justify a £6 or £5 franchise—or one even lower.[68] In the terms one Liberal used in an earlier round in this argument, paying a rent of £7 a year did not "coincide with any natural division of society."[69] "If the Bill falls, we fall," Gladstone had told the Cabinet, and after it was voted down the government resigned, passing the task of reform to the Conservatives.[70] As the historian Robert Saunders has shown, when Disraeli managed to get his reform bill passed the following year, it was because he had found a formula that *did* correspond to a "natural division of society." In other words, Disraeli's formula aligned with judgments about the relative "fitness" of different sections of the working class that were both clear and plausible to a majority of MPs.

The idea, which was not Disraeli's own and which had been floating around for several years, was to base the franchise in urban (borough) constituencies on rates (local property taxes) rather than rent. There were practical reasons for using rates as a guide, but the Small Tenements Rating Act of 1850 furnished a symbolic hook. Tenants whose houses' rating value was less than £6 a year paid their rates indirectly through the landlord, a practice called "compounding." Those whose houses' rating value was £6 or more paid their rates themselves, in person.[71] A man who paid his rates in person did not necessarily contribute more than a compounder, but he had to manage his own money. The distinction between personal ratepayers and compounders, was, supporters argued, that between the independent and the dependent. There was, as Saunders writes, "a seductive logic to claims of a moral distinction between compounders and personal ratepayers." It was politically appealing for its apparent finality. A man either paid rates personally or he didn't: this test was not subject to endless downward revision in the way Gladstone's £7 rental was. It was thus "a ledge on which to rest," Lord Carnarvon told Disraeli: a point beyond which there would not be further movement towards manhood suffrage.[72]

Gladstone, who was not troubled by the idea of future incremental additions to the electorate, failed to grasp the symbolic power of paying rates in person, and worried away at the details and arbitrariness of the distinction.[73] The most consequential of the technical elements proposed involved tenants opting out of compounding to pay their rates in person—if this was a test of character, compounders had to have a path towards becoming ratepayers. Disaggregating rates and rent proved so complicated that a Liberal backbencher proposed doing away with compounding and obliging every tenant to pay their rates in person. Disraeli accepted the amendment. Few MPs objected, though the change caused chaos in local taxation. The moral significance of paying rates in person prevailed over administrative tidiness. More importantly, it meant that MPs supported a reform bill that enfranchised far more working-class men than the rejected Liberal bill of the previous year would have. The ideal of the responsible householder swept away all the cautious calculations about the expanded electorate.[74]

So the Second Reform Act, Disraeli's "leap in the dark," enfranchised urban male householders. For most of the legislative process, a tax bracket had served as a proxy for the ideal of the responsible working man. Although it was a Conservative administration that had delivered franchise reform, the idea that there was a connection between the obligations imposed by the tax system and the rights and responsibilities that went with the franchise had deeper roots among Liberals and Radicals, and it was a common theme in reform agitation outside Parliament.[75] The Radical John Bright built a cross-class alliance for franchise reform by linking representation to taxation.[76] "I believe," Bright told the House of Commons in March 1867, "that the solid and ancient basis of the suffrage is that all persons who are rated to some tax . . . should be admitted to the franchise." As usual, a claim on behalf of one group entailed a distinction from the unworthy. Bright argued that the impoverished "residuum" should not be enfranchised, because they had "no independence whatsoever."[77] Other politicians pointed to the prudence and self-control manifest in institutions such as building societies and co-operatives as evidence of working-class men's "fitness" for the vote.[78] Everyday economic life was a space in which working-class men—like landowners, industrialists, and professional men—developed and demonstrated the implicitly and often explicitly masculine quality of "character" so central to Victorian Britain.[79] Formal education mattered less, at least before the "public schools"—the most exclusive independent boys' schools—emerged as character-factories of national significance later in the nineteenth century.[80] For Mill and other proponents of electoral reform, the franchise itself was a force for education.[81] Though Mill believed that "universal teaching must precede universal enfranchisement," he also thought that it was through "political discussion, and collective political action," that the manual worker with few other intellectual opportunities, "learns to feel for and with his fellow-citizens, and becomes consciously a member of a great community."[82]

Three years after the Second Reform Act, the Liberals introduced legislation to extend the provision of elementary schooling. W. E. Forster described his Education Bill as shoring up the constitution: "I am one of those who would not wait until the people were educated before I would trust them with political power . . . but now that we have given them political power we must not wait any longer to give them education." Yet this was not Forster's driving concern. He made this remark late in a lengthy speech, and very few participants in the protracted debate on the bill made a connection between education and the franchise.[83] (Similarly, Robert Lowe's oft-quoted remark during the debate on what ultimately became the Second Reform Act—"I believe it will be absolutely necessary that you should prevail on our future masters to learn their letters"—was an isolated remark. Lowe said it was a disgrace that no other speakers in the Commons debate had addressed the question of education.)[84] Forster's legislation was much less ambitious than the nation-building education laws of other European countries at this time. After all, it was extending education in a society that already had comparatively high levels of literacy, and it made no attempt to dislodge religious authority in favor of the national and the secular, as was the case in Third Republic France.[85] Forster's act provided for a national elementary education system by supplementing existing private and church-run schools, not by replacing them. Much of the debate in and out of Parliament concentrated on staples of Victorian political discussion: religious freedom and the established church; voluntarism, charity, and state compulsion; and funding and efficiency. And as the 1870 settlement was revisited by Liberal and Conservative governments in later decades, the main points of contention were the extent to which the religious education provided in elementary schools was non-denominational, and the competing claims of Nonconformist Protestants and the Church of England—not the potential of schools to produce sound citizens.[86] The older idea of education as a bulwark against disorder endured, but the advocates of public education were animated by the ideal of national progress rather than anxieties about the dangerous classes.[87]

While popular education was not part of the project of constitutional reform, there clearly were analogies between the two. Intellectuals who took an interest in working-class reading—a subject to which the restlessly omnivorous Victorian journals of opinion returned many times— often made connections with the franchise question or drew their guiding metaphors from it. Thus the spread of literacy amounted to an extension of "the literary franchise" and the late-nineteenth-century explosion of popular literature was an effect of the "democratic wave which was spread over all society."[88] At the turn of the twentieth century, John Garrett Leigh was appalled that so few working-class people kept abreast of political news ("The only daily paper which is at all widely read is the sporting daily") and were therefore "utterly unfitted to exercise their privilege of government." The "elementary equipment of reading" was "being utilized in a manner which almost makes us wish that the masses could not read." Leigh even mentioned the idea of a civic test for eligibility to vote: "If ever there was a time when a certificate suffrage was defensible it is the present, for the fact is undeniable that great persons in politics have an influence far outweighing the influence of the causes which they espouse." The fear expressed by some Liberals in 1867: that an ignorant electorate would yield to demagogues or defer to aristocratic authority, rather than practicing the strenuous judgment of the responsible citizen,[89] was reiterated by Leigh: "The men do not trouble . . . to understand political questions. It is sufficient for them that this or that leader thinks this or that."[90]

Leigh went further than most when he admitted he could imagine regretting that the masses could read at all, but other commentators also expressed disappointment at the world mass literacy had made. The underwhelming quality of working-class literacy was in part a consequence of the failure of the state and civil society to complement elementary education with further opportunities for learning.[91] For both sexes, the years between leaving school and "taking charge of a household" were the most important phase of life, wrote George R. Humphery: "It is at this time that the character is moulded."[92] (This time in a person's life would be a focus of concern in obscenity trials as well.) Middle-class commentators such as Humphery, as well as some working-class autodidacts, remarked that too many working people read merely for amusement and what would later be called "escapism."[93] Judgment as well as intellect was ill-served by penny papers. Humphery, who claimed authority from twenty years' involvement with "a library connected with a factory," wrote that the "'penny dreadful' trash . . . fills their heads with unattainable ideas." It distorted understandings of the world and their place in it.[94]

Working-class reading was, inevitably, a cause of concern for antivice campaigners. The increase in popular literacy, combined with the repeal of the taxes on newspapers and periodicals, had opened up a vast expanse of opportunities for purveyors of suspect literature. A Conservative-leaning newspaper editorialized in 1888: "Until what is called education had become nearly universal, the possibilities of harm which were latent in printed matter had not attracted public attention. The children of the lower classes read with difficulty, and did not read for amusement. That has all been changed. . . . We have now to face an agent of moral corruption, no longer confined to persons willing and ready to be corrupted, but obtruding itself on everybody."[95] This editorial was a response to Henry Vizetelly's conviction for obscene libel for publishing cheap translations of Emile Zola's novels. Vizetelly's two trials, in 1888 and 1889, encapsulate the way these Victorian ways of thinking about literacy, social class, and self-control governed obscenity law in practice.

The National Vigilance Association and the Vizetelly Trials

The Vizetelly trials were portentous in signaling that not just dirty ephemera but also novels by authors whom the monthly and quarterly reviews took seriously would be vulnerable to destruction orders. The old Vice Society had largely been true to Lord Campbell's word in not going after contemporary novels or classics. The antiobscenity crusaders of the

1880s made no such exceptions, targeting the publisher of an abridged but not expurgated version of Boccaccio's *Decameron* at the same time as they pursued Vizetelly.[96] The Vizetelly prosecutions were representative of a moment of powerful antivice activism in the later decades of the nineteenth century, a moment when the interests and organizational efforts of feminists, working-class radicals, and ministers and lay people from a span of Protestant denominations and the Salvation Army converged on certain issues. One of the great feminist causes had been the repeal of the Contagious Diseases Acts, which subjected suspected prostitutes in garrison and port towns to medical examinations to limit the spread of venereal disease. The Contagious Diseases Acts institutionalized the sexual double standard, invasively controlling women while treating men's sexuality as a fact of life whose negative consequences the state could manage. Clergymen could agree with feminists that the acts were an evil that had to be resisted, on the grounds that "the law of chastity is binding upon man as upon woman," and different elements of the "social purity" coalition were united in their efforts to curb child prostitution.[97] The alliance was contingent. In the 1870s, the feminist Josephine Butler and the Methodist lay leader Percy Bunting were partners in setting up the British, Continental and General Federation for the Abolition of Government Regulation of Prostitution; a decade later, Bunting had come to embody for Butler "some of the more objectionable features of the Nonconformist conscience—in particular, its surprising new confidence in law enforcement as a means of bringing the righteous community into existence."[98]

At this time, 1886, Bunting was chairman of the new National Vigilance Association (NVA), a successor to the ailing Society for the Suppression of Vice. The association's secretary, William Coote, was likewise a strong believer in the reforming powers of the criminal law. Coote was the driving force behind the NVA's campaign to curb the sale of indecent publications, recruiting retired police officers to gather intelligence and appearing regularly before the magistrates himself.[99] Coote was a working-class Londoner who had been born again. His determination and sense of his vocation enabled him to carve out a remarkable career as the NVA's chief organizer despite the objections of grandees who thought the secretary should be a gentleman who did not need a salary. Coote owed his chance to prove himself to the patronage of W. T. Stead, who paid him £4 a week to compensate for the loss of wages from his day job as a compositor.[100] Stead was editor of the *Pall Mall Gazette* and a hero of the movement against vice. His 1885 exposé of child prostitution helped pressure Parliament into raising the age of consent and introducing new restrictions on prostitution. "The Maiden Tribute of Modern Babylon," as Stead's series of articles was titled, was a prime example of the sensationalism and muckraking of what came to be called the New Journalism. Like *The Confessional Unmasked* and any number of subsequent exposés, "The Maiden Tribute" combined outrage and prurience. Stead's articles marshalled the cultural power of Victorian melodrama to shock the nation into moral awakening.[101] In the months after publication, Stead used his profile to help get the National Vigilance Association up and running.[102] As Stead's newspaper helped bring the NVA into existence, it and other periodicals became an engine for the association's campaign against "pernicious literature."

When the NVA member and Liberal MP Samuel Smith raised the subject of "the rapid spread of demoralizing literature in this country" in the House of Commons in 1888, he quoted a recent *Edinburgh Review* article on "The Literature of the Streets," and presented his own initiatives as in dialogue with those exploring the subject of popular reading in the great reviews. In turn, his speech in Parliament prompted an essay in another publication.[103] The real audience of a speech in the House of Commons, Smith wrote in his memoirs, was the newspaper readers who would learn of it the next day. Ideally, the weekly and monthly magazines would take it up, and the issue would return to Parliament after gathering force in the press.[104] Smith sought to pressure the police into enforcing the Obscene Publications Act. "The Act called Lord Campbell's Act, if vigorously worked, would do a great deal to suppress this class of literature; but it was not vigorously worked, it had been allowed to fall into disuse."[105] Smith called out Henry Vizetelly, whose publishing operation the *Pall Mall Gazette* had been needling for months.[106] Smith's speech in Parliament set in train a process that would see Vizetelly committed for trial for obscene libel before the end of the year. At first the authorities refused to act, so Smith and the NVA initiated a prosecution of their own. The attorney general then changed his mind and took over the case. The prosecution was conducted by the solicitor general, Sir Edward Clarke, assisted by the future Liberal Prime Minister H. H. Asquith.[107]

Born in 1820, Henry Vizetelly had followed his father into the engraving and printing business. After completing his apprenticeship, he had run his own journals, and was a veteran of the fight against the "taxes on knowledge," holding office in an organization that campaigned against the paper duty in the 1850s.[108] He spent time in Paris as correspondent for the *Illustrated London News*, reporting from the besieged city during the Franco-Prussian War. Returning to London, he established himself as a book publisher, commissioning translations of French novels and selling them directly to a mass market. "I . . . introduced to English readers hundreds of volumes translated from foreign authors whose writings until then had been sealed books to the multitude," Vizetelly wrote a few years afterwards.[109] He was less high-minded in his advertisements, which made it clear that he was offering readers something illicit.[110] Vizetelly was, then, another radical publisher and bookseller who had ridden the logic of capitalism and the logic of nineteenth-century British politics to the trade in salacious books.[111] All the same, Vizetelly's translations of Zola's *Nana, La Terre*, and *Pot-Bouille* were in fact slightly expurgated. The most offensive pages Vizetelly published, according to the jurors in his first trial, was a scene in *La Terre* where a bull is having difficulty mating with a cow until a farm laborer, Françoise, intervenes.[112] A literal translation of the French is: "She grasped the bull's member and straightened it. And when he was ready, his strength regathered, he penetrated deep with a single thrust."[113] Vizetelly's version merely says that Françoise "aided the animal in his efforts, and he, gathering up his strength, speedily accomplished his purpose."

As Katherine Mullin observes, "The NVA seemed keenest to police borderline cases" rather than the most explicit—the same course the NVA's predecessor had followed three decades earlier when Lord Campbell's Act was passed.[114] In its first few years, the NVA initiated proceedings against a newspaper that published spicy details of a divorce case and a barrow trader selling photographs of nude statues that had been exhibited in Parisian galleries. Contemporary French literature was itself borderline, in the judgment of Stead's *Pall Mall Gazette*: "It is sometimes difficult in these days to distinguish between high class French fiction and mere pornography."[115] The NVA was concerned about borderline readers, too. As the association's *Vigilance Record* explained, Vizetelly had brought the "immoral French novel" within reach of "lads at school and college," "city clerks," "shop girls" and "all the promiscuous multitude of unmarried or other readers who may buy cheap books."[116] Young men at vocational colleges were at that vulnerable stage of life George Humphery identified, that time of early adulthood when their character was being molded.[117] So, implicitly, were those multitudinous unmarried readers. Contemporaries found the "shop girl," a creature of Victorian consumerism, both culturally resonant and hard to place.[118] Clerks were models of precarious in-between-ness in British fiction.[119]

Vizetelly pleaded guilty, was fined, and undertook not to publish the three offending Zola novels or anything similar again. The NVA kept up the pressure on the authorities, though, and, failing to get the desired response, launched another private prosecution six months later against Vizetelly and three other publishers and booksellers. Again Vizetelly pleaded guilty. This time he served three months in prison for publishing other Zola novels and works by Guy de Maupassant and Paul Bourget. The NVA's counsel in the second trial explained that Vizetelly's crime was to make Zola's novels available to "the common market," by translating them and packaging them in affordable formats, instead of catering to "the select literary class."[120] There was no parallel effort to restrict access to the French originals.[121] The cultivation that entailed a command of French was indexed to social position, and the middle and upper classes could be counted on to exercise self-government as they read.[122] This trust evidently extended to women of these classes. The eminent monthly and quarterly reviews discussed Zola's novels calmly and at some length, and a good deal of this critical writing was by women.[123] Not long after the Vizetelly trial, another publisher issued translations of Zola's novels in expensive editions on hand-made paper. These editions were not retailed publicly but sold by subscription. They were thus not available to "the ordinary English public," the publisher reassured. These deluxe editions did not attract prosecution.[124]

The explorer and orientalist Richard Burton, who introduced British readers to the *Kama Sutra*, monitored Vizetelly's travails and clipped newspaper reports on the case.[125] When Burton published an unbowdlerized translation of the *Arabian Nights*, he sought advice from a lawyer and took the precaution of selling his translation by subscription, just as the publishers behind the Zola translations printed on hand-made paper did. To cover himself, Burton used the same words as Cockburn had in *Hicklin*, saying in the prospectus that his was "emphatically a book for men and students [of Islamic society]; and nothing could be more repugnant to the translator's feelings than the idea of these pages being placed in any other hands than the class for whose especial use it has been prepared." Although he took these precautions, Burton saw his translation of the *Arabian Nights* as "a declaration of war against the proponents of purity," a public endorsement of a freer sexual culture. That was why he put his own name to the book.[126] Burton's posthumous publications did not go out into the world so boldly. His widow approached William Coote and together they combed through Sir Richard's unpublished manuscripts deleting sentences to which Coote took exception.[127]

Samuel Smith was not convinced that immoral literature could circulate safely in expensive editions: the logic of the market meant that it would always be profitable to produce cheap versions for mass circulation.[128] All the same, in making judgments about whether a borderline book should be suppressed or not, judges and the police often treated its price and market as the determining factor. Age and gender were as important as social class, but class, insofar as it corresponded to disposable income, was the variable most useful to officials in making these decisions. High prices and limited editions could more or less place a volume out of the reach of working-class readers; it was much less feasible for the modern British state to ensure that women would not be exposed to a questionable book while keeping it available to men. There is a parallel with the disparity Paul Johnson has noted between the strict regulation of working-class financial institutions and personal indebtedness and the more forgiving regime of bankruptcy law and limited liability that governed middle-class finances after the 1860s. This "stark inequality," Johnson argues, "came to be justified by the alleged difference in the moral characteristics of the rich and the poor."[129] Financial regulation was statutory: the class bias was written in from the beginning. In the Vizetelly trials, by contrast, contemporary assessments of the respective "characteristics of the rich and the poor" were penciled into a legal maxim that, in Cockburn's hands, had been more concerned with youth and age. These assumptions became embedded in the law, governing the rules of thumb police officers and justices of the peace followed, even though they were never stated expressly in the legal digests they relied on.[130]

Library Censorship

Both Vizetelly's cheap editions and Burton's subscription-only *Arabian Nights* bypassed the dominant institutions of the Victorian book trade: the circulating libraries.[131] These were not public libraries but subscription services. The Victorian middle classes borrowed rather than bought new novels, and most publishers' decisions were geared towards the library market. With a family clientele, the libraries were very cautious about novels that might give offense.[132] When dealing with authors, publishers therefore had to anticipate any objections from the libraries. Many novelists accepted that some subjects were off-limits, or learned obliqueness, out of a sense of social responsibility. Others accepted these constraints as a cost of doing business, and some openly complained about "library censorship."[133]

Among the latter was George Moore. Much influenced by Zola, whom he met while living in Paris, Moore sometimes acted as an intermediary between Zola and Vizetelly. Moore's 1883 novel *A Modern Lover* was reviewed favorably, but Mudie's Circulating Library refused to carry it, supposedly because "two ladies in the country" wrote to Charles Mudie saying they disapproved of it.[134] Missing out on the library public was a disaster for Moore. Publishers issued novels in three volumes, which fitted the libraries' business model but made them discouragingly expensive for individual buyers: to publish a novel in three volumes was, in effect, to rule out retail sales.[135] Moore's next novel was published by Vizetelly in a cheap edition to circumvent, and defy, the circulating libraries. Moore published a polemic, "A New Censorship of Literature," in the *Pall Mall Gazette* in 1884. The "literary battle of our time," he wrote, "lies not between the romantic and realist schools of fiction, but for freedom from the illiterate censorship of a librarian." His only regret was "that a higher name than mine has not undertaken to wave the flag of Liberalism and to denounce and to break with a commercial arrangement that makes of the English novel a kind of advanced school-book, a sort of guide to marriage and the drawing-room."[136] One sign of the conventions' power was that among the readers and editors who advised Thomas Hardy to tone down his early novels were eminent Liberals and men who had gone through their own confrontations with Victorian norms.[137] Both descriptions fitted Leslie Stephen, who published Hardy in the *Cornhill Magazine*. Hardy's approach seems to have been to bide his time until he had the power to dictate his own terms, which he attempted to do, with partial success, with *Tess of the D'Urbervilles* between 1887 and 1891. *Tess* expanded the range of the acceptable, but the libraries retained their ability to set the moral tone of publishing into the early twentieth century.[138]

The six largest libraries banded together in 1909 to set up an overt censorship scheme after H. G. Wells's *Ann Veronica* and other "sex-problem novels" sparked a controversy that brought together the NVA and the *Spectator*.[139] This Circulating Libraries Association included Mudie's and the *Times* Book Club, whose subscribers tended to be solidly middle-class, and also companies that catered to the larger lower-middle-class market. The W. H. Smith and Boots chains operated libraries attached to their retail outlets—railway bookstalls and news agencies in Smith's case, chemists' shops in Boots."[140] They profited from the growing supply of cheaper books, a change Mudie's never adjusted to and the reason for its decline in the early decades of the twentieth century. The Circulating Libraries Association sorted books into three categories: A, circulated with no difficulty; B, not displayed on counters but supplied "on special application"; C, not supplied in any event.[141] *Ann Veronica* was placed in category C, along with several other novels featuring extramarital affairs and illegitimacy.[142]

Janet Hogarth, who resigned as librarian of the *Times* Book Club in response to the censorship scheme, alerted the press, and the Circulating Libraries Association backed down.[143] They then reactivated their censorship several years later, placing a novel by the bestselling author Hall Caine in category B, supplied on application. The Circulating Libraries Association assured the Society of Authors that in the preceding two years fewer than ten books had been proscribed or restricted. A representative of W. H. Smith declared: "The C.L.A. are not 'Censors'. A Censor is one who has power over others to prevent publication. The C.L.A. have no power to prevent publication."[144] In the face of continuing bad press, the libraries retreated again, but they did not dismantle their censorship system altogether.[145] Going beyond self-defense, the Circulating Libraries Association supplied the Headmasters' Conference, which represented independent schools, with lists of books suitable and unsuitable for school libraries. Later, at the request of W. H. Smith's librarian, the association forwarded these lists to the National Vigilance Association.[146]

Fear of the libraries also stopped publishers taking on books in the first place, or at least gave them an excuse. In 1912 William Heinemann wrote to D. H. Lawrence rejecting *Sons and Lovers* on account of its "want of reticence." "The tyranny of the Libraries," Heinemann said, "is such that a book far less outspoken would certainly be damned (and there is practically no market for fiction outside of them)."[147] Lawrence consented to extensive cuts to get the novel accepted by another publisher. With *The Rainbow*, in 1915, Lawrence managed to dodge many of the requests for changes that the publishers Methuen made at the proof stage, but the novel was not stocked by libraries and kept off the bookstalls. Reviewers said it was an outrage that an immoral book should circulate at a time when young men were dying for liberty.[148] The director of public prosecutions sought a destruction order under the Obscene Publications Act. The case was so enveloped by wartime feeling that an MP who asked a parliamentary question about the proceedings thought they had been instituted under the Defence of the Realm Act.[149] The magistrate at Bow Street granted the destruction order.[150] Lawrence was devastated. His book had been condemned and he had lost his livelihood.[151] "They were robbing me of my freedom," he said later.[152]

Increasingly, Lawrence and other writers who transgressed moral or formal conventions would look beyond established British publishers, to continental Europe and to heterodox small presses.[153] Censorship, actual and expected, governed the publishing history of modernism.[154] The censorship controversies of the beginning of the twentieth century pointed towards the future in another way as well. Taking a leaf out of the Circu-lating Libraries Association's book, the emerging film industry recognized the protective potential of self-regulation and set up the British Board of Film Censors. It is also possible that the library censorship scheme and the forced withdrawal of *The Rainbow* had consequences we will never know about. "People say, 'Few novels have been suppressed of late,'" the art critic Clive Bell remarked in his 1923 polemic *On British Freedom*. "How many have never been written?"[155]

CHAPTER TWO

The Censorship versus the Moderns

1918–1945

VICTORIAN OBSCENITY LAW was haunted by popular literacy and the extension of the franchise. The moment in the early twentieth century when offensive books became a subject of acute official concern was the struggle to stabilize British society at the end of the First World War. Strikes and rioting in England and Wales and revolt and repression in Ireland raised the alarming question of whether the violence the war had called forth could be contained.[1] Many of the men involved in this unrest now had the vote. The electorate trebled with the Representation of the People Act of 1918, adding to the existential fears of an outnumbered middle class.[2] This was a moment of seething class conflict and of apprehension about masculinity and femininity. The disruption of prewar assumptions about femininity by women's wartime labor, the extension of the vote to most women over thirty, and the spectacle of the stylish female consumer apparently liberated by the postwar dispensation was profoundly disturbing to many in positions of power (and a source of opportunity for others).[3] The reception of literary modernism in the 1920s was caught up in these more general cultural concerns.

The men chiefly responsible for the state's vigorous enforcement of obscenity law were also engaged in struggles against other forms of modern misrule, and modernist writing was seen as part of the broader pathology of post-war Britain. These men were assisted by campaigners connected with international networks dedicated to suppressing the traffic in obscene publications. They were resisted by liberals outside the government—and, cautiously, by some within government who began to have second thoughts—and by a coterie of dissident printers. Small presses calculatingly conformed to the principle of "variable obscenity," producing challenging work in limited editions issued "at a revolting price & printed in a disgustingly exquisite way" that kept them from falling into the hands of the poor, and at the same time tried to establish a new kind of publishing, free of the inhibitions of the mainstream.[4] The British film industry wanted *only* a mainstream, and set up its own censorship system to constrain and protect the exemplary modern art form.

The Post-War Men

Stanley Baldwin, the three-time Conservative prime minister who set the political tone of the twenties and thirties in Britain more than anyone else, spoke of those "hard-faced men who had done well out of the war."[5] There was also a cadre of men whose response to the challenges of coming out of the Great War—the conflict in Ireland, the industrial action and civil unrest of 1918/1919, the unraveling of the Lloyd George coalition government—saw them placed in positions of responsibility through the next decade. Three of them worked in concert against obscene publications in the twenties: Sir William Joynson-Hicks, Sir John Anderson, and Sir Archibald Bodkin.

Joynson-Hicks elicited derision from many contemporaries and posterity has found little reason to think differently.[6] He was, it is generally agreed, pompous, authoritarian, intolerant, and lacking in self-awareness. Born William Hicks in London 1865, he was an evangelical Anglican and total abstainer. He was a solicitor by profession, that is, a lawyer who advised clients and handled their affairs but did not appear in court himself. Hicks married Grace Joynson, the daughter of a Manchester industrialist. Hicks added Grace's surname to his own and got his entrée into Conservative politics through her father. Earlier morals campaigners in British politics (Samuel Smith, for instance) tended to be Liberals; since the late nineteenth century the Conservatives had indulged "the people's pleasures."[7] If Joynson-Hicks's temperance activism set him apart from many Conservative MPs, in other respects he was a caricature of a hardline Tory. During the First World War he advocated the use of Zeppelins to bomb German civilian populations indiscriminately. He supported the general responsible for the 1919 Amritsar massacre and urged a firm hand against Irish nationalists.

For much of his time in Parliament, Joynson-Hicks was a marginal figure. He secured ministerial office only after he thought his political career was effectively over. As one of the Conservative backbenchers working to undermine the Lloyd George coalition, he was a beneficiary of that government's fall in 1922. The new Conservative prime minister, Andrew Bonar Law, made him a parliamentary secretary. When the Conservatives returned to power after the short-lived first Labour government, Baldwin made Joynson-Hicks home secretary. Joynson-Hicks's grandiosity and hectoring were very different from his prime minister's manner. "Baldwin's aim," Philip Williamson has written, "was to invert the style and values which had long been expected from democratic politics—to deflate demagogy and establish a different, safer, demotic idiom. Power, strength, public spirit and truth were to be identified with restraint, humility, moderation, and common sense."[8] Yet the home secretary's crusades against nightclubs and obscene publications were consistent with Baldwin's efforts to reassert the nation's moral values and link the Conservative Party's defense of property and order with the protection of conventional social standards.[9] Joynson-Hicks believed fiercely that the law was "founded upon public morality." If morals deteriorated, civic order and national strength would follow.[10]

The administrative head of Joynson-Hicks's department was Sir John Anderson, another veteran of the crisis years at the end of the First World War. A year into the Anglo-Irish war, Anderson was tapped to be the highest-ranking civil servant at Dublin Castle. Much of the time he was effectively the head of the British government in Ireland. Unlike Joynson-Hicks, Anderson was not an enthusiast for martial law, and he worked hard to tame the violence and indiscipline of the British forces. In Dublin, Anderson established a reputation as a good manager of emergencies. Capable, cool, and forceful, he would go on to oversee the logistics of the government's response to the General Strike of 1926, and to serve as Governor of Bengal through the challenging years from 1931 to 1937. After his return from India Anderson was drafted into Parliament and served as home secretary for a year after the outbreak of the Second World War, thus earning the unusual distinction of having led the Home Office both as a civil servant and as secretary of state.[11] The suppression of indecent publications does not appear to have held the personal significance for Anderson that it did for Joynson-Hicks. He was a strong and decisive enforcer of the law, not a policy innovator or a department head working to subvert or moderate his minister.[12]

Sir Archibald Bodkin combined something like Anderson's diligence with Joynson-Hicks's moralism. Bodkin was director of public prosecutions (DPP) from 1920 to 1930. The post was established in 1879, part of a wider trend away from private prosecutions toward, but never arriving at, a state monopoly on instituting criminal proceedings. Most prosecutions were brought by local police forces and the DPP's office usually limited itself to cases of national significance. Bodkin interpreted national significance broadly. His commitment to the policing of public morals as well as his general mania for work explains the effort he put into obscenity cases. Another barrister who shared Bodkin's social conservatism and who also had a keen eye for the limitations of people more successful than himself remarked: "His two failings were that he could not delegate, and so tried to do all the work himself; and that, through prosecuting with hardly any relief and without any other interest, he gradually developed almost the mind of a super police inspector, until he forgot that methods which were necessary in war time were not justified in normal conditions."[13] Bodkin became DPP in large part thanks to the support of Lloyd George and his attorney general, Gordon Hewart, who had been impressed with Bodkin's work preparing war crimes indictments against German officers.[14] Since the Second World War, the DPP has operated at arm's length from the Home Office. Before that, it was perfectly legitimate for the Home Office to ask the DPP to initiate a prosecution, and Bodkin worked closely with Anderson.[15]

The Home Office was assisted in its efforts against indecent publications by allies in the press, especially the vigilant editor of the *Morning Post*. H. A. Gwynne was a true die-hard, implacably opposed to any measure of self-government for India and Ireland. The *Morning Post's* owner, Lady Bathurst, was active in Conservative politics and supported Gwynne's editorial adventures in the Unionist cause. Bathurst let Gwynne stay in the editor's chair despite his conviction under the Defence of the Realm Act—and putting the *Morning Post* at risk—for plotting a coup that would replace Lloyd George's government with one led by Field Marshal Sir William Robertson.[16] Both proprietor and editor were anti-Semites, a quality they shared with Joynson-Hicks, and in 1920 Gwynne helped legitimate the *Protocols of the Elders of Zion*. He published them in the *Morning Post* and used them as a weapon against Jewish critics of the paper's campaign to defend the Amritsar massacre.[17] Writing in 1921, the journalist Philip Gibbs described the newspaper that Gwynne and Bathurst made as one "published exclusively" for "the old type of John Bull Englishman": reactionary, authoritarian, and chauvinist.[18] Bathurst then sold the paper to a consortium led by the Duke of Northumberland, an anti-Bolshevik conspiracy-monger whose pamphlets the *Morning Post* had printed in previous years.[19] Gwynne stayed on as editor and continued to champion

Stanley Baldwin, a service that the prime minister acknowledged.[20] Symbolic of Gwynne's support for Baldwin's government was turning the *Morning Post*'s plant over to Winston Churchill to produce a government newspaper, the *British Gazette*, while publication of other newspapers was suspended during the 1926 General Strike.[21]

Class warriors rubbed shoulders with culture warriors. To many conservative critics, the formal experiments of new writing, painting, and music of this period were affronts to society as well as artistic travesties. More was at stake than literary taste and even public decorum.[22] The very reality of feeling and experience was under attack. Critics of contemporary culture as well as literature and art returned repeatedly to this theme. Picking over the case of Edith Thompson, whose 1922 trial (she was charged alongside her lover for the murder of her husband) made public her immersion in popular novels, which helped her reflect on her life and imagine new possibilities, the journalist James Douglas wrote that Thompson exhibited "a mania for self-analysis in copious epistles . . . that reeked of the theatre and the novel." "Nourished on melodramatic novels and melodramatic plays," she was "the creature and creation of a hectic and hysterical age that lives on films, headlines and humbug. . . . This is the world begotten by the Great War!"[23] The sexual frankness of some modernist novels was the main charge against them—like psychoanalysis, modernism was offensive in giving more emphasis to baser human drives than many contemporaries found acceptable—but formal experimentation, too, provoked disquiet. The authorities who had to judge whether to allow an artwork to circulate freely sometimes confused novelty of form with moral heterodoxy or assumed that the one followed the other. The incomprehensibility of Joyce's *Ulysses* as well as its manifest obscenity counted against it in the decisive British legal opinion on the novel.

From Ulysses *to* The Well of Loneliness

Sir Archibald Bodkin was asked for his opinion of *Ulysses* after a copy of the Paris edition published by Sylvia Beach of Shakespeare and Company was intercepted by a Customs officer at that scene of interwar intrigue, the Croydon aerodrome. Customs sought the Home Office's judgment about *Ulysses* and the Home Office sent the book to Bodkin.[24] He had heard of the novel months earlier and expected it would cross his desk at some stage. Receiving the copy seized by Customs, Bodkin read Molly Bloom's soliloquy and promptly reported:

As might be supposed, I have not had the time nor, I may add, the inclination to read through this book. I have, however, read pages 690 to 732. I am entirely unable to appreciate how those pages are relevant to the rest of the book or, indeed, what the book itself is about. I can discover no story, there is no introduction which might give a key to its purpose, and the pages above mentioned, written as they are as if composed by a more or less illiterate vulgar woman, form an entirely detached part of this production.

In Bodkin's opinion, the book went beyond "mere vulgarity or coarseness" and was full of "unmitigated filth and obscenity."[25]

Sidney Harris at the Home Office mulled over "whether we ought not to ask the Police to make discreet enquiry among booksellers in London as to whether the book is being obtained." He decided against it on the grounds that "a prosecution might only give the book further publicity."[26] The Home Office told Customs to seize any further copies brought into the United Kingdom.[27] At Folkestone in April of 1923 Customs officers seized 499 copies of the second Paris edition, published with the imprint of the Egotist Press, and burnt them.[28] The home secretary signed a warrant instructing postmasters to intercept packages reasonably believed to contain copies of *Ulysses* and send them to the General Post Office. The postal archives show that they managed to do this, identifying suspicious packages sent from Switzerland and, more impressively, from Ipswich.[29] The warrant was renewed every few years and circulars went out to post masters around the country.[30]

Bodkin was drawn back to *Ulysses* in 1926 when an academic at Cambridge decided to test the ban. F. R. Leavis was preparing a course of lectures on modern English prose and persuaded a bookseller in the town to ask permission to import copies.[31] The request went as far as Anderson, who expressed doubts about the novel's "suitability for the education of the boy and girl undergraduates who may attend the lectures." Anderson was "inclined to think that so far from removing the ban we should take active steps to prevent the lectures taking place."[32] Bodkin told the university's vice-chancellor that *Ulysses* was not a fit subject for lectures, let alone discussion by "a mixed body of students."[33] The vice-chancellor, Albert Seward, called Leavis in for an interview and was evidently satisfied by his explanation. Seward declined to oblige Bodkin and left Leavis to go about his business, albeit without his own copy of *Ulysses*.[34] It was fitting that a sortie in the long struggle over *Ulysses* should involve an undergraduate course: both censorship and canonization are forms of recognition and misrecognition.

Busy and high-ranking officials devoted such close attention to *Ulysses* because of the cultural significance of an explicit and confounding book. Looked at in terms of criminal penalties, the Customs infractions or even the common-law misdemeanor of uttering an obscene libel were minor matters unworthy of the time and effort of the chief prosecutor for England and Wales. Several years later Bodkin committed a good amount of his time and police resources to suppressing *The Sleeveless Errand*, Norah C. James's novel about jaded heterosexual bohemians. The *Sleeveless Errand* case illustrates the coordination between the *Morning Post*, the Home Office, and the DPP. The *Morning Post*, like many other newspapers, received a review copy at the beginning of 1929. Someone in the office brought it to Gwynne's attention, and Gwynne tipped off Joynson-Hicks, who evidently asked Anderson to deal with the matter.[35] Anderson sought a legal opinion. Bodkin found the novel appalling, though there was room for doubt about its illegality. "It is astonishing that such a book could be written by a woman. . . . There is a certain amount of psychology in the treatment of Paula as a character, and in a much less degree that of Bill, and, shorn of its foulness, the theme of the book, though exaggerated, is not without some interest. . . . It would be somewhat difficult, I think, to regard the book as corrupting in the sense that it would tend to make people who read it indecent or immoral." Here Bodkin took the *Hicklin* test seriously, asking whether the book was actually likely to deprave and corrupt its readers. While the book had some merit, it also contained some indecent material and profanity. "Imagine this book finding its way into the hands of decent young women!"[36] The language of the *Hicklin* test— "into whose hands a publication of this sort may fall"—surfaced again: Bodkin had arrived at a decision about the book's obscenity.

With Anderson's support, Bodkin prepared to seek a destruction order. He got the police in Hertfordshire, where *The Sleeveless Errand* had been printed, to examine the printers' order books so that if the magistrate granted a destruction order, police throughout England and Wales could be informed of all the bookstores stocking it.[37] Briefing the barrister who would represent him at Bow Street Magistrates' Court, Bodkin stepped back to comment more generally: "There has been a marked decadence of late years in certain ranges of literature, unnatural practices between men and women, filthy language and indecencies not infrequently found, and it is thought that the time has certainly come when a strong stand should be taken against the degradation of English literature by such productions as . . . the present book." Like Cockburn in *Hicklin*, Bodkin invoked vulnerable or impressionable young people, especially young women, as the hypothetical readers to be considered in obscenity cases (as he had already done in his first comment on the book, the opinion he wrote for Anderson). Being a novel, *The Sleeveless Errand* might "lie on anybody's table and be picked up and read by a youth or a girl. . . . Imagine a daughter in a respectable English household reading . . . page 227 and coming across the passage 'We're bored with people who aren't bawdy. We call them prigs and prudes if they don't want to talk about copulation at lunch time and buggery at dinner.'"[38] Describing the book for counsel, Bodkin suggested that the outrage of the book was its "fast" attitude, its representation of "unnatural practices" without authorial condemnation.[39] *The Sleeveless Errand*, like so many productions of the twenties, offered up forms of femininity that were deeply disquieting to many traditionalists. "There are people still existing," Bodkin wrote, "who look upon women as delicate and refined, and yet into the mouth of the principal character of this book there are [put] odious words and odious sentences." Bodkin was also unsettled that the publisher "should without hesitation distribute it through the trade in the ordinary course of business"—implying that the book might have been less objectionable had the circumstances of its publication been different (if it had been issued as a limited edition, say).[40] He told counsel he should "in the strongest terms denounce the scandal which the publication of such a book as a piece of literature undoubtedly amounts to. It must not be forgotten that this is published as a novel."[41] These sentences are ungainly (probably a function of Bodkin's habit of dictating his ruminative briefs to a secretary), but together the apparently unnecessary reminder that *The Sleeveless Errand* was a novel and the reference to its being published "as a piece of literature" indicate that part of the book's danger lay in its claims to legitimacy. *The Sleeveless Errand* was not mere pornography, but a novel that might be taken seriously by responsible readers.

The magistrate at Bow Street, Rollo Graham Campbell, had no doubt the novel was obscene. Where Bodkin had at first queried whether *The Sleeveless Errand*, despite being repellent, satisfied the "deprave and corrupt" test, Graham Campbell, after quoting *Hicklin*, pronounced himself "certain that the book in question would suggest to the minds of the young of either sex, or even to persons of more advanced years, thoughts of a most impure character."[42] Thanks to the efforts of multiple police forces and the cooperation of the publisher, printers and wholesalers, practically the whole of the print run of eight hundred had been confiscated.

The books were put through a mechanized guillotine owned by the civil service.[43]

Though the Metropolitan Police acted assiduously in doing Bodkin's bidding, when operating on their own they could be more reserved. They were mindful of the confusion and uncertainty generated by English obscenity law. Their archive affords glimpses of the force trying to keep up with the rules of a sometimes unpredictable game.[44] Constables could also lack the literary knowledge, and the time to read, that was necessary to save themselves from errors of judgment and their superiors from embarrassment. A police lawyer whose distinctive but illegible signature appears in the comments pages at the beginning of a great many files from the twenties and thirties wrote wearily of "these troublesome dirty book cases." He made this comment after sorting out which classics seized from a bookshop on Buckingham Palace Road—Petronius's *Satyricon*, Rabelais, a Plato volume with an indecent illustration—should be the subject of legal action. "By returning the Rabelais we take away from the defense the chance of ridicule."[45] As a matter of policy, he said, the assistant chief constable should be notified "before a search warrant is applied for in a case in which there is a possibility of a literary high-brow argument."[46] Following up seven months later, he wrote: "If the case involves anything that can be dignified by the term 'literature' then, in the absence of some special reason, the case is for the Director every time. . . . The ordinary 2nd rate dirty photograph case is quite different and is one, as a rule, for Messrs. Wontners," the solicitors who conducted police prosecutions.[47]

Destruction orders were granted by magistrates' courts or police courts with summary jurisdiction. (Prosecutions for obscene libel called for trial by jury in courts presided over by bigger judicial fish such as recorders and high court judges.) Magistrates typically came from the criminal bar and tended to be severe.[48] Ronald Powell at Westminster Police Court could be counted on to take a stand against immoral books. So could Sir Chartres Biron, one of Graham Campbell's fellow magistrates at Bow Street. Biron had a good working relationship with Joynson-Hicks and thought highly of him: "As a busy solicitor, his work had taken him a good deal to the police courts, and he had a thorough knowledge and understanding of the actual work the magistrates do, which very few Home Secretaries have." Joynson-Hicks was receptive to Biron's appeals for help with the administration of the magistrates' courts, especially children's courts.[49]

Biron presided over the magistrates' court hearing in the most famous twenties obscenity case about "unnatural practices," the saga of Radclyffe Hall's novel about a lesbian relationship, *The Well of Loneliness*. This too was a joint effort by the Home Office, the director of public prosecutions, and a vigilante in the press. In the case of Hall's novel, however, Joynson-Hicks himself was more actively involved, and the newspaperman who set the wheels turning was not Gwynne but James Douglas, star columnist for and nominal editor of the *Sunday Express*. The novel had been soberly and sympathetically reviewed until Douglas launched a tirade against it.[50] Douglas said he would rather give "a healthy boy or a healthy girl a phial of prussic acid than this novel. Poison kills the body, but moral poison kills the soul."[51] Specifying the type of poison was surely a homage to Lord Campbell's comparison of pornography with prussic acid when he derailed a debate on the Poisons Bill in 1857 with his call for legislation against obscene publications. Poison, pollution, plagues, putrefaction, perversion, paganism; cleaning the Augean stables, giving literature a carbolic rinse, calling in the "sanitary inspector of literature": Douglas was proficient in the late-Victorian and Edwardian language of degeneration and national hygiene as well as the twenties journalistic art of the tease.[52] *The Well of Loneliness* was not the first book he declared to be one "that must be suppressed"—his attack on Lawrence's *The Rainbow* was quoted extensively in the court proceedings against the novel—nor the last.[53] As we have seen, Douglas also had form for seeing heterodox or unfamiliar conduct by women as a sign of cultural decline.

Douglas did not have a direct channel to the home secretary as Gwynne at the *Morning Post* did: he induced Hall's own publisher to raise the matter with Joynson-Hicks. The Friday before his column appeared, Douglas wrote to Jonathan Cape to let him know what was coming. The *Sunday Express*'s daily stablemate carried an announcement of the forthcoming article, posters went up in London, and the Saturday edition of the *Evening Standard*, another newspaper in the same stable, offered cross-promotion.[54] Errand boys from bookshops queued outside Cape's trade department for copies on the Saturday morning.[55] When Jonathan Cape read the much-anticipated column the next morning, he wrote two letters without consulting Hall first.[56] One was a long letter to the *Daily Express* (for Monday's paper) and the other a short one to the home secretary enclosing a copy of *The Well of Loneliness* and the text of his letter to the *Express*, which invited Joynson-Hicks to forward it to the director of public prosecutions if he believed the book broke the law.[57] Cape said he was willing to withdraw the book, but "not at the behest of the Editor of the *Sunday Express*": it was up to the home secretary and the DPP. Cape took issue with Douglas's line about giving poison to a healthy boy or girl: "But why should anyone give this book to a boy or girl? It is not intended for boys and girls. . . . The result of the 'Sunday Express' article . . . can only be to nullify our most careful attempts to see that this book reaches the right class of reader. . . . A wide and unnecessary advertisement has been given to the book," Cape told the *Express*, "and all the curious will now want to read it. . . . The smut-hounds will be anxious to read it so that they may lift up their hands in indignation that such things can be allowed."[58]

Cape was in earnest. He took Hall seriously when she told him that she wrote *The Well of Loneliness* "from a deep sense of duty." She was "proud indeed to have taken up my pen in defence of those who are utterly defenceless": "sexual inverts." The novel was a stylization of Hall's own experience and acquaintance, punctuated by impassioned pamphleteering ("God . . . give us . . . the right to our existence!") A pious Catholic, she went to mass to pray for the book as it went out into the world to do its work.[59] That the smut-hounds found something in it to gnaw on distressed her. To keep them at bay, Cape had, with Hall's approval, produced the book in black binding with a plain dust jacket, and priced it at 15 shillings—double the standard price of a new hardcover novel.[60] Cape was indeed not seeking a mass audience for the book. He sent review copies only to the "serious" newspapers and weekly journals and told the novelist Hugh Walpole, a powerful shaper of what was coming to be called middlebrow opinion, "I realize that the publication of *The Well of Loneliness* may be called into question unless it is soberly and carefully published."[61] As publisher of an expensive abridgement of *The Seven Pillars of Wisdom* by T. E. Lawrence, Cape had experience in using cost and exclusivity to keep a book away from the attention of ordinary readers and their self-appointed tribunes.[62] Cape knew, or thought he knew, how to use the antidemocratic assumptions of English obscenity law in the service of something like freedom.

Douglas now sought to put pressure on Joynson-Hicks with a column, in the same Monday edition of the *Daily Express* as Cape's letter, about the "Home Secretary's Duty" to ban *The Well of Loneliness*. His efforts proved unnecessary.[63] Joynson-Hicks sought a legal opinion immediately. Bodkin was away and his deputy, Sir Guy Stephenson, handled the matter. Using the familiar *Hicklin* phraseology, Stephenson said he believed that "this book would tend to corrupt the minds of young persons if it fell into their hands." It would do so through its overall message rather than any conventionally obscene passages: *The Well of Loneliness* was, "in effect . . . a plea not only for toleration but also for the recognition of sexual perversion among women." Hall's sincerity and courage did not matter: under the *Hicklin* test, only the "tendency" of the text counted, not the motivation of the author. Stephenson thought there was a reasonable chance a jury would convict.[64] This consideration was important even if the DPP sought only a destruction order and did not prosecute Cape or Hall for obscene libel: to issue a destruction order, Section 1 of the Obscene Publications Act required a magistrate to be satisfied that the material in question was sufficient grounds for an indictment for obscene libel. Stephenson added that he had "informally consulted" the chief magistrate at Bow Street, and Biron was willing to grant process. Two days later, Arnold Bennett saw Biron at the Garrick Club, talking to none other than James Douglas. "I set violently on Jimmy about his attack on Radclyffe Hall's Sapphic novel," Bennett wrote in his journal. "Jimmy was very quiet and restrained but Biron defended Jimmy with *real* heat."[65] It would be some months before *The Well of Loneliness* would come before Biron's court, however. Joynson-Hicks discussed Stephenson's opinion with the lord chancellor and they were both of the view that the book was indecent. "I wrote to the publishers asking for its withdrawal," Joynson-Hicks wrote in red ink at the end of Stephenson's opinion, "If they decline proceed at once."[66]

Cape complied, though he did not quite surrender. He was well aware of the opportunities that publication in Paris or Florence offered to circumvent the British authorities. He leased the rights to *The Well of Loneliness* to a contact in Paris, John Holroyd-Reece, who would publish them through his firm, the Pegasus Press. Cape arranged for the printers to make molds of the type and had his business partner take them to Paris.[67] Holroyd-Reece's edition was printed within three weeks. Pegasus Press sent circulars to British booksellers whom Cape had identified as comparatively safe, including those who had put in advance orders for the third printing that Cape had been forced to cancel. Copies began to enter Britain. Joynson-Hicks signed warrants directing the opening of mail from Pegasus Press's office in Paris. When Customs seized a consignment at Dover, the Home Office told the solicitor representing Holroyd-Reece and Hall that if they wanted to challenge the confiscation they should take it up with the Board of Customs and Excise.[68]

It turned out, however, that Customs and Excise did not see the matter the same way as the Home Office. The board members read *The Well of Loneliness* and Sir Francis Floud told his minister, Churchill: "The subject is treated seriously and sincerely, with restraint in expression and with great literary skill and delicacy." The story was tragic and "does not seem calculated to arouse sexual emotion or to corrupt morals by encouraging the practice of sexual inversion. If the subject is one that can permissibly be treated at all in a novel, it is difficult to see how it could be treated with more restraint." And if the subject was not acceptable for a novel, "it will be difficult to know where our censorship is to stop." "If we were left to ourselves," Floud concluded, Customs would have "come to the conclusion that . . . the book is not one that should be stopped on the ground of indecency or obscenity."[69] Floud was aware that Customs would embarrass Joynson-Hicks if it released the shipment of copies of a book that the home secretary had declared in breach of the law of obscenity. With Churchill's backing, Floud met with Anderson to work out a way for the Home Office rather than Customs to take action about *The Well of Loneliness*.[70] A convoluted sting operation eventually led to the hearing in Biron's courtroom at Bow Street on November 9, 1928.[71]

The DPP had applied for a destruction order rather than a prosecution for obscene libel. Jonathan Cape Ltd and the Pegasus Press challenged the application in Biron's court. Hall had no standing. Counsel for the publishers attempted to get Biron to heed the voices of other authors. The solicitor for both Cape and Holroyd-Reece, Harold Rubinstein, wrote to 160 authors, clergymen, doctors, and other eminences asking to testify in support of *The Well of Loneliness*. Forty said yes, many for the sake of freedom of expression rather than out of a belief in Radclyffe Hall's art.[72] E. M. Forster and Virginia and Leonard Woolf were among them. Forster and Leonard Woolf had organized an open letter immediately after the *Sunday Express* article.[73] Then, Hall had expressed her gratitude to Forster and Woolf, but "reject[ed] any support that while including a number of important names would not involve any support of my book's decency or of its literary merit."[74] Some of the same people who signed the letter Forster and Woolf prepared now assembled at Bow Street.[75] Cape's barrister, Norman Birkett, argued that Biron should admit the evidence of the expert witnesses Rubinstein had recruited. Biron was skeptical: "The test is whether it is likely to deprave or corrupt those into whose hands it is likely to fall. How can the opinion of a number of people be evidence?" Birkett said that if he was "not allowed to call the evidence it means that a magistrate is virtually a censor of literature." Biron told him: "I don't think people are entitled to express what is merely an opinion upon a matter which is for the decision of the court." Though unpersuaded, he entertained the experiment briefly and allowed Birkett to call Desmond MacCarthy, a widely respected reviewer.[76] Birkett got as far as asking him, "In your view is it obscene?" before Biron said, "No, I shall disallow that." Eustace Fulton, representing the DPP, "contended that it was entirely a question for the magistrate whether a book was obscene or not."[77] Fulton and Biron were probably right on the law as it stood at the time.

Deprived of the chance to examine his witnesses, Birkett fell back on arguing that *The Well of Loneliness* had been written "out of a sense of duty, with a high-minded desire" to deal with lesbianism "as a fact of life." He submitted "that the theme of the book is a theme which ought to be discussed just as any other phase of life ought to be discussed in order that it may be understood."[78] Biron reserved his decision and, then, a week later, granted the destruction order. Explaining his reasons, he restated the legal commonplace that obscenity law was not a form of censorship because the book had not been vetted by officials before publication. Biron accepted Birkett's claim that *The Well of Loneliness* "had some literary merit," but said that this was beside the point: "Otherwise the preposterous position would arise that, because it was well written, every obscene book would be free from proceedings." The "mere fact that the book dealt with unnatural offences between women would not in itself make it an obscene libel. But in the present case there was not one word which suggested that anyone with the horrible tendencies described was in the least degree blameworthy." The lesbian characters "were presented as attractive people." Worse, "certain acts were described in the most alluring terms." Biron went on to quote many passages from the novel. Eventually Radclyffe Hall, sitting in the gallery—she was not, after all, a party to the legal proceedings— shouted: "I protest. I emphatically protest." Biron said he must ask her to be quiet. "I am the author of this book—" she began. Biron cut her off, threatening to have her removed if she could not behave herself. "Shame!" shouted Hall. Biron wound up his judgment with an incantation of the *Hicklin* maxim: "SIR CHARTRES . . . had no hesitation in saying that the book was an obscene libel, and that it would tend to corrupt those into whose hands it should fall."[79]

Cape and Leopold Hill, the Charing Cross Road bookseller acting as the Pegasus Press's representative in Britain, lodged an appeal, and a month later a bench of twelve magistrates constituting the court of quarter sessions considered the matter. In court the Crown was represented by no less a figure than the attorney general, Sir Thomas Inskip. Inskip was a close ally of Joynson-Hicks. They were fresh from their successful campaign against the revised Anglican prayer book, which they opposed for its liturgical accommodations of Anglo-Catholicism.[80] Inskip read from *The Well of Loneliness* and said of one passage: "This is more subtle, demoralizing, corrosive, corruptive, than anything that was ever written. . . . I hardly need ask what is the picture conjured up to minds that are open to immoral influence." The magistrates took only ten minutes to agree that the appeal should be dismissed with costs. Sir Robert Wallace, the bench's chairman, agreed with Inskip that the book's subtlety made its representation of "unnatural practices" all the more dangerous.[81] This was a clear victory for the Home Office and the DPP, though Bodkin recognized that "the appellants will have derived very considerable profits." Still, "at least the standard of decent literature in this country has to some extent been maintained."[82]

The ordeal of *The Well of Loneliness* was, as Laura Doan observes, a pivotal moment in the making of lesbian identity. James Douglas did not tap into a panic about lesbianism so much as engineer a controversy. The ensuing media coverage, not least the lavish photographic profiles of Hall and her partner Una Troubridge, "changed [life] utterly for *all* women who lived with other women, or *all* women drawn to masculine styles of dress, whether lesbian or not."[83] The affair had a lasting impact on the law. Though a magistrate's court hearing could not set a precedent on a point of law, Biron's refusal to entertain Birkett's witnesses convinced many observers that it would be unrealistic to expect a court to admit expert witness testimony about a book's literary qualities.[84] Making literary merit a defense against obscenity charges became a goal of law reformers.[85]

D. H. Lawrence and the Small Presses

At this time a network of small presses and bookshops in central London was running a guerrilla campaign against what they called "the Censorship."[86] The anarchist bookseller Charles Lahr acted as an informal liaison between them. They included a handful of expatriate Australians: Eric Partridge, the publisher of *The Sleeveless Errand*, and Jack Lindsay and P. R. Stephensen of the Fanfrolico Press. Stephensen then struck out on his own with the Mandrake Press. Censorship was both a hindrance to the kinds of art Stephensen approved of and a symbol of the culture he wanted to change. He published a book-length critique, Bernard Causton and G. Gordon Young's *Keeping It Dark, or The Censor's Handbook*, and he took on books that pushed the boundaries of what was legal—above all, work by D. H. Lawrence. Lawrence attracted people who regarded bourgeois civilization as bankrupt but who had not settled on an alternative ideal.[87] Or, to put it another way, people who were politically available in the volatile years between the war and the side-taking that went on after the Nazi seizure of power. When he met Lawrence, Stephensen was on the way from communism to the pro-Nazi and pro-Japanese positions he would take after his return to Australia in the early thirties.

In his last years (he died in 1930) Lawrence himself was hungry to confront British censorship.[88] *Lady Chatterley's Lover* is an example of what the literary scholar Celia Marshik calls the "censorship dialectic": the way censorship shaped modernist literature rather than simply restraining the circulation of texts produced independently of the legal system.[89] The novel was a deliberate challenge to censorship, an escalation in response to Lawrence's previous brushes with obscenity law.[90] *Lady Chatterley's Lover* was first published in Florence and produced in a utilitarian print shop in the city (direct speech appeared inside guillemets: the printer must not have had enough double quotes).[91] Pirated editions proliferated. Lahr, who had connections with other shady publishers and booksellers in Europe, kept Lawrence informed of the pirated versions in circulation. In January of 1929, Lahr proposed a German edition to compete with the pirates. Then, perhaps at Stephensen's urging, Lahr changed his mind and suggested an English edition. Lawrence agreed. Stephensen managed to find a printer near Euston Station. He produced five hundred copies that claimed to be the work of the Tipografia Giuntina, the shop in Florence that printed the first edition. Though the edition had Lawrence's endorsement, it was so secret it was long regarded as a pirate version.[92]

Stephensen put own his name to another book of Lawrence's the same year, an unexpurgated edition of a collection of satirical and sometimes scatological poems entitled *Pansies*. Lawrence angrily resolved to publish *Pansies* uncut after the Post Office opened a package sent to Lawrence's agent containing the typescript.[93] Lahr obliged and produced a limited edition with Stephensen's name and address on it instead of his own: Stephensen wanted to be the defendant in any legal action.[94] The Post Office was monitoring the booksellers F. J. Joiner and Alan Steele, having caught them the previous year posting copies of *Lady Chatterley's Lover*, and now postal workers opened a parcel from them containing three copies of the unexpurgated *Pansies*.[95] They notified the Home Office, and Anderson sought an opinion from the DPP. Bodkin thought the poems were "of the nauseous and disgusting kind rather than the corrupting and immoral kind." A magistrate might well decline process under the Obscene Publications Act, so it was advisable, Bodkin concluded, to rely on the Post Office regulations instead and "keep a strict look-out for those going through the post." Bodkin also noted: "if it be correct that the present edition was for private circulation to subscribers then the case stands differently from a book which is on every bookstall for indiscriminate publication."[96] Stephensen did not get the test case he thought he was provoking: the trick of publishing in a limited edition was too effective.

Stephensen would self-consciously exploit the cover that a limited edition could provide a borderline book one more time, in 1929. The high production values of the books put out by Mandrake, Lahr's Blue Moon Press, and the others were not simply instrumental—their directors and backers had succumbed to the allure of the book-as-objet-d'art—but they did serve a strategic purpose.[97] When the Mandrake Press issued a volume of reproductions of Lawrence's paintings to coincide with their exhibition at Dorothy Warren's gallery in London, Stephensen or an ally prepared a list of arguments for the defense in the event of legal trouble, as some of the paintings were nudes and showed pubic hair. The document acknowledged that the paintings were "unusual in treatment and subject, and that consequently only persons of intellectual maturity could view them with advantage." The volume was "issued for subscription only by connoisseurs and collectors of objects of art," and sold at a high price (ten guineas) that "prevents any possibility of the book ever reaching a wider market."[98] The lessons learned from the Vizetelly prosecutions had become part of the institutional knowledge of the publishing trade. "Intellectual maturity" and discernment correlated with disposable income. Selling a book by subscription to the cognoscenti was a sign of a publisher's good faith, as it meant it there was little chance of such a book falling into the hands of the many—"a wider market"—whose minds were open to immoral influences. The exhibition was raided and some of the paintings seized, but Mandrake's book survived.[99]

New Media

Film censorship had its origins in building safety rules rather than obscenity law.[100] Cinema's predecessors, kinematograph and bioscope shows, shared venues with other kinds of entertainment, and, before recorded sound became standard, films had musical accompaniments, so municipal governments treated them as comparable to music halls and other businesses they had to monitor. Managing the fire danger was the biggest challenge that cinema posed for councils: early film stock was highly flammable and the lighting sources unreliable. As the film industry consolidated, around 1906/1907, and standalone picture palaces were constructed in many towns, the legal rationale for treating cinemas like music halls became shaky, and councils called for legislation that would allow them to license cinemas. The resulting Cinematograph Act dealt only with safety considerations, but local governments treated it as permission to impose license conditions relating to other matters such as Sunday observance.[101]

The Court of King's Bench held those conditions to be valid.[102] The court's reasoning also enabled municipalities to act as film censors, and they began to do so.

In 1912 the film industry took matters into its own hands by establishing a British Board of Film Censors. The Home Office took an interest, sending Sidney Harris to take part in the discussions that set up the board (after his retirement from the Home Office in 1947, Harris became president of the BBFC), but the board was never an arm of central government.[103] The plan for a national system of censorship required municipalities to defer to the BBFC. Many newly empowered councils were unwilling to do so. The turning point came in 1921 when the London County Council agreed to make it a condition of a cinema license that no film without a BBFC certificate be shown without the council's express permission. In effect, the council delegated film censorship to the BBFC while reserving the power to overrule it in any given case.[104] Other councils followed London's example, though some, such as Manchester, ran their own independent film censorship operations.[105]

The Lord Chamberlain's Office was an obvious model for the new film censorship board. Theater directors had to submit scripts to the Lord Chamberlain's Office, where they were assessed by a reader who could recommend an outright refusal or specific cuts. In the silent film era, the BBFC could similarly demand cuts or simply refuse a certificate. After talkies became the norm at the end of the twenties, British filmmakers could submit scripts before production, as theatrical companies did to the lord chamberlain, so that the examiners could give an indication about whether a scene would be acceptable before the producers went to the trouble and expense of shooting it. (Of course, the board had no input into the development of the Hollywood movies that dominated the British screen—with foreign films it could only assess the finished product.) The BBFC's first president, G. A. Redford, was a veteran of the Lord Chamberlain's Office. While there, his judgment was vigorously attacked by George Bernard Shaw and G. K. Chesterton, and the lord chamberlain, Lord Althorp, disliked him and seems to have edged him out.[106] Some of Redford's few explicit rules for films—no depiction of Christ, no offensive portrayal of a living person—derived from the lord chamberlain's rules for plays.[107]

Very conscious that cinema was a mass art form with many patrons who were young and without much formal education, the BBFC not only exercised moral guardianship but did its best to shore up the standing of public institutions and authority figures.[108] This attitude was especially pronounced in wartime, but it was a constant. The report for 1926 included the following reasons for cuts:

Travesties of familiar Biblical quotations and well-known hymns.
Propaganda against Monarchy, and attacks on Royal Dynasties.
White men in state of degradation amidst native surroundings.
Incidents which reflect a mistaken conception of the Police Forces in
    this country in the administration of Justice.
Subtitles in the nature of swearing and expressions regarded as
    objectionable in this country.
Workhouse officials shown in an offensive light.
Girls and women in a state of intoxication.
"Orgy" scenes.
Nude and semi-nude figures, both in actuality and shadow-graph.
Marital infidelity and collusive divorce.
Dangerous mischief, easily imitated by children.[109]

Redford died in 1916. His successors were all former politicians or senior civil servants, and they took pains to show that the board and the film business were politically responsible. The board frequently consulted government departments and kept in touch with the Public Morality Council, a pressure group presided over by the bishop of London.[110] Welcoming a new BBFC president in the thirties, the bishop, Arthur Winnington-Ingram, spoke of his warm relations with his predecessors. "Dear old T. P. O'Connor used to come down and have lunch with me when he was in doubt about a film. Then there was Mr Shortt, and now Lord Tyrrell."[111] The board excised slurs on the Salvation Army as well as the Church of England: it was not just in the business of propping up establishment institutions but of minimizing offense and controversy more broadly. Avoiding "controversial politics" was another of the lord chamberlain's directives.[112] Lord Tyrell reflected after his first year as president: "We may take pride in observing that there is not a single film showing in London today which deals with any of the burning questions of the day."[113] This sentiment was very much in keeping with the cultural style of Baldwinite Conservatism, a politics in which controversy was trouble-making and tended to be caused by proponents of change.[114]

Imperial and international relations lent themselves to controversy and the board was concerned not to offend sensibilities in India and continental Europe. The BBFC filtered the cultural products of the competing exemplars of the future, the Soviet Union and the United States. Complementing the quota system that limited the number of American films British audiences were exposed to, the censors kept a vigil against

American treatments of sex and violence.[115] The threats posed by American flashiness and directness paled in comparison with the dangers of Bolshevism, of course. The BBFC banned *Battleship Potemkin*, *The End of St. Petersburg*, and other Soviet films. They could only be seen at screenings run by film societies that secured permission from local councils to show them "privately" to members. A Federation of Workers' Film societies was founded in 1929 to provide access to left-wing films made in the Soviet Union and elsewhere. The London County Council's permission to screen films without a BBFC certificate did not extend to films that had been submitted to the BBFC and rejected, and the window for viewing Soviet films narrowed quickly.[116]

The British Broadcasting Corporation did not exercise censorship in the sense that the BBFC did, since it was the producer of everything that went out legitimately over the airwaves rather than a third-party gatekeeper. Nevertheless, the corporation does bear comparison with the British Board of Film Censors in its determination to minimize controversy. Where the film business was trying to earn respectability, the BBC was trying to earn authority. Sir John Reith, the BBC's first director, believed that the partisanship and pushiness of the press, or commercial radio elsewhere—really, in the United States—were inappropriate for a national institution with a monopoly over a powerful new medium. In its news coverage, the BBC was neutral in a way that favored the status quo. The corporation deferred to the government at times of crisis such as the General Strike and the Munich conference, though it should be noted that most of the British press was also complicit in appeasement. The Talks Department took more liberties in exploring contemporary social problems, and though the BBC's leadership clamped down on it, there remained pockets of challenging, socially engaged broadcasting, especially in the regional studios.[117] The BBC was most like the film censors or the circulating libraries or cautious publishers when it came to light entertainment. Performers were told they could not make jokes about sex, alcohol, clergymen, or politics (comedians struggled to comply). In radio as well as film, censorship and editorial policy made for a mass culture that excluded reference to swathes of human life.[118]

International Exchanges and the Thaw in British Censorship

The struggle against obscene publications was an international one. From the late nineteenth century, representatives of different countries had been meeting to draft agreements to cooperate in suppressing the traffic in obscene publications. After the First World War, these meetings took place under the auspices of the League of Nations. Bodkin and Harris represented the United Kingdom at a conference in Geneva in 1923 that produced a new accord on obscene publications, which the Home Office invoked when it alerted government agencies throughout the empire to the possibility that copies of *The Well of Loneliness* were heading their way.[119] States' responsibilities under the agreement were not onerous, and the Home Office was underwhelmed by the cooperation it received from the French authorities in suppressing Paris-based publishers of English-language articles for import into Britain.[120] The League of Nations committee responsible for obscene publications dealt primarily with the trafficking of women and girls. The earlier international agreements dealt with both problems, and some pressure groups did as well.[121] The secretary of the National Vigilance Association in the thirties, F.A.R. Sempkins, was previously secretary to the International Bureau for the Suppression of the Traffic in Women and Children, which the NVA absorbed in 1925.[122] Sempkins went to Geneva for meetings of the corresponding League committee. In the twenties and thirties the NVA was in regular contact with its counterparts in continental Europe, the United States, Canada, and India. They shared foreign models of good practice such as Danzig's law against obscene literature.[123] They tipped each other off about meretricious books and birth control literature.

Many such items reaching Britain originated in the United States, and the NVA sought and received information about them from the American Social Hygiene Association. NVA members imported single copies and forwarded them on to the secretary, who passed them on to Harris at the Home Office. The Eugenics Publishing Company of New York was the source of many of these. Its catalogue also included such not very eugenicist books as Petronius's *Satyricon* translated by Oscar Wilde: like antipopery before it, eugenics and associated health-and-efficiency movements provided cover for erotic material.[124] When sexological material came before the English courts it triggered variable-obscenity judgments about the danger it posed to working-class readers. In the 1935 case over Edmund Charles's *Sexual Impulse*, the magistrate asked a witness whether a quoted passage was "fit and decent for people of the working class to read."[125] Another magistrate condemned the distributors of a book entitled *Sane Sex Life and Sane Sex Living*, which a member of the NVA independently solicited from New York, for exercising "no sort of discrimination . . . in the manner in which it was brought to the attention of the public."[126]

The National Vigilance Association cooperated with the Public Morality Council—not without mutual suspicion—and, buoyed by the outcome
of the *Well of Loneliness* case, the two organizations stepped up their lobbying of the Home Office at the end of the twenties.[127] At this point, the
civil servants began to push back.[128] Briefing Joynson-Hicks before he
received a deputation from the Public Morality Council and the NVA in
March of 1929, Harris warned of the difficulties of proceeding against distributors of books that could be regarded as literature. One risk was raising "the suspicion that the right to free expression of opinion and the free
development of art is being challenged." Harris now suggested to Joynson-
Hicks that the most effective way of staunching the flow of "border-line
book" sales was by "informing and stimulating public opinion" against
indecency, rather than by legal action.[129] Both Harris and another civil
servant, H. Houston, deplored the tendency of schoolmasters and others
to demand that the Home Office take action against indecent magazines:
"The present tendency of aunts, mothers, and schoolmasters to thrust
their own duties upon our shoulders is a matter of regret and ought to be
discouraged. . . . There was no such tendency in Victorian days."[130] Houston's sidelong reference to the Victorians is telling. Britons in the second
half of the nineteenth century did see the setting of moral standards as the
responsibility of public opinion, families, and those in loco parentis, rather
than the state. The late twenties turn in the Home Office's thinking seems
like a reversion to older liberal assumptions that had been checked, possibly in reaction to the social destabilization of the war and its immediate
aftermath, possibly a result of the discipline John Anderson imposed on
the department.[131]

By 1932 Anderson had gone to Bengal. Joynson-Hicks left office after
the general election at the end of May 1929. His Labour successor, J. R.
Clynes, made it clear that he would not be targeting suspect literature. In
his first month as home secretary, Clynes canceled the warrant allowing
the opening or seizure of postal packets from the Pegasus Press.[132] Clynes
also sent the Public Morality Council a letter, probably drafted at least in
part by Harris, that signaled a change of direction. "You will bear in mind,"
he wrote, "that my predecessor did take one or two well-known books into
Court and the comments even of reputable newspapers did not indicate
any large measure of support." Clynes told the council that the best service it could render was to "inform and strengthen public opinion on this
subject."[133]

Bodkin, too, left his post around the same time and Clynes appointed
his successor. E. H. Tindal Atkinson was a successful barrister but did not

have much experience with criminal law, and he approached the DPP's job with caution.[134] He was certainly diffident about initiating obscenity proceedings.[135] When an anonymous complainant sent him a copy of Pierre Louÿs's *Aphrodite* in 1932, he pulled a file from 1928 which detailed the action Bodkin had taken against the book's earlier distributors. Atkinson asked the Home Office if they wanted him to do anything about the booksellers currently selling it, Fudge and Co. "I think it is just possible," he said, piling on the deadpan, "that according to present standards the book may not be regarded quite in the same light as it was regarded in 1928."[136] In a public lecture, Atkinson speculated that public-interest defenses might be possible in obscenity cases.[137] His position aligned with Fitzjames Stephen's suggestion that publishing or displaying obscene or disgusting material was justified "if their exhibition or representation is for the public good," conducive to justice, religion, or science, and so on.[138]

The *Ulysses* ban ended the same year as Atkinson delivered his lecture. This time input from the United States worked to relax censorship rather than reinforce it. The book's prospects in Britain improved after Judge John Woolsey handed down his decision in *United States v. One Book Called "Ulysses"* in New York in 1933. Woolsey held that the novel was not obscene because Joyce lacked pornographic intent. He was being true to an artistic experiment, and that ambition put *Ulysses* in a different category from other books that used four-letter words and described sexual matters in detail. Woolsey wrote:

> Joyce has attempted—it seems to me, with astonishing success—to show how the screen of consciousness with its ever-shifting kaleidoscopic impressions carries, as it were on a plastic palimpsest, not only what is in the focus of each man's observation of the actual things about him, but also in a penumbral zone residua of past impressions, some recent and some drawn up by association from the domain of the subconscious. He shows how each of these impressions affects the life and behavior of the character which he is describing.
>
> What he seeks to get is not unlike the result of a double or, if that is possible, a multiple exposure on a cinema film, which would give a clear foreground with a background visible but somewhat blurred and out of focus in varying degrees.[139]

No English judge was going to get into this kind of literary criticism, but Joyce's advisors took Woolsey's judgment as an omen that *Ulysses* could soon be published safely in Britain. T. S. Eliot and his employer Geoffrey Faber sounded out the solicitor general, Donald Somervell. Faber forwarded a copy of the *Saturday Review of Literature* that reprinted

Woolsey's judgment.[140] J. F. Henderson of the Home Office was noncom-
mittal, but two years later when John Lane's firm The Bodley Head went
ahead with a British edition of *Ulysses*, Henderson recognized the force of
the literary arguments likely to be made in court: by evoking "the gradual
transition from complete consciousness to a state of dream" and its attempt
to portray "the 'stream of consciousness,'" *Ulysses* was "Freud in novel
form." He went on to argue that "serious adults should not be prevented
from reading a book which may not be suitable for the young." Henderson
had already "had a preliminary word with the D.P.P. about it, rather on the
lines that a book costing either £6.6.0 or £3.3.0 was not likely to get into
the hands of anyone likely to be corrupted by it, and the prudent course
was to do nothing." The booksellers Foyles then issued a circular claiming
that Lane had consulted the Home Office before publishing—Foyles were
presumably trying to reassure prospective customers—but this was not the
case, and the Home Office was placed in an "extremely awkward situation."
Quietly declining to take action was no longer feasible.[141]

Henderson therefore met with the DPP, Atkinson, and Somervell,
recently promoted to attorney general. Somervell said that the *Hicklin*
definition of obscenity was "inadequate" and "the question of intention
has to be taken into account as in the criminal law generally. . . . If he were
challenged in the House of Commons his answer would be on the line that
it was a well established principle of law that the intention of a writer had
to be taken into account." This was an interpretation of the law that the
courts would reject for decades to come. But on the question of whether a
case should go to court in the first place, the attorney general was the final
arbiter. Somervell said that, having taken into account the author's intention—by which he seems to have meant Joyce's intention to create a work
of art—and the context of the edition, as well as the novel's "established
position now in literature," he was satisfied *Ulysses* was not obscene. More
generally, Somervell thought, "no book which had any pretensions to be
treated as a serious work" should be the subject of prosecution by a local
police force: all such cases should be referred to the DPP.[142] Customs and
the Post Office were informed, and the home secretary's warrant against
Ulysses was cancelled.[143] The Home Office sent a circular to chief constables instructing them: "If in the execution of a search warrant issued
under the Act of 1857 a book of any literary merit is seized which has
been published in this country, the book should be referred to the Director."[144] Legal proceedings against avant-garde books did not cease with
the departure of Bodkin, Joynson-Hicks, and Anderson, but the postwar
moment when the most powerful national authorities took the lead in the
suppression of offensive literature had passed.

Hanley and Forster

In the thirties James Hanley exerted something like D. H. Lawrence's transgressive, ambiguous attraction. Hanley was an Irish seaman who fetched up in Liverpool and then moved to a village in North Wales, where he wrote short stories and novels about the sea and working-class life, and the varieties of bullying and survival found in cramped ships and claustrophobic families.[145] The Popular Front left tried to claim him as an authentic working-class voice, and the Dionysian right were captivated by his boldness. "God Almighty, you leave nothing unsaid or undone, do you?" the other famous Lawrence, T. E., exclaimed to Hanley, "I can't understand how you find brave men to publish you."[146] In the early thirties, Hanley's brave publishers were Charles Lahr, Eric Partridge, and F. J. Joiner, who published his stories in limited editions fancily printed on handmade paper. They were soon joined by the new firm of Boriswood, a partnership between Terence Bond, John Morris, and C. J. Greenwood who, like so many others, were carried away by Hanley's writing.[147]

The novella *Boy*, which told the story of a young sailor's brutalization and rape, was a book that only a very daring publisher would accept. Hanley had previously tried The Bodley Head, whose reader described it as "nothing but buggery and brothels and filth."[148] Boriswood published a costly limited edition and the book circulated without legal attention, despite the fact that late in 1931 Hugh Walpole made it an example of what was wrong with modern fiction, saying Hanley was trying to "out do the Lawrentians or Joyceans." He theatrically tore up a copy in a London bookshop.[149] (Jonathan Cape was wise to get Walpole onside when he published *The Well of Loneliness*.) Boriswood then took a chance and published a trade edition with some scenes toned down and offensive words cut. Still no trouble. Then, in 1934, the firm repackaged the partly expurgated text in a cheap edition with a provocative cover depicting the scene in which the sailors visit a brothel in Alexandria.[150] A man named George Franks bought copies for his small chain of provincial lending libraries.[151] In the thirties most working- and lower-middle-class people still got most of their reading matter from newsagents or commercial lending libraries— national chains like Boots, "twopenny libraries" attached to corner shops, and middling suppliers like Franks.[152] Franks had a library in Bury and the local police heard that *Boy* was being much discussed in the town.[153]

Boriswood's Greenwood assured Franks that because *Boy* had been out for three years with good reviews, the Bury justices of the peace would content themselves with "asking you to withdraw the book from circulation in this particular district."[154] Franks's solicitor was not so sanguine: "The subject matter of the said work is one which is strictly forbidden, relating as it mainly does to intimacy between members of the male sex . . . no Bench in this Country would hesitate to designate the said work as 'obscene.'"[155] He advised Franks to plead guilty to mitigate the fine and to try to push most of the blame onto the publishers.[156] The justices at Bury committed Franks and the Boriswood directors for trial at the Manchester assizes for uttering an obscene libel. Two different lawyers advised Greenwood, Bond, and Morris that a Manchester jury would feel obliged to "vindicate . . . the honour of Lancashire." There was a strong chance they would go to prison.[157] They therefore pleaded guilty, as did Franks. Mr. Justice Porter fined Franks, Greenwood, Bond, and Morris £50 each and fined Boriswood £250.[158] Without consulting or paying Hanley, Boriswood then sold their rights in *Boy* to the Obelisk Press in Paris, whose niche was English-language books that fell foul of censorship in their countries of origin.[159]

Hanley's case became a modest cause célèbre. E. M. Forster, whose novel about a homosexual relationship, *Maurice*, was not published during his lifetime, spoke about *Boy* at the International Congress of Writers in Paris later in 1935. The congress was intended to show that communists valued intellectual freedom. Forster told his audience that English freedom was "race-bound and . . . class-bound." "If you invite the average Englishman to share his liberties with the inhabitants of India or Kenya, he will reply, 'Never,' if he is a Tory, and 'Not until I consider them worthy' if he is a Liberal." Forster did not say anything equivalent about the class-bound nature of freedom, but the Liberal position he described—when they're worthy—had guided the class politics of the extension of the franchise in the nineteenth century, and was the key to what Forster called one of the "mysteries of English law": why the buyers of the limited edition of *Boy* were able to read it but the clients of an inexpensive commercial library in Bury were not. Forster praised *Boy* as a "serious and painful piece of work" and added, as critics of obscenity proceedings were practically obliged to do, that Hanley's novel was, in truth, a moral book, though Forster could not carry this ritual off unequivocally (the book's "'moral', if it had one, was definitely on the side of chastity and virtue"). The publishers, he told the congress, were nearly ruined, and although they had withdrawn the book, they remained liable for the copies already sold and still circulating. They might be fined another £400 in Cheshire or Devon, and this could go on for years: "I am not telling you a fairy tale out of Swift or Voltaire. I am telling you what can happen in England, the home of free speech."[160]

The prosecution was ridiculous, said Forster, even more ridiculous than the proceedings against *The Well of Loneliness*. Therein lay the possibility of change. Protest—ridicule—might mobilize public opinion against future prosecutions and open up a space for the serious—and the comic—treatment of sex in creative work.[161] In the years to come, Forster would work together with other members of the Society of Authors and the National Council for Civil Liberties to bend public and parliamentary opinion against legal censorship.[162]

CHAPTER THREE

Protecting Literature, Suppressing Pulp

1945–1959

THE WARTIME STATE needed a lot of censors. By the end of the Second World War there were more than six thousand people working in the Postal and Telegraph Censorship Department; nearly all of them were let go or redeployed in the months after the end of hostilities and the department was wound up.[1] The Ministry of Information ran censorship operations, and the Defence Regulations gave the state new powers to constrain the press. Defence Regulation 18B also permitted the imprisonment of writers and publishers who, in peacetime, ran afoul of the common law.[2] The interned included Arnold Leese of *The Fascist*, the defendant in a sedition trial about anti-Semitic publications in 1936.[3] Police action against obscene publications fell during the Second World War as a result of the pressure of other work, and there were inevitable inconsistencies. James Hadley Chase was convicted of obscene libel for his novel *Miss Callaghan Comes to Grief* in 1942; the same author's *No Orchids for Miss Blandish*, also gruesome, was left undisturbed and became probably the most widely read book in the armed forces as well as the civilian population.[4]

After the war, the police, courts, and Customs contended with a growing market for pornographic magazines and dirty postcards, and with the moral threat presented by American pulp. A new generation of comic books from the United States led precipitately to new powers to confiscate printed matter, and American gangster fiction and knockoffs by British writers were subjects of serial prosecutions. In debates about popular reading, as in other reaches of British culture, "Americanization" was a proxy for concerns about the "affluent society," and especially its effects on young people. Police and prosecutors' vigilance about American-style pulp swept up other writers and publishers, giving the appearance of a concerted crackdown on literature and heterodoxy. A spate of prosecutions of mainstream publishers in 1954 was, the Labour MP Roy Jenkins said, "associated with various other acts of illiberalism which took place during that year," such as the trial of Peter Wildeblood, Lord Montagu of Beaulieu, and Michael Pitt-Rivers for homosexual offenses.[5] The campaign to reform obscenity law that Jenkins and the Society of Authors embarked upon at the end of 1954 was conceived of as a defense of literature. These efforts resulted eventually in the 1959 Obscene Publications Act, which empowered defendants to call expert witnesses to testify that publication of a contentious book was for the public good. The 1959 legislation ensured that subsequent obscenity trials would turn into public "seminars" interrogating cultural change.[6]

The confluence of different kinds of "illiberalism" and the conspicuous enforcement of obscenity law can make the fifties look like a replay of the twenties, with American mass culture replacing literary modernism as the culturally alien threat and a new cohort of reactionary home secretaries to rival Sir William Joynson-Hicks. Such claims were made at the time, and they have been echoed too easily by historians.[7] To do so distorts the agendas of ministers and government lawyers during the Conservative Party's long period in government between 1951 and 1964. It also misses a critical change in the administration of the criminal law. After the Second World War, the home secretary could no longer order the director of public prosecutions to institute proceedings. New regulations placed criminal proceedings at arm's length from the Home Office.[8]

The change happened quite unexpectedly. Early in his tenure as director of public prosecutions, Sir Theobald Mathew took it upon himself to update the regulations under which his office worked. They dated from 1886 and no longer reflected actual practice. Mathew also wanted to refine the reporting obligations of police chiefs around the country.[9] His draft Prosecution of Offences Regulations preserved the clause that obliged the director to commence criminal proceedings if so instructed by the attorney general or the home secretary. Donald Somervell, still attorney general in the last months of the wartime coalition, intervened to have this clause removed. Somervell thought it was "wrong in principle" for the home secretary to be able to order a prosecution.[10] While attorneys general and home secretaries alike were appointed from within the ranks of the government, attorneys had a "quasi-judicial" obligation to advise on legal matters, sometimes in ways that confounded government policy.[11] Usually they were not members of Cabinet as were home secretaries, and serving as attorney general was not traditionally a stepping stone to higher political office, unless it was to the position of lord chancellor, which uniquely combined executive, legislative, and judicial functions.[12] Indeed, it had been traditional for a current or past attorney general to be offered the post of lord chief justice when it fell vacant.[13] The knighthood customarily conferred on appointment reflected the attorney general's status as a quasi-judicial semi-politician: High Court judges were knighted right after their appointment, but politicians were usually knighted only after they had departed the front bench or the House of Commons for good. Making public prosecutions subject to the judgment of the attorney general alone was, in Somervell's eyes, a safeguard against the appearance of politically motivated proceedings.

The cautionary tale, mentioned often as the regulations were revised, was the Campbell case of 1924, in which sedition proceedings against the editor of the *Workers Weekly* were instituted by Sir Patrick Hastings, the attorney general in the short-lived first Labour government.[14] Baldwin's Conservatives hounded the government over the attorney's handling of the matter and signs of the prime minister's involvement in the decision to prosecute, and the controversy was a factor in the fall of the government at the end of that year. Yet the incoming Conservative home secretary, Joynson-Hicks, secured Cabinet backing for the principle that in cases involving national security the home secretary and attorney general should "co-ordinate." Somervell may have been mindful of the excesses of the Joynson-Hicks years as well as the Campbell case.

The new regulations were put on hold when the government went into caretaker mode for the 1945 general election. In the new year, civil servants placed them before the new Labour home secretary, James Chuter Ede, who, like his predecessor Clynes, was wary of the powers of the office. Ede assented with no comment beyond his signature.[15] Although the Home Office expected little practical change to follow from the revocation of the home secretary's power to order prosecutions, relations between the Home Office and the DPP became less intimate after 1946. Mathew made the most of the independence he had not sought.[16] There could be no repeat of the close collaboration between Joynson-Hicks, Sir John Anderson, and Sir Archibald Bodkin in the twenties.

Policing Obscenity in the Postwar Years

All the same, *policy* on obscene publications, as distinct from decisions to prosecute in individual cases, remained part of the home secretary's portfolio. When changes to the system were mooted, civil servants at the Home Office took the lead in responding. And it was the Home Office that collected statistics on prosecutions and destruction orders and liaised with chief constables throughout England and Wales about censorship questions. One purpose of that liaison work was to ensure that the police did not seize the wrong kinds of books and magazines. Periodically the Home Office sent chief constables a confidential list of books and magazines that had been the subject of destruction orders.[17] After the Swindon magistrates granted a destruction order for an edition of the *Decameron*, a decision that was widely mocked, the Home Office did some preliminary work on a "whitelist" of classics that should not be subject to destruction orders, before abandoning the project as counterproductive.[18] As the Metropolitan Police's lawyers knew, taking a Boccaccio or a Rabelais volume before a magistrate would expose them to ridicule: and it was public ridicule, E. M. Forster suggested at the Paris congress, that could breach the defenses of the censorship system. Sir Frank Newsam, the top civil servant at the Home Office, was very sensitive to the danger that derision in the press posed to the law and to his minister.

Both the projected whitelist and the list of titles that had been declared obscene were assembled from a card index the Home Office maintained. The information the Home Office collected from police forces and the director of public prosecutions in the postwar years yielded an unusually comprehensive account of the enforcement of the law. The number of convictions and destruction orders under the 1857 act grew immediately after the war; by the mid-fifties, numbers of successful obscenity proceedings had crept back down to prewar levels.[19] Table 1 shows the number of proceedings, and the numbers and types of items destroyed, for the years before the war and the first half of the fifties.

The increase in convictions and orders up to 1950 was probably a consequence of police forces returning to peacetime operations and peacetime staffing levels.[20] The surge in proceedings beginning in 1951 and reaching its peak in 1954 was a result not only of diligent enforcement, but also more products arriving on the market—and more customers entering the market. Sexually suggestive comic postcards were a British tradition, associated above all with the seaside.[21] With more workers in a position to take

Table 1. Destruction Orders under the Obscene Publications Act 1857 and Convictions for Obscene Libel, 1935–1939, 1950–1956

	1935	1936	1937	1938	1939	1950	1951	1952	1953	1954	1955	1956
Number of destruction orders	39	33	44	66	11	67	271	113	154	152	38	58
Number of articles destroyed:												
Books and magazines	900	1,506	5,314	24,727	3,006	40,404	65,277	31,842	44,130	167,293	3,056	2,110
Photographs	8,547	11,492	8,737	2,064	344	7,182	28,956	8,329	20,141	10,503	7,412	3,059
Postcards	78	7,874	Nil	17	Nil	297	11,662	16,029	32,603	16,646	1,214	22,598
Miscellaneous	176	705	622	5,006	7	160	2,150	2,546	1,950	18,609	151	1,745
Number of convictions for obscene libel	39	18	31	39	7	19	51	34	49	111	43	42

Source: TNA, CUST 49/4712

summer vacations, the market for these postcards grew after the war.[22] "Although it is open to question whether many of these are obscene," a group of civil servants wrote, "experience has shown that magistrates will frequently order their destruction."[23]

Magazines accounted for an increasing proportion of the material seized and destroyed. Magazines had been gradually displacing individual photographic prints as the medium of pornographic images since 1918.[24] The spike in the number of books and magazines destroyed in 1954 was caused by the seizure from the printers in Leeds of 108,000 copies of a monthly magazine entitled *A Basinful of Fun*.[25] Schoolchildren and adolescents dominated its readership. The magistrate granted a destruction order because of its "lavatory jokes," but was not persuaded that the photographs of women in bikinis—a novelty that was often mentioned as a sign of the times—were obscene. The illustrations were "no worse than those of film actresses which one saw on the hoardings."[26] The formula of a few photographs of naked or semi-naked women, spaced out with jokes, line drawings, and short fiction was also standard for magazines catering primarily to adult men.[27] Newsagents carried such magazines. For more explicit material, customers had to turn to mail-order firms, or to shady contacts.[28] A good deal of pornography was smuggled into Britain in small consignments by individual seamen.[29]

The import trade in pornography seldom showed up in the criminal justice system. When Customs and Excise officials discovered pornography and impounded it, they did not need to seek destruction orders. The onus was on importers to contest the decision to confiscate, and they seldom did. Only two confiscation cases involving books were challenged in the courts between the midthirties and the midfifties, and on both occasions the courts sided with the commissioners of Customs and Excise. The department relied on its powers of confiscation to curb the flow of obscene material, and brought few prosecutions for importing indecent matter—between zero and three each year between 1952 and 1956.[30] Customs officials—in Whitehall if not at Dover and the Croydon aerodrome—took into account the class and education of the likely reader and how many copies were being imported, which was a variation on the question of class and education: were these items destined for collectors, or for a wide sale? A civil servant explained the department's policy: "The general character *ad captandum vulgus* [to attract the masses], and numerousness of copies, are special reasons for detaining indecent books. . . . There may be a Rabelais, or Boccaccio, for men of letters, which should be admitted, and another for apprentices, which ought to be stopped." Even "the most aggravated indecency" might not result in confiscation if the book or artwork was extremely rare or "a valuable illustration of human manners." An item of this sort might still find "a place in the library, where it will be carefully kept from the common eye. Such works are not merchandise but the prizes of the private collector."[31]

As in the interwar period, Customs frequently intercepted books published in Paris but written in English.[32] Customs were especially vigilant about anything published by Maurice Girodias's Olympia Press. Girodias was the son of Jack Kahane, whose Obelisk Press took Hanley's *Boy* off Boriswood's hands. The son's list was a mix of books that other people judged pornographic, such as Henry Miller's *Tropic of Cancer*, and books that Girodias himself judged pornographic.[33] The Home Office described them as works "of a gross obscenity previously only met in typescript or manuscript books or letters."[34] (Copying a pornographic text out by hand, or, from the interwar period, typing and duplicating, made it possible to do without printers who might refuse to set it. Producing pornography by hand or on a duplicator obviously limited the number of copies possible, but the there was nevertheless a flourishing clandestine trade in "Soho typescripts.")[35] The Home Office, as the designated authority under the international agreement to suppress the traffic in obscene publications (which survived the expiry of the League of Nations), appealed to the French Ministry of the Interior to take action against Olympia, drawing particular attention to *Justine* and *The Bedroom Philosophers* by the Marquis de Sade, several titles by Guillaume Apollinaire, the eighteenth-century English novel *Fanny Hill* by John Cleland, a magazine that Olympia Press published entitled *Paris Teaser*, as well as Samuel Beckett's *Watt* and Henry Miller's *Plexus*.[36] The French government does not appear to have been as helpful as the British would have liked, and the Home Office arranged for one of its civil servants to visit the Ministry of the Interior for an update while he was in Paris on other business.[37] This appears to have had the desired effect. Girodias was visited by the vice squad and some of his books were proscribed by the Ministry of the Interior.[38] In 1955, Olympia would publish Vladimir Nabokov's *Lolita*, copies of which appeared before magistrates in England several times. The question of what would happen when a British firm published *Lolita* loomed over debates about censorship in the second half of the fifties.

Horror Comics and Hank Janson

The Olympia Press's output reached only a handful of British readers, but American and American-style comics and gangster fiction had a huge market in the United Kingdom. The horror comics of the early fifties such as *Tales from the Crypt* and *Haunt of Fear* ratcheted up the gore. They also relaxed their grip on the crime-does-not-pay lessons that legitimated other exploitation literature. The most notorious strip, "The Orphan," told the story of an American girl who witnesses the murder of her abusive father by the girl's mother and her lover. The protagonist, Lucy, then informs on the murderers and expresses satisfaction when the pair of them go to the electric chair. Lucy ends up in the custody of her aunt, happy to live in a nice house with nice furniture and all the toys she wants.[39] The subject matter, the values expressed, and young people's enthusiasm for these comics were all affronts to the idea of childhood innocence.

As such the comics were a lightning rod for the concerns about juvenile delinquency, adolescent sexuality, changes in gender norms, and the effects of affluence on traditional (working-class) values that caused alarm in many countries in the fifties.[40] The new American comics ignited public controversies across Europe and the English-speaking world. In the middle of the decade, the United Nations Educational, Scientific, and Cultural Organization resolved to collect and share information on efforts to protect children from the adverse effects of mass communications. The United Kingdom opposed the idea of an international body to study the problem, but the Home Office paid attention to research coming out of UNESCO, in particular Philippe Bauchard's *The Child Audience*.[41] In former dominions such as Australia and New Zealand, where the British taboo on pre-publication censorship held little sway, the state moved quickly to suppress offensive comics.[42] In the United States itself, comic book publishers resorted to the motion-picture industry solution of self-regulation. A code of conduct was agreed ("1. Crime shall never be presented in such a way as to create sympathy for the criminal") and a former New York City magistrate was installed as "Comic Book Czar," much as the Motion Picture Association of America had recruited the postmaster general, Will Hays, three decades earlier.[43]

Foreign service officers in Washington, DC, and London plied the UK Foreign Office with information on American efforts to combat the evil, and British campaigners against horror comics liaised with their American counterparts. The most famous document in the attack on comic books, *The Seduction of the Innocent* by the American psychiatrist Fredric

Wertham, was swiftly republished in London. The Labour MP Horace King met with Wertham in New York to discuss proposed legislation to curb the new imports.[44] Wertham was at war with comic books generally, not just the horror comics that emerged after he began his research and advocacy. He criticized superhero comics as quasi-fascist exaltations of strength and violence. Comics glamorized drug-taking and distorted the development of children's understanding of sex. They retarded children's literacy and cut them off from the resources of culture.[45] *The Seduction of the Innocent* was an arsenal that could equip a variety of combatants.

The British campaign against horror comics brought together quite different interest groups: clergy, Conservative MPs, English teachers, and communists. A handful of Communist Party (CP) members, including several teachers and a full-time cultural affairs officer for the party, laid the groundwork and then, once the campaign began to gather steam, the CP members deliberately pulled back and let the National Union of Teachers drive the campaign. Cominform policy was for communist parties outside the Soviet Union to emphasize national independence and national traditions. Going after comics was a way of attacking the "American way of life" and contesting the Americanization of British culture. Peter Mauger, a party member and English teacher, took comic books to task for their xenophobia and glorification of power: "It is by appealing to the best instincts of ordinary decent people that we can stop this American vulgarization."[46] Mauger thus echoed earlier critics of juvenile literature and anticipated Wertham; and he used the anti-Americanization language acceptable to other English teachers who weren't members of the Communist Party.

School teachers in mid-twentieth-century Britain were expected to exercise moral leadership and they took their status in the community seriously. Many teachers of English believed that they had a special responsibility to help their pupils resist the depredations of popular fiction, the movies, and advertising. The culture industry traded in manufactured emotions and encouraged their consumers to settle for the easy and ersatz. The industrial metaphor was not uncommon: many teachers and critics saw mass culture as the equivalent of the "leveling down" and "standardization" that Fordism brought to manufacturing. This critique of mass culture was developed most fully by the literary critics F. R. and Q. D. Leavis and others connected with the journal *Scrutiny*, above all Denys Thompson, who edited an English teachers' journal.[47] But a larger constellation of educationalists turned public figures held similar positions, including several participants in the agitation against horror comics. Horace King, who had a doctorate in English literature, was a grammar school headmaster before entering Parliament. Edward Blishen taught at one of the secondary modern schools established after the war for young people deemed less academically able; he wrote a novel, *Roaring Boys*, about his experience teaching them.[48]

The campaign against horror comics was remarkably successful in mobilizing support in Parliament, despite the fact that there was no need for fresh legislation. Chief constables had not sought new powers to deal with comics, and the idea that the existing law covered only representations of indecency, not violence, came from a non-lawyer. The archbishop of Canterbury persuaded the Conservative home secretary, Gwilym Lloyd George, that new legislation was needed because the *Hicklin* test did not extend to depictions of non-sexual violence.[49] Churchill himself, in his last year as prime minister, took an interest in the subject, apparently at the urging of his friend Brendan Bracken.[50] Legislation was duly drafted and sent to the attorney general, Reginald Manningham-Buller. His legal advice was that the draft Children and Young Persons (Harmful Publications) Bill was too wide in scope and in any case unnecessary. Apart from an Australian case that had no bearing in Britain, there was no judicial precedent "restricting the meaning of 'obscene' to matters relating to sex," so the existing law was quite capable of dealing with horror.[51] Cabinet preferred the archbishop's view to the attorney general's and went ahead with the Harmful Publications Bill.

The bill hurtled through Parliament. Lloyd George kept his speeches on the subject short—"so as to lessen the opportunity for debating the law of obscenity"—much to the frustration of the Foreign Office, which wanted him to acknowledge that the US Air Force had deferred to a British request to withdraw objectionable comics from Post Exchange stores in bases in Britain.[52] "Although less political capital is being made about the American origin of the comic than had at one stage seemed possible," an officer at the American desk wrote, "there is still a tendency in some quarters to equate horror comics with American comic publications in general." The bill passed without trouble. The Children and Young Persons (Harmful Publications) Act added new powers of search and seizure, prescribed summary offenses for sellers of comics, and prohibited the importing of comics themselves or the matrices used to print them.[53] (Most horror comics sold in Britain were printed locally from matrices bought from the American publishers.)[54] It is unclear whether the new confiscation powers were used much. There were very few prosecutions.[55]

Gangster fiction was the other malign American (and Americanizing) genre of the war years and postwar period. The boom in paperback gangster novels was one cause of the increase in obscenity proceedings in the first half of the fifties.[56] Unlike the horror comics, which were actually of American origin, albeit printed in Britain, many of the pulp novels sold in Britain were written by British writers who found that reading hard-boiled fiction and reference books was sufficient preparation for writing convincing crime stories set in Chicago or Los Angeles. A number of self-taught gangster authors came from the "popular writing" scene of middle- and lower middle-class freelancers who bulked out the fiction columns of Britain's weekly press.[57] Stephen Frances was one of them, placing an ad in *The Writer* offering the services of his fly-by-night literary bureau. Frances was the creator of Hank Janson and wrote most but not all of the Hank Janson stories. Frances tried his hand at westerns—another popular genre that could be practiced without personal experience of American life—before settling into a groove chronicling the sometime reporter Hank Janson's adventures with crooks and dames.[58]

Gangster fiction was sometimes described, like comics, as objectively fascist—Orwell called one of James Hadley Chase's novels "a daydream appropriate to a totalitarian age"—so it comes as some surprise that Frances was a socialist throughout the thirties and a conscientious objector during the war (he refused to fight other workers).[59] His publisher was not a natural fit for strongman stories either. Julius Reiter was a Jewish refugee from Nazi Germany. He ran a newspaper distribution business. Frances supplied Reiter with manuscripts and Reiter took care of the printing and sales. When paper rationing was lifted in early 1950, Frances and Reiter went into business with Reginald Carter, a sales rep at a company with an underemployed rotary press that would be capable of printing paperbacks in much larger runs than Reiter's twenty thousand. Carter would handle the printing and Reiter the distribution. When the operation was at its peak, a new Hank Janson went onto the market in an edition of one hundred thousand every six weeks.[60]

The huge numbers of Hank Janson books in circulation—and their lurid covers—made them conspicuous targets. Frances hoped that avoiding four-letter words and not being explicit about the most repellent acts of his characters (the exact details were left to the reader's imagination, though the reader didn't have to have much of an imagination to get the picture) would keep the books just on the right side of the law. After a handful of destruction orders were granted in towns across England, Frances, Reiter, and Carter devised self-policing guidelines. Any "scene, action or words used" had to be "commonplace and generally accepted in society." "If a naked girl was mentioned in a book, it could be shown that widely-read magazines also featured a naked woman," and so on.[61] Reiter repeatedly showed manuscripts to detectives, hoping to get a definitive answer on whether a work was obscene or not, but they always refused to give assurances.[62]

As was the way with obscenity cases, courtroom discussions sometimes turned from the paperbacks and their producers to their readers. In 1952, police on the Isle of Man, working from the Home Office list of titles against which destruction orders had been granted, charged booksellers with selling obscene books. Many of them were Hank Janson novellas. The high bailiff asked the police inspector presenting the case if he had read the bestseller of the previous year, Nicholas Monserrat's *The Cruel Sea*: "There's a passage in that which could hardly be more obscene." The officer replied that *The Cruel Sea* was not likely to fall into the hands of young people on vacation at the Isle of Man. The high bailiff decided he had a point and a week later granted a destruction order.[63] Like late nineteenth-century commentators on popular literacy, the police officer identified young adulthood as a time when working-class readers were particularly impressionable. The distinction between *The Cruel Sea* and the sort of book that would fall into the hands of young holidaymakers was a judgment about class as well as age: Janson's novels would not be found in respectable bookshops but in newsagents' shops. The previous year, when Carter and Reiter were tried in Blackburn alongside their competitor Irene Turvey of Modern Fiction (the publisher of Hank Janson's rival Ben Sarto), Turvey's barrister asked the court: "Is the standard to be different in the case of books printed in stiff covers and in the reach of the pockets of the limited class, and in the case of the working man's literature in a paperback cover?" He got nowhere.[64]

These proceedings in provincial courts led eventually to a more substantial response from the center. Officers from the Metropolitan Police raided the printing facility, and a month later Carter and Reiter were indicted on seven counts of publishing an obscene libel. The seven books— *Accused, Auctioned, Persian Pride, Pursuit, Amok, Killer,* and *Vengeance*— had already been the subject of multiple destruction orders.[65] The proceedings were undertaken by the director of public prosecutions and the trial would take place at the Old Bailey. The DPP provided counsel with a page of notes on each of the seven novels, with page references under several headings such as "Sexual Descriptions," "Brutality," "Whipping," and "Murder," together with short summaries and comments: "This book is a continuation of 'Auctioned' much on the same lines. Brutality and sex is the main theme"; "This is about the worst book that Hank Janson has written. The raping of a young girl that the killer kidnaps is about as obscene as it could be."[66] This time there was no suggestion that different readers might be affected by these books in different ways. The judge, Sir Gerald Dodson, thought that *anyone* could be depraved or corrupted by Hank Janson.[67] The jury convicted on all counts. Dodson sentenced Carter and Reiter to six months in prison and fined their companies £2000 each.

Carter and Reiter's barrister argued along the lines of Frances's own guidelines—that scenes in the Hank Janson stories were no worse than other publications that never attracted legal attention. Their counsel was Christmas Humphreys, a striking combination of second-generation criminal barrister and pioneering British Buddhist.[68] Humphreys asked permission to introduce some comparison books as evidence for the jury to read. The judge turned him down. After the verdict, Humphreys tried to argue in mitigation of the sentence by pointing out that Hank Janson was much in demand in the armed forces, and the troops did not buy their own books: they were bought on their behalf "by some representative of the Government." He continued, "These are not books which are sold under the counter in small shops in the back streets round the Charing Cross Road and the like. They were openly sold to Smiths bookstalls, and the like."[69]

This attempt to normalize Hank Janson had unintended consequences. When the case went to the Court of Criminal Appeal, the judges took up the question of whether other books could be admitted as evidence. Lord Goddard said that this struck him as "absolutely wrong" and cited a recent Scottish decision, *Gellatly v. Laird.* Although that case involved a Scottish statute, it applied a close paraphrase of the *Hicklin* test and the principles were the same.[70] In *Gellatly v. Laird,* the defense had tried to compare the books complained of to others available at the Paisley public library. On appeal the lord justice general held that examining other books "would be endless and futile. If the books produced by the prosecution are indecent or obscene, their quality in that respect cannot be made any better by examining other books, or listening to the opinions of other people with regard to those other books." Goddard endorsed the lord justice general's remarks as a statement of the law "in this country as it is in Scotland."[71] Goddard added, however, that the books Humphreys mentioned for comparison "might be proper subjects for proceedings."[72]

The 1954 Prosecutions

The DPP then referred these novels to the senior treasury counsel, who would represent the Crown if any case went to court. The advice came back in favor of proceeding. The DPP accordingly launched prosecutions against their publishers, and against Secker and Warburg, the publishers of another novel, found obscene on the Isle of Man, where the authorities remained vigilant about indecent publications.[73] Norman St John-Stevas, a critic of the law on obscene publications, fulminated: "For the first time since the period of Joynson-Hicks at the Home Office, a full-scale campaign of prosecutions was opened against publishers who were admitted by all parties to be of the highest standing and repute."[74] Later observers have also taken up the idea of a concerted campaign.[75] It gels with the notion that public morals agitations occur cyclically—the early fifties as a return to the Joynson-Hicks twenties. Theobald Matthew and David Maxwell Fyfe (during his time as home secretary) star as authoritarians in Jeffrey Weeks's argument that law enforcement conducted a "purge of homosexuals" in London in the first half of the fifties.[76] John Springhall merges Weeks's story of a witch hunt led by the DPP and the home secretary with his own story of a "crusade against supposedly pornographic fiction."[77]

These claims do not stand up. Even if the Conservative home secretaries and Cabinet lawyers of the fifties had been in the Joynson-Hicks mold and Mathew had been all-in like Bodkin, the criminal prosecution system was much less centrally coordinated after 1946 and the opportunities for top-down public morals initiatives correspondingly diminished. The historian Matt Houlbrook has demonstrated that the rise in charges for homosexual offenses correlates with the Metropolitan Police's resumption of peacetime operations. He finds no archival evidence that the DPP or home secretary ordered increased vigilance.[78] Nor is there any paper trail of a concerted campaign against established publishers. A campaigner for the reform of obscenity law described the Home Office as a "spectator," "in no way responsible for the 1954 'big five' prosecutions."[79] Mathew was usually cautious about obscenity proceedings. Up to this point, he had prosecuted for obscene libel only when the material was being produced on a large scale, as it was with Carter and Reiter. He did not "normally take proceedings against a reputable publisher, author or retailer in respect of a work which might be on the border-line."[80] For instance, Mathew opted not to take action against André Deutsch for publishing Norman Mailer's *The Naked and the Dead*, and weathered a certain amount of criticism in consequence.[81] Mathew felt obliged to act on Goddard's "suggestion."[82] "As you know, there were special reasons" for the prosecutions of 1954, he told Sir Frank Newsam.[83]

The first case to come to trial concerned the novel condemned on the Isle of Man, Stanley Kaufman's *The Philanderer* not one of the books Goddard suggested the DPP take a look at.[84] Kaufman's novel explored the emptiness of a New York ad man's sexual adventuring. Fredric Warburg knew there was a risk in publishing it. Several other publishers had passed on it. The book "shocked at least one reader" in Warburg's office, but "the final decision was to publish."[85] The Metropolitan Police bought a copy from Foyles at the beginning of January 1954, but did not apply for process until nearly five months later. At the trial, the jury acquitted. Better still, from the Society of Authors' point of view, was the summing up by Mr. Justice Stable (another of the expressive Dickensian names that the history of British censorship turns up).[86] Stable made a succession of points that critics of the law had made since *Hicklin*. He attempted to narrow the scope of the *Hicklin* test, saying that "to deprave or corrupt" had to mean something more severe than "to shock or to disgust." He also took issue with *Hicklin*'s reference to "those whose minds are open to such immoral influences and into whose hands a publication of this sort may fall." Asking, "Are we to take our literary standards as being the level of something that is suitable for the decently brought up young female aged fourteen?" Stable's answer was an emphatic no. He thus rejected a staple of prosecutors' rhetoric: "Would you put this book into the hand of your 16 year old daughter[?]"[87]

Stable even questioned whether books could put ideas in people's heads, and—like Home Office officials pausing to rethink their task in the wake of Joynson-Hicks's tenure—he suggested that the responsibility for young people's moral wellbeing lay with parents and teachers rather than the law. A "mass of literature, great literature," was unsuitable for adolescents, and might shock or disgust adults with its hard truths. Stable recognized a special role for literature in providing a way of understanding "the society when it was written." Fitzjames Stephen had offered the same justification for being able to read the classics unexpurgated: Juvenal, Swift, Defoe, Rabelais, Chaucer, and Boccaccio were full of obscenity, but publishing them uncut was justified by "the consideration that upon the whole it is for the public good that the works of remarkable men should be published as they are, so that we may be able to form as complete an estimate as possible of their characters and of the times in which they lived."[88] Stable did not quote Stephen, but he did channel another Victorian luminary, Matthew Arnold: "The literature of the world . . . represents the sum total of thought of the human mind." Stable argued that the principle applied to novels that showed "how life is lived and how the human mind is working in those parts of the world which are not separated from us in point of time but are separated from us in point of space, and, at a time like to-day, when ideas and creeds and processes of thought seem, to some extent, to be in the melting pot and people are bewildered and puzzled to know in what direction humanity is headed." Stable endeavored to reinstate the distinction between literature and pornography that Lord Campbell had acknowledged in the debates over the 1857 act, but which the Vizetelly prosecutions had blurred. Literature might include unseemly material, but it was animated by thought. Mere "filthy books," in contrast, had "no message . . . no inspiration . . . no thought."

Hopes that the law was evolving dissipated with the next trial, also at the Old Bailey.[89] Dodson, the judge who presided over Carter and Reiter's trial, expressly rejected Stable's contentions, which the defense counsel had quoted at length. Literary standards *were* to be determined by a book's effects on "a callow youth or a girl just budding into womanhood." "The definition is designed to protect the weak rather than the strong," Dodson declared.[90] In a third case, two successive juries failed to reach a verdict, and another prosecution resulted in an acquittal. Printers became even more cautious about liability and hired additional readers to vet jobs sent by publishers.[91] The Society of Authors swung into action and so, anticipating their push for reform, did the civil service.

The Making of the Obscene Publications Act 1959

The figurehead of the Society of Authors' campaign wanted to call their reforming legislation the Protection of Literature Bill.[92] This was a campaign on behalf of writing recognized as aesthetically valuable by establishment publishers, academic critics, and the men and women of letters who commanded the reviews pages of the "quality" newspapers. It was not about protecting Hank Janson. Indeed, the Society of Authors took up the cause of law reform because a censorship that was legitimate when applied to pulp novels and pornographic magazines had crossed over into a different category of text: literature. A literary casualty of the previous generation was a touchstone for the efforts. The treatment of Radclyffe Hall and *The Well of Loneliness* had become part of the literary profession's corporate memory, and as they sought to change the law Society of Authors and its supporters mentioned Hall's case again and again. They demanded three things that Hall had been denied: the right of the author to speak on a book's behalf in hearings over applications for destruction orders; license to defend a book on the grounds of its literary merit; and the power to call expert witnesses to attest to the value of the book. The literary orientation of the campaign made it an umbrella under which people on the left could cooperate with Conservatives who were impatient with officialdom or cant.[93] There were more radical libertarian and libertine opponents of censorship out there (one of them, Alec Craig, probably knew more about the operations of obscenity law than anyone else), but they wielded little influence.[94]

The committee convened by the secretary of the Society of Authors was always referred to as "the Herbert Committee," no doubt for its official ring. A. P. Herbert had been the Society of Authors' man in Parliament before the Oxford University seat was abolished along with other instances of plural voting in 1950. He was a humorist and non-practicing barrister whose satires on the law, "Misleading Cases," had a faithful following. Herbert was also an inveterate writer of letters to *The Times* and a firm believer in the paper's correspondence columns as a public forum.[95] The committee's parliamentary representative was the Labour backbencher Roy Jenkins, whose two books on British political history qualified him for membership in the Society of Authors. Jenkins educated himself about obscenity law and honed his parliamentary tactics. The Obscene Publications Bills that he and others introduced were drafted by Norman St John-Stevas. Stevas was an academic lawyer. He was Catholic and would become a prominent contributor to Catholic debates about homosexuality, contraception, and euthanasia. He was also one of those younger Conservatives seeking to modernize the party.[96] The Herbert Committee stalwart with the most unusual career was C. R. Hewitt, pen name C. H. Rolph. Hewitt deferred his dream of becoming a full-time writer until after he had completed twenty-five years in the City of London police. He then joined the *New Statesman*, surely the only retired chief inspector to become a staff writer on a left-wing paper. He had long been interested in censorship.[97] Hewitt, Stevas, Herbert, and Jenkins were the committee's key members. They would spend five years, Herbert would later quip, "playing Snakes and Ladders with the Home Office."[98]

The Herbert Committee's bill, drafted by Stevas, would have codified obscenity law for England and Wales, updating the destruction order procedures in the 1857 act and replacing the common law misdemeanor of obscene libel with a statutory offense. The bill included the three *Well of Loneliness* demands. First, authors would be granted the right to be heard in proceedings against their publishers or distributors, who were almost always the defendants in obscenity cases. Second, courts would be obliged to take into account the "literary or other merit of the publication." Here Stevas adapted Fitzjames Stephen, whose authority he invoked in an explanatory piece in the *Author*.[99] Stephen had submitted that the publication of obscene books could be justified if it was "for the public good, as being necessary or advantageous to religion or morality, to the administration of justice, the pursuit of science, literature, or art, or other objects of general interest."[100] And third, Stevas's bill would empower defense counsel to call experts to testify about a work's literary qualities.[101] A note in Roy Jenkins' files indicated the kind of people the Herbert Committee had in mind: "Professors of lit, critics, novelists, etc. R. Mortimer. H. Nicolson."[102] (Raymond Mortimer and Harold Nicolson were both eminent book critics in newspapers.) Stevas's bill also required courts to consider the "dominant effect" of the publication, not just cherrypicked rude bits. The phrase "dominant effect" was taken from Judge Woolsey's judgment giving *Ulysses* its freedom in the United States, and it was incorporated into an Australian statute.

The bill also made demands that, in time, the Herbert Committee would trade away. One was making an intention to deprave and corrupt (as distinct from an intention to publish something that magistrates or juries later decided was likely to deprave and corrupt) an essential component of the offense. Mixing erudition with wishful thinking, Stevas argued that this was the true common-law position and to think otherwise was a misreading of *Hicklin*.[103] This would be a hard to sell to government lawyers. The bill also required the attorney general or DPP to approve all prosecutions for obscenity. The stated purpose of this provision was to ensure consistency across the country, but it would also have slashed the number of prosecutions. Only a minority of obscene libel cases in England and Wales were led by the DPP; the rest were initiated by local police forces.[104] Requiring the attorney general's consent would also rule out private prosecutions. This too would meet with resistance.

In Britain the government—the party or coalition of parties commanding a majority in the House of Commons—more or less controls the legislative agenda. Opposition MPs or government backbenchers might succeed in amending bills in Parliament, but it is much harder—often literally a lottery—for legislation originating with the opposition or government backbenchers to get a hearing. These "private member's bills" can be starved of time for reading and debate if the leadership of the government chooses, because the government manages the parliamentary schedule. A Cabinet committee would consider whether to entertain a private member's bill, and, if not, would block it by asking a government MP to speak until the time allotted for the bill's first reading ran out. In March of 1955, Roy Jenkins succeeded in introducing the Herbert Committee's draft legislation into Parliament as a private member's bill under the "ten-minute rule."[105] The text was sent to the Home Office, which greeted it with a sigh. "It will only revive interest in this matter, which is a pity," one civil servant wrote on the file.[106]

Sir Frank Newsam had already taken steps to pre-empt the Herbert Committee. As early as November of 1954, Newsam wrote to the DPP and other department heads suggesting the formation of an interdepartmental working party to review the law on obscene publications.[107] "This is definitely an issue in which S of S [the home secretary] should proceed on the policy 'festina lente' [rush slowly]," said Sir Austin Strutt, the working party's chair.[108] Strutt and his colleagues were not persuaded that the law as it stood had led to injustice or "the unnecessary suppression of works of literary merit." Moreover, Stevas's bill was "very much an *author*'s Bill, prepared in their interest and not in that of the general public."[109] The government blocked the bill.[110]

The Herbert Committee regrouped. A new recruit, the Conservative MP Tony Lambton, introduced a revised bill in the next parliamentary session with the support of Jenkins and handful of liberal or intellectual Conservatives such as Angus Maude and Sir Edward Boyle, as well as two Conservative MPs who were also publishers: Nigel Nicolson, son of Harold and a principal at Weidenfeld and Nicolson; and Maurice Macmillan, who, like his father Harold, soon to be prime minister, was a partner in the family publishing firm.[111] By the time the new bill got its chance at a second reading in March 1957, the Home Office detected a shift in public and parliamentary opinion.

Newsam and Strutt began to entertain the possibility that reform was desirable, even if the Herbert Committee's successive bills were not the right way to go about it. Strutt conceded that the existing law was "open to serious objection" and that "a purely negative attitude will merely make us ridiculous to a highly articulate section of the public."[112] Strutt said he could put up with the dominant effect requirement, though he would prefer to say that a book should be judged "as a whole." "Notwithstanding a scene of revolting sadism where a character's eyes are gouged out in full view of the audience, the effect of 'King Lear' *as a whole* is not corrupting." Strutt doubted whether literary merit was "in strict logic relevant to the liability of a work to corrupt," but he recognized that "it does not conduce to the authority of the law that a work which is suppressed in one generation is acclaimed in the next as one of the glories of literature or art (e.g. 'Ulysses' or 'Jude the Obscure' or 'Dejeuner sur l'Herbe')."[113] Newsam recognized that the debates on the horror comics bill showed that MPs of all parties harboured "uneasiness and misgivings about the anomalies of the present system and its uncertainties." Ever alert to the dangers to the Home Office of being on the wrong side of public opinion, Newsam now said he could accept changes to the law if they were limited to a requirement that a book be assessed as a whole and that the courts "should be enabled to hear expert evidence on either side as to the literary or scientific merit of the work."[114] These two reforms were the ones that mattered most to the Society of Authors.

There was a change at the top of the Home Office too. Lloyd George was replaced as home secretary by R. A. Butler, a far more accomplished policy maker and operator. Butler agreed that the government should be open to reform of some kind if there was cross-party support in the Commons.[115] Butler anticipated strong resistance from the attorney general.[116] However, when the Legislative Committee discussed the subject, most of those present were broadly supportive. Newsam then sketched out a way forward. Assuming that the Lambton bill's flaws were too serious to be fixed at the standing committee stage, it should go to a select committee, an ad hoc parliamentary body with investigative powers that a routine standing committee lacked. Newsam recommended that Jack Simon, the junior Home Office minister who would be representing the government, should hold back and observe how the debate ebbed and flowed; then, if there turned out to be substantial cross-party support for change, he should intervene and recommend the Lambton bill go to a select committee. Butler discussed the matter with the chief whip and they agreed.[117] The debate in the house unfolded as Newsam had foreseen. Jenkins saw the danger of a select committee. It would take time to complete its task, and if it did not report before the end of the parliamentary session, the bill would lapse. If that happened, a revised bill that emerged from the select committee would need to start the journey through the legislative process from the beginning. Jenkins asked for an expression of goodwill from the government to set aside the necessary parliamentary time if it turned out that way. Simon said he could not give any commitment. Jenkins expressed his disappointment but had to accept. The bill was read a second time and committed to a select committee.[118] Down the snake it slid.

The select committee took a year to complete its work, so Lambton's bill did indeed expire. The select committee got on with interviewing senior officials from the relevant government departments and the Metropolitan Police. The Public Morality Council's representatives came to talk about photographic pornography. Unlike their interwar predecessors, they were not worried about "serious works of art" that pushed against contemporary moral expectations.[119] T. S. Eliot and E. M. Forster reminisced about *The Well of Loneliness*. On some questions a consensus emerged. The select committee, like the Home Office, accepted the Society of Authors' call for courts to take the whole book into account and for an author's right to be heard. It recommended tweaking the *Hicklin* definition of obscenity rather than starting again, a stance the Society of Authors could reconcile itself to. Appearing before the select committee, Hewitt said that the Society did not like the *Hicklin* test, but no longer saw much profit in trying to devise alternatives: "We should find ourselves in the courts forced back on the use of dictionaries and, following the inevitable circle, coming right back to where we began."[120] That left a defense of literary merit and the power to call expert witnesses. On these demands, the select committee was divided and could not make any firm recommendations.[121]

The Home Office made no public response to the select committee's report. Given that Newsam and Strutt could now accept a literary merit defense, and given Butler's record as a problem-solver, it seems likely that the reason for their inaction was not an obstinate return to *festina lente* but the difficulty of getting any reform past the attorney general. In November, Cabinet's Home Affairs Committee considered a revised bill the Herbert Committee had drafted in response to the select committee report. Manningham-Buller objected to the requirement the DPP or attorney general sign off on all prosecutions.[122] Manningham-Buller thought it a "fundamental principal [*sic*] of English criminal law that proceedings may be instituted by private individuals."[123] This was one of those semi-constitutional principles that did not apply throughout the United Kingdom: private prosecutions were very rare in Scotland.[124] The meeting agreed to block the bill, while taking steps to reassure Jenkins "that this did not mean that the Government had decided, at this stage, to prevent the Bill from proceeding at a later date." In the meantime, the lord chancellor—Viscount Kilmuir, formerly David Maxwell Fyfe—would chair a subcommittee that would "consider the position in more detail."[125] Kilmuir was one of Butler's closer colleagues in the parliamentary party.[126] When Jenkins's bill came up for a second reading the following week, several Conservative MPs objected, and the bill stalled.[127]

Over the next month, Manningham-Buller and Kilmuir raked over the recent history of obscenity law. Manningham-Buller lent Kilmuir a copy of Walter Baxter's novel *The Image and the Search*, the subject of one of the 1954 prosecutions. A jury had failed to reach a verdict, so Manningham-Buller had been forced to decide whether to push on with a retrial. He told Mathew to persist. The second jury also failed to agree and the publishers were formally acquitted. Would Kilmuir have made the same call? The lord chancellor thought *The Image and the Search* in bad taste but could not imagine anyone being depraved or corrupted by it, and so would not have supported prosecuting.[128] Manningham-Buller's stated reason for taking the case to a jury a second time had less to do with Baxter's book than with the next one. If the DPP had given up trying to get a conviction over *The Image and the Search*, he "would feel he could not properly give his consent to a prosecution in respect of a similar book. He would only do so in relation to books which were even worse. Consequently every time a prosecution failed there would be a lowering of standards."[129] Despite his truculence (his nickname was "Bullying Manner"), the attorney general based his decision on a perception of the criminal law's frailty.[130]

The subcommittee was "deeply divided," just as the select committee had been. Everyone acknowledged that "the political pressures which have developed make it necessary to adopt a constructive attitude towards Mr. Roy Jenkins' Bill," but the measures the committee could agree on fell far short of the Herbert Committee's demands. Not everyone on the subcommittee was persuaded that legislation was needed: the prosecutions of 1954 occurred in exceptional circumstances, and the mixed record of convictions and acquittals made it "unlikely that similar prosecutions would be undertaken in the future." They all found the idea of a defense of literary merit "unacceptable." Some members found the idea of any special defense undesirable; others were open to a defense of good faith or the public interest. Others objected that a defense of good faith would smuggle in the question of literary merit and an argument that publication was in the public interest was "too vague to be workable." Manningham-Buller even dissented from the principle that a potentially obscene book should be judged "as a whole." Manningham-Buller thought that this "could open the way to pornography by enabling obscene passages or pictures to be included in works otherwise unobjectionable"—what a Customs official called "the 'ingredient' problem."[131] Kilmuir's report could not do more to chart a way forward than recommend that the whips make time for a second reading for Jenkins's bill, and hope that a standing committee could sort out all the problems that the select committee and the Home Affairs subcommittee had failed to resolve.[132]

The external pressure on the government intensified. Maddened by the decision to block the second reading of the latest bill, A. P. Herbert announced his intention to stand as an independent in a looming by-election. "You may not care much about books, whether pure or pornographic," he wrote in an open letter to the voters of East Harrow, "But you must agree that this is not the way in which the land should be governed or the laws be made."[133] As a writer and public figure Herbert had a large Conservative fan base. While he was unlikely to win East Harrow, the Conservative whips worried about how many votes he would siphon away from them.[134] Herbert's return to his old trouble-making ways roused Butler to rush less slowly. The day after Kilmuir's subcommittee reported, Butler addressed the House of Commons on obscene publications. He declared an intention to act on the select committee's recommendations—Kilmuir's report remained confidential—though he warned that many difficult questions remained unresolved. Chuter Ede retorted that Butler's speech "was so inconclusive . . . that I see no reason for Sir Alan Herbert to feel that he should now withdraw from the East Harrow by-election."[135]

In fact, Butler's speech in the Commons *was* enough to persuade Herbert to withdraw from the East Harrow contest.[136] Butler resolved to treat Jenkins's bill—rather than a bill initiated by the government—as a suitable vehicle for reforming the law on obscene publications. He was doubtful he could bring the attorney general along.[137] Manningham-Buller indicated that he expected the bill to be substantially re-written once it went to a House of Commons standing committee.[138] Partly, it seems, to circumvent Manningham-Buller, Butler did not let the bill go straight to committee. Instead, he and his officials met with Jenkins and others from the Herbert Committee a number of times over the winter of 1958/1959. Believing they needed more legal guidance, the Herbert Committee brought in Gerald Gardiner, a prominent civil libertarian and someone whom Butler and the Home Office's lawyers took seriously.[139] The civil servants and the Herbert Committee representatives hammered out compromises, and Butler had the parliamentary counsel draft new clauses.[140] Butler did not like the idea of a defense of literary merit, but he thought a public-good defense was workable. In this he was guided by the 1955 working party.[141] Butler said he was advised that it was "held in some quarters that it is a good defence under the present law to show that the publication of matter prima facie obscene is for the public good because it is necessary or advantageous to religion, science, literature or art, provided that the manner and extent of publication do not exceed what the public good requires." The courts were yet to give an authoritative ruling: this was an inference "derived from the corpus and the digest of law."[142]

Neither Butler nor the working party named the source of the proposed defense, but Hewitt recognized that it was Stephen's *Digest of the Criminal Law*. Explaining this to the rest of the Herbert Committee, Hewitt pointed out that Stable had also relied strongly on Stephen's reasoning in the *Philanderer* case.[143] Hewitt went on: "A defence of public good which sought to establish literary 'good' would necessarily involve the calling of witnesses who would be widely recognised as knowing literary merit when they saw it. Either by this route, therefore, or by way of a frankly admitted 'defence of literary or artistic merit', the expert evidence would get in."[144] Meeting with Butler two weeks later, Jenkins insisted on explicit provision for expert evidence, saying that the Herbert Committee would "certainly break off negotiations if we could not get this." Butler brought up the public good defense, apparently implying that it would make expert testimony admissible. Jenkins said they preferred explicit literary merit, reflecting the overwhelmingly literary concerns of the Herbert Committee.[145] Gardiner too thought literary merit preferable to public good, and urged them to "fight hard" for the former.[146] By the end of the meeting, the parties seemed close to "a compromise under which public good was made the main defence but literary and artistic merit was specified as a special division of this and expert evidence was made clearly admissible."[147] Jenkins, Hewitt, and Stevas had a further discussion with Home Office lawyers that confirmed this compromise. The right of the author to be heard in applications for destruction orders—Radclyffe Hall's predicament—was provided for.[148]

The standing committee held two surprises for Jenkins, one a setback and the other a stroke of luck. The setback was that the government's representative was not one of Butler's junior ministers, as Jenkins had expected, but Sir Harry Hylton-Foster, the solicitor general and thus, in effect, Manningham-Buller's deputy.[149] But then, when the hearings got underway, Jenkins found that he was often in the majority because most of the Conservative members did not turn up.[150] Jenkins wondered fleetingly whether this was the work of Butler, "that most ambiguous of politicians."[151] The Conservative no-shows meant that Jenkins and his allies were able to prevail over Hylton-Foster in most of the divisions, including the vote on the admissibility of expert evidence. Manningham-Buller was staunchly opposed to allowing testimony about subject matter on which "no expert corpus of opinion exists," and he and Hylton-Foster harbored a more general aversion to tampering with the law of evidence.[152] Having failed to defeat the reform effort through the select committee, Manningham-Buller seems to have gone back to Butler, who informed Jenkins several weeks after the standing committee wrapped up that he could not accept an expert evidence clause. Butler explained that it would be either otiose—Home Office advisers had long said that expert witness testimony might drag out hearings but would make little difference to the outcome—or an undesirable and unprecedented interference with the courts' discretion about what evidence to admit—Manningham-Buller's line.[153] The climax came when the attorney general called Jenkins to a meeting and the two of them made a deal. Manningham-Buller agreed that expert evidence could stay in the bill if the clause requiring the attorney general's consent to prosecutions were struck out.[154] That Manningham-Buller was willing to concede expert witness testimony indicates that he really did think that the right to bring private prosecutions was fundamental.

The bill then went to the House of Lords, where the government proposed further amendments. With a combination of helpfulness and menace, Butler assured Jenkins that the amendments were merely technical and that he should accept them. Jenkins and company knew they were in danger of running out of parliamentary time and were willing to accept losses on some minor points.[155] The bill received the royal assent two days before the end of the parliamentary session. A few weeks later, Jenkins expressed his gratitude to Butler: "Without your flexibility and desire to help we might easily have got shipwrecked in the difficult negotiations during the week before the Report Stage."[156] That was right when Butler was ostensibly endorsing Manningham-Buller's position. Butler appears to have played a subtle game throughout.

The Obscene Publications Act 1959 was Jenkins's triumph, but Butler's input was critical—not just his tactical manipulation, but his insistence on the public-good defense over the Herbert Committee's preference for literary merit. The act took Fitzjames Stephen's proposal—its very wording and made it law. Here is Stephen:

> A person is justified in exhibiting disgusting objects, or publishing obscene books, papers, writings, prints, pictures, drawings, or other representations, if their exhibition or publication is *for the public good*, as being necessary or advantageous to religion or morality, to the administration of justice, the pursuit of *science, literature, or art, or other objects of general interest.*

And here is the 1959 act:

> 4(1) A person shall not be convicted of an offence against section two of this Act, and an order for forfeiture shall not be made under the foregoing section, if it is proved that publication of the article in question is justified as being *for the public good* on the ground that it is in the interests of *science, literature, art* or learning, *or of other objects of general concern.*[157]

Stephen's advice had gone unheeded for the better part of a century. Then, when change seemed inescapable, the Home Office's lawyers went with Stephen over the authors' proposal. The public-good defense meant that courts would hear testimony not only from "Professors of lit, critics, novelists," but also what one disgusted Conservative called "experts in social service, whatever that is."[158] The public good defense opened the way to courtroom debates about the social, educational, and psychological value of explicit or discomfiting books. It was this that made obscenity trials forums for exploring sexual morality and cultural change in the decades to come.

Lolita

Lolita would not be the subject of one of those trials. When, at the end of 1958, Nigel Nicolson spoke in the main House of Commons debate about obscene publications, he mentioned the risks he faced in contemplating publication of Nabokov's novel. The next day the top civil servant in the Law Officers' Department briefed the attorney general on the legal situation: George Dudman, told Manningham-Buller that if the edition of *Lolita* that Weidenfeld and Nicolson planned to publish was not materially different from the Olympia edition that had been the subject of a successful obscene libel prosecution in 1956, "it would be the duty of the Director of Public Prosecutions to institute proceedings against them."[159] Nicolson made the publication sound hypothetical, but in fact it was well underway. Worried that the appearance of a British *Lolita* would derail negotiations over the Obscene Publications Bill, a barrister on the Herbert Committee had a word with Nicolson's partner George Weidenfeld and talked him into postponing publication until after the current parliamentary session.[160] Several months later, with the new act in force, Weidenfeld and Nicolson scheduled publication for November, and Manningham-Buller's department arranged a meeting to discuss what action, if any, to take. The sensitivity of the situation—the as yet untested Obscene Publications Act, the fact that the novel had been discussed in Parliament, and the fact that a Conservative MP was the publisher—is indicated by the personnel present. The attorney general and the solicitor general were there, as was Dudman. The director of public prosecutions attended, as did the senior treasury counsel, Mervyn Griffith-Jones. Griffith-Jones had conducted the prosecutions of Carter and Reiter as well as Secker and Warburg and all the other mainstream publishers involved in the trials of 1954. Those trials had gone ahead on his recommendation to Mathew. He now advised against proceeding over *Lolita*.[161] Dudman too recommended against prosecution after reading the novel. His remarks show how much things had changed since he last advised on the legal position regarding Nabokov's novel ten months earlier: "Even if I thought there were reasonable prospects of obtaining a conviction, I should be opposed to the institution of criminal proceedings in respect of this book." Dudman explained that in the debates over the Obscene Publications Bill, the lord chancellor let it be understood that the criminal law should be directed at "the commercialised and deliberate use of filth for filth's sake," and that this was "the general view of the law."[162] At the end of the meeting, Manningham-Buller declined to give Mathew any direction, and Mathew resolved not to prosecute.[163]

The decision not to prosecute Weidenfeld and Nicolson suggested that the act was working as its backers intended, preventing trials over "serious works of art." But the *Lolita* decision was the result of consultations between the DPP and his senior prosecuting counsel, the attorney general and the solicitor general, and these officers' legal advisor. Without such coordination, there was no guarantee that the system would have yielded the same outcome. Criminal prosecutions in postwar Britain were not the work of the Home Office calling the shots: they emerged from relations between different actors answering to distinct and only partially overlapping authorities. At the end of 1959, Penguin Books decided that the new act made it safe for them to include *Lady Chatterley's Lover* in their edition of the works of D. H. Lawrence. A provincial chief constable referred a proof copy of the book to Mathew, who sought Griffith-Jones's opinion. Griffith-Jones recommended prosecution, and Mathew initiated proceedings. The first major trial under the Obscene Publications Act of 1959 concerned precisely the kind of book that the Society of Authors and its allies had sought to protect.

CHAPTER FOUR

The *Lady Chatterley's Lover* Trial

1960

THE 1960 PENGUIN BOOKS trial was a contest over the authority of a patrician elite that Mervyn Griffith-Jones personified all too amply. It was also a contest *within* the establishment.[1] Indeed, ever since that term had been popularized in the mid-fifties to refer to the "interlocking circles" of Britain's governing classes and its professional and intellectual elites, commentators had doubted whether there was a single, coherent establishment.[2] Contemporary efforts to reform the laws of divorce and homosexuality, as well as of obscene publications, were spearheaded by liberalizing elites challenging traditions dear to others of their class. The barristers in the *Lady Chatterley* trial were political opposites and social doppelgangers. Mervyn Griffith-Jones was educated at Eton and at Trinity Hall, Cambridge; Penguin's counsel, Gerald Gardiner, went to Harrow and to Magdalene College, Oxford. Griffith-Jones was senior treasury counsel, in effect the top prosecuting barrister in England and Wales; Gardiner was at the end of a two-year term as chairman of the General Council of the Bar.[3] Gardiner was also one of the leading lights in the Society of Labour Lawyers and, as we have seen, he had advised the Herbert Committee as it neared its goal of a new Obscene Publications Act.[4]

The expert evidence section in the new act enabled Penguin's legal team to call distinguished authors, bishops, and other eminent people in support of Lawrence's novel. Shrewdly, the defense recognized the breadth of cultural authority in the Britain of 1960, and recruited witnesses from outside the traditional haunts of the establishment, most notably Raymond

Williams and Richard Hoggart. Williams was a Welsh railwayman's son who won a place at an academically selective grammar school and then Cambridge. Hoggart was an orphan from a poor quarter of Leeds who also went to a grammar school and then to Leeds University. As Stefan Collini has observed, at a time when social mobility, the future of the working class, and the tendencies of popular culture were much debated, a "special premium was attached to those who embodied as well as analysed" the changes of the postwar period.[5]

That Hoggart and Williams became influential interpreters of contemporary Britain was also testimony to the heft of literary criticism in the mid-twentieth century.[6] This was partly a consequence of the way F. R. Leavis and his many pupils and admirers in adult education and the grammar schools showed how close reading of texts could illuminate and expose the manipulations of advertising and the entertainment industry.[7] The "left Leavisites" of the fifties went further. Hoggart in *The Uses of Literacy* used the close reading of texts from popular songs to Hank Janson novels to tease out changes in the outlook and emotional life of the urban working class.[8] Williams's *Culture and Society* assembled critiques of the world wrought by industrial capitalism.[9] Dieter Pevsner at Penguin recognized how Williams demonstrated the reach of modern literary criticism. "The book is at once a literary study of the thought of certain writers of the period he discusses, and a sociology, or perhaps rather sociological history, of certain aspects of British society during that period," Pevsner enthused, urging his superiors to buy the paperback rights to *Culture and Society*. The book's method, Pevsner noted, was to focus on words such as "industry," "democracy," "class," "art," and "culture," and track their changing usage from Burke to Orwell to arrive at "a sharp picture of the development of certain of the main attitudes of the modern, industrial, consumers', welfare society."[10] As Wolf Lepenies has observed, literary criticism functioned as a "concealed sociology" in Britain.[11] *Culture and Society*, like *The Uses of Literacy*, was more or less workshopped in evening classes. Hoggart and Williams were experienced adult education teachers. The adult education movement's sensibility pervaded Penguin's nonfiction list. W. E. Williams, the closest advisor to Penguin's founder Allen Lane, was a veteran of the Workers' Educational Association.

Lawrence was a major figure in the critical tradition surveyed in *Culture and Society*. His novels were a profound influence on Leavisite thinking about life under "industrial society," and how popular culture in the twentieth century was subject to the same industrial logic as manufacturing. *Lady Chatterley's Lover* is shot through with adverse judgments about mass culture. Many of these occur in connection with Sir Clifford Chatterley's celebrity in "the illustrated papers" as a modish short story writer. Members of the *Scrutiny* group and their imitators often quoted the overwhelming description of Constance Chatterley's drive through the mining village attached to her husband's estate:

> The car ploughed uphill through the long squalid straggle of Tever-shall, the blackened brick dwellings, the black slate roofs glistening their sharp edges, the mud black with coal-dust, the pavements wet and black. It was as if dismalness had soaked through and through everything. The utter negation of natural beauty, the utter negation of the gladness of life, the utter absence of the instinct for shapely beauty which every bird and beast has, the utter death of the human intuitive faculty was appalling. The stacks of soap in the grocers' shops, the rhu-barb and lemons in the greengrocers! the awful hats in the milliners! all went by ugly, ugly, ugly, followed by the plaster-and-gilt horror of the cinema with its wet picture announcements, "A Woman's Love!," and the new big Primitive chapel, primitive enough in its stark brick and big panes of greenish and raspberry glass in the windows.[12]

The novel's descriptions of sex probe the question of whether meaningful human relationships are possible in this ugly, mechanical world in which emotion is "counterfeit"; whether sex can transcend industrial society.[13]

Sexual relations tangle with class relations. The affair between Constance Chatterley and Oliver Mellors crosses class lines, and so does the complicated relationship between Clifford and his nurse, Mrs. Bolton. The two Tevershall natives, Mellors and Mrs. Bolton, themselves have complicated class affiliations. Mellors has served in the army in India and then renounces his new status as an officer, and to some extent his old one too, when he returns to the place he was born and simultaneously withdraws from it by taking the lonely job of gamekeeper on Clifford Chatterley's estate. In conversation he switches abruptly from Derbyshire dialect to "educated" English. After Mrs. Bolton's husband dies in a mining accident, the company—then run by Clifford Chatterley's father—pays her compen-sation in instalments, denying her dream of buying a shop with the lump sum, whereupon, against the odds, she trains as a nurse, achieving a status and independence unusual in a mining village. She seethes with resent-ment toward the upper class and also craves their attention. Nursing Clif-ford, who is paralyzed from the waist down from a war injury, gluts both her anger and her desire. *Lady Chatterley's Lover* spoke as no other novel could to postwar Britain's compounding questions about sex and class;

literature and the authority of intellectuals; and whether wives and servants should be licensed to read what responsible men could.

The Decision to Prosecute

Penguin's list mixed the popular and the edifying, and some of the firm's big successes blurred the line between the two categories—just as Allen Lane could see himself as a questing autodidact *and* an entrepreneur who grasped the importance of design, branding, and economies of scale.[14] As well as Penguin Classics, the firm produced a separate line of uniform editions of the complete works of major authors. W. E. Williams oversaw Penguin's D. H. Lawrence series, which the firm now proposed to complete with the third, and most explicit, version of *Lady Chatterley's Lover*. The firm was emboldened not only by the new legislation, but the decision of an American court not to bar Grove Press's unexpurgated edition of the novel.[15] The American judgment had no effect on the legal position in Britain, but it looked like a sign of the times. As with *Ulysses* a generation earlier, a decision in the United States District Court for the Southern District of New York served as a cue for publishers in Britain.[16]

Penguin paid £1000 to Lawrence's estate and prepared to print 200,000 copies, which would place *Lady Chatterley's Lover* in the best-seller league.[17] One of the compositors complained about the material they were having to set, and after a contentious board meeting the firm broke its contract with Penguin (it had been burned before, by a libel action).[18] The Conservative MP James Pitman, heir to the shorthand empire, stepped in and arranged for a subsidiary of Sir Isaac Pitman and Sons to print the novel as a matter of principle, and informed the home secretary of his decision.[19] In the meantime, an anonymous informant, presumably an employee of the original printers, sent a proof copy to the Peterborough police.[20] The chief constable knew that the book had previously been deemed obscene and was surprised to find that Penguin were bringing out an edition "which includes all the passages to which Courts have taken exception in the past." Seeing that W. H. Smith and other reputable firms would be selling it, he "thought it possible that some more recent decision had caused a broader view to be taken."[21] (W. H. Smith's share of the retail market—like Boots, it had long abandoned its library business—and the steps the firm took to avoid stocking titles that were legally risky prompted one member of the book trade it call it an "unofficial Ministry of Information.")[22] Peterborough's chief constable followed the regulations and referred the book to the office of the director of public prosecutions. The deputy director, Maurice Crump, was non-committal. "I am not prepared to say that a book by so distinguished an author is necessarily in all circumstances obscene though clearly in some it might well be." Crump said that prosecutors were obliged to consider the context of sale: "If the book is hawked round school children, that is one thing. If it is offered by responsible people for sale only to responsible people, it is quite another."[23]

The circumstances of sale became clear when Penguin began advertising in June. "It had become apparent," a DPP official noted, "that a wide publication at 3s/6d. was intended."[24] In June 1960 Mathew referred the book to Griffith-Jones for his opinion on the wisdom of prosecuting and the likelihood of a prosecution.[25] A month later, Griffith-Jones furnished this two-sentence opinion:

> In my opinion the unexpurgated version of "Lady Chatterley's Lover"—a proof copy of which I have read—is obscene and a prosecution for publishing an obscene libel would be justified. Indeed if no action is taken in respect of this publication it will make proceedings against any other novel very difficult.[26]

On the strength of this opinion, Mathew resolved to institute proceedings. The attorney general gave him no direction one way or the other. Manningham-Buller was aware that the matter was under consideration, but he did not intervene, and Mathew did not consult him.[27] Manningham-Buller does not seem to have been promptly informed of Mathew's decision. A month after Griffith-Jones delivered his advice, Manningham-Buller dashed off a note while on a train, telling Mathew that he was up to chapter four and "if the remainder of the novel is of the same character, I have no doubt that you were right to start proceedings & I hope you get a conviction."[28] It is surprising that Mathew did not consult the attorney general, as the possibility of a prosecution had been raised in Parliament in February and again in April.[29] There may have been some undocumented back-channeling via Jack Simon, who had been a junior Home Office minister in 1958 when the select committee on obscene publications reported and was now solicitor general. Manningham-Buller asked Simon to read *Lady Chatterley's Lover*, and after he received his copy Simon wrote to Mathew to say: "perhaps we could have a word about tactics if you are free sometime next week."[30] George Dudman, the legal secretary to the attorney general and the solicitor general, does not appear to have been involved, whereas he had taken part in the deliberations over *Lolita*. He wrote "This is balls" in several places in the margins of a postmortem on the case that was possibly written by Manningham-Buller's private secretary.[31] The Home Office learned about the prosecution from the newspapers.[32]

Why did Mathew go ahead with proceedings? He was cautious and mindful of the toll that embarrassing cases could take on the law's reputation. But he was also deferential to others' professional judgments. Perhaps most important was the matter of policy that Griffith-Jones raised: "If no action is taken in respect of this publication it will make proceedings against any other novel very difficult." In the *Philanderer* case, Griffith-Jones had been reproved by Mr. Justice Stable for suggesting in his closing speech that the jury, by its decision, would be having a say about the kinds of books that could be published in the future. Stable told the jurors their task was "absolutely nothing of the kind." They were there to make a judgment about whether one book satisfied a legal test. "We are not here to say whether we think it would be a good thing if books like that were never written."[33] Stable was applying the law correctly, but Griffith-Jones had a point: publishers could indeed be expected to base future decisions on past verdicts. His thinking was consistent with Manningham-Buller's observation that declining to proceed against one novel would make it difficult for the director to prosecute over a similar book, so every failed or forgone prosecution would mean an easing of standards.[34] *Lady Chatterley's Lover* posed the question more acutely: if you don't prosecute over a book that includes a scene of anal sex, describes genitalia explicitly, and uses the words "fuck" and "cunt" repeatedly, what are you going to prosecute?

Under the new Obscene Publications Act, there was an answer to that question: "You prosecute a book that includes scenes and language like that but which was not written by a canonical author and won't be able to attract the support of authoritative literary critics." Mathew may have felt that it was improper for him to anticipate the defense's probable use of the public-good defense, and that he should make the decision purely on whether there was a case to answer. This was the spin that the Law Officers' Department put on the matter when briefing the leader of the government in the House of Lords after the trial was over: "If, having regard to the nature of a book and the extent of the publication of the book and all other relevant circumstances, the director of public prosecutions considers that there is a prima facie case of an offence against the Obscene Publications Act, 1959, it is his duty to prosecute. It is for the accused to raise the defence that publication is for the public good."[35] If this was what happened, it would be consistent with Mathew's characterization of the prosecution as a test case under the new legislation, and his decision to depart from the usual practice and charge only Penguin Books and not its directors as well, which would have made them liable to imprisonment. Mathew's conduct suggests someone committed to process rather than a zealot. When it was all over he shared a crude joke about the novel with Allen Lane.[36]

Critics and Lawyers

If Mathew deliberately disregarded likely defense arguments in deciding whether to prosecute, he and his staff had to anticipate them and work out counterarguments as the trial approached. Maurice Crump interviewed John Holroyd-Reece, who had published the Paris edition of *The Well of Loneliness* and, after he moved to Hamburg, an edition of *Lady Chatterley's Lover*.[37] The eccentric Holroyd-Reece gave Crump some ideas about the failings of *Lady Chatterley's Lover*, and Crump wrote up some literary-critical notes on *Lady Chatterley's Lover* reflecting Holroyd-Reece's canons—the importance of good grammar, how well the background of the characters was fleshed out, whether the word choices in the dialogue were true to the time—and passed them on to Griffith-Jones. Penguin gave advance notice that they would be calling expert witnesses,[38] and when rumors of their identity circulated in the press, DPP staff looked the names up in *Who's Who*.[39] For a time the prosecutors hoped to call experts of their own. Mathew wrote to the Oxford literary scholar Helen Gardner and the provost of King's College, Cambridge, Noel Annan, asking if they were willing to assist the prosecution. Both wrote back the following day saying that they supported Penguin's action.[40] Mathew's office also attempted to make contact with T. S. Eliot and Lord David Cecil "with a view to sounding them [out] as to the possibility of their giving evidence for the prosecution," but both proved elusive.[41] Nevertheless, the DPP's office supplied Griffith-Jones with an article by Cecil and Eliot's *After Strange Gods*, both critical of Lawrence and both written not long after his death in 1930.[42]

Griffith-Jones also received excerpts from *The Dark Sun* (1956) by the Cambridge critic Graham Hough.[43] Though Hough later testified for the defense, the DPP found the misgivings he articulated in *The Dark Sun* promising. The use of the "four-letter words not commonly seen in print" had some literary function, Hough accepted. "They are all put into Mellors' mouth, and are meant to show his frank carnality and its vivifying power." But they were "part of the extra-curricular activity of bringing 'sex out into the open', and like all such secondary purposes in a work of fiction they are . . . an irrelevance."[44] Hough did not disapprove of Lawrence's desire to create a "proper vocabulary to discuss sex," but writers have to respect the nature of language, and no writer "can alter the connotations of a whole section of the vocabulary by mere fiat; and the fact remains that the connotations of the obscene physical words are either facetious or vulgar." Hough insisted that Lawrence's battle against censorship, which manifested itself in Constance's dance in the rain as well as the sex scenes and the profane philosophizing speeches, was "extraneous" to properly literary purposes. The passages written to provoke the censors were comparatively brief and "do little to affect the book as a whole." Indeed, Hough went on, "to my mind, even the expurgated edition, where most of the specific sexual detail is cut out, and there is therefore considerable loss, suffers less by the omissions than has often been alleged."[45] The DPP's office briefed Griffith-Jones: "Counsel may think that the general conclusion to be gathered from this extract [from *The Dark Sun*] is that its author regards 'Lady Chatterley's Lover' as a good novel which contains a number of undescribable irrelevancies . . . If this is so it does add strength (in spite of Lawrence's own argument in 'A Propos of Lady Chatterley's Lover') that the expurgated edition contains all that is important in the book."[46] Penguin's solicitors were notified that "Treasury Counsel proposed to seek the authority of the Court to make available to each member of the jury not only an unmarked copy of the Penguin edition, but also a copy marked to show the deletions and alterations made for the expurgated Heinemann edition." The solicitors instructed Penguin's barrister to resist such an application "most strongly."[47] In the event, Griffith-Jones did not follow through with a detailed comparison of the different versions.

The architect of Penguin's defense was Michael Rubinstein, whose firm, Rubinstein, Nash, and Co., had a long record of representing publishers. Michael Rubinstein's father Harold was Jonathan Cape's solicitor at the time of the *Well of Loneliness* case. In preparation for the hearing before Sir Chartres Biron, Harold Rubinstein had appealed to more than a hundred eminent writers, clergymen, and other authorities on sex and morals, in the unfulfilled hope that their testimony might be admitted.[48] With the passing of the 1959 Obscene Publications Act, his son was able to pursue the same strategy successfully: the *Lady Chatterley's Lover* trial was yet another replay of the *Well of Loneliness* case. Michael Rubinstein worked assiduously to recruit "As wide as possible a range of witnesses."[49] He recognized better than anyone else the opportunities the public-good clause in the Obscene Publications Act offered. Roy Jenkins had seen the public good defense as a just-good-enough substitute for the literary merit clause he wanted; even Gerald Gardiner had not seen its potential when he advised the Herbert Committee in the early months of 1959.[50]

In Rubinstein's plan, the testimony of the various experts would advance an argument about the function of literature and the need for the law to respect that role. That argument was the same one Mr. Justice Stable had made in his summing up in the *Philanderer* case. In his brief for Gardiner, Rubinstein quoted repeatedly and in bulk from Stable. The reason the courts' imagined reader should not be "a fourteen-year-old schoolgirl," Stable had contended, was that in shielding the vulnerable, the criminal law would block access to "the sum total of human thought throughout the ages and from all the varied civilizations the human pilgrimage has traversed." What Stable said of *The Philanderer* applied equally to *Lady Chatterley's Lover*: "This . . . is a book which obviously and admittedly is absorbed with sex, the relationship between the male and the female of the human species." Addressing the jury, which, like the jury in the *Lady Chatterley's Lover* trial consisted of nine men and three women, Stable said he trusted that they shared his hope that society would approach "this great mystery" in a way that would lead to "personal happiness between individuals of the opposite sex in millions of homes throughout this island, which, after all, is the only possible foundation upon which to build a vigorous, strong, and useful nation."[51] Stable's opinions, and his cadences, were not so different from those of forward-thinking clergymen. He provided a template for Gardiner's arguments and for a consideration of the social value of frankness about sex, and a conclusion to which the questioning of the expert witnesses would lead.

This conception of literature as exploration and documentation of "the human pilgrimage" would also guide the examination of the literary critics who testified for Penguin. Literature was writing with a message (Stable's word) about human experience; the fact that it is a way of doing things with words was secondary.[52] This was an approach to literature that many lay people were comfortable with.[53] And it kept the emphasis on the book as a whole, not its most explicit passages, which was tactically important. Rubinstein was insistent about this. "Every attempt by the prosecution at any time during the trial to draw the attention of the jury—or of witnesses—to particular passages or words in the book should be strongly challenged," he instructed Gardiner. "If this prosecution has been brought because certain passages and/or words in the book are allegedly obscene then it has not properly been brought in accordance with the provisions of Section 1(1) of the Act where the test of obscenity is specifically related to the effect (of a book) 'taken as a whole.'"[54] The novel's narration made it easier for the defense to make a case based on Lawrence's message—easier, that is, than another candidate for a test case. *Lady Chatterley's Lover* has a third-person narrator, whereas *Lolita* is narrated by its "nymphet-loving" protagonist. *Lady Chatterley's Lover* could be (and was, in the trial) said to articulate its author's philosophy; *Lolita*'s ambivalence and indirectness would have been much harder to defend on these terms. Moreover, as one critic pointed out several years after the trial, Lawrence "never once, *as narrator*, uses obscene words: he uses them many times in dialogue . . . but never in his own person as controlling and omnipotent novelist."[55]

The defense did not confine itself to literary merit and invoked the other parts of the public-good defense ("in the interests of science . . . learning, or . . . other objects of general concern") as well.[56] Rubinstein enlisted clergy to talk about the ethical value of having *Lady Chatterley's Lover* freely available. The first to testify was John Robinson, bishop of Woolwich and a theologian associated with situational ethics. As the historian Sam Brewitt-Taylor has remarked, "It was the first major appearance of the radical Christian ethical tradition in post-war national debate." Robinson testified that Lawrence was trying to portray sex "as something sacred, in a real sense as an act of Holy Communion." He was not really equating sex with the Eucharist so much as exalting the "transcendent potential" of human love and noninstrumental relationships "above fixed moral rules."[57] The novel, Robinson said, stressed "the real value and integrity of personal relations as such. That sex is not just a means of using other people but as a means of respect for them."[58]

Rubinstein approached other Anglicans besides Robinson. He wrote to Martin Jarrett-Kerr, an Anglican monk and literary critic, author of *D. H. Lawrence and Human Existence*, published under a pseudonym at his superior's behest.[59] Jarrett-Kerr "understood Lawrence's intent to have been to reassert the importance of sex within a loving relationship against those moralists who separated mind from body and placed the mental and spiritual above the physical aspects of love."[60] In the event, Gardiner decided to wrap up Penguin's defense without calling Jarrett-Kerr, which left the monk relieved: his testimony would have been more equivocal than Robinson's.[61] Jarrett-Kerr and Robinson were in the theological avant-garde, but they also reflected a widespread Anglican unease about the Church's connection with the criminal law. As Matthew Grimley has shown, the crisis over the Prayer Book in 1927/1928—in which Joynson-Hicks had been a combatant—had left a generation of Anglicans wary of state involvement in church matters and vice versa.[62]

Given the belligerent common sense that lawyers liked to attribute to English juries, it seems unlikely that the defense team thought that the jurors in the *Lady Chatterley* trial would accept the idea of sex as holy communion. Rather, the mere fact that ministers of religion were willing to support the novel might blunt the charge that the novel was likely to deprave and corrupt its readers. Teachers and social workers provided a different line of defense against suggestions that frank representations of sex and the use of four-letter words would corrupt people, especially adolescents. These witnesses would point to the practical value of the honesty and frankness that another clergyman stressed.[63] In the course of interviewing potential witnesses, Penguin's solicitors met with a marriage guidance counsellor who regularly spoke to youth groups. One of the difficulties in getting young people to talk about sex, love, and marriage was the lack of a frank vocabulary that could be used without shame or embarrassment in mixed company. However, the trust essential to a marriage guidance counsellor's work meant that none would take the stand in court. Rubinstein advised counsel to use another witness to make the same point: "As Mr. Cammaerts, a Grammar School Headmaster, will say, unless he used the only words his pupils use freely amongst themselves he cannot communicate with them in regard to sexual problems." Counsel should "make what use he can of Mr. Cammaerts' evidence to support what were Lawrence's intentions in bringing the words in question out into the open."[64] A teacher at a girls' grammar school, Sarah Jones, and an educational psychologist, James Hemmings, both testified that *Lady Chatterley's Lover* was a salutary corrective to the sexual education teenagers picked up from mass culture.[65] This was a sex-education take on Lawrence's attempt to "purify" the words "fuck" and "cunt" and burn away repression and shame.[66] Throughout, the defense team treated Lawrence as an earnest reformer. In this they mimicked a tactic used in defamation cases—presenting the offending words as a sincere expression of opinions that some people could take the wrong way.[67]

Thus Rubinstein and Gardiner devised a way of defending a novel in a manner that was not especially literary. With nearly all the witnesses testifying about literary merit, Gardiner avoided the text altogether. Instead, he asked questions about Lawrence's purpose in writing *Lady Chatterley's Lover*, how the novel rated against his other works, and whether Lawrence ranked among the greatest of twentieth-century authors. Gardiner took this approach with academics as well as with representatives of the metropolitan literary world, such as E. M. Forster, Rebecca West, and literary journalists such as Anne Scott-James and Dilys Powell. All these witnesses made claims about the stature of the book, and the defense counsel made claims—implicitly but obviously—about the stature of the witnesses. Only the witnesses influenced strongly by Leavis—Raymond Williams and Richard Hoggart—engaged in textual analysis as part of their prepared testimony.[68]

Even with Williams and Hoggart, however, Penguin's counsel began with questions of purpose and context. Gardiner's junior, Jeremy Hutchinson, led Williams through an overview of his chapter on Lawrence in *Culture and Society*. Williams told Hutchinson: "I think Lawrence . . . believed that industrial civilisation had destroyed or weakened normal human relationships, including sexual relationships, and I think that is the way in which he would have put it; that the whole effect of a civilisation based, as he saw it, on money and that kind of materialism was inevitably fatal to genuine and immediate human feeling between people of all kinds." Lawrence had tackled the theme before, but in *Lady Chatterley's Lover* "he attempted to take it to a kind of experience not normally openly discussed in polite literature because he felt it was part of the central truth about what industrial civilisation does to people or can do to people."[69] Hutchinson invited Williams to expand on the terms "sex" and "sensuality" that kept recurring in the trial. "I think the real difficulty here," Williams replied, "is that both these words, both sex and sensuality, have been specialised to one kind of meaning, and that a bad meaning. . . . I think one of the main purposes of this book was to challenge the bad meaning in the interests of a possible good meaning." Rebutting Griffith-Jones's insinuation that the novel's treatment of sex was simple indulgence, Williams suggested it was a kind of cultural critique. To illustrate the point about Lawrence's use of the word "sensuality," he quoted the following passage: "It was not really love. It was not voluptuousness. It was sensuality sharp and searing as fire, burning the soul to tinder. Burning out the shames, the deepest, oldest shames, in the most secret places." Williams explained: "Quite clearly what is meant there by sensuality is not the common association of the word, the over-mastering interest in an isolated physical thing, but in the kind of human experience available in this way."[70] Here was another instance of Lawrence trying to bend the language to his moral purpose, reconfiguring potent abstract nouns as well as purifying swear words. Turning over cruxes like this, Williams was worrying away at excessively meaningful words, as he had to such effect in *Culture and Society* and as he would do in full dictionary mode much later in *Keywords*.[71]

Griffith-Jones's way of dealing with the expert witnesses was either to ignore them—he chose not to cross-examine most of the literary journalists—or to try to make them look devoid of ordinary common sense. If he lost the jury with his wife-or-servants gaffe, he tried to regain them through anti-intellectualism, a potential source of solidarity across the class divide. Diatribes against challenging writing often appealed to the authority of "the plain man," and Griffith-Jones played the part of the plain man impatient with the games of intellectuals.[72]

His heaviest barrage was directed at Richard Hoggart. Hoggart ventured that Lawrence's "insistence . . . on arriving at relationships of integrity" placed him within "the English Non-Conformist Puritan tradition," which Hoggart claimed as "my own background too."[73] He developed this idea at length, with short, helpful responses and prompts from Hutchinson, who acted more like an interviewer on a radio arts program than a barrister examining a witness. Like Williams, Hoggart was modeling the kind of cultural and historical reflection that the attentive scrutiny of words could make possible. When it was his turn, Griffith-Jones asked Hoggart to confirm that it was his "considered view" that the novel was "highly virtuous and almost puritanical." Permission granted, Griffith-Jones was away. "I thought I had lived my life under a misapprehension as to the meaning of the word 'puritanical'," he said to Hoggart. "Will you help me?" Hoggart's answer harnessed Lawrence's (and Leavis's) thinking on the social life of language, and asserted the authority of literary scholarship:

> Yes. Many people do live their lives under a misapprehension of the meaning of the word "puritanical". This is a way in which language decays. In England today and for a long time the word "puritanical" has been distended to mean somebody who is against anything which is pleasurable, particularly sex. The proper meaning of it to a literary man or to a linguist is somebody who belongs to the tradition of British puritanism generally, and the distinguishing feature of that is an intense sense of responsibility for one's conscience, and in this sense this book is puritanical.

Griffith-Jones replied: "I am obliged for that lecture."[74] He used the put-down again, possibly going too far the second time. "The question is quite a simple one to answer without another lecture," he reproved Hoggart. "You are not at Leicester University at the moment." Sybille Bedford italicized "Leicester" in the account of the trial she wrote for *Esquire* to indicate the "thin distaste" in Griffith-Jones's voice. The way Hoggart remembered it, Griffith-Jones paused slightly before the name of the university, "as if he had to recover the name of so insignificant a place from the depths of his memory. . . . He saw himself as cross-examining someone who taught at a provincial and therefore inconsiderable place, for inconsiderable people."[75]

The cross-examination then settled into a routine in which Griffith-Jones read out parts of the sex scenes and then asked Hoggart: "Is that a puritanical passage?"; "More puritanical stuff?"; "Puritanical?" Each time, Hoggart replied in the affirmative, right up to the last one, about Constance's wonder at her lover's balls:

> Q: That again, I assume, you say is Puritanical?
>
> A: It is Puritanical in its reverence.
>
> Q: What! Reverence to the balls? Reverence to the weight of a man's balls?
>
> A: Indeed yes.[76]

Hoggart remained determinedly patient, but Griffith-Jones had at least got him to say plenty of things that plain men would have found preposterous. Griffith-Jones's bafflement was probably put on. The DPP's research addressed the question of puritanism, and the prosecution's exhibits included *The First Lady Chatterley*, published in New York with a preface in which Lawrence's German wife Frieda called the novel "the last word in Puritanism." "Only an Englishman or a New Englander could have written it," she said.[77]

In advancing the "puritan" argument, Hoggart had invited a searching cross-examination. With another academic, Graham Hough, Griffith-Jones was less ambitious, quoting embarrassing bits of prose and half-asking Hough's opinion. "I suppose that is good writing, or is that ludicrous?" he said after reading a short passage. "Not to me," Hough replied. Griffith-Jones persistently asked questions along the lines Maurice Crump had suggested after interviewing John Holroyd-Reece: Why does a good writer have to be so repetitive? Is the dialogue realistic? Verisimilitude had special significance in an obscenity trial, since Stable, whom Gardiner quoted in his opening speech, had (like Fitzjames Stephen) said that the literature of a period was "the only real guidance we get about what people thought and behaved over the ages."[78] Reminding the jury of Stable's remarks, Griffith-Jones read Hough the scene in which Constance's father lunches with Mellors. Sir Malcolm asks Mellors what sex with Constance was like, and, on being told it was good, exclaims: "I'll bet it was! Ha-ha! My daughter, chip of the old block, what! I never went back on a good bit of fucking, myself."[79] Griffith-Jones put the question to the witness: "Do you think any future generation reading that conversation will get anything approaching an accurate picture of the kind of way in which Royal Academicians conducted their conversation?" Hough declined to play along and replied that he had said in *The Dark Sun* that this was "a disastrously bad passage."[80]

Gardiner must have thought Hough would make an effective witness, or he would not have put him first, though the performance received little publicity at the time or in later accounts. Hough's responses appear to have made Griffith-Jones change tactics in one respect. Griffith-Jones read him a series of adverse judgments by Katherine Anne Porter, whose essay "A Wreath for the Gamekeeper" in the January 1960 issue of *Encounter* was among the ammunition the DPP's office had given him.[81] He evidently expected Hough to be intimidated by Porter's reputation. Hough said Porter was a very distinguished short-story writer but he had never thought of her as a critic. He described one of her comments about *Lady Chatterley's Lover* as "fatuous" and another as "an eccentric opinion."[82] Griffith-Jones did not try to use Porter, or other critics, on subsequent witnesses. Rather than seek to undermine the authority of the critics on the stand with quotations from other critics, he would rely on the text itself, appealing to the jurors to read the novel in the way he modelled, rather than the ways the expert witnesses did.[83] No one would call Griffith-Jones a literary critic, but his case depended much more than the defense's did on "the words on the page."

Although he read many short passages to the witnesses, trying to chip away at their credibility, he saved the longest excerpt for his closing speech. This was Griffith-Jones's most devious move, but one that has been mistaken for an act of absurd naivete. Griffith-Jones asked the jury to find in their copies a passage that he had not referred to before, and which he thought no one else had (in fact Raymond Williams had touched on it). It was the anal sex scene. It begins:

> It was a night of sensual passion, in which she was a little startled and almost unwilling: yet pierced again with piercing thrills of sensuality, different, sharper, more terrible than the thrills of tenderness, but, at the moment, more desirable. Though a little frightened, she let him have his way, and the reckless, shameless sensuality shook her to her foundations, stripped her to her very last, and made a different woman of her.[84]

The writing continues in this fierce but oblique way. Griffith-Jones interspersed his reading with remarks such as: "Not very easy, sometimes, not very easy, you know, to know what in fact he is driving at in that passage." He finished: "I do not know what it means; you will have to think."[85]

It is part of the folklore of the *Lady Chatterley's Lover* trial that Griffith-Jones did not know what that scene was describing.[86] He did. Griffith-Jones's copy of the Penguin edition, Exhibit 1 from the trial, has the word "BUGGERY" written in capital letters down the margin of the page where this scene begins.[87] Saying over and over that it was difficult to know what Lawrence meant was a way of prodding the jurors to work it out for themselves. Doing it this way saved the jurors the embarrassment of having it spelled out.[88] Moreover, reading this scene out right at the end of the trial meant that the jury confronted it without the mediation of literary critics (or a rejoinder from the defense, as, at this time, the prosecution made its closing speech after the defense).[89] Gardiner tried to stop him, protesting, "This passage was not read in opening; it was not put to a single one of [the] witnesses; apparently it has been saved up for final speech." Mr. Justice Byrne backed Griffith-Jones: "On the question of obscenity the book is the only evidence before the jury."[90]

Deference and Equality

The way the two sides approached the text and how to read it was a mirror image of their substantive positions. The prosecution appealed to the jurors' own judgment as readers, telling them to set aside the opinions of lecturers and bishops and read as ordinary men and women.[91] Griffith-Jones trusted that an ordinary person's way of reading was the aggressively "plain man's" reading he practiced in court. Yet he was, of course, seeking to deny ordinary readers outside Courtroom 1 of the Old Bailey the opportunity to read *Lady Chatterley's Lover*. Penguin's case was built on deference to expertise and authority, even though its objective was to defeat the paternalism of English obscenity law.[92]

As we have seen, the idea that a book could be condemned as obscene when published for a mass audience but might pass unmolested in an expensive edition was never formulated as a maxim in legal digests, but it was the guiding assumption of obscenity law and policing, and it was widely known.[93] Because Penguin was, if nothing else, a publisher of cheap books, its publication of *Lady Chatterley's Lover* was always going to raise this issue in a way that Weidenfeld and Nicolson's hardcover *Lolita* was not.[94] Horace King, the Labour MP and campaigner against horror comics declared: "As an Englishman I am opposed to censorship, particularly a censorship which allows 'Lolita' to be published because it costs 25/- but has a court case over 'Lady Chatterley's Lover' because it costs 3/6."[95] In its brief for counsel, the DPP's office described the book as being

so obscene that "its publication on a 3/6d Penguin [was] unjustifiable"—
the implication being that a more expensive edition might have been tolerated.[96] Griffith-Jones floated such a hypothetical in his opening remarks,
telling the jury that they had to consider "how freely" the book would be
distributed: "Is it a book that is published at £5 a time as, perhaps, an
historical document, being part of the works of a great writer, or is it, on
the other hand, a book which is widely distributed at a price that the mer-
est infant can afford?"[97] Griffith-Jones repeatedly mentioned the price of
three shillings and sixpence, driving home the point that anyone might
read this book.[98] Mocking Dilys Powell's claim that *Lady Chatterley's
Lover* treated sex "on a holy basis," Griffith-Jones asked whether it was
realistic to think the novel would be read that way by "the young boys and
men leaving school, thousands of them, tens of thousands every year, I
suppose, leaving school at the age of fifteen, going into their first jobs."[99]
Young people at a crossroads in their lives had been the kind of borderline
reader that obscenity law attended to since the Victorian period; and of
course young people of both sexes were the subjects of considerable anxiety through the fifties, not least during the horror comics agitation.

Griffith-Jones's remarks were as much about class as about age. Practically everyone leaving school at fifteen and going into full-time paid
employment was working-class. Griffith-Jones's imagined adolescent
reader was not the socially mobile young man or woman at an academically selective grammar school whose teachers worried about how to talk
to them about sex, but the teenagers marking time in secondary modern
schools, where those who failed the eleven-plus test went. (One of the
people Martin Jarrett-Kerr sought advice from before deciding to testify,
the increasingly pessimistic educationalist Leslie Paul, asked rhetorically:
"What happens when the Secondary Modern School boy uses f . . . in his
essays with the intention of challenging the master, and defends himself
because it's in a book he just bought? There are some roaring boys who
ache daily to do this kind of thing.')[100] In his summing up, Mr. Justice
Byrne echoed Griffith-Jones. If the novel was published, he said, it would
not remain in "the rarefied atmosphere of some academic institution where
the young mind will be perhaps directed to it and shewn how to approach it
and have indicated to it the real meaning of it, and so forth; it finds its way
into the bookshops and on to bookstalls, at three-and-sixpence a time, into
public libraries, where it is available for all and sundry to read."[101]

The defense had prepared for a battle over the cheapness of the book.
In his brief to counsel, Rubinstein sketched an argument to neutralize the
issue of class. Although Rubinstein said it would be hypocritical to claim

that a hardback edition "would not have been obscene, while the Penguin edition is obscene, because of a different range of persons likely in all the relevant circumstances to see two such editions," his main point was that this was inaccurate. Nowadays even teenagers could afford to buy a cloth-bound book; the distinction between paperback readers and readers of hardcover books no longer corresponded with social differences. In court, Gardiner made a much bolder argument than this. Griffith-Jones's conduct of the prosecution placed the question of class front and center, and in his closing statement, Gardiner confronted the class politics of obscenity law directly.[102]

After quoting Griffith-Jones's rhetorical question about wives and servants, Gardiner remarked: "I cannot help thinking this was, consciously or unconsciously, an echo from an observation which had fallen from the bench in an earlier case: 'It would never do to let members of the working class read this.'"[103] He teased Griffith-Jones that there were "a certain number of people nowadays who as a matter of fact do not have servants" and then shifted his tone abruptly to a piercing earnestness:

> The whole attitude is one which Penguin Books was formed to fight against . . . this attitude that it is all right to publish a special edition at five or ten guineas, so that people who are less well off cannot read what other people do. Is not everybody, whether they are in effect earning £10 a week or £20 a week, equally interested in the society in which we live, in the problems of human relationships, including sexual relationships? In view of the reference made to wives, are not women equally interested in human relations, including sexual relationships?[104]

Many of the cross-examinations of literary critics had lingered over Lawrence's intense repetition of keywords such as "sensuality" and "tenderness." Gardiner had done the same himself with "equal," a central term in Penguin's synthesis of democracy and commerce. The company's success, Gardiner said, was based on Allen Lane's insight that "there are students of literature in every section of the community." If it was right that *Lady Chatterley's Lover* should be read," Gardiner argued, "it should be available to the man who is working in the factory or to the teacher who is working in a school."[105] The factory worker and the teacher together, with their implied elite foil not quite in view: Gardiner's rhetoric recalled the wartime celebration of ordinary people, a cross-class progressivism that Penguin itself had captured so well.[106]

In Gardiner's speech the entitlement of factory workers and teachers to read what the well-off did was, among other things, a consumer right.

In the United States, an alliance of librarians and the American Civil Liberties Union (ACLU) had campaigned for a "right to read" that shrewdly linked the protections for dissent in a Cold War climate to the rights of the consumer during the postwar boom.[107] Gardiner had sterling credentials as a civil libertarian, but a sweeping argument like the ACLU's was not appropriate in the *Lady Chatterley's Lover* trial. To unpick the social judgments of variable obscenity, and the prosecution's flagrant restatements of them, it made sense to argue on the basis of equality and the social merits of a great novel more than a generalized liberty. In any case, the hard-won Obscene Publications Act recognized freedom of expression only as a means to the end of art or debate, not for its own sake. As the historian Jon Lawrence remarks, "In many ways the trial was as much about challenging Britain's traditions of authoritarian paternalism as it was about upholding the right to freedom of expression."[108]

Verdict

The trial lasted five days. Mr. Justice Byrne was thought by many to be as "out of touch" with contemporary manners and morals as Griffith-Jones, but his summing up was not one of the most tendentious. The jury deliberated for three hours and returned a verdict of not guilty. "And that is the verdict of you all?" the clerk asked ritually. "Yes," the foreman answered. Gardiner asked for an order for costs, noting that Griffith-Jones had described the prosecution as a test case for the new act. Byrne declined to make an order for costs and gave no reasons.[109] He may have decided that Penguin could afford to subsidize the justice system's test of Section 4. The lawyers' fees were high, over £13,000, but Penguin sold two million copies of *Lady Chatterley's Lover* in the six weeks before Christmas.[110]

English juries' deliberations are supposed to remain secret, and it is not possible to know whether the jury in the *Lady Chatterley's Lover* trial were swayed by any of the things that seemed so important to articulate contemporary observers and to posterity: Griffith-Jones's question, Gardiner's closing speech, Hoggart's performance of critical intelligence and northern unpretentiousness. But it is clear that the missteps of the prosecution and the successes of the defense provided firm lessons for prosecutors—and pressure groups. In 1963 the Metropolitan Police proposed to prosecute the British publishers of Henry Miller's *Tropic of Cancer* "to avenge the repulse we suffered in the Lady Chatterley case."[111] The Public Morality Council had resolved not to take any action against the book, "lest by so doing we might make it a cause celebre, rather like Lady

Chatterley's Lover."[112] Griffith-Jones gave his opinion, and this time he *did* take the likely defense into account. "Even if the book should be considered by some to be 'obscene,'" he wrote, "I think it extremely doubtful whether a conviction would ever be obtained. In its curious style I find it well written—better written than 'Lady Chatterley's Lover'—and with considerable humour so that the question of its literary merit would present difficulties. The author is apparently well recognized as a writer of distinction. It would appear that in the event of a prosecution there would be no shortage of distinguished 'experts' ready to speak on behalf of the book." He was right: the publisher had lined up more than a dozen expert witnesses.[113] "For these reasons," Griffith-Jones concluded, "I advise that no criminal proceedings be instituted."[114]

Griffith-Jones' infamous question about wives and servants, Gardiner's firm answer to it, and the audible laughter from jurors fatally discredited class-based variable obscenity. The expert witness provisions of the Obscene Publications Act made possible a new kind of courtroom discussion; but it was Griffith-Jones's ill-judged question, making the unsaid embarrassingly explicit, that prised open a space in which the underlying assumptions of English obscenity law could be challenged. This was a substantial change and one that lends support to the popular idea of the trial as a symbolic threshold to the social and cultural transformations of the sixties.[115] But the trial faced backwards too. As he dismantled the Victorian principle of variable obscenity, Gardiner argued within the terms of that tradition, the qualification of different types of citizen to read heterodox books, rather than the cultural libertarianism for which "the sixties" became a byword. And in its combination of democratization and deference, the trial epitomized the cultural politics of the fifties. As Michael Bell has observed, that decade was "one in which the older hierarchical assumptions of social leadership overlapped with a new openness as to who might perform this function."[116] The sixties unsettled the assumptions about social leadership, and the ideas about art and culture, that Penguin's defense curated in Courtroom 1 of the Old Bailey. A decade later, the spectacle of middle-aged male academics, even ones of working-class origin, earnestly parsing Lawrence on sex would have seemed as out of touch as Griffith-Jones's question about wives and servants.

CHAPTER FIVE

The Liberal Hour

1961–1969

SITTING RIGHT IN THE middle of the period bracketed by the Suez fiasco of 1956 and the Profumo scandal of 1963, which fatally weakened Harold Macmillan's premiership, the trial of Penguin Books quickly became a symbol of the decline of establishment authority. At the same time, widespread affluence threatened the deference that sustained not only a patrician mode of leadership but also conformity.[1] The very idea of "conforming" to traditional moral codes and social expectations was an allusion to public religion just like the term "the establishment." Even many Church of England clergy were wary of state enforcement of Christian doctrine, and the Conservative Party, in power from 1951 to 1964, wrestled with the problem of how to reconcile affluence with traditional morals.[2] The unravelling of deference and conformity was a process that would extend over at least two decades, but already by the midsixties more confident assertions of freedom of expression were audible in the arts, at least: among novelists, dramatists, film clubs, publishers, and their lawyers, and in and around the Arts Council, the public funding body established at the end of the Second World War. This chapter examines that change and also shows how the unfinished business of fifties liberal reformers played out in the next decade.

Philip Larkin wrote that the early sixties' changes in sexual morality—what came to be called the "permissive society"—arrived too late for someone of his age.[3] It's true that the standard bearers for the new irreverence of the early sixties were the young men of the "satire boom," and the underground—the British counterculture—that took shape later in the decade was primarily a young people's culture.[4] But middle-aged people too had a hand in the making of the permissive society, especially where censorship was concerned. Lawyers such as Michael Rubinstein and John Mortimer—and many others who rallied to the defense of the publishers John Calder and Marion Boyars—made the wholesale repeal of print censorship a cause of the arts establishment. The year Larkin singled out with mock seriousness as the moment sex really began, 1963, was also a pivotal year for the most important opponent of permissiveness. For Mary Whitehouse the disgrace of John Profumo laid bare a decline in moral standards in public life. The publication that same year of *Honest to God* by John Robinson, one of the defense witnesses in the *Lady Chatterley's Lover* trial, made it clear to Whitehouse that the church could not be counted on either.[5] From this point onwards, campaigns for and against censorship would involve a greater variety and number of actors than the campaign that resulted in the Obscene Publications Act.

The Unfinished Business of Fifties Liberalism

During the Conservatives' long period in government through the fifties and early sixties, many reformers' games of Snakes and Ladders remained unfinished. As home secretary, R. A. Butler successfully introduced new legislation on betting and made progress with penal reform, but he and like-minded ministers such as Iain Macleod, who insisted that the people should be treated as "grown-ups," repeatedly came up against grassroots members' support for flogging and other "Victoriana."[6] The decriminalization of sexual acts between men, the legalization of abortion, divorce reform, the suspension of capital punishment, and the abolition of theater censorship all had to wait for the Labour government of 1964–70 led by Harold Wilson.[7] None of these reforms was official Labour policy, but the government engineered them nonetheless. Roy Jenkins recruited most of the sponsors for these bills during his tenure as home secretary between 1965 and 1967, and he succeeded in getting the parliamentary time the legislation needed—even if only in the dead of night.[8] Jenkins had support from other senior members of the government, including Gerald Gardiner, whom Wilson drafted into the House of Lords.[9] On becoming lord chancellor, Gardiner set about establishing the Law Commission, which would put law reform on a more systematic basis. He also found time to advance civil liberties bills in the House of Lords and to cajole home secretaries.

Two of the changes the incoming government pursued bore directly on the question of free speech: the abolition of the lord chamberlain's powers of theater censorship and the introduction of a law against "incitement to racial hatred." These matters were important in their own right; they were also referred to repeatedly in debates over obscenity law.

Racist leaflets and posters emerged as a concern after the race riots of 1958. Neofascist groups posted stickers and leaflets with racist messages around Notting Hill, one site of the rioting, and Caribbean organizations and a cross-party caucus of MPs lobbied for criminal penalties. The issue flared up in 1962 after a contentious rally in Trafalgar Square led by the neo-Nazi Colin Jordan.[10] The Conservative Henry Brooke, R. A. Butler's successor as home secretary, rejected calls to amend the Public Order Act to make illegal "words inciting hatred of any section of the public."[11] To take that course, Brooke told the House of Commons, would infringe freedom of speech and turn the police into censors.[12] The Labour MP George Brown retorted that the police were already censors: the laws against obscenity and blasphemy empowered them to restrict people's freedom of speech. Brown said it was time to consider "whether uttering words of race hatred . . . should be put in the same category as obscenity and blasphemy—as things which we ought not to do."[13] Where the Obscene Publications Act made it possible to move *Lady Chatterley's Lover* out of the category of smut and into the category of debate on fundamental human problems, a measure against inciting hatred would make it possible to move racist speech and writing out of the category of debate or commentary. At around the same time, the Society of Labour Lawyers proposed criminalizing utterances that went "beyond the borders of comment"— again, thinking in terms of a category of debate and a category of unacceptable or unprotected expression.[14]

The Labour Party committed to legislation that would outlaw incitement to racial hatred and curb discrimination in places of public resort.[15] After returning to government in 1964, Labour introduced its bill as part of a "package deal" of legislation on race and immigration: the Race Relations Bill was a "positive integration measure" balancing another bill that restricted immigration.[16] The law against incitement did not lead to a flood of prosecutions. One result of the handful of early trials was to push racist groups to modulate their rhetoric, moving away from what could be taken to be crude invective and back within "the borders of comment." Some people were disappointed when the Conservative politician Enoch Powell did not face charges over his 1968 "rivers of blood" speech, but that was never likely.[17] Powell delivered that speech to a Conservative Association meeting, and political meetings were the very paradigm of freedom of expression in Britain for much of the twentieth century. The Race Relations Act 1965 affirmed the idea of freedom of speech as the freedom to debate right at the time more expansive conceptions of freedom, and of expression, were beginning to be articulated in Britain and other parts of the world.

The Lord Chamberlain's Office was part of the Royal Household, and theater censorship arose from the lord chamberlain's historical duty to ensure that the theater did not disrespect the monarchy. The appointment typically went to men with long and distinguished records in public life—Lord Cobbold, the incumbent in the sixties, was a former governor of the Bank of England. The lord chamberlain's readers were Guards officers, another signal of old-fashioned privilege. Playwrights and directors had long complained about the lord chamberlain's cuts and rewrites, but their discontent deepened in the second half of the 1950s with the advent of more confrontational theater, often with working-class settings. Many of these plays, beginning with John Osborne's *Look Back in Anger* (1956), were staged by the Royal Court Theatre. When the lord chamberlain rejected a script or demanded changes that the playwright or the Royal Court's directors could not accept, the play would go ahead as a notionally private performance to a theater club. Patrons would sign up as members of the English Stage Society for a small fee. For years this "subterfuge," as a member of the lord chamberlain's staff called it, had gone on with the acquiescence of the lord chamberlain and the Home Office, which saw it as a safety valve that defused anticensorship campaigns.[18] However, with the staging of Osborne's *A Patriot for Me* and Edward Bond's *Saved* ("A revolting amateur play about a bunch of brainless, ape-like yobs with so little individuality that it is difficult to distinguish between them," said one of the lord chamberlain's readers) as productions for members only, the ruse was too overt.[19] Cobbold felt that the director of public prosecutions had to charge the theater with showing an unlicensed play, or it would look as if the law was not being enforced, and then Cobbold would be honor-bound to tell the House of Lords that he could no longer carry out his duties.[20]

Thus began a series of maneuvers within the Labour government. Gardiner arranged for Noel Annan, one of his witnesses in the *Lady Chatterley's Lover* trial, to open a debate in the House of Lords on theater censorship. The Wilson government had elevated Annan to the Lords, but he was not a member of the Labour Party, and that made him good choice to lead a debate that would "afford an opportunity for liberal opinion to express itself and for public reactions to be judged," as the minutes of the Home Affairs Committee put it.[21] Only Cobbold spoke out in support of theater censorship.[22] As planned, the matter was sent to a select committee with members from both houses. Gardiner, Annan, and Arnold Goodman, chairman of the Arts Council, were on it; Norman St John-Stevas was among the Conservative members. The committee took written evidence and examined witnesses, including John Osborne, the director Peter Hall, and the critic Kenneth Tynan. Nearly everyone who gave evidence to the committee wanted an end to the lord chamberlain's powers over the theater. The chief exceptions were theater managers, for whom the lord chamberlain's endorsement of a play protected it against the possibility that a provincial town's watch committee would take against a production and shut it down—just as a BBFC certificate shielded a film from local government.[23] The submissions from Conservatives included not only a memo from Viscount Dilhorne, the former Reginald Manningham-Buller, in favor of censorship, but also a vigorous critique of the present regime from the Bow Group, an incubator of socially liberal and free-market Conservatism. "The central argument for theatre censorship," wrote the Bow Group's Peter Lloyd, "is the alleged need for somebody to prevent the staging of material believed to be destructive of morals and social relationships. We do not believe that it is really possible for such a function to be carried out in a liberal and heterodox community." "The Lord Chamberlain's role," Lloyd claimed, "is no more nor less than the reinforcing in the theatre of those pressures towards conformity which are already quite strong enough."[24] The joint select committee duly recommended repealing the Theatres Act and allowing "freedom of speech in the theatre." "Political censorship of any kind will cease."[25] Censorship, that is, in the British sense of prior restraint; playwrights and producers would now become subject to the same sanctions as the Obscene Publications Act applied to print and entitled to the same public-good defense.

The joint select committee's confident use of the future tense now collided with reservations the queen had communicated to Wilson.[26] She was apprehensive about the loss of the lord chamberlain's power to suppress plays about living persons at a time when the satire boom showed no signs of abating.[27] Wilson told Cabinet the Palace was worried about skits about the Duke of Edinburgh, the queen's husband; according to Wilson, the Palace also cited "Mrs Wilson's Diary," the scurrilous magazine *Private Eye*'s regular feature that purported to chronicle the prime minister's doings in the amiable manner of the long-running radio program *Mrs Dale's Diary*.[28] A stage version was in the works. As the Cabinet minister Richard Crossman recorded in his own less amiable diary, Wilson had seen the script, "which made him out to be a complete mugwump."

To Crossman it was obvious that Wilson "wanted censorship as much as the Queen."[29] A standoff between Wilson and Roy Jenkins ensued. It was resolved a year later while Wilson was opportunely overseas. The government arranged sufficient parliamentary time for Gerald Strauss's Theatres Bill to abolish the lord chamberlain's oversight of the theater. In the House of Lords, Cobbold continued to support measures against character assassination of the living. He was not acting in self-interest—Jenkins claimed in his memoirs that every time the two met afterwards, Cobbold thanked Jenkins for putting him out of an impossible job—but representing the interests of the Royal Household. The queen seems to have worried that Edward Bond's latest play, *Early Morning*, which the lord chamberlain banned and then briefed her about, was a portent. The play was a violent eminent-Victorians phantasmagoria in which Disraeli and Prince Albert plot to murder the queen and Victoria rapes Florence Nightingale. Despite the queen's concerns, conveyed to the lord chamberlain and Wilson with unusual directness, Strauss's Theatres Bill passed, and the queen gave it the royal assent, as she did every other bill approved by Parliament. The Royal Court staged a production of *Early Morning* the following year.

The decriminalization of sexual acts between (most) men also influenced arguments about censorship.[30] The Sexual Offences Act 1967 implemented recommendations made by the Wolfenden Committee ten years earlier, which R. A. Butler had then judged too far in advance of public opinion. The committee, chaired by Sir John Wolfenden, a university vice-chancellor and former public school headmaster, had an outsized influence on discussions of censorship and civil liberties generally. "Unless a deliberate attempt is to be made by society, acting through the agency of the law, to equate the sphere of crime with that of sin," the Wolfenden Committee argued, "there must remain a realm of private morality and immorality which is, in brief and crude terms, not the law's business." This was not to "condone or encourage private immorality," they insisted. "On the contrary, to emphasise the personal and private nature of moral or immoral conduct is to emphasise the personal and private responsibility of the individual for his own actions, and that is a responsibility which a mature agent can properly be expected to carry for himself without the threat of punishment from the law." This restatement of classical liberalism informed the committee's findings on prostitution as well as homosexuality. Wolfenden recommended a clampdown on soliciting accompanied by a softening of criminal sanctions for commercial sexual activity that took place off the streets and the legalization of homosexual acts by "consenting adults in private."[31] The contention that the state should not regulate private, consensual sexual activity formed a template for liberal positions on obscenity and censorship in the coming decades.

The attention the Wolfenden Report attracted was sustained by the debate it set off between two prominent jurists. In a widely reported lecture, the judge Patrick Devlin rejected Wolfenden's notion of a "realm of private morality." He shifted the terms: "Morality is a sphere in which there is a public interest and a private interest, often in conflict, and the problem is to reconcile the two." The "true principle" was that the law existed "for the protection of society," not of individuals. He went on: "It does not discharge its function by protecting the individual from injury, annoyance, corruption, and exploitation; the law must protect also the institutions and the community of ideas, political and moral, without which people cannot live together." Devlin argued that a society was held together "by the invisible bonds of common thought. If the bonds were too far relaxed the members would drift apart. A common morality is part of the bondage. The bondage is part of the price of society; and mankind, which needs society, must pay its price."[32] This was a vision of public order long implicit in English criminal law: the idea that "the queen's peace" entailed a sort of moral equilibrium as well as the absence of overt disorder. To this tradition Devlin brought a Catholic sensibility—an "enduring recourse," the historian Alana Harris has written, "to an Augustinian understanding of the 'earthly city' as echoing (sometimes dimly) a divine order."[33]

Responding to Devlin in a broadcast talk, Oxford's professor of jurisprudence H.L.A. Hart contended that there was not "the slightest reason for thinking of morality as a seamless web: one which will fall to pieces carrying society with it, unless all its emphatic vetoes are enforced by law." Hart reaffirmed John Stuart Mill's insistence on the importance of freedom of expression and the social value of open discussion.[34] He restated Mill's harm principle ("the only purpose for which power can be rightfully exercised over any member of a civilized community, against his will, is to prevent harm to others")[35] in terms that made it clear that challenges to majority sentiment did not count as harm, because open critical discussion and confronting alternative positions were conducive to self-criticism.[36] Hart jabbed away at the lack of proof for the "vague nostrum" that morality was public and indivisible and moved on to the "wider, perhaps deeper criticism" that Devlin's appeal to popular feeling and majority sentiment courted oppression. Citing Tocqueville as well as Mill, Hart concluded: "It is fatally easy to confuse the democratic principle that power should be in the hands of the majority with the utterly different claim that the majority, with power in their hands, need respect no limits."[37] The argument

Hart outlined on the radio and developed in *Law, Liberty, and Morality* (1963) made him a public figure, joining A. J. Ayer as an avatar of secular liberalism.[38]

Morals Campaigners in Changing Times

The early sixties were also the making of the great scourge of secular liberalism, Mary Whitehouse. Whitehouse was an Anglican evangelical and a veteran of Moral Re-Armament, which was a conduit for American evangelical activism in the early postwar decades.[39] She started the Clean Up TV Campaign with Norah Buckland. They were both mothers of three, as they pointed out when stating their credentials. Whitehouse was a teacher in Wolverhampton and Buckland was a vicar's wife in Stoke-on-Trent. As the campaign grew beyond the Midlands, Buckland stepped back, and Clean Up TV became the National Viewers' and Listeners' Association (NVALA). Whitehouse characterized herself as a housewife speaking for other housewives, though her experience as a teacher was also part of her persona and perhaps her civic authority. Before she gave up her job to devote her time to her cause, Whitehouse taught in a secondary modern school. She thus worked with the kinds of adolescents who figured as readers susceptible to immoral influences in the fifties and sixties. Boys at secondary moderns were the borderline readers of *Lady Chatterley's Lover* that Leslie Paul had worried about ("What happens when the Secondary Modern School boy uses f . . . in his essays with the intention of challenging the master, and defends himself because it's in a book he just bought?") and they were who Griffith-Jones had in mind when he asked how the novel would be read by "young boys and men . . . leaving school at the age of fifteen, going into their first jobs."[40] (Most secondary moderns did not teach beyond the age of fifteen.) In an article for an education journal in 1963, Whitehouse described the sex-education program her school had launched to fortify its pupils against "the onslaught of dirty, materialistic atheism which attacks them on every side." How, she asked rhetorically, "do you help girls not to tease and tantalise? How do you help boys to assess the girls' behaviour for what it is and be firm enough to withstand it?"[41] Sex education remained on Whitehouse's radar, but television was her main target as an activist.[42]

The BBC in the sixties under Hugh Carleton-Greene's leadership was an agency of the secularist onslaught Whitehouse was committed to resisting. Whitehouse repeatedly attacked it for tolerating blasphemy and indecency, and for not always being on the right side of history. She wrote to the prime minister criticizing the BBC for anti-American bias in a report on Vietnam and negative portrayals of white mercenaries in the Congo.[43] Members of her organization were invited to monitor television programs and complete questionnaires that included this question: "Was authority upheld or ridiculed, an object of fear or an object of respect?"[44] Whitehouse's mission was to defend and reassert "the Christian character of our country."[45] Her preferred abbreviation of her organization's name was "National VALA," to sound like "national valour." It was supposed to be a national, nonpartisan movement, giving voice to the provinces rather than swinging London.[46] As a national institution, the BBC was an appropriate focus of the campaign's efforts. It was "a public service and should be responsible to the people for what it does. . . . We have a right to say to the B.B.C. what we do and do not want."[47] Prospective members were reminded that television license-holders were "shareholders" in the BBC and so could hold it to account. Whitehouse made good use of the language of consumer rights, not least in calling her organization a "viewers' and listeners' association." Across the Atlantic, civil libertarians had successfully repackaged freedom from censorship as a consumer right. In Britain organized opposition to censorship tended to be confined to literary and legal circles: only in the seventies was there an effort, and (as we will see) not a very effective one, to make create a popular movement based on freedom of expression. Whitehouse was far more successful in mobilizing people using the rhetoric and methods of the consumerist age she deplored.

Yet the similarities between the NVALA and consumer organizations only go so far. The BBC had no advertisers and did not answer to the market. Whitehouse and her supporters sought to exert pressure through letters to the government and the BBC's leadership, approaches to local newspapers and church newspapers, which provided clergy with material for sermons.[48] This was the traditional repertoire of public morals activism. What set NVALA apart was Whitehouse's personal media presence. She achieved a celebrity that no other morals campaigner in the twentieth century did (or sought). The appetite for confrontation and flair for provocation that made Whitehouse good copy also alienated potential allies. The Reverend Kenneth Greet, secretary of the Methodist Church's Department of Christian Citizenship and a leader of the Public Morality Council (PMC), was a forthright critic, and he encouraged the ecumenical (though Protestant-dominated) British Council of Churches to establish a broadcasting committee of its own that would displace the NVALA.[49] The Mothers' Union and the Catholic Teachers' Federation were supportive of

Whitehouse at first and then pulled back after finding her and her allies "not open to argument" and unfair and unrealistic in their concentration on the BBC.[50] NVALA membership, which skewed older and female and was probably mostly middle-class, reached 7000 in 1968, which was substantial but not necessarily "the voice of the silent millions." The branch structure was exiguous and the executive practically unchanging.[51] Whitehouse's complaints to the BBC about offensive items were usually rebuffed, and politicians explained over and over that they had no say in BBC programming.[52] Whitehouse surely grasped this. Perhaps the real function of the complaints was to remind the authorities that the NVALA was keeping watch (literally, with the questionnaires they completed as a sort of vigilante audience research survey). Throughout the sixties, the NVALA maintained its focus on the BBC: it was not until the following decade that Whitehouse took to the courts to contend with morally repugnant films, plays, and publications.

Until Whitehouse broadened her remit in the 1970s, the struggle against indecent publications was mostly kept up by other organizations. These included youth charities and organizations led by young people. Across the north of England, Young Action and Youth Watch branches protested newsagents selling indecent magazines and sent copies of pornographic publications to their MPs.[53] The committee of management for Dr Barnardo's Homes for destitute children felt "great anxiety . . . at the undesirable literature which was having a disastrous effect on children and young people."[54] Sir Cyril Black, a Conservative MP, Baptist lay preacher, and member of the PMC leadership, was prevailed on by his old friend General Sir Arthur Smith to get the PMC to act.[55] Late in 1963 the PMC hosted a conference on pornography, by which they meant "glamour" or "pinup" magazines, nude photographs sold in packets, and American paperback novels.[56] The conference brought together a wide range of religious and charitable organizations and a corresponding mix of perspectives. Members of the PMC leadership other than Black were willing to entertain different Christian ideas about sex, which was one reason for the friction between them and Whitehouse.[57] Kenneth Greet's brief for the conference was to outline a positive way forward. Pornography was not "any book or pictures dealing with sex," he said. "Erotic stimulation" was not pornographic in itself but could become pornographic "if its deliberate intention is to produce sexual excitement unrelated to real personal relationship." Drawing a line between what was pornographic and what was not was difficult because of the "interplay of objective facts and subjective judgments and motives."[58] The only real solution to pornography was "a sound attitude to sex itself," and this was an area in which the Christian churches had been neglectful.[59] Greet's answer to the question "What can and should the law attempt to do?" was "very little." He made a few suggestions such as criminalizing the possession as well as the distribution of obscene material: "So far as the law is concerned it would seem to me wise to concentrate our attention on the plainly pernicious, and the obviously trashy material which deliberately exploits human weakness for monetary gain, rather than works for which some kind of reasoned defence can be submitted."[60]

Only months after the conference, the PMC began to fall apart. Its long-serving secretary died and a period of administrative chaos ensued. His replacement, Edward Oliver, moved quickly to shift the organization's focus away from public morals, renaming it the Social Morality Council. Oliver distanced himself from his past as head of the London Council against Obscenity; an ordained office-holder in the PMC followed Oliver's lead, mocking the PMC's concern with dirty postcards in a speech to the renamed organization.[61] Oliver, a Catholic with connections with Catholic bishops, succeeded also in wresting the organization from Anglican oversight and turning it into a rival to the British Council of Churches. As the historian Callum Brown observes, the passing of the PMC signaled "the end of organised moral vigilante work by the British religious establishment to combat the liberalisation of sexual representation in the arts, cinema, television and public life."[62]

The Freedom of Vision Teach-In

Another conference three years later showed how anticensorship thinking was changing. In October of 1966 the pressure group Freedom of Vision held what it called a "teach-in" at Hampstead's Old Town Hall. Representatives of the lord chamberlain, the DPP, the Home Office, and Customs and Excise declined their invitations,[63] and the teach-in was dominated by artists, authors, small-time publishers, film buffs, representatives of activist groups, and interested members of the public who spoke from the floor. In the chair was the new Labour MP Ben Whitaker, who had unseated Henry Brooke as member for Hampstead earlier that year. As he opened the proceedings, Whitaker declared his own position: censorship was "an infringement of human liberty." He disagreed with what Enoch Powell and John Gordon had to say, but he would "defend to the death their right to say it."[64] This maxim, commonly attributed to Voltaire but actually from an early twentieth-century commentary on Voltaire, would become a staple of British position taking about censorship. John Gordon was the James Douglas of the postwar period. Gordon occupied Douglas's old job—outraged columnist for and nominal editor of the *Sunday Express*—as well as the same cultural role.[65] He was one of the first British commentators to denounce *Lolita*.[66]

Freedom of Vision's active membership consisted only of Jean Straker and his wife Elizabeth. She was a Manchester University graduate with experience in educational administration; he was a photographer.[67] Jean Straker specialized in female nudes. He saw himself as an artist and not a pornographer. The Strakers had become activists through Jean's struggles with the law. Jean was in and out of court for breaches of the Obscene Publications Act and the Post Office Act. He represented himself. In 1963 Straker satisfied a court that the Obscene Publications Act did not cover photographic negatives. The government promptly moved to close the loophole.[68]

At this time Jean Straker was pushing the argument that British law infringed the European Convention on Human Rights. At the beginning of the year the teach-in was held, the government declared that it would grant anyone under United Kingdom jurisdiction the right of individual petition to the European Court of Human Rights in Strasbourg. This was apparently Gerald Gardiner's doing.[69] Straker emphasized that Article 10 of the Convention declared that freedom of expression included the right "to receive and impart information and ideas without interference by public authority and regardless of frontiers." He claimed that British courts' constructions of the Obscene Publications and Post Office Acts were "such as to deny me the right to impart information and ideas."[70] This was a stretch. The rights and freedoms articulated in the Convention were subject to restrictions that could be "necessary in a democratic society," including those on the grounds of "the protection of health or morals," which plainly legitimated measures against publishing or mailing indecent material.[71] Indeed, the European Convention was drafted in large part by David Maxwell Fyfe, who had expressed little doubt about the legitimacy of British obscenity law while attorney general, home secretary, and lord chancellor.[72] It would not be until the mid-seventies that the Strasbourg Court, or the European Commission of Human Rights which considered petitions first, accepted a freedom of expression case from the United Kingdom.

Though nothing came of Jean Straker's attempt to engage the European Court of Human Rights, his contention that censorship was a drag on ideas and information resonated with others at the Freedom of Vision teach-in.[73] Edward Bond suggested that the theater was peculiarly suited for exploring basic human questions at a time when the consensus—a Victorian consensus, Bond thought—about what "an ideal, conscientious human" being was had collapsed. Live theater forced the audience to concentrate, and out of that concentration "you get a close examination of human nature; this exploration is in the nature of an experiment, for the dramatist, in looking at human nature, is experimenting with it." Bond then pressed the metaphor on to a moral:

> If a scientist were to produce an experiment or a set of equations, and somebody were to tell him:—
>
> > "No, you can't have an equation like that—we don't like it; you can't do this particular experiment—we don't like it,"
>
> Everybody would begin to be seriously concerned about this—not just a few people. They would say:—
>
> > "But isn't the scientist pursuing something called 'truth'?"

The same applied to theater: to pursue truth, a dramatist needed "freedom to experiment properly and honestly."[74] That "properly and honestly" hinted that Bond was abiding by an old convention for defenses of artistic freedom: positing a genuine art with an implicit or explicit foil—mass culture or pornography—that was pernicious and did not deserve protection, or, in some variants, would wither away once the real thing was freely available (Straker claimed that nudes like his would make cheap pornography redundant).[75] In fact, though, Bond did not rely on such a foil. He called pornography "an art form, just as satire is," and thought it possible that pornographers, like other artists, might arrive at "helpful solutions" to "human problems." Bond said he could not understand why people got so upset about pornography, because there was no evidence it affected behavior. He doubted literature could "corrupt" people either. There was no evidence that in the six years since the *Lady Chatterley's Lover* trial "all our servants have been hopelessly corrupted."[76]

This egalitarianism was not shared by every speaker at the teach-in. Fraser Smith of the International Federation of Film Clubs argued that censorship had a legitimate function: protecting the ignorant. The theater was a minority pursuit and "the ignorant in society stay away," but the cinema was an art form "exposed to practically every member of the population . . . without any discrimination at all."[77] Film clubs, whose interests Smith spoke for, were comparable to theater clubs in the final phase of the lord chamberlain's regime in that films to be screened in clubs could bypass the BBFC's costly and intrusive process. Unlike the theater clubs, however, film clubs were real organizations, serving a public intensely interested in challenging films from continental Europe. Smith's address to the teach-in was elaborate but incoherent. He drew attention to the anomaly that a film passed by the BBFC to screen at the Academy Cinema—a well-established "art house" cinema with a jazz club in the basement—would have fewer cuts than if it was showing at the popular cinemas at the other end of Oxford Street, but he was "all in favour of people who can appreciate critically having free access to their art" without censors or vigilantes obstructing them. Smith did endorse the traditional opposition between mass-market indecency, which should be banned, and serious art.[78] When Whitaker opened the floor to questions, a man whom Elizabeth Straker could not identify when she was transcribing the tapes said that "artists in general do tend to run away with themselves—and if they write plays or novels or take photographs or make paintings or films that are in advance of their time, I don't think they have any right to press these things on the public." A voice in the crowd interrupted him, and the following exchange unfolded:

> A WOMAN'S VOICE: But they can go home if they want to; why should they protect me from doing what I like doing?
>
> THE MAN CONTINUES: Because very often the public don't know what they're getting until they get it.
>
> THE WOMAN CONTINUES: Well, when they get it they can walk out— they can turn their tellys off; surely you mustn't protect me from something I might want to see. Why should you protect people? They'll never learn anything. If they find they don't appreciate it when they go out to see it, let them go home.
>
> ELIZABETH STRAKER: If you don't allow people to be in advance of their time how can time advance?
>
> THE MAN CONTINUES: I don't agree with censorship in principle; there's nothing to stop them, you know, from writing their plays, and painting their photographs, or drawing their pictures—they can do that; it's only that they mustn't expect the public to want to see these things.
>
> THE WOMAN: No one drives the public to see them.[79]

The man's position is close to that of the Wolfenden Report: artists should be allowed to be artists, as long as they are not foisting their work onto an unconsenting public. The woman does not reject that principle:

she thinks that people can give or withdraw their consent by choosing to leave the television on or walk out of the theater. As significant as her argument is the fact that she was making it. Women had been prominent campaigners *for* censorship from the early days of the National Vigilance Association through to the National Viewers' and Listeners' Association, and Whitehouse stressed that her organization represented women's perspectives in particular. In contrast, the organized opposition to censorship was practically monopolized by men. Gerald Gardiner spoke for women ("Are not women equally interested in human relations . . . ?") just as jurymen were invited to act on behalf of the women in their lives ("your wife," "your sixteen-year-old daughter") when reaching a verdict in an obscenity trial. Male jurors stood in for women just as propertied men "virtually represented" those without the vote in the nineteenth century. Here, in the Hampstead of 1966, was a censorship debate animated by more than one woman's voice.

It is not clear from the transcript whether the unnamed woman who spoke a few minutes later was the same person; that woman, on hearing someone else express concern about the idea of "protecting the ignorant," interjected: "Who are the ignorant?" Elizabeth Straker replied:

> Apparently it has been defined for us into those who can go to the Academy Cinema and those who go lower down Oxford-street; one lot are the elect and the other lot are outside.
>
> Now, how, if you are ignorant, do you acquire knowledge, if knowledge is withheld from you?
>
> That is what is worrying me—and it does seem to be better that knowledge should be allowed to be sorted out by the people, freely for the people to acquire, than it should be the perquisite of the few who have been brought up to it and form a kind of elect class.
>
> To me this is the most dangerous thing in the world; this is the thing which sets up dictatorships; this is the thing which gets rid of every kind of freedom, not merely to look at the sort of pictures you want, but freedom to vote how you wish, freedom to bring up your children in the way you want; these are fundamental freedoms to which you are born.[80]

Straker worried that attempts to protect the ignorant inhibited people's ability to grow. The idea of culture—or knowledge, as Straker put it, like her husband—being allocated only to an elect was unacceptable coming from the film-club cognoscenti as well as the paternalistic state. Here Straker spoke the human-rights language of fundamental freedoms and alluded to the lessons of totalitarianism, another feature of the public discourse of freedom. But her reference to raising children the way one wanted hints at a more vernacular conception of liberty that was taking shape in early sixties Britain even before the flourishing of the underground and second-wave feminism.

Elizabeth Straker's disagreement with Fraser Smith implied that censorship was not simply the work of "the establishment" and big companies such as W. H. Smith, as some other speakers at the teach-in contended.[81] Francis Carr, the publisher of the magazine *Past and Future*, described the *Lady Chatterley's Lover* trial as a hammer blow to the establishment's moral authority comparable to the Profumo scandal.[82] Speaking from the floor, an unidentified man said he was "very dubious about the analysis of the 'Establishment' that Francis Carr gave us, a sort of blanket 'Establishment', as the thing we're up against."[83] The novelist Sean Hignett broke in to say that the politician who was harassing him in Parliament and in the press about the blaspheming and swearing in his novel *A Picture to Hang on the Wall* was "a working-class Labour MP."[84] Exactly, said the man who had taken issue with Francis Carr: "What we're up against is a whole puritan tradition that's not confined to the 'Establishment.'"[85] Mary Whitehouse was a critic of the establishment, not its creature. Her claim to speak as an ordinary woman for ordinary women prompted Avril Fox, a Labour councilor whose beliefs "meshed Sufi, feminism and science fiction" to call her counter-Whitehouse pressure group the Harlow Housewives League.[86] The Harlow Housewives League soon changed its name to COSMO. Its treasurer spoke at the Freedom of Vision teach-in to brief the audience on Whitehouse's agenda.[87]

Michael Rubinstein's performance at the Freedom of Vision teach-in bore little resemblance to the cautious brief he wrote for the *Lady Chatterley's Lover* case, where he hewed closely to Mr. Justice Stable's summing-up in the *Philanderer* case to make arguments about safeguarding literature that explored "the human pilgrimage," all the while accepting as axiomatic that pornography must be suppressed.[88] Rubinstein told his Hampstead audience that in "a so-called civilised society such as ours," the problem of censorship had two solutions. Either we decide that "we cannot really answer for anyone else," or we draw arbitrary lines. And letting someone else draw those lines inhibited one's self-development. "If you have censorship, if you have 'big brother'"—a figure absent from British discussions of censorship before this, but subsequently ubiquitous— "saying what you may or may not see, what you may or may not read, then the individual has no real prospect of maturity, because he always, she always, from the earliest years has to defer to somebody else's judgment. . . . It seems to me that to grow up . . . is to be able to decide for yourself—not that you have to—what may or may not be shown to you."[89] Maturity and responsibility—the maturity and responsibility of a male head of household—were prominent in nineteenth-century debates on the franchise and literacy. Perhaps there is an attenuated Victorian liberalism in Rubinstein's arguments; or perhaps he was simply invoking that common-sense or vernacular liberalism that Iain Macleod did when he said that governments should treat people like grown-ups. Given his long-standing, even hereditary commitment to the liberties of authors and publishers, it seems unlikely that Rubinstein had experienced an awakening: rather, the terms of debate had shifted sufficiently for him to be able to contest the premises of censorship in a way that would have been counterproductive for a lawyer a decade earlier as serial Obscene Publications Bills stalled in Parliament.

Last Exit to Brooklyn

Jean Straker's troubles notwithstanding, there had not been a major obscenity trial since *Lady Chatterley's Lover*. Over the course of 1966, a new one was brewing, and a string of police raids on galleries sparked concern among participants at the teach-in and people in high places alike.[90] A raid on an art dealership in London attracted the most attention. The Robert Fraser Gallery was exhibiting works by the American pop artist Jim Dine, including a series of drawings and collages referencing the kinds of graffiti found in public toilets.[91] These works were visible through the gallery's windows, which made them subject to the Vagrancy Act 1824. "This is not as dotty as it sounds," one civil servant told another. "Section 4 of the Vagrancy Act is the one which . . . makes it an offence for any person 'willfully to expose to view in any street, road, highway, or public place any obscene print, picture, or other indecent exhibition.'"[92] Robert Fraser was a big player in "swinging London," which may have been one reason the DPP consulted the attorney general. Both the DPP and the attorney approved the raid, and the Metropolitan Police visited the gallery and seized Dine's drawings and collages. The *Listener*'s art critic likened it to the raid on the Lawrence exhibition at the Warren Gallery in 1929; Ben Whitaker put a question down on the parliamentary order paper; and Jennie Lee and Lord Goodman called on Roy Jenkins at the Home Office.[93]

Jenkins was untroubled by the Dine case, as there was no suggestion that the police would have acted if the gallery had not been flaunting the art works to passers-by.[94] But Lee and Goodman were two people he had to mollify. Britain's first minister for the arts, Lee was a totemic figure on the Labour left, and she had the prime minister's ear. In Lee's hands politics was the art of the only-just-possible—she conjured the Open University into being through improvisation and force of will. She had installed Goodman, her friend, neighbor, and solicitor, as chair of the Arts Council.[95] Goodman was a former partner at Rubinstein, Nash and Co. and he was legal advisor to the British Board of Film Censors.[96] He was a prodigious networker and became a familiar figure on boards and the quangos—quasi-autonomous non-governmental organizations—that proliferated in the fifties and sixties. Goodman's politics, insofar as he articulated them, were not really Labour, but senior Labour figures came to rely on him as an advisor and mediator.[97] The interest Goodman took in the Dine case foreshadowed interventions he made against censorship later in the sixties.

Both Goodman and Lee were aghast at reports of police officers snooping round the Tate Gallery and the Victoria and Albert Museum.[98] Jenkins reassured Lee and Goodman that a detective in the Dine case had gone to the Tate to verify that Dine was a bone fide artist, with work displayed in a national collection. The Metropolitan Police commissioner himself visited the V&A on being told that the originals of the Aubrey Beardsley drawings in a book seized under the Obscene Publications Act were currently exhibited at the museum. So the police were trying to make an informed judgment about art and standards—not necessarily a bad thing, Jenkins said.[99] He warned Lee and Goodman that an overhaul of the Vagrancy Act would take time, but that meanwhile he would be able to help with another matter they were concerned about—Sir Cyril Black's attempt to suppress *Last Exit to Brooklyn* by Hubert Selby, Jr.[100]

Last Exit to Brooklyn was a string of vignettes about drug-taking, sexual transgression, industrial conflict, and poverty in the projects. The component stories aroused distinct worries: in some denunciations, *Last Exit* was a book about homosexuality; in others, it was an education in drug use. Selby's novel was first published in the United States in 1964 by Barney Rossett's Grove Press. A British edition followed two years later under the imprint of Calder and Boyars, which published many of the same authors as Grove Press (the pair of them often reprinted books first published in Paris by Maurice Girodias). In his partnership with Marion Boyars, and earlier under his own imprint, John Calder was the leading British publisher of the European and American avant-garde. Taking Marguerite Duras, Nathalie Sarraute, and Alain Robbe-Grillet on a tour of university towns and unexpectedly filling Coventry's town hall gave Calder the idea of holding a writers' conference in his hometown, Edinburgh.[101] He convinced the director of the Edinburgh Festival to allow the conference to run in parallel with the festival in 1962. The resulting International Writers' Conference showcased a new overtness in discussions of sexuality, especially male homosexuality. A confrontation between Alexander Trocchi, one of Calder's authors, and the grand old *enfant terrible* Hugh MacDiarmid would reverberate through Scottish letters for decades. British readers were introduced to William S. Burroughs, another of Calder's authors. And a whole day was spent discussing censorship. Girodias made an appearance and told the conference that the distinction between "political censorship" and "moral or sexual censorship" was misleading, as "these two types of repression are always complementary."[102]

Given Calder's list, it was only a matter of time before he had legal trouble. His firm dodged an obscenity trial when Griffith-Jones recommended against prosecuting, judging Miller's *Tropic of Capricorn* well written and likely to attract impressive supporters.[103] Calder was not so lucky when *Cain's Book*, by Trocchi, was seized with other material in Sheffield. In the subsequent trial, three magistrates held that obscenity was not limited to sex, and that a book could count as obscene if, like Trocchi's novel, it featured frank representations of drug use. (A decade earlier, Manningham-Buller had argued that the horror comics legislation was unnecessary as there was no case law "restricting the meaning of 'obscene' to matters relating to sex.")[104] The Court of Criminal Appeal affirmed the Sheffield magistrates' ruling.[105] This made *Last Exit to Brooklyn* vulnerable. The director of public prosecutions became aware of Selby's novel as early as April 1964, probably because Customs were intercepting copies of the American edition.[106] When Calder and Boyars notified the DPP of its forthcoming publication in Britain, the department gave it extensive consideration. Michael Evelyn, who moonlighted writing detective fiction under the name Michael Underwood, reported:

> It is crude, ugly and violent, and obviously intended to be. It is not erotic. The author uses words, as a modern painter does paint, to depict life in the raw amongst people whose animal instincts dominate their lives. . . . In that it did from time to time make its impact on my imagination, I suppose it might be said to have literary merit. . . . See pp. 82–83 for sheer ugly violence: pp. 88–89 for violent sex (straightforward): pp. 146–147 for violent sex (homosexual—Alberta is male—at least I think so!): pp. 230–233 for a general sample of this strange book.

Both Evelyn and Maurice Crump worried how it would look if they brought proceedings against *Last Exit* when they had recently decided to take no action against Burroughs's equally notorious *Naked Lunch*. Crump remarked: "While failure to prosecute the Naked Lunch could not be cited against us in Court it would be cited in public as evidence of the incredible inconsistency of the Establishment and this would be generally damaging to the administration of justice."[107] While *Last Exit* was, in his judgment, obscene, "that is only the beginning of the matter."[108] He went on: "The literary world feels so strongly that there should be no such Acts as the Obscene Publications Acts that on a prosecution under them many distinguished persons will always be prepared to bend towards giving evidence of a book's literary merit simply in order to circumvent their hated Acts."[109] Norman Skelhorn, Theobald Mathew's successor as DPP, wobbled, but eventually decided not to prosecute.[110]

Black then decided to take the matter into his own hands. He applied for a destruction order against *Last Exit to Brooklyn* in the Marlborough Street Magistrates Court.[111] In the postmortems on the *Lady Chatterley* trial it was said that the prosecution should have matched the defense "bishop for bishop and don for don."[112] Black accordingly recruited the bookseller Sir Basil Blackwell, a doctor, and current and former parliamentary colleagues connected with literature and publishing.[113] Calder and Boyars were not able to call expert witnesses of their own: the public-good defense was only available in cases where the publishers were charged with a crime under the Obscene Publications Act. Black had merely applied for a destruction order; he was not trying to have the publishers fined or imprisoned.

In the debates on the 1959 act and the 1964 amendments to it, it was assumed that any private citizen seeking to bring the law to bear on a publisher would prosecute, and so bring the matter before a jury. A destruction order was "simply . . . a means for dealing conveniently and expeditiously with pornography in bulk."[114] The Publishers' Association was alarmed at the implications of Black's action for the "freedom to publish." They declared: "That the sole judgment of a single Magistrate (whose views on obscenity may be well-known) may be evoked by a private citizen (in this case an M.P. who knows that the D.P.P. does not intend to prosecute), makes nonsense of the law."[115] Jenkins, and perhaps his advisors at the Home Office too, regarded it as "an abuse for a private individual to use it to test a particular work with claims to literary merit."[116] Once the magistrate at Marlborough Street issued the destruction order at the end of 1966, the Home Office moved to add a provision to a miscellaneous criminal justice bill that would deprive private individuals of the right to seek destruction orders.[117]

Formally, the destruction order applied only to three copies of *Last Exit to Brooklyn* acquired from Calder and Boyars' offices. Calder and Boyars' solicitors told Skelhorn that the publishers "have decided not to appeal against the decision, but to continue to publish the book and to invite the Director of Public Prosecutions if he thinks fit to institute criminal proceedings against them" under Section 2 of the Obscene Publications Act—that is, charging them with the publication of an obscene item, which would enable them to call evidence about literary merit.[118] The lawyers had exceeded their instructions.[119] They followed up with an apology for the "unintentionally aggressive tone" of this letter. Calder and Boyars also backpedaled: rather than continuing to sell the original edition of *Last Exit to Brooklyn*, they were having it reprinted with an introduction by Anthony Burgess, to be sold at a higher price. By pricing copies at 42 shillings, they would lose sales to imports from America and continental Europe. In a further gesture of their good faith that harked back to the old practices of variable obscenity, they would "limit distribution to recognised established Book Sellers and to keep it away from undesirable and back street shops specialising in erotic literature."[120]

These conciliatory moves came too late. Skelhorn consulted the attorney general and solicitor general shortly after the "unintentionally aggressive" letter and decided to prosecute. "In view of the solicitors [*sic*] letter on behalf of the publishers inviting us to prosecute under s. 2, it has been decided that we should do so," Skelhorn noted in the file.[121] A member of his staff glossed the decision differently: once Calder and Boyars resolved to continue publishing *Last Exit*, criminal charges were unavoidable.[122] (All the same, Calder and Boyars changed solicitors, becoming clients of Arnold Goodman's firm, Goodman, Derrick and Co.) The DPP's office effectively agreed with Sir Cyril Black that once an experienced metropolitan magistrate had found the book obscene, the director would have to prosecute in the event of further publication.[123] Between them, Black and the publishers had forced the DPP's hand. Once again, the public prosecutor was backed into a high-profile obscenity case.

"Another full-dress case under the Obscene Publications Act goes to court," reported *The Times*. "The publishers . . . are mustering eager expert witnesses, 'social workers, historians, doctors, literary people.'"[124] Boyars told reporters *Last Exit* was "like a religious tract." "This is a book about violence and it helps us to understand violence," Calder said.[125] The critic

Ian Hamilton remarked that Calder and Boyars pretended Selby was a social worker, just as Penguin had pretended *Lady Chatterley's Lover* was "a hymn to marriage." Both publishers did so, Hamilton observed astutely, in order to make a "utilitarian defence": "to plead, in other words, that their books really belonged to, and had a useful role to play within, the court's scheme of morality. 'Don't be fooled by the vocabulary, these books are on your side,' was the dominating argument."[126]

That argument did not save *Last Exit to Brooklyn*. Though the judge seemed sympathetic to Selby's book, the jury convicted the company. One of the defense witnesses, the poet A. Alvarez, speculated later that the case was already lost before any of them took the stand. On the first day the jurors were told off for trying to read the book too quickly and were sent back to study it more closely—"a grim enough task for a trained reader, one which they seemed not to take to." Alvarez was the third of thirty defense witnesses, and when he was in the box the jury already seemed "depressed beyond words or hope . . . bored out of their skulls." Alvarez suspected that the book's formal difficulty and the narrator's detachment counted against it: "Had *Last Exit* been more obviously what it was accused of being—more depraving, more corrupting: that is, more titillating, more pornographic—it might have stood a better chance. At least the jury might have known better where they stood and warmed to or against it."[127] The legal definition of obscenity also called for exegesis that was beyond the jurors. At least, this was the ground of Calder and Boyars' appeal—that the judge had not explained how the legal meaning of obscenity differed from a dictionary definition and had not given adequate guidance about the public-good defense.[128] Goodman, Derrick instructed a new barrister for the appeal, John Mortimer. A successful playwright with a rebel-Tory sensibility, Mortimer had much in common with A. P. Herbert. As a writer, Mortimer too got a lot of comic mileage out of the law's foibles, but unlike Herbert, he had a flourishing legal practice. Mortimer succeeded in persuading the Court of Appeal that the judge's summing up in the *Last Exit* trial was defective, and the conviction was quashed. Delivering the judgment of the Court of Appeal, Lord Justice Salmon remarked that the trial judge threw the jury "in at the deep end" of the public good section "and left them to sink or swim in its dark waters."[129] The 1959 act had not been considered by the appellate courts, so the trial judge "was without guidance from authority." Salmon's attempt to provide such guidance created an opening for a new critique of obscenity law under the auspices of the Arts Council.

The Arts Council Working Party

While the *Last Exit* appeal was still pending, the chairman of the Arts Council sponsored a review of the obscenity laws. Lord Goodman was alive to disquiet in the arts sector, though he was himself was not opposed to all censorship. He thought that in cases like the Jim Dine matter it would be good for the police to have to run requests for search warrants or prosecutions past "a literate official or body such as an ad hoc Home Office Committee specially selected for the purpose."[130] Goodman outlined this idea in a speech to the Publishers' Association at the beginning of 1968, and the president and secretary thought the idea a good one.[131] Goodman wrote to the Arts Council's literature director, Eric W. White, saying with pro forma tentativeness that "it might be a good idea to have some sort of symposium on this important subject."[132] White and his assistant Frances Jenkins began organizing a conference that took place in June that year.

Close to one hundred people took part. Most of them represented organizations and companies. A few were individuals with an interest in censorship.[133] When Mary Whitehouse inspected the list of delegates to the conference, she realized it was going to result in "another of those 'loaded' reports." The BBC was invited but not the commercial television companies; the Schoolmasters' Association, but not the National Union of Teachers, which, Whitehouse noted pointedly, "contains women as well as men." She questioned the decision to invite the Albany Trust (which agitated for homosexual rights) and Freedom of Vision, which she described as Jean Straker's "pornographic photography cult."[134]

The conference wound up resolving to appoint a working party to investigate changes to the law. Officially, the working party was a body "set up by a conference convened by the Chairman of the Arts Council of Great Britain," not an Arts Council committee.[135] Eric White had to explain that it was "not really an Arts Council report."[136] But it inevitably carried some of the Arts Council's aura.

When the working party convened, several months after the Court of Appeal quashed Calder and Boyars' conviction, it was obviously stacked in favor of liberalization, though the likes of Freedom of Vision did not have representatives. John Calder was there as the nominee of the Defence of Literature and the Arts Society, an anticensorship group that began life as the Free Art Legal Fund ("Phase One: 'Last Exit to Brooklyn' Trial appeal; Phase Two: A Permanent Legal Fund for the Arts").[137] John Mortimer was one of the Arts Council nominees on the working party. C. R. Hewitt was there for the Society of Authors, and one of the two representatives of the Publishers' Association was Frederic Warburg, defendant in the *Philanderer* case.[138] The chairman was John Montgomerie, another partner in Goodman, Derrick. The working party did contact organizations supportive of censorship—while Whitehouse declined, the former Public Morality Council, now renamed the Social Morality Council, was keen to engage. Frances Jenkins also tried unsuccessfully to arrange a meeting with the Moral Law Defence Association, which Sir Cyril Black had recently founded after splitting from the Social Morality Council ("long story—libellous," Jenkins scribbled).[139] Nevertheless, the witnesses whose testimony the working party emphasized (and excerpted in its report) tended toward liberalization. An important figure here was John Trevelyan. Trevelyan came to the British Board of Film Censors after service as a local education director, but despite this point of departure he moved steadily towards permissiveness during his tenure as BBFC secretary between 1958 and 1971.[140]

The stage was set for a predictably liberal outcome: the Arts Council had rounded up the anticensorship crowd and Goodman had put a partner from his law firm in charge to keep them in line. Then, to everyone's surprise, Goodman and the Arts Council lost control. Early on, the working party agreed to divide into two subcommittees.[141] The first would present a case for abolishing the obscenity laws and the second would devise proposals for reform. The two groups were not evenly matched. Sub-Committee A (for Abolition) included Calder, representatives of the writers' advocacy group PEN, the Writers' Guild, the Society of Young Publishers, the Institute of Contemporary Arts, and the Library Association, along with the playwright and former Labour MP Benn Levy. Twenty years earlier, Levy sponsored a private member's bill to revoke the lord chamberlain's powers over the theater, but he had not been prominent in the struggle that had culminated in the Theatres Act.[142] The abolition subcommittee included no lawyers and no one from the Arts Council. Sub-Committee LR (for Law Reform) was more high powered. It was chaired by Montgomerie and included the literary critic Frank Kermode, an Arts Council member in whose judgment Goodman and the Literature Panel staff set great store; Reginald Davis-Poynter of the same panel; and John Mortimer wearing his Drama Panel hat rather than his barrister's wig. Also on the subcommittee were Hewitt for the Society of Authors; both Warburg and the lawyer R. H. Code Holland for the Publishers' Association; J. E. Morpurgo of the National Book League; and Tony Smythe of the National Council for Civil Liberties.[143]

The disparity in clout between the two subcommittees suggests that the serious work lay in proposing viable reforms, and that abolition was being entertained as a thought experiment or a way of making the reform options look middle-of-the-road. Montgomerie drafted legislation that would mitigate some of the failings of the Obscene Publications Act and limit the use of what his subcommittee called the "fringe laws" such as the Vagrancy Acts and the Post Office Act to circumvent the public-good defense in the Obscene Publications Act.[144] Levy drafted a critique of the law's premises and circularity, his tone veering between the forensic and the mocking.[145] Levy grasped, as E. M. Forster and Sir Frank Newsam had in their very different ways, how vulnerable obscenity law was to ridicule. Levy made a forceful case, and at a thinly attended meeting of the full working party in April 1969 everyone present voted "in favour of the repeal of all legal sanctions against literature, drama and the visual arts." They agreed that the draft would become the working party's final report, subject to some further revision by Levy and Montgomerie "with a view to ensuring that it was meticulously accurate from the legal point of view."[146]

The Arts Council staff then contacted some of the many members of the working party who missed the voting and asked if they would support the decision to recommend abolition rather than reform. William Gaskill of the Royal Court Theatre said yes.[147] Kathleen Nott, PEN's representative, said yes; she had experience as a defense witness in an obscenity trial.[148] Mortimer, who had missed several meetings because he was in Swansea defending the Free Wales Army in their distended trial under the Public Order Act, said he agreed wholeheartedly: "There is no really reasonable alternative to total abolition."[149] Other heavy hitters expressed reservations but said they would go along with the decision. Code Holland telephoned the Arts Council and left the following message: "Not going to oppose. (Doesn't agree that there's a hope in hell.) Personally convinced by BWL's [Benn Levy's] argument. But more likely to get away with reform. [Publishers' Association] wd. not want to appear to be opposed to abolition, but wd. not want to suggest it—1/3 wd. be v. much agin it."[150] Kermode, on sabbatical in the United States, wrote to Eric White: "I was a little surprised by the peripeteia in our deliberations, but on reading the papers I understand it. I will go along with the decision to recommend abolition, with no bet-hedging."[151] Hewitt said it would be a shame to throw away all Montgomerie's work. Montgomerie's draft bill "represents the *possible*, which a recommendation for abolition does not. If we want abolition or nothing, we shall get nothing; legislation, like politics, being the art of the possible." Hewitt was not even certain that total abolition would be good thing even if it were possible, and he suspected Frederic Warburg felt the same way.[152] Over the next month, he came round. He told Elizabeth Barber of the Society of Authors that he still thought that it was "crying for the moon" to call for abolition, but nevertheless there was a case, after all, "for the Arts Council to say 'This is what we think you should do about censorship—abolish it'. . . . So, slightly surprised, I found myself voting for the report. It's far better that it *should* be unanimous of course."[153]

With Hewitt on board, the working party could claim publicly that the case for abolition had been endorsed without dissent.[154] Responsibility for the report was collective: there was no sign in the published document that Levy was the principal author, and so readers could assume that it was largely the work of a lawyer such as Montgomerie or, more likely Mortimer, since much of the text went back over cruxes from the *Last Exit* appeal. Readers were encouraged to believe that those responsible for the administration of obscenity law also thought that the law was unsatisfactory and misconceived. The report gave pride of place to the statement by a "distinguished legal witness" that "Obscenity is incapable of objective definition and is therefore an unsatisfactory subject for the criminal law." In his interview with the working party, the witness said that "all obscenity laws should be abolished. This, however, was probably an impractical proposal in present circumstances, but some improvement could be achieved." The so-called fringe laws such as the Vagrancy Act could be repealed. "The ideal to work for, however, was complete abolition."[155] A summary of the interview and a follow-up statement from the unnamed witness appeared as an appendix to the final report.[156] Early drafts named him, but the final report kept him anonymous "owing to his official position, which is relevant to this whole subject."[157] This was disingenuous if not an outright lie. The witness, C. H. Lewes, was not meaningfully involved in the administration of obscenity law.[158] Nor was he a criminal lawyer. Lewes worked in the Restrictive Practices Branch of the Treasury Solicitor's Department. He dealt with the Net Book Agreement, which seems to have been his only connection with the world of publishing. Lewes was an old friend of Eric White, who secured his invitation to the initial conference and suggested him as a possible member of the working party.[159]

Levy noted in the report that the *Last Exit* appeal succeeded because the trial judge had not explained the law sufficiently. The problem, Levy suggested, was that a thorough explanation of the law would strike the jury as absurd. Explaining the public-good defense meant giving guidance about how much depraving and corrupting could still be for the public good.[160] The judge in the *Last Exit* trial "apparently felt himself unable to recite this conundrum from the bench with a straight face."[161] When statutes are "impracticable or vacuous," judicial pronouncements "fill the vacuum." In attempting to gloss "corruption" in the *Last Exit* appeal, Lord Justice Salmon turned a law that was "dangerously vague" into one that was "dangerously specific."[162] Salmon had listed four types of corruption: "(1) to induce erotic desires of a heterosexual kind, or (2) to promote homosexuality or other sexual perversions, or (3) drug-taking, or (4) brutal violence." Thus, said Levy, "ordinary sexual desire" itself became a form of corruption, and drug use and violence became obscene.[163] To regard violence and drug use as obscene was to redefine the obscene as the antisocial.[164] This made a mockery of the idea, expressed most firmly by Mr. Justice Stable in the *Philanderer* case, that "deprave" and "corrupt" were terms of art whose meaning exceeded those of "shock" and "disgust." In Levy's account, Salmon took the "two elusive words" "deprave" and "corrupt" to mean "merely . . . what is unacceptable in the age in which we live."[165]

Levy wanted to have it both ways: in this part of the report he argued the Court of Appeal had diluted Stable's exacting interpretation of the "deprave and corrupt," and elsewhere he claimed that the troublesome words could never be defined satisfactorily. "Nobody knows what this means," a queen's counsel and part-time judge told the working party. "Obscenity" was an inescapably subjective term and the courts had resorted to an inscrutable phrase in an attempt to define it. The meaning of "obscenity" and "deprave and corrupt" was forever deferred. Judges and parliamentary draftsmen could "only offer us question-begging periphrasis."[166] The problem was intractable: the obscenity laws could not be reformed.

This was the working party's justification for repealing the Obscene Publications Act. The working party recommended leaving the British Board of Film Censors and the existing broadcasting oversight regime as they stood. The Children and Young Persons (Harmful Publications) Act would remain on the books. The fringe laws would go, and in their place would be a new offense of exhibiting an indecent item in a public place so as to offend people who see it.[167] The working party's conclusions were recognizably "post-Wolfenden," as the historian Lawrence Black observes, and nowhere more tellingly than in the exceptions they allowed for.[168] Retaining restrictions on what children could see and read, and limiting public displays of sexually explicit material were both consistent with the Wolfenden principle that the state should not regulate what consenting adults did in private. If the zone of freedom was defined by adulthood, privacy, and consent, it was legitimate for the state to shield nonadults from sexually explicit material and to prevent people walking past a cinema from seeing explicit posters advertising a pornographic movie. Those passersby were not necessarily consenting to the experience. Privacy and consent interlocked.[169]

Roy Jenkins's successor as home secretary, James Callaghan, made it clear that there was no prospect of government legislation on the subject, given the sizable body of public opinion against further liberalization.[170] As Hewitt appears to have recognized, Levy's purpose was not to bring about practical change in the short term but to move the window of publicly defended positions on censorship. The report was an essay in quango-sponsored politicking.[171] The conference launching the report received some exposure in the press. Whitehouse showed up and told the hundred or so people present that repealing the obscene publications laws would expose children to "a diet of depravity." She cited the lessons of Nazism: "The permissive free-for-all of the Weimar Republic in Germany had paved the way for Hitler."[172] Parables about Nazism were common among advocates of censorship; opponents of censorship could counter with the spectacle of Nazi book-burning.[173] As Whitehouse spoke, the BBC's Martin Esslin burst in. "I happen to know something about the Weimar Republic," said Esslin, who lived in Vienna until the Anschluss. "Hitler came to power on your ticket," he told Whitehouse.[174]

The Vacuum

The "vacuum" of which the Arts Council working party spoke was the defining quality of modern British obscenity law. Because obscenity was a severe term for which it proved impossible to establish generally agreed criteria, it became a receptacle for strong social judgments. For a long time, the conceptual incoherence of British obscenity law was shored up by those same social judgments. Assumptions of social hierarchy allowed the essentially Victorian obscenity regime to perpetuate itself through the first half of the twentieth century without serious challenge, even when the anomalies it threw out caused headaches for the police and others working in the system. When those hierarchical assumptions began to unwind as patrician leadership faltered and deference declined, the law's "subjectivity" and "question-begging" led even sober lawyers like Montgomerie and Code Holland to put their names to a case for repeal. A comparable loss of confidence in the system can be seen in Skelhorn's doubts and Crump's pessimism as the DPP's office hesitated over *Last Exit*. In each man's reaction there is the sense of a system creaking, becoming unworkable.

This was a response quite different from John Trevelyan's gradual conversion to the idea that censoring films for adult audiences was undesirable as a matter of principle. Yet these two kinds of response could converge, and the Arts Council working party's report documents a convergence between seeing the mechanics of censorship as malfunctioning and seeing censorship as a bad thing in itself. Outside the spheres of government departments and quangos, as the Freedom of Vision teach-in showed, there was an increasing willingness to disavow censorship, whether in the language of Victorian liberalism, human rights, or a more demotic insistence on being treated as a grown-up. The underground press of the late 1960s and early 1970s was one of the forums, or playgrounds, in which the claims of a new libertarianism was thrashed out, and it was, accordingly, the target of a rearguard attempt to extend obscenity law to a wider range of "antisocial" behavior. This was the *Oz* trial. John Mortimer represented the defendants.

CHAPTER SIX

Subversion from Underground

1970–1971

OZ ATTRACTED COMPLAINTS and police attention from its first issue in 1967.[1] The director of public prosecutions held off until *Oz* number 28 appeared in May of 1970. "School Kids Issue," the cover announced. *Oz*'s editor, Richard Neville, believed in democratizing the underground press like everything else. He was also lazy, which was another reason to outsource the content of the magazine. "Occasionally we would get very bored," recalled Felix Dennis, another editor, "and we couldn't do it or we didn't feel like doing it so we would invite nutters to produce issues." Hence the flying saucers issue.[2] They placed an advertisement in the magazine saying that they were feeling "old and boring" and invited readers under eighteen to apply at the *Oz* office to edit an issue: "You will enjoy almost complete editorial freedom. OZ staff will assist in purely an administrative capacity."[3] The school kids given temporary control of the magazine made the most of the opportunity to shock their elders. Their own writings and drawings, as well as the ads for sex toys and pornographic magazines, spurred the DPP to prosecute.[4] In previous obscenity trials, young people were hypothetical readers: "Would you put this book into the hand of your sixteen-year-old daughter?" An offensive publication actually written by people aged 14 to 16 made for a new kind of contest.

Another novelty that made the *Oz* trial a distinctive piece of theater was the presence of the editors in the dock and the ringleader of the school kids—who was nearly indicted alongside the editors—in the witness box. In the *Lady Chatterley* trial, the author was of course long dead, and the publishers were treated with restraint: Griffith-Jones reserved his scorn and browbeating for the expert witnesses. Hubert Selby and Alexander

Trocchi did not testify at trials over their books, and John Calder received courteous treatment. The *Oz* editors, by contrast, were attacked vigorously by the prosecuting counsel, Brian Leary. Neville relished this combat; Dennis coped with it well; Jim Anderson, the third editor-defendant, was cowed. He was terrified that Leary would force him to admit that he was gay. Leary opted to go only as far as tormenting insinuation: "That's a male organ, isn't it, Mr Anderson?" he said, pointing to a picture in the magazine. "Very attractive, male organs, are they, Mr Anderson?"[5] In other ways, the *Oz* proceedings bore some resemblance to the *Lady Chatterley* trial, as contemporaries were quick to point out. It was not difficult to characterize Leary as the new Griffith-Jones, and Judge Michael Argyle resembled Mr. Justice Byrne of the *Lady Chatterley's Lover* trial in his periodic testiness and incomprehension, real or put on, at much of the expert witness testimony. (Among other things, Argyle claimed to be unfamiliar with the words "dildo" and "cunnilingus." Everyone who writes about the trial takes him at his word, though it is just possible that Argyle, eight years in the army and many more at the criminal bar—his clients included the Great Train Robber Ronnie Biggs—was feigning unworldliness.)[6] As with Byrne in the earlier trial, Argyle's obvious disapproval obscured how indulgent he was towards the defense witnesses, whom he routinely permitted to speechify on matters of principle remote from their claims to expertise.[7]

This was one reason the *Oz* trial was the longest obscenity trial in British history. The other reason the proceedings dragged on was that Neville represented himself, while John Mortimer represented Dennis and Anderson. Neville presented this as a gesture of rebellion, but it was part of a scheme. It would buy the defendants an extra speech for the jury, and Neville could say things that a barrister could not.[8] Neville remained a client of the solicitor instructing Mortimer, David Offenbach. Geoffrey Robertson, an Australian lawyer in Britain as a Rhodes Scholar, worked with Offenbach to edit Neville's closing speech and prep nearly all the witnesses.[9] Mortimer was able to question the witnesses Neville called, and vice versa, which provided a further kind of complementarity.

The parade of witnesses Mortimer and Neville called collectively made the argument that kids were different today, and though adults might be offended by their manners, sexuality, attitude to authority, and experimentation with drugs, they should try to understand rather than criticize. (Neville recited that verse of Bob Dylan's "The Times They Are a-Changin'" in his closing address.)[10] It was better for society as well as individuals if these things were out in the open rather than repressed. The defense called teachers and social workers to illuminate contemporary school life, especially the culture of the comparatively new comprehensive schools, which were progressively replacing academically selective grammar schools and secondary modern schools, their poor relations in the postwar system. (A lot of controversy attached to comprehensives, but the move away from the two-tier system enjoyed substantial public support.)[11] If the average age of the jurors was around sixty, as one of the defense team later claimed plausibly,[12] many of them would have finished school before the establishment of secondary moderns, let alone comprehensives.[13] The defense enlisted psychologists to assess whether there was any danger in teenagers reading about sex or drugs, and to comment on the broader issue of repression. Neville also called a philosopher and a legal theorist to talk about freedom, responsibility, and morality in a liberal society.

The *Oz* trial was thus another courtroom seminar, albeit one with several professors. Yet the *Oz* defense was not the exercise in cultivating deference to intellectual authority that Gardiner and Michael Rubinstein had orchestrated. The times were less propitious, and so was the publication in question. Gardiner's combination of force and earnestness was certainly not Neville's style, or Mortimer's. Often Mortimer would act blasé, bemused by his own witnesses, as if the comic playwright in him was getting the better of the barrister.[14] However, in their different ways both Mortimer and Neville were able to make arguments for freedom of speech with an overtness that had not been possible for Gerald Gardiner in the *Lady Chatterley* trial. The *Oz* defense harked back to the Freedom of Vision teach-in in its rejection of censorship on principle and in the convergence of liberal lawyers and the producers of questionable material.[15]

Why Oz *and Not* Penthouse?

The *Oz* editors insisted that they were not pornographers. They certainly weren't making the kind of money that proprietors of pornographic magazines were.[16] All the same, for Neville and company there were few types of rebellion or heterodoxy that could not be illustrated effectively by naked women.[17] Still, it was fair to ask, and the defense did, why the DPP should target *Oz* rather than *Penthouse*.[18]

The British pornography market was much influenced by developments in Scandinavia. In 1964 Danish authorities prosecuted the distributors of the ribald eighteenth-century English novel *Fanny Hill*.[19] They were found not guilty and on appeal the Danish Supreme Court upheld the acquittal. Danish publishers and booksellers set about energetically pushing the boundaries of the law, and the Ministry of Justice appointed a commission to examine the law. Reporting in 1966, the commission recommended the relaxation of Denmark's censorship laws, citing psychiatric research finding insufficient evidence of a causal link between indecent publications and crime and mental health problems. The Danish parliament duly abolished most forms of print censorship between 1967 and 1969. Denmark's decision became a touchstone for British discussions of pornography and censorship, pro and con, for the next decade. Benn Levy's report referred to it only briefly, but the Arts Council staff took the trouble to get briefings and background information from the Danish embassy.[20] Scandinavian magazines flooded into Britain; to compete, British pornography became more explicit.[21]

By the early seventies, observed a Home Office lawyer, the glossy magazines had "reached a point where, if the legal definition of obscenity has any meaning at all, one would have thought that many of them contravened the present law."[22] And yet they were ubiquitous, sold by "respectable corner-shop newsagents" as well as shops in red-light districts such as Soho.[23] When W. H. Smith was distributing these magazines, it was not feasible for the police to suppress the trade.[24] In London this was a matter of policy. In the wake of the raid on the Jim Dine exhibition, Skelhorn, the DPP, concluded that public opinion was becoming more tolerant, and he prevailed on the Met to be less aggressive in their enforcement of the Obscene Publications Act and the Vagrancy Acts. A Home Office lawyer observed that the police showed "very little initiative in this field." They limited themselves to occasional arrests in Soho "on a fairly selective and arbitrary basis."[25] They did, however, pay close attention to the underground press, the voice of British counterculture.[26]

The trailblazing underground paper was *IT*, which was popularly supposed to be short for *International Times*, but which, according to its founder, Barry Miles, stood for nothing in particular.[27] Miles ran an alternative bookshop and was in touch with American counterculture luminaries via the City Lights bookstore in San Francisco and papers such as New York's *East Village Other*. Miles also knew Jim Haynes, the American who ran Edinburgh's Paperback Bookshop and worked with John Calder on the 1962 Edinburgh writers' conference.[28] With a handful of others, they launched *IT* in 1966 as a platform for a London scene open to cultural experiments, including those enabled by LSD. Other self-described underground magazines addressed the same public and drew on the same contributor pool, though with different emphases. Where *IT* devoted a lot

of attention to drugs, *Friends* (*Frendz*) concentrated on music. The latter
was conceived as a London satellite of *Rolling Stone*, produced by British friends of the American original, but Jann Wenner and Mick Jagger
quickly dropped it.[29] *IT* and *Friends* were produced out of offices in Notting Hill and Ladbroke Grove, the center of London's underground. With
its large Victorian houses in a kind of market limbo before gentrification
began in earnest, Notting Hill had been a "reception area" for people from
the Caribbean in the fifties, and its shabbiness and edginess also made
it a reception area for different sorts of newcomers as the music, drug,
and underground press scene took shape.[30] John Hopkins's club night, the
UFO (more flying saucers) functioned as a hub. Hopkins was also one of
the instigators of the London Free School, a forum in which white counterculture people mixed with black artists and activists such as Courtney
Tulloch, Horace Ove, as well as Michael de Freitas/Michael Abdul Malik/
Michael X, who progressed from slumlord's henchman to Black Power
leader.[31]

Oz made its base in Notting Hill too but for at least the first few years
it was regarded as an interloper. *Oz* was, among other things, an expatriate Australian enterprise. The magazine's title played on the name of the
ringleaders' home country as well as the wizard's domain. Richard Neville
and Jim Anderson were from Sydney and knew Germaine Greer and Clive
James from back home. *Oz* itself was an expatriate, the reincarnation of
a magazine Neville had founded in Sydney with the same title. Martin
Sharp, designer for the London *Oz*, was an alum of the Sydney *Oz*, as was
Marsha Rowe, who started working in the Notting Hill office right after
the School Kids issue came out.[32] Like the London bohemian scene of the
twenties, the underground had plenty of space for people from the settler
colonies. Neville had been features editor on the University of New South
Wales student newspaper. The Sydney *Oz*, which he started after gradu-
ating, extended the boyish provocation of student papers at the time.[33]
It was much influenced by *Private Eye* in its ethos and in specific tricks.
Quite a few covers of the Sydney *Oz* followed the *Private Eye* pattern of
newspaper photographs with speech bubbles added.[34] Where *Private Eye*
attracted libel suits, the Australian magazine drew obscenity charges: the
Old Bailey trial in 1971 was not Neville's first experience in the dock. It was
not difficult to provoke the Australian authorities. Because a majority of
the books available in Australia were imports, the Customs department's
censorship regime was very powerful. Even when the censorship board
recommended a book be allowed into the country, the Cabinet minister
responsible was able to overrule it. The censorship board approved the

Penguin *Lady Chatterley's Lover*, but Cabinet, not simply the minister, said no. The prime minister, Robert Menzies, insisted on it. It followed that C. R. Hewitt's book about the trial, which quoted barristers and witnesses quoting the novel, remained banned too. In April 1965 two Sydney booksellers arranged for contacts in Britain to break a copy of *The Trial of Lady Chatterley* into eight bundles and mail them separately to Australia, whereupon they were reassembled and used to print an Australian edition. The Australian government lifted the ban on *The Trial of Lady Chatterley* and *Lady Chatterley's Lover* itself later that year.[35] That was the federal government. The states had their own obscenity statutes. The Australian *Oz* ran afoul of the New South Wales Obscene and Indecent Publications Act. The cover of the February 1964 issue of the Australian *Oz* showed Neville and his co-editors pretending to use Tom Bass's sculpture on the wall of the P&O building in central Sydney as a urinal. (As in the British satire boom, staid institutions trying to get "with it" came in for mockery.) This image, the magistrate found, was "designed to attract certain types of adolescents and perhaps immature and unhealthy minded adults." On the inside, there was bad language, blasphemy, and filthy drawings.[36] The editors were convicted but were released on bail pending an appeal, which overturned their convictions.[37]

When *Oz* was reborn in London several years later it was not so very different.[38] David Widgery, a member of the International Socialists, heard from someone that "there was this guy from Australia and he was publishing some sort of student magazine," which Widgery suspected, correctly, would be an outlet for the denunciation of hedonistic London that he wanted to write.[39] In time, the editors tuned in to the underground. Neville's feel for shock tactics converged with the sensibilities of the Yippies he had met in the United States in 1968.[40] Sharp threw himself into psychedelic art.[41]

The minutes pages—part index, part summary—of the DPP file on *Oz* chart the magazine's evolution as refracted through the officials' usual disconcerting combination of the broad-minded and the narrow-minded.

> [February 1967]
> From what I have heard about the magazine "OZ" it is an imitation by Australians of the English "satirical" journal "Private Eye."

> [December 1967]
> I felt that this was on a par with various articles on drugs in International Times which you will remember was seized in bulk by the police and on which it was decided to take no action. . . . The present article

while giving what is no doubt undesirable advice about the use of LSD is not, I think, an unqualified invitation to indulge in drugs. . . . I do not feel that it can necessarily be regarded as obscene & likely to deprave & corrupt.

[May 1968]
The emphasis is more political, being a re-hash of the magazine's favourite topics— . . . Vietnam, Rhodesia, . . . the Greek régime etc. The slant on these topics remains the same, veering from extreme leftism to the various brands of anarchism. The emphasis is, as before, anti-"Establishment." . . . Mr Julian Snow MP complained to the A-G . . . about page 15 of no. 11. Under the guise of a "readers medical advice column" reprinted from the "Los Angeles Free Press" the article discusses the pros and cons of anal intercourse. Distasteful though the article is, I don't think that it can be held to be an incitement to commit an unnatural offence as the article does point out the dangers.

[June 1968]
There is little if anything in this number that seems obscene. This number consists really of three psychedelic broadsheets, much of it incomprehensible.

[July 1968]
Re Enoch Powell's complaint—public figures must expect to be caricatured. This one does not come anywhere near obscenity.

[February 1969]
Has it become obscene yet?[42]

The complaints against *Oz* reflected the recent widening of the scope of obscenity to encompass non-sexual varieties of supposedly antisocial behavior, especially drug use. Manchester police alerted the DPP to an issue of *Oz* given over to articles about drugs after finding a copy in the possession of a suspected drug dealer.[43] Sex between men could also be treated as antisocial behavior, despite its partial decriminalization in 1967.[44] *IT* was raided after the paper carried gay contact ads, and the company charged with conspiracy to corrupt public morals.[45] Anachronistic as it may seem, this common-law crime was in some senses a creation of the sixties. Just as the 1959 act came into effect, a man named Frederick Shaw was prosecuted for publishing a directory of London prostitutes, the *Ladies Directory*. He was convicted of publishing an obscene book, living off immoral earnings, and conspiracy to corrupt public morals. It was a matter of debate whether the conspiracy offense had existed in the common law before the judicial committee of the House of Lords recognized it in Shaw's final appeal.[46] One of the law lords in *Shaw* envisioned the counterrevolution while the revolution was some way off. "Let it be supposed," Viscount Simonds said in 1961, "that at some future, perhaps, early, date homosexual practices between adult consenting males are no longer a crime. Would it not be an offence if even without obscenity, such practices were publicly advocated and encouraged by pamphlet and advertisement? Or must we wait until parliament finds time to deal with such conduct? I say, my Lords, that if the common law is powerless in such an event, then we should no longer do her reverence."[47] Patrick Devlin, by this time a law lord himself, hailed the case as a classic example of the way the way the evolving common law expresses morality. Juries would act as a safeguard against overreach: if they disagreed with particular laws that enforced morals, they would vote to acquit. Shaw's case, Devlin argued, "makes the jury a constitutional organ for determining what amounts to immorality and when the law should be enforced."[48]

The conspiracy conviction in *Shaw* prompted Roy Jenkins to seek an assurance that the DPP would not use charges of conspiracy to corrupt public morals as a way of bypassing the public-good defense in the Obscene Publication Act. Jenkins was told such an assurance was unnecessary, and indeed there was no immediate surge in conspiracy prosecutions. However, in the late sixties and early seventies, the DPP brought conspiracy charges more often, using the common law offense's elasticity to cover new situations, such as clandestine cinemas showing pornographic movies.[49] After *IT* was prosecuted in 1970 for doing what Viscount Simonds foresaw, "encouraging" sex between men by advertisement and without obscenity, the company appealed to the House of Lords, seeking to overturn *Shaw*. Instead, their lordships affirmed it, effectively accepting that the courts had a "residual power" to "make punishable conduct of a type hitherto not subject to punishment."[50] The *Oz* editors were indicted on a count of conspiracy to corrupt public morals as well as breaches of the Obscene Publications and Post Office Acts.

The School Kids issue was antisocial to the point of sedition rather than obscenity. Frederick Luff, the detective in the *Oz* case, argued along these lines when he pushed for the School Kids issue to be referred to the DPP:

> The whole theme and message is directed to young students urging them to revolt against society and to discard morality, responsibility and self-discipline in every sense. Further, that this type of publication

is much more harmful than the Danish and Swedish "hard core" pornography, in that . . . "Oz" No. 28 attacks the very roots of society and because of its open sale and distribution is[,] within the meaning of the obscenity laws, proportionately more obscene.[51]

Here, then, was the answer to the question "Why *Oz* and not *Penthouse*?": challenges to the established order, not smut, were what was truly corrupting.

And the fact that this message was directed to school-age readers made it easier to answer yes to the question "Has it become obscene yet?" John Gordon, still going strong, remarked in his *Sunday Express* column that *Oz* was "a crude, nasty, erotic and in parts obscene publication aimed normally at kinky adults," but this issue was "blatantly aimed at children."[52] (Gordon said, "I have had sent to me a magazine called *Oz*," as if by an informant, but he was a subscriber, no doubt waiting for an outrage like this.)[53] Individual teachers wrote to the DPP, the National Union of Teachers had its solicitors express the union's disapproval, and two headmasters who held office in educational organizations produced statements attesting to "the destructive effects of this magazine on young people." In one of his legal opinions, Leary mentioned these condemnations from teachers, as well as evidence from the police that the issue "has been circulated in a large number of schools." Because a prosecution under the Obscene Publications Act had to prove that the material would tend to corrupt those likely to read it, it was important to gather evidence that the School Kids issue was reaching school children.[54] The police took statements from a geography teacher and a cleaner at one school, the cleaner testifying: "About two weeks ago I saw two notices in red crayon on notice boards in the fourth year classrooms. On these notes were the words either 'Buy Oz' or 'By Oz'. At the time I thought these notices were about school plays."[55]

Against Repression

The school kids who answered the ad in *Oz* knew full well that it offered an opportunity to revolt, or at least a break from conforming. Charles Shaar Murray, who became a prominent music journalist not long afterwards, saw it as a way of getting away from his hometown of Reading. He came down to London for an initial meeting where Neville, Anderson, and Dennis asked the teenage volunteers what they were interested in, what they thought about education and everything else. The urbanity of the other school kids impressed Murray as much as the editors' cool. Several of the contributors went to school at Holland Park, near *Oz*'s base.[56] Holland Park School had been the flagship comprehensive; many in the progressive elite sent their children there. After making the cut—it's not clear if anyone didn't—Murray and the others made further trips to the *Oz* office and Neville's flat, culminating in a four-day write-in where the young people put the issue together. The editors seem to have kept their promise to provide administrative support and not try to direct the content.[57]

For young people, issues of freedom and constraint inevitably touched on schooling. At the introductory meeting, would-be contributors described their school as well as their musical tastes and any experience with drugs or sex when they introduced themselves to the *Oz* team.[58] The School Kids issue printed reports on the climate at eight British schools. It also ran a piece entitled "School Atrocities," a cartoon of a male teacher masturbating as he touched boys' bottoms, and a description of armed-forces cadet units in schools as the "British Hitler Jugens."[59] Even when they wrote about these social attitudes outside the context of education, their work bore the imprint of school. One of the issue's most forceful contributors was by Anne Townsend of Farnborough, someone's sixteen-year-old daughter. According to her contributor bio, Townsend "Says . . . 'I want all the freedom I can get,' but will conform to anything as long as she gets something out of it.'"[60] The article she submitted was a plea for more "freedom of sexual expression in public." Although contemporary British society was "labelled permissive (by society itself)," it was not free enough to permit sex in public places. "Animals perform the act every day in public, so why not let humans have the same freedom if they wish it?" Having sex in public, or "dancing at a funeral," would be an assertion of freedom from "the system" and "tradition." For most people, "This society is closing in on you and taking you over. It is a safe bet that you obey someone who is your equal but holds a higher position than you. Why not start a freedom campaign in your area now and just do as you wish? . . . Live in the moment and not the future. Be free and tread on anyone who stands in your way. Your true identity is sure to come to the surface. Don't become Mr. and Mrs. Average. Live a little before it's too late."[61] Calling for freedoms that not every repressed person secretly craved, like dancing at funerals, Townsend's piece was rebellious in content but compliant in form: its rhetorical moves recall the provocative essays or debate speeches solicited by edgier English teachers in the sixties and seventies. Among other things the School Kids issue of *Oz* was an unchained version of a school magazine.

Vivian Berger, a fifteen-year-old at the independent school where a cleaner had mistaken the *Oz* notices for announcements of school plays, contributed anecdotes that sat within the long literary tradition of schoolmaster sadism: "He once took us rowing when there was lots of snow"; "he caned me once & I had to bend over and put my hands on a chair so the muscles in my arse would be tense and it would hurt more."[62] Berger was also responsible for a collage in which Rupert Bear, a beloved children's book character, was pasted into a Robert Crumb cartoon—lifted, as copy and images commonly were, from the American underground press. The resulting comic strip showed Rupert having sex with someone who was both a granny and a virgin. Uninhibited puerility doubling as countercultural transgression, it was one of the most offensive things in the whole issue. At the trial, Leary had some success in wrong-footing witnesses who defended the cartoon as "youthful genius," in Jim Anderson's ill-advised phrase.[63] Other witnesses were less willing to play along. Michael Schofield, the author of *The Sexual Behaviour of Young People* and *The Strange Case of Pot* (and, earlier, under the name Gordon Westwood, *Society and the Homosexual*) refused to agree with Leary that Rupert Bear was a child.[64] "It's an unreal question: you might as well ask me how old is Jupiter." Leary persisted, and Schofield replied: "I don't know whether he goes to school or not. I'm sorry but I'm obviously not as well informed as you are about little bears."[65]

There was an argument for charging Berger alongside Neville, Dennis, and Anderson for conspiracy to corrupt public morals. Leary reasoned. "If a conspiracy to corrupt public morals by the production of OZ 28 be established in this case then clearly on his own admission Vivian Berger was party to the conspiracy." Vivian's mother, Grace Berger, the chairman of the National Council for Civil Liberties, intervened with the DPP personally.[66] The DPP decided not to charge Vivian Berger, citing his age, and opted to call him as a witness instead.[67] The DPP official who conducted the committal hearing at the magistrate's court thought that Vivian Berger's statement was an asset to the prosecution: "It tends to show the depravity of the contributors and the level to which the contributors hope the reader will sink."[68] In the event, Berger proved more useful to the defense.[69] Asked by Mortimer why he made the Rupert Bear cartoon, Berger replied: "I think that, looking back on it, I subconsciously wanted to shock your generation: to portray us as a group of people who were different from you in moralistic attitudes." Older people would have taken Rupert Bear as a symbol of idealized innocence and the cartoon showed him "just doing what every normal human being does." Mortimer asked if he was trying to "show that there was a more down-to-earth side of childhood than some grown-up people are prepared to think." Yes, said Berger enthusiastically. "This is the kind of drawing that goes around every classroom, every day, in every school."[70]

If school kids were already making cartoons like Berger's, seeing them in *Oz* was not going to corrupt them further. Mortimer stressed that young people's experiences were radically different from their elders', and for the sake of Britain's future, adults needed to understand them. The School Kids issue offered a glimpse of "the true state of mind of teenagers living in a big city, going to big State schools, grammar schools and comprehensives. Are we going to say, subsequently, well, that's true; that's what those kids think; that's what they think and that's how they feel, but don't for goodness sake let's ever let it be known? Let's shut our minds to it; let's go on as if all the boys thought of nothing but cricket bats and all the girls thought of nothing but knitting patterns. Is that really how we want to view life?" Clearly not: "It may be for the public good of all as parents, as teachers, and as human beings, to know how our children really feel and really behave."[71]

This was familiar territory for Mortimer. The *Oz* trial began as he was finishing up his defense of *The Little Red School-Book* against obscenity charges.[72] Another Scandinavian import, *The Little Red School-Book* gave young people frank advice about sex and drugs (and homework). It openly challenged adult authority. A group of teachers and older school students revised the English translation to add information specific to Britain.[73] *The Little Red School-Book*'s British publisher was Richard Handyside, who also published books by Fidel Castro and Che Guevara. The circumstances of publication suggested that *The Little Red School-Book* was an insurrectionary publication, as did title's nod to Mao.[74] Handyside saw it as "a political book, its message being that what is wrong with schools is what is wrong with society as a whole and can be changed only if society is changed."[75] Combining subversion, schooling, and sex education, it engaged many of Mary Whitehouse's concerns, and she complained to the DPP.[76] He initiated proceedings under the Obscene Publications Act 1959. Handyside opted for a summary trial before a magistrate, apparently out of concern about the costs of a jury trial (the *Oz* defendants received legal aid). Despite Mortimer's efforts, the magistrate convicted Handyside and fined him £50. When legal costs and the confiscation of stock were taken into account, Handyside faced a loss approaching £5000.[77] A destruction order was issued against copies taken from a progressive bookshop in

Brighton, but a court in Glasgow declined to order the destruction of copies taken from a radical information exchange there.[78] Handyside took his case to the European Court of Human Rights to argue that the Obscene Publications Act infringed his right of free communication.[79] It was only the second petition the Strasbourg court heard from the United Kingdom. The court ruled that the British legislation fell within the limits permitted by Article 10 of the European Convention.[80]

The Little Red School-Book unsurprisingly sparked controversy among teachers and children's advocates.[81] The *Oz* defense team approached some of them so that Mortimer could back up his arguments about the generation gap with testimony from those on the educational barricades. Michael Duane had been headmaster of Risinghill, an early comprehensive school in a deprived part of North London. At Risinghill Duane attempted to involve pupils and parents in the governing of the school. He abolished corporal punishment, provided frank sex education, and tried to make the most of his pupils' creative impulses. Duane's goal was, as he put it in his job application, "the development of an education nearer to the real powers and needs of children."[82] Duane's methods met with fierce opposition from the press and some parents, and he had trouble with the school inspectorate. The Inner London Education Authority closed Risinghill after only five years in the course of a restructure of education in Islington and Finsbury, but the real purpose, Leila Berg claimed in her book about Risinghill, was to shut down Duane's experiment.[83] Berg testified for the defense in the *Oz* trial. She and Duane were both advisors to the magazine *Children's Rights*, along with other teachers influenced by Ivan Illich and Wilhelm Reich, though Berg's interest in radical pedagogy ran back to the thirties, when she discovered the work of Susan Isaacs; she had been an active Young Communist.[84] Berg was one of many whose ideas were decisively shaped by the thirties and came into their own in the sixties, and then found themselves overtaken. In time the children's rights movement drew in people influenced by antipsychiatry, another current in the late sixties and early seventies underground.[85] Questioning the teacher-pupil binary altogether took the idea of "deschooling" further than Duane and Berg could countenance. They broke with *Children's Rights* when it published articles encouraging vandalism and giving advice about how not to cooperate with the police.[86]

The children's rights movement was grist to the mill of those for whom progressive education and comprehensive schools symbolized a breakdown in standards in society at large.[87] It was reasonable to suspect that an Old Bailey jury would also condemn the movement. Mortimer was making an audacious move in hitching the defense to educational figures who could be discounted as extremists. Duane was practically a pariah. Under cross-examination by Leary, Duane told the court that in the five years since Risinghill's closure, he had applied unsuccessfully for thirty headmaster posts and eight to ten principal positions at small training colleges.[88]

Duane told the court that no harm would come from the mockery of teachers and headmasters in the School Kids issue.[89] He elaborated: "My experience of young people is that the more they are prevented from expressing their real feelings about authority the more likely they are to develop real feelings of frustration and desires to do something damaging or to express themselves in more violent ways. The more access they have to the expression of their points of view about authority the more likely they are to develop rational ways of coping with that authority."[90] In his experience, Duane said, children "came out with the most extraordinary fantasies; and if these are at all repressed, they cause difficulty for the child later on. But if brought out into the open and discussed, they don't become a problem." That was the role of this issue of *Oz*: "to give some sort of scope to youngsters to give vent to their feelings in public."[91] Echoing Duane, Berg testified that bad language of the kind in *Oz* amounted to a "release of tension," which was "the first step toward education." If *Oz* incited adolescents into anything, it was into thoughtfulness about their society: "Our society, far from being permissive, is exploitive, manipulating and forbidding."[92]

Children also wanted a say in how their lives were run. This was one of the demands in the charter of children's rights that Berg was promoting at the time. It was a cause that had support from the National Council for Civil Liberties. Duane, the cause's martyr, knew Grace Berger through the same campaign. On the stand, Duane was able to gloss a jaded but broadly sympathetic article in the School Kids issue about the Schools Action Group.[93] "I'm very often invited to speak to it. . . . It is a kind of incipient trade union for school pupils. . . . Their central programme is to ask for participation in the running of schools."[94] The democratization of schools had long been an ambition of progressive education, one realized most fully at A. S. Neill's Summerhill. The appearance of the School Kids issue prompted readers to ask for more information about the Schools Action Group and, in one case, to call at the *Oz* office about jobs in progressive schools. Marsha Rowe passed on the contact details of someone at Dartington Hall, a famous progressive school in Devon; Rowe then followed up with a letter to Dartington Hall asking why the school did not subscribe to *Oz*.[95]

Psychologists reinforced the message that repression was unhealthy. The psychologists who appeared for the defense also testified that there was little or no scientific support for the notion that articles about drugs or sexually explicit pictures had damaging effects. Josephine Klein acted surprised that anyone could think that a magazine could kindle perverted desires, and routinely shut down Leary with responses like "this really is a bit silly" and "this isn't a proper discussion."[96] Lionel Haward believed that "young people who are exposed to sexual pictures and books are less likely later to show sexual psychopathology or sexual deviance." Haward read the Rupert Bear strip, which evidently validated the preconceptions of everyone who looked at it, as an indirect critique of the inadequacy of sex education.[97] The most famous of the psychologists who testified was Hans Eysenck, almost a household name as a consequence of his television and radio presence.[98] As Mathew Thomson has shown, Eysenck was a champion of "value-free" psychology, but his research usually landed on the "permissive" side of controversies—for instance, about smoking, the causes of crime, and the effects of TV violence.[99] There is an interesting parallel with two high-profile positivists in other disciplines, A. J. Ayer in philosophy and H.L.A. Hart in law: rigorous positivist analysis tended to result in secular liberal positions on issues of public interest. Eysenck was also something of a hired gun: in research funded by the tobacco industry, he found that the connection between smoking and cancer was that people genetically disposed to developing lung cancer were also genetically predisposed to take up smoking.[100] Testifying for the Oz editors, Eysenck said that it was extremely unlikely that the images in Oz could shape readers' sexuality, or "create a lesbian from any young person" as Mortimer glossed the prosecution argument.[101] Pornographic material was usually sought out by people who were already heading in a pathological direction, Eysenck said. None of the psychologists took issue with the assumption that homosexuality was a psychopathology. The only witnesses who contested it vigorously were the Oz editors. Felix Dennis told Leary: "Your constant insistence that homosexuality is a perversion—is not in my opinion." "I wouldn't agree with word 'pervert,'" Jim Anderson said in response to a question about Oz's small ads. "I prefer the words erotic minorities; sexual minorities."[102]

Eysenck was asked whether he thought Oz pornographic, and he said no, partly because it did not go as far as stuff that would usually be called pornographic, but also because of the intention behind it "One doesn't get the feeling that it was written in order to be salacious, but that sex is made use of in, perhaps, a semi-political context. The impression I gained from it was an opposition to authority and the Establishment. And since the Establishment tends to be against free love and the open expression of sex, sex is brought in as one of the issues to beat the Establishment with."[103] Friends and enemies alike recognized that, as a Home Office lawyer put it, "the underground press . . . deliberately challenges many of the bases of current society including the code of sexual morality," and "resort[s] to pornography as an essential aspect of the expression of their views."[104]

A Case about Dissent

At the outset, Mortimer said that this was "a case about dissent." He claimed a connection between religious dissenters "who, in past times, used to thunder their denunciations in dark clothes and rolling phrases from the pulpits of small chapels. Now, the dissenters wear long hair and colourful clothes and dream their dreams of another world in small bed-sitting rooms in Notting Hill Gate. In place of sermons with their lurid phrases about damnation, we have magazines reflecting a totally different society from that in which we live."[105] Mortimer snorted at Leary's statement that that the proceedings were not an attack on freedom of speech: "For myself, I find it impossible to comprehend how a case that places young men in the dock because of their editorship of a small magazine, which, it is conceded is not hard core pornography and which is attacked because of the views it puts forward about sex and drugs, can possibly be held *not* to be an attack on the freedom of speech." In his closing address, Mortimer quoted the dictum attributed to Voltaire about defending to the death someone's right to say something one disagrees with. Mortimer did not mention John Stuart Mill by name, but he affirmed one of the planks of Mill's *On Liberty*: "Tolerance means protecting minority opinions, particularly the opinions of minorities with whom we disagree."[106]

Mortimer did not go as far as putting living philosophers into the witness box, but Neville did. Richard Wollheim, a professor of philosophy at University College London, agreed to testify. So did Hart's successor as professor of jurisprudence at Oxford, Ronald Dworkin.[107] Wollheim was asked to comment on the article "I Wanna Be Free," which asked rhetorically why people weren't allowed to have sex in the streets. Wollheim told the court that "I Wanna Be Free" was probably the best thing in the issue:

I say that because I think that one does find here an attempt to try and come to grips with certain subjects which are extremely important for people of this age in helping them to form their own moral views. It is partly concerned with morality as such, and partly concerned with the rather different issue of how far morality should be enforced by law. . . . I think that it proceeds by a method used by many moral thinkers. It shows how something which is forbidden is really very like and very close to something which is not forbidden, thus raising the question that if the one is allowed, why is the other forbidden. And this allows people to arrive at a reasoned conclusion. And that, in itself, is an essential element in the formation of an individual's moral conceptions.

Neville broke the spell with a follow-up question to confirm that Wollheim did not think the article would provoke "a sudden outbreak of fucking in the streets." "No," replied Wollheim.[108]

The other defense barristers then had the opportunity to examine Wollheim. Yes, he told Mortimer, using exaggerated propositions to start a debate was an established technique, one used by "some of the greatest moral thinkers of our civilisation." Responding to another question, Wollheim said: "In a liberal society like ours, we are partly interested in getting people to conform to rules which we think to be reasonable, and we are partly interested in people forming their own moralities, forming their own conceptions of human life and of what a human being should do."[109] These interests could come into conflict, but it was important to have discussions like that of "I Wanna Be Free" to help articulate the reasons for conformity and to help individuals "work out some morality of their own."[110] Before Wollheim left the stand the judge let Neville ask him another question: what effect he thought this prosecution might have on the community. That was irrelevant, Argyle told Neville. "No barrister would be allowed to ask that question." Neville insisted: "That's what the case is all about, two mentalities fighting each other." The judge gave in. "Ask any question you like," he said. Wollheim hesitated, then stated that he thought the *Oz* trial might be damaging in two ways. It threatened to endanger "the morality of toleration which is a large part of the morality of a society like ours." He also worried that it might encourage "the kind of polarisation in our society which we already see in existence in other societies such as America."[111]

Dworkin, whose evidence was brief, touched on the same themes. He said that "a concern for toleration and freedom of expression" was central to the way young people thought about morality. *Oz* was part of a movement that "takes as its end, to increase the role that morality plays in public and private behavior." Neville then ventured to ask Dworkin, an

American, how he thought a case like the present one would fare in an American court. This was another question that no barrister would have been allowed to ask. Again, Argyle made a show of umbrage followed by leniency: "Well, if you think you can ask that question, go ahead and ask it." Neville repeated the question and Dworkin replied that "this prosecution would be unconstitutional in the United States by virtue of the First Amendment, which prohibits the infringement of the freedom of speech."[112] Leary did not cross-examine. Argyle's belated comeback in his summing-up was: "But we are not, as yet, an adjunct of the United States."[113]

Verdict, Sentence, and Appeal

Dworkin's testimony seems unlikely to have done the defendants any favors with a jury whom the lawyers sized up as conservative and unsympathetic.[114] The same could be said of many of the other witnesses, such as the comedian who audibly called Argyle a "boring old fart" as he left the courtroom.[115] Having to listen to so many witnesses must also have taxed the jury's patience and concentration.[116] Even then, the defense had more witnesses in reserve, including Germaine Greer, David Hockney, more school kids, and the sociologist Stanley Cohen, whose book *Folk Devils and Moral Panics: The Creation of the Mods and Rockers* came out the year after the *Oz* trial.[117] The conduct of the defense suggests that the "seminar" aspect of the trial was more important than securing an acquittal. "I knew that the trial would go on outside the courtroom," Neville said later: "there would be a great big public out there and we needed to get our point of view across."[118] The witnesses' ideas might not impress the jury but could reach a much larger audience through media coverage of the trial. There is a distant analogy with parliamentary speeches by backbench campaigners: the real audience was not the handful of members in the house at midnight, but the next day's newspaper readers. Friends of *Oz*, run by Sue Miles of *IT* and Stan Demidjuk, another expat Australian hand on the London *Oz*, organized carnivalesque demonstrations outside the Old Bailey and issued press releases. A publicist connected with *Oz* gave Miles a crash course in writing copy. For all the strenuous irreverence, Friends of *Oz* was a serious public relations operation.[119]

However well *Oz* and its friends played this long game, the defense lost the short game. The jury convicted on the obscenity and postal charges.[120] The defendants were acquitted on the charge of conspiracy to corrupt public morals. Rather than pass sentence then and there, Argyle remanded Neville, Dennis, and Anderson in custody for a psychiatric evaluation.

This surprised everyone, including DI Luff, who told them as they left for Wandsworth prison: "I'm sorry you've been sent to the nick because I didn't think it would come to that. I think on the whole you're not actually bad young lads, but you've been led astray." Dennis said he would have felt better if Luff had gloated.[121] In jail a barber cut their hair, a symbolic de-hippie-ing that provoked a minor outcry.[122] After the three editors had spent a week in jail, Argyle was ready to pass sentence. The assessments he requested turned up nothing negative. The prison's medical officer reported no signs of mental illness and no drug problems; the "social enquiry report" by a probation officer described them as polite, articulate, and committed to *Oz* "as a platform for reformative views" rather than a way of making money.[123] Argyle confounded expectations again by imprisoning the editors rather than imposing suspended sentences or fines.[124] Neville was sentenced to fifteen months in prison and recommended for deportation, "banish[ing] him to Botany Bay," as a group of Australian writers working on Fleet Street put it in a letter of protest.[125] Anderson was born in Britain and could not be sent back to Australia. He got twelve months in prison and Dennis nine months. The judge also fined Oz Publications Ink Ltd £1000, which was £240 more than the company's net assets.[126]

Neville, Dennis, and Anderson appealed against conviction and sentence. Mr. Justice Griffiths granted them bail while waiting for the appeal hearing on condition they not work on the magazine in the meantime.[127] Griffiths granted bail partly because the custodial sentence was unusual for an obscenity case, and partly because there was a danger Dennis would already have served most of his sentence before the Court of Appeal delivered its judgment. The Court of Appeal heard the case three months later, in early November of 1971. Now the convolution of the defense became an asset, because the volume of evidence made it more likely that Argyle had made mistakes in summing it up for the jury, and the Court of Appeal might decide that those mistakes called the verdict into question. Mortimer and Robertson identified scores of errors Argyle had made in parsing the expert witnesses' testimony. The Court of Appeal took these mistakes seriously and criticized Argyle's attitude to the expert witnesses. Lord Chief Justice Widgery—no relation of the *Oz* writer—noted: "There are in a number of cases sentences, asides almost, in the course of the summing up which tend to denigrate the witness in question. It may be in some instances these asides were justified . . . but they are frequent and give the impression that the Judge was biased against experts as a group and was inclined to make little of their evidence." Where other judges would have ruled out a line of questioning, or sent the jury out so counsel could make legal arguments about its validity, Argyle let the examination proceed and cast aspersions afterwards.

This led him into a mistake about the law. Whether a publication was obscene or not was supposed to be a question for the jury; the publication itself was the only evidence of obscenity. This was the position both before and after the 1959 act. The defense could call evidence to show that, while obscene, the publication was redeemed by some contribution to the public good, but it was not supposed to call evidence on the question of whether the publication was obscene or not. In another Old Bailey trial in 1971 involving a book entitled *The Mouth and Oral Sex*, as soon as counsel asked a witness (the novelist Margaret Drabble) whether she thought the book was likely to deprave and corrupt, the judge ruled the question out of order as one for the jury alone.[128] In the *Oz* trial, the Court of Appeal held, "a majority of the expert evidence . . . bore no relation to the defense of public good under Section 4 [of the Obscene Publications Act 1959], but was rather directed to showing that the article was not obscene. In other words, it was directed to showing that in the opinion of the witness it would not tend to deprave or corrupt." The psychologists, for instance, all testified about whether the School Kids issue was likely to have an adverse effect on young readers. The Lord Chief Justice went on: "Now whether the article is obscene or not is a question exclusively in the hands of the Jury, and it was decided in this Court in *Calder & Boyars* . . . that expert evidence should not be admitted on the issue of obscene or no."[129] Mortimer had of course represented Calder and Boyars at the *Last Exit* appeal. He knew better than anyone, certainly better than Judge Argyle, that expert witnesses were not supposed to hold forth on "the issue of obscene or no." Argyle failed to heed another lesson of the *Last Exit* case. Then, Mortimer had persuaded the Court of Appeal to set aside the conviction because the trial judge had failed to explain the legal meaning of obscenity. He was able to repeat the argument in the *Oz* appeal. When the *Oz* jurors asked for clarification of what constituted obscenity, Argyle read them a dictionary definition. It was possible Argyle gave the jury the impression that, in law, "obscene" was synonymous with "indecent." He did not remind them of the stipulation that an obscene publication was likely to deprave and corrupt, rather than just shock and disgust.

The Court of Appeal judges accepted Mortimer's argument that this made the verdicts under the Obscene Publications Act unsafe and quashed the convictions. That left the convictions under the Post Office

Act, which related to sending material that was merely "indecent." The Court of Appeal let those convictions stand but suspended the sentences for two years. That is, the defendants could go free, and provided they were not convicted of other offenses punishable by imprisonment in the next two years, the sentences would expire. The Court of Appeal cancelled the recommendation that Neville be deported, now that his sole conviction was an infringement of the Post Office Act.[130]

The Fall of the Obscene Publications Squad

"The case of 'Oz' magazine . . . did immeasurable damage to the proper administration of the law in this field. After a trial which was more like a circus . . . the remanding in custody, the ritual hair cutting, the wholly ill-judged observations of the Judge, and the sentences themselves all served to turn the persons responsible into public martyrs and in some quarters even heroes."[131] This was the assessment, six years later, of David Tudor Price, Leary's successor as senior treasury counsel. Outrage at the prison sentences, and the haircuts, was a persistent theme of the critical commentary in the media, and in the complaints that ordinary citizens made to the authorities. Lynda Anderson, who described herself as "in no way 'hippy' but a fairly 'straight' 23 year old Personal Assistant to the Sales Director of an international company in London," wrote in a letter to the director of public prosecutions that the haircuts and the psychiatric evaluations were abuses of civil liberties and the sentences out of all proportion to the charges. Anderson was a regular reader who agreed "with many opinions put forward in OZ which, whilst being on occasions a sexually daring magazine, has always a *majority* content of intelligent, important, and relevant political and social comment." The people who read *Oz*, she added, chose to do so, whereas "I have to walk down Soho's Berwick and Brewer Streets each day to get to work and there—not by choice—I am forced to see these life size 'blown up' photographs of women fondling their own breasts and similar provocative sights."[132]

The Conservative home secretary, Reginald Maudling, was alarmed by "the volume of opinion that is asking why certain publications such as 'Oz' and the 'Red School Book' are singled out for prosecution, while at the same time not all that much is done about the hard core pornography openly on sale on a large scale in Soho." Maudling was "mindful of the fact that it is not for him to decide about prosecutions," but the Home Office still oversaw law enforcement and Maudling asked the DPP and the Metropolitan Police commissioner, Sir John Waldron, to explain.[133] As the deliberations over *Last Exit to Brooklyn* and the early *Oz* complaints showed, the DPP's office in Skelhorn's time was wary of prosecutions under the Obscene Publications Act. When challenged about "the apparent discrepancy between the convictions of 'Oz' and 'Little Red Schoolbook' and the relative inviolability of Soho," Skelhorn conceded that he could bring more prosecutions, but they were costly and the penalties imposed by the courts were usually meagre.[134] Prosecutions were less effective at suppressing pornography than the combination the police had been using since the early 1950s: destruction orders and disclaimers, under which a retailer agreed to forfeit material after a raid and the matter did not go to any court. The police, the DPP, and the Home Office recognized that it was not certain that the disclaimer procedure was legally watertight, but they all agreed it was convenient.[135]

Waldron let the Home Office know that he thought his officers did not get enough support from the DPP. Of 305 cases the police referred to the DPP in 1971, the director's office took no action—not even a caution—in 123 of them.[136] Although the Metropolitan Police had acceded to Skelhorn's wishes after the Fraser Gallery raid and taken a less aggressive approach to obscene publications, the more permissive policy clearly rankled: "About twelve months ago I did contemplate mounting a special exercise to try and clear up the whole of the Soho areas, particularly in regard to pornography but because of manpower problems and the liberal view taken in regard to 'Love Camp 7' and 'Oh Calcutta' I decided against it."[137] Waldron was making his own version of the discrepancy argument: if the DPP was not going to act against the nudity of *Oh! Calcutta!*, the revue orchestrated by the drama critic Kenneth Tynan, or against a women's-prison exploitation movie set in the Third Reich, it would be inconsistent of the police to go after Soho.[138]

Waldron ordered a report from George Fenwick, the head of the Metropolitan Police's Obscene Publications Squad, to address the home secretary's concerns about the new round of "Why *Oz* rather than *Penthouse*?" questions. Fenwick wrote that it was "an unfortunate fact of life that pornography has existed for centuries" and it was "unlikely that it can ever be stamped out." Underground papers presented a more serious threat. "In this country at the minute there are somewhere in the region of 80 publications which advocate what in the current idiom is called the alternative society. Of these about 25 can be termed 'underground' press and a number of them contain articles which can be described as indecent. . . . However, by far the worst of these are Oz, Frendz and IT, in that order. These in fact are the only ones against whom action has been taken or indeed contemplated in the last twelve months." *The Little Red School-Book* did not deal merely with sex but called for "a change in the structure of society."[139] Fenwick's distinction between the underground press and unambiguous pornography was in line with Detective Inspector Luff's recommendation that the *Oz* editors be prosecuted: unlike Scandinavian pornography, the School Kids issue attacked "the very roots of society." Though the charges involved morals, the deeper threat was the social order, which—Luff would have agreed with Devlin—depended on a common morality.

Luff, who had since transferred from the Obscene Publications Squad to Notting Hill police station, genuinely believed that immorality and subversion had to be suppressed.[140] It soon emerged that Luff's erstwhile colleagues in the Obscene Publications Squad—the "Dirty Squad," as they liked to call it—took a different view, at least of pornography. Fenwick and others were running a protection racket with Soho porn traders, exploiting the disclaimer procedure under which the police agreed not go to court for a destruction order if seller gave up the seized items. The Soho porn bosses paid the Dirty Squad bribes, and the detectives tipped the protected porn distributors off about impending raids. Confiscated pornographic movies provided the entertainment for Friday night drinks with other officers in the division.[141] Fenwick was ultimately sentenced to ten years in prison, together with Bill Moody, who handled the Jim Dine case, and Leslie Alton, who oversaw the first raid on *IT*.[142]

It was later claimed that the harassment of *Oz* and *IT* was a diversionary tactic to protect this illicit trade. Fenwick was surely too cunning to attract unnecessary attention. Staged and selective raids had worked well enough to keep the Metropolitan Police hierarchy and non-bent detectives like Luff in the dark. It is more than possible that Fenwick and the others did think that *Oz* or *The Little Red School-Book* had to be suppressed or that they believed that enforcing moral conventions for ordinary people, not special men like themselves, was essential to preserving the social order. This is why it is unwise to assume that Judge Argyle really did not know what cunnilingus was; or that Mervyn Griffith-Jones could read a description of anal sex and not recognize it for what it was. To assume that enforcers of censorship must be either ageing naïfs or hypocrites is to overlook their sense of the importance of public morals to "the peace."

The Dirty Squad's corruption was discovered by a tabloid newspaper and corroborated by a private investigator working for the antipornography campaigner Lord Longford. As the Metropolitan Police attempted to put its house in order and the DPP and Home Office regrouped, many others, from Longford and Mary Whitehouse to anticensorship bodies like the Defence of Literature and the Arts Society, as well as the Greater London Council's film licensing department, would seize the opportunity to reshape the system.

CHAPTER SEVEN

Campaigners and Litigants

1972–1977

THREE MONTHS AFTER the *Oz* appeal, Ronald Dworkin discussed censorship with a Conservative MP on BBC Radio 3.[1] Michael Havers had written a report on obscenity for the Society of Conservative Lawyers.[2] Havers's working party was tasked with responding to the way people in Britain had, within only a few years, become routinely exposed to sexually explicit material—in newsagents' shops especially. They proposed a new offense, public indecency, and they sought to redefine obscenity as that which affronted community standards of decency.[3] In the interview, Dworkin doubted that any moral consensus existed in contemporary Britain. Objections like Dworkin's did not stop morals campaigners in the seventies from trying to replace the troublesome "deprave and corrupt" definition of obscenity with majority standards. This was the goal Lord Longford, who led a pseudo-official commission of inquiry into pornography, of the serial litigant Raymond Blackburn, and of the evangelical-dominated Nationwide Festival of Light.

Where the Festival of Light was a social movement that dabbled in litigation, the Defence of Literature and the Arts Society was a legal defense fund trying to reinvent itself as a movement and make freedom of expression a cause important to more than a literary and legal minority. Nevertheless, its primary activity remained supporting defendants in censorship cases, and it mobilized on behalf of *Gay News* and its editor when Mary Whitehouse prosecuted them for blasphemy. *Gay News* was the latest in a sequence of cases relying on previously obscure or dormant offenses instead of the Obscene Publications Act. At the same time, with the British Board of Film Censors under pressure for its alleged permissiveness, private prosecutors succeeded in bringing film censorship within the reach of the common law. Raymond Blackburn had his greatest victory when he forced the Greater London Council to bring its liberal film censorship regime into line with the common law of conspiracy to corrupt public morals. By the late seventies nearly everyone with an opinion on the subject agreed that censorship in Britain was dysfunctional.

Lord Longford's Rejoinder to the Arts Council Working Party

Frank Pakenham went over to the left with other members of the upper class in the thirties. He converted to Catholicism around the same time. Three decades later, as the seventh Lord Longford, he had gained a reputation as an eccentric, idealistic to the point of delusion. His advocacy for the "Moors murderer" Myra Hindley, whom he believed to have repented, raised many eyebrows. Yet he was sufficiently with it to be a cabinet minister and Labour's leader in the House of Lords for four years under Harold Wilson, and, from 1970, as chairman of Sidgwick and Jackson he transformed a specialist publisher into a major generalist one. Campaigning against pornography, he made the most of his standing and connections as a peer and politician.[4]

Longford assembled a "study group" of eminent and interested persons: educationalists, doctors, social workers, authors and publishers. There were Christian lay people and ministers from various denominations, a rabbi, and some literary figures whom no one would have identified closely with religion, such as the novelist Kingsley Amis, and David Holbrook, an inspirational school teacher whose campaign against pornography grew out of his recent reading of heterodox psychiatry and his long-standing Leavisite and communist critique of capitalist culture.[5] To avoid seeming out of touch, Longford's group co-opted two celebrities from the world of pop, the singer Cliff Richard and the DJ Jimmy Savile.[6] The feminist paper *Spare Rib*, which Marsha Rowe founded in reaction against *Oz*, interviewed three "ordinary" women on the committee.[7] Did they actually agree with Longford? One said, "she was against the commercial aspects of porn but not against it artistically." A second was "sardonic" and the third "admitted coyly, 'I'm for nice porn, that is, pornography which is pro-sex.'"[8]

The study group was commonly referred to as the Longford Committee, which made it sound like an official "departmental committee," one of those bodies of experts and respected citizens that government departments appointed to consider thorny issues of public policy (the Wolfenden Committee, for instance). Lord Longford and other well-connected members of the committee sought briefings from government departments. Sir Philip Allen at the Home Office resolved to supply Longford with no more information than the Home Office would provide any other MP or peer, writing: "This is a private inquiry, with no official locus, and no Government spokesman should get involved."[9] Newspaper editors and owners took the committee seriously enough to grant them interviews.[10] Longford engaged a market research firm and also hired a private detective, Matthew Oliver, to find out how the pornographic bookshop business worked. Oliver discovered that Soho magnates were paying about £1000 a week to a group of police officers. His findings confirmed what journalists on the *Sunday People* had discovered about the Dirty Squad.[11] Although critics said that it was disingenuous for the Longford Committee to call itself a study group when it obviously had an axe to grind, it did do a lot of research.

Longford was keen to reassess the Danish experiment in decensorship. Several years earlier the Arts Council working party had seized on early evidence from Denmark that lifting restrictions on pornography had not had any adverse consequences. The Longford Committee stressed that the Danish reforms were barely underway when the Arts Council working party produced its report. Longford and several of the others traveled to Denmark and witnessed live sex shows, a form of research that attracted predictable derision back home.[12] The Danish embassy in London and the British embassy in Copenhagen arranged meetings with Danish government officials, the Copenhagen police, and the Institute for Criminal Science at the University of Copenhagen, which had played a part in the research that led to the reform of Danish obscenity laws.[13] The *Longford Report* acknowledged the findings of the Danish psychologist Berl Kutchinsky—in research commissioned by the US Commission on Obscenity and Pornography—that since the law changed, the incidence of "two types of sex crime, namely peeping and (physical) indecency towards girls" had declined. Longford noted, however, that this fell short of the Arts Council working party's sweeping claim that "the incidence of sexual crime" was down 25 percent. And, as the Longford Committee hastened to point out, the numbers of reported sex crimes had been dropping for years before the 1967–1969 reforms. The committee was impressed by the high-ranking police officer who thought the sexual openness of the times had made members of the public less likely to report crimes such as indecent exposure and "minor offences against children." The Longford Committee declared the Danish experience a draw, not conclusive evidence for or against censorship.[14]

The treatment of Denmark by the Longford Committee reflected the fact that the *Longford Report* was an answer to the Arts Council working party's report. Both were partisan documents that traded on the appearance of official authority. Longford's committee contacted members of the Arts Council working party and gave them the opportunity to recant. John Montgomerie did not, but C. R. Hewitt did.[15] The common complaint that things had "gone too far" had special force when it came from a reformer who did not expect things to go further than *Lady Chatterley's Lover*.[16] Longford's committee used critiques advanced in the Arts Council report to argue for the repeal of the Herbert Committee's great achievement, the public-good defense. The Arts Council working party had argued that the conviction in the *Last Exit* case was quashed because the trial judge could not explain "with a straight face" how the jury was supposed to weigh depravity and corruption against the public good.[17] Like the Arts Council document, the *Longford Report* proceeded as if deprave and corrupt was language the Herbert Committee had wanted, rather than historical baggage they were willing to carry to get a defense of literary merit onto the statute book.[18] The Arts Council working party contended that the logical tangle of the existing law could not be unraveled and the only thing for it was abolition. The Longford Committee proposed a different solution. First, repeal the public-good defense: nothing could be simultaneously obscene and in the public good, and as a practical matter Section 4 of the Obscene Publications Act had "led to justice being obstructed by the calling of totally inadmissible evidence and the resultant confusion of juries."[19] Second, replace the "deprave and corrupt" test with an appeal to orthodoxy. The Longford Committee recommended that a publication or performance be deemed obscene "if its effect, taken as a whole, is to outrage contemporary standards or decency or humanity accepted by the public at large."[20]

They borrowed this definition of obscenity from Havers' report for the Society of Conservative Lawyers, but went a lot further (Havers did not recommend getting rid of the public-good defense). For all its reasonable-man prose, the *Longford Report* was as extreme a document as the legal satire that Levy wrote in the name of the Arts Council. Like the Arts Council report, Longford's was an attempt to shift the parameters of debate about censorship.[21] Longford could throw his weight around—he succeeded in shutting down a conference on obscenity law organized by Brunel University in conjunction with *Forum*, the text-heavy stablemate of

Penthouse, by telephoning the vice-chancellor and threatening to make life difficult for him—but he was not very interested in lobbying and litigating to get individual books or films banned. Whitehouse, in contrast, was turning increasingly to the courts in the seventies. So were some in the Nationwide Festival of Light.[22]

The Nationwide Festival of Light and Indecent Displays

As the name suggests, the Festival of Light was originally conceived as a one-off event. Peter Hill was inspired by a dream of young people marching in London for Christ. An Australian, Hill was a missionary in India for four years, and when he arrived in Britain he was dismayed by the moral state of the country. The warning sign was an indecent display: a hoarding in the Dover ferry terminal with a beer advertisement showing a woman wearing very little. Hill talked about the march for Christ with Eddy Stride, a former shop steward who was now an evangelical vicar. Stride convinced Hill that pornography was an issue that would galvanize people to march and urged him to approach Mary Whitehouse. She put him in touch with the professional iconoclast and recent Christian convert Malcolm Muggeridge, who was also on the Longford Committee.[23] With their encouragement, Hill and Stride began organizing public events which culminated in a rally and march in London. Up to 35,000 people gathered in Trafalgar Square in September 1971 to hear proclamations exhorting the churches, media, and government to stand against permissiveness. The crowd then marched to Hyde Park, where the American preacher Arthur Blessitt addressed the crowd and Cliff Richard performed.[24]

Anglicans dominated the leadership and were the denomination represented most among the rank and file. Their participation reflected an increased concern with issues of sexual morality among evangelical members of the Church of England, a shift catalyzed by the National Evangelical Anglican Congress at Keele in 1967.[25] And as Blessitt's participation suggested, the Festival of Light owed a debt to American evangelism. Some of its early members had belonged to Moral Re-Armament as Whitehouse had. The Festival of Light's leaders were under no illusion that a majority of the population went to church regularly, but they believed Christian morality continued to guide ordinary people in Britain.[26] The organizers worked to maintain momentum and by 1974 the Nationwide Festival of Light was a registered charity with a small full-time staff and over one hundred regional coordinators.[27] The staff was led by O. R. (Ray)

Johnston. Like Whitehouse, he was a teacher before he became a full-time campaigner.[28]

Johnston brought organizational discipline to the Festival of Light. It joined with the National Viewers' and Listeners' Association to collect 1,350,000 signatures on a petition for public decency, which they submitted to the prime minister in 1973.[29] The petition was in support of the pending Cinematograph and Indecent Displays Bill. This was the legislation that eventually emerged from the Society of Conservative Lawyers report. As the name of the bill suggests, it dealt with film screenings as well as advertising. The bill included curbs on film clubs, which offered a way around the BBFC and local government's regulatory powers.[30] There were signs that this loophole was being used to show pornographic movies as well as arthouse films. The Cinematograph and Indecent Displays Bill was a government bill rather than a private member's bill, and it cleared its second reading. But then Prime Minister Edward Heath called an election. The parliamentary session ended, and along with it the Cinematograph and Indecent Displays Bill. Roy Jenkins, returning to the Home Office after Labour's election victory, said bluntly that the new government would not revive it.[31] Private members tried again in the succeeding years, but not until Margaret Thatcher was in Number 10 would the goal of an indecent displays law be realized.[32]

At a local level, Festival of Light members pressed newsagents to keep pornographic magazines off their shelves. "Operation Newsagent" in the early seventies and a follow-up later in the decade were blamed by the editor of *Forum* for a spike in police raids in many British towns.[33] The Festival of Light office in London in London printed an "Appeal to Newsagents" for members to distribute. On the last page was a list of titles, some of which are now so obscure that they sound made-up (*Probe Spring Spread*, *Pentact Unisex*), that had been subject to destruction orders by magistrates around the country. The pamphlet then backtracked and said that "You know and we know that the law is not the best answer," and that only "voluntary self-restraint" and caring for one's neighbor could solve the problem of pornography, or the problem of which pornography was a symptom.[34] But the law was a good stopgap for some in the Festival of Light.

Citizens Enforcing the Law

The seventies were a time when individuals conspicuously took to the courts, often without legal representation, to contest the actions of the bureaucratic state and institutions exercising public functions. Their actions were of a piece with the middle-class activism of the seventies, which, a contemporary researcher observed, challenged the "centralisation and remoteness of centres of decision-taking, the development of 'administrative' politics in Whitehall and town halls of an almost invisible kind."[35] These litigants found a sympathetic judge in the ubiquitous Lord Denning, who regarded it as "a matter of high constitutional principle that if there is good ground for supposing that a government department or a public authority is transgressing the law . . . then in the last resort any one of those offended or injured can draw it to the attention of the courts of law and seek to have the law enforced."[36] Denning's conservatism did not translate into deference to precedent: he was a Tory whose suspicion of inert and abstract systems led him to extend the common law in creative ways. He saw himself as a servant of "practical justice." He believed that stringent rules about standing were inappropriate in an age where non-state bodies—trade unions as well as quangos—wielded more and more power over citizens.[37]

The period's most accomplished litigant in person was Raymond Blackburn. He was briefly a solicitor. After becoming politicized during the Second World War, he was elected as a Labour MP in 1945, and then just as quickly became disenchanted. He left the Labour Party in 1950 and Parliament in 1951.[38] Blackburn spent years battling alcoholism, serving time in prison for fraud, and discharging bankruptcy. He was struck off as a solicitor.[39] He then re-emerged in public life, appearing to others as a morals campaigner but seeing himself as an anticorruption crusader insisting on the rule of law.[40] Blackburn's weapons of choice were two prerogative writs: mandamus (an action to compel officials to discharge their duty) and prohibition (an action to compel an authority to cease practices that contravened the law). Blackburn saw in mandamus actions a means of limiting the abuse of police discretion. In 1968 he sued the Metropolitan Police to get them to drop their policy of selective enforcement of a gambling law.[41] In 1972 he brought a similar suit concerning their enforcement of the Obscene Publications Act in Soho. That case became an authority on police discretion, but its effects on obscenity policing in London were overtaken by the exposure of the Dirty Squad.[42] Lord Denning heard both these cases, and indeed every single suit of Blackburn's that reached the Court of Appeal. This was no accident: as master of the rolls, Denning controlled the docket.[43]

Denning also presided over all of Ross McWhirter's cases in the Court of Appeal. With his twin brother Norris, Ross McWhirter owned and edited the *Guinness Book of Records*. He was a Conservative Party activist and sometime (unsuccessful) parliamentary candidate. He campaigned against the Irish Republican Army, Britain's membership in the European Community, compulsory trade union membership for journalists, and the replacement of grammar schools by comprehensives. He was a member of the NVALA and joined the Nationwide Festival of Light.[44] On occasion he represented the Festival of Light in meetings about censorship.[45] In 1973 McWhirter tried to prevent commercial television airing a documentary about Andy Warhol and his entourage.[46] After an advance screening for journalists, newspapers described the "permissive shocker" that viewers would see the following Tuesday. There was bad language, transvestism, and Brigid Berlin making one of her "tit prints" by dipping her nipples in paint and dragging them across a canvas.[47] The newspapers approached Whitehouse, Longford, and the Festival of Light for comment and reported their condemnations.[48] The day the press reports appeared, McWhirter went to court seeking an injunction to stop the broadcast.

The commercial television legislation, which was more stringent than the rules governing the BBC, required the Independent Broadcasting Authority (IBA) to be satisfied that no program offended public decency or good taste.[49] Like Blackburn with the Met, McWhirter argued that the authority was not living up to its obligations. The judge did not accept that merely having paid the television license fee gave McWhirter standing and he refused to grant an injunction. Moving fast, McWhirter managed to get the Court of Appeal to consider his application that afternoon (*Warhol: Artist and Filmmaker* was scheduled to screen at 10:30 the same evening). The majority—Denning and Lord Justice Lawton—held that by not viewing it themselves beforehand, when there had been adverse public comment, the IBA's members had not done as much as they could have to satisfy themselves that the documentary complied with the law. The two judges were prepared to grant the injunction even though McWhirter did not have the support of the attorney general, as actions of this kind were supposed to have. The dissenting third judge, Lord Justice Cairns, said briefly that it was still the law that a private individual could not enforce the responsibilities of a public body like the IBA without the support of the attorney general.[50] Cairns was in the minority and the court granted the injunction. The documentary did not air.

By the time the court reconvened several weeks later to consider whether to lift the injunction, the attorney general had agreed to give his formal support. For this longer and more involved hearing, McWhirter instructed a barrister, Godfray Le Quesne, who was a member of the Longford Committee and possibly the author of its legal recommendations.

Denning's opinion struck notes in harmony with those of Longford, the Festival of Light, and Whitehouse: the IBA should respect the "silent majority of good people" as well as "the vociferous minority who, in the name of freedom, shout for ugliness in all its forms"; an indecent television program beamed into McWhirter's home was an invasion of his privacy.[51] (TV as "an intruder into private houses" was a favorite theme of NVALA members.)[52] However, the court had little choice but to lift the injunction, as the authority members had now viewed the documentary themselves and stood by the original decision to broadcast. One of the regional television companies signaled that it would not show the documentary. Its chairman, Lord Shawcross, was a leader of the antipermissive Responsible Society alongside David Holbrook and another member of Lord Longford's committee, the psychiatrist Mary Miles.[53] The head of the IBA brought Shawcross to heel, and, after a cooling-off period of six weeks, every ITV station broadcast *Warhol*. It drew more viewers than late-night documentaries usually did.[54]

Edward Shackleton's action against Bernardo Bertolucci's *Last Tango in Paris*, a film that the Festival of Light had campaigned against in multiple towns around the country, did not meet with even temporary success. Shackleton was retired and did a lot of work for the Salvation Army—as a social worker, according to the rather vague press reports. He had a law degree from Durham.[55] Shackleton contended that *Last Tango in Paris* was obscene because it was sadistic. Marlon Brando's character "is determined not to know the girl as a human being, but as an object. . . . She is of an age to have been his daughter, and he treats her as a sort of prey for sex without love or emotion. . . . His immediate aim is to degrade. . . . There is an occasion when he performs an act of sodomy on her, making her repeat, while he assaults her, such blasphemies and obscenities which on the spur of the moment he imagines."[56] Much later Bertolucci admitted that he and Brando kept Maria Schneider in the dark about how they would do the scene "because I wanted her reaction as a girl, not as an actress. I wanted her to react humiliated."[57] Shackleton did not know this, of course. He brought a private prosecution against the distributors, United Artists Corporation.[58] Shackleton believed he had found a loophole in the Obscene Publications Act: though the law plainly did not apply to film *screenings*, a distributor passing the print on to the exhibitor might count as "publishing" under the legislation.[59] This sounds far-fetched, but it reflected a slippage between two paragraphs in the act, and it was an interpretation that the Home Office had held to quietly for some years.[60] Shackleton represented himself at the committal hearing, and then instructed a queen's counsel for the Old Bailey trial. United Artists retained Jeremy Hutchinson, who had been Gerald Gardiner's junior in the *Lady Chatterley's Lover* trial. After hearing legal arguments, the judge threw out the case. Shackleton faced an enormous legal bill.[61]

It was not irrelevant that Bertolucci was an Italian (as well as a communist). The obscenity controversies of the early seventies took place at the same time as the debates over British membership of the European Community. The Festival of Light did not take an official position on the 1975 referendum on remaining in the European Community, but its leaders did express concern that "continental standards of conduct," as glamorized in Scandinavian pornography and the *Emmanuelle* films, would "become more and more pervasive in Britain." They were mindful that Ernest Wistrich, a leader of the campaign to vote yes to continued European Community membership, was the husband of Enid Wistrich, the anticensorship censor at the Greater London Council between 1973 and 1975.[62] Independently, both McWhirter and Blackburn unsuccessfully challenged the constitutionality of EC membership in the courts.[63] Norris McWhirter continued to fight for his brother's causes after the IRA assassinated Ross McWhirter in November of 1975.

Inside Linda Lovelace

Despite his failure to suppress *Last Tango in Paris*, Shackleton became the Festival of Light's honorary legal advisor.[64] He also belonged to—perhaps was half the membership of—the Action Group against the Abuse of Law (AGAL). Its leader was Hugh Watts, a retired barrister living in Worthing. According to Sussex Police, AGAL aspired to be

> judge and jury on the current attitude towards pornography in this country, and it would appear that it is attempting to use the police as a lever in achieving its object. Inspector RANGER of Worthing knows Mr. WATTS well, and has informed me that he (WATTS) is very eccentric, and has lately devoted his life to running a personal vendetta against the FINLAY (Tobacconists) chain of shops where questionable pornography in book form is on sale. It is also believed that the Director of Public Prosecutions maintains a file on Mr. WATTS, and there may be another at Force Headquarters.[65]

Shackleton gave Watts advice about obscenity cases and offered to accompany him to meetings with officials. Ray Johnston of the Festival of Light reminded the DPP of the gigantic petition for public decency and repeatedly pressed him to act on Watts's complaint about *Inside Linda Lovelace*, a copy of which he bought from a Finlay's outlet in Brighton.[66]

This book was a confected confession and sex manual ostensibly by the star of the American pornographic movie *Deep Throat* (1972). Lovelace, real name Linda Boreman, later testified that she had been raped throughout the filming. She inevitably appears as a joyous hedonist in the book that bears her stage name. The publication of *Inside Linda Lovelace* coincided with Boreman's UK tour in 1974/1975. She was photographed at Ascot and Lord's. Her host was Jimmy Vaughan, the Englishman who owned the rights to *Deep Throat*.[67] A Festival of Light press release observed: "Miss Lovelace is the spearhead of an intense campaign to make hard-core pornographic films . . . acceptable in the High Street cinemas."[68] Vaughan was involved in plans for a symposium on censorship at the National Film Theatre at which *Deep Throat* would be screened. The conference never eventuated, embarrassing the organizers, and in any case, the print of *Deep Throat* was held up by Customs.[69]

Watts was frank about his objective in going after *Inside Linda Lovelace*: "I want to engineer a situation wherein the case becomes an authority on the practice to be observed under Sect 4 of the 1959 act and the limitations of the section." The law was becoming "unworkable" because of the abuse of the expert evidence provision. Watts had in mind not only the "circus" of irrelevant witnesses but also the "therapeutic defense" advanced on behalf of pornography that lacked any plausible artistic or political claims.[70] The therapeutic defense was that pornography provided a safe masturbatory outlet for disturbed men. The Sussex Police suggested Watts bring a private prosecution if he felt so strongly, pointing out that as a barrister he was well able to do so. Instead, Watts pressured the DPP to charge the book's publisher, Heinrich Hanau. Asked for his opinion, Brian Leary said that the book could be held to deprave and corrupt, but it was not "of the most diabolical sort," and "so much will depend on the constitution of the jury." The DPP's office waited for further advice from Leary, and made plans to question Hanau "on as friendly a basis as possible"—"no search warrant and no seizures."[71] This was in August of 1974. For reasons not documented in the DPP file, the case went to court the following year. Hanau's counsel, Geoffrey Robertson, offered to destroy all remaining copies if the indictment were withdrawn. Leary thought this would be a good outcome, but the DPP rejected the offer.[72]

Hanau's case was heard by a jury of nine men and three women. The defense counsel—John Mortimer joined Robertson—made thirteen peremptory challenges in jury selection.[73] In none of the major seventies obscenity trials were women a majority on the jury. The defense barristers' rule of thumb was that young men were the most likely to acquit in obscenity cases and middle-aged women the most likely to convict.[74] They used their right to challenge potential jurors accordingly. Whitehouse knew this and documented the practice in her book *Whatever Happened to Sex?*[75] Ros Schwartz, who wrote a rare published account of a British juror's experience, described the procedure in a 1982 obscenity trial in which Mortimer appeared for the defendants: "The defence had used twelve objections to ensure as large a proportion of men on the jury as possible." Before her jury service Schwartz had been only "a feminist of sorts" and had not given pornography much thought. That changed after she had to read a succession of rape fantasies in the jury room. She was disturbed by the other jurors as well as the books. "Some of the men," she wrote, "spent the week lying on their stomachs while they read—was this stuff giving them a hard-on?"[76]

As expected, Hanau's defense called a parade of witnesses. They included a novelist, a GP, a psychologist, and, less predictably, Johnny Speight.[77] Speight was the creator of *Till Death Us Do Part*, the TV sitcom centered on the bigoted opinions of Alf Garnett. Speight had sparred with Mary Whitehouse for years about swearing, blasphemy, and disrespect for the royal family in *Till Death Us Do Part*.[78] Speight was there "to laugh the case out of court," as a DPP official summarizing the proceedings put it. Anna Coote, "a person who campaigns for women's rights," testified that "women should take the initiative in deciding which position to adopt when making love 'rather than just lying there in the missionary position thinking of England.'"[79] (Coote had also edited a National Council for Civil Liberties handbook.)[80] Hanau himself claimed that he published the book to inform readers on a matter of current public debate, and hoped the verdict would "prove that it is only in communist societies that men can still be branded as criminals for publishing ideas and arguments."[81] Appearing with Hanau at the committal hearing, John Calder stated: "We live in a pluralistic society where there are different acceptable codes of conduct and different ways of facing life and I think information about less conventional life styles is important, because we live in a more tolerant society and this has been created to a certain extent by writers to enable us to understand how other people live without having to repeat that experience themselves."[82]

The jury retired for several hours and then returned seeking a clarification of the law. Once the judge explained "the law about the 'number of people likely to be depraved etc' the foreman said words to the effect of 'Ah, we should be able to bring in a verdict shortly.'"[83] Although some jurors may have found the book repellent, they apparently could not go as far as agreeing that it would deprave significant numbers of readers. "It was upon the terminology of the actual law that the prosecution case foundered," the DPP's office recognized. Watts had tried to engineer the retrenchment of Section 4, but the actual outcome was to dash any remaining confidence in the definition of obscenity that the 1959 act had adapted from *Hicklin*: "It may be concluded that with the Act as it presently stands, no article will be found obscene."[84] Skelhorn and his successor as DPP, Sir Tony Hetherington, resolved that in the future their default position would be not to institute obscenity proceedings over prose.[85]

The Defence of Literature and the Arts Society

John Calder was there with Hanau because his case was the latest cause taken up by the Defence of Literature and the Arts Society (DLAS). It began as the Free Art Legal Fund established to support Calder and Marion Boyars through the *Last Exit* appeal. The plan was for the money left over to go into an enduring legal defense fund for artists and writers.[86] DLAS brought together veterans of earlier stands against censorship. Geoffrey Robertson was the de facto legal officer. Michael Rubinstein was periodically active though not a core member, as was Benn Levy until his death at the end of 1973. Bruce Douglas-Mann, the solicitor who had to back down from his challenge to the DPP over *Last Exit*, was on the committee—there were apparently no hard feelings after Calder and Boyars cut him loose—and reminded waverers of the importance of the principle of free speech.[87] Douglas-Mann was now a Labour MP as well—he represented North Kensington, where he had previously been a councilor, and was involved in Notting Hill's antiracism Community Workshop.[88] Ben Whitaker and another Labour MP active in the anticensorship cause, William Hamling, were active members. With Whitaker in the chair, DLAS meetings often took place in the House of Commons.

The remains of the longstanding distinction between literature worth protecting and worthless pornography had collapsed: a change signaled in the Freedom of Vision teach-in of 1966 was fully realized in DLAS's activities in the following decade. By the midseventies, DLAS was describing its mission as "to work towards changes in the law to safeguard freedom of speech and expression in Britain" and to give "moral and practical support" to writers, artists, publishers, "and all others whose work is censored or under attack on moral, political or similar grounds."[89] They really did mean "and all others." In a departure from the original policy ("A responsible national society of this kind must be selective if it is to have any teeth. The battle to free pornography is a completely different battle"), the executive courted members of the Kingsley Committee, an informal alliance of pornographic magazine publishers.[90] The "committee" took its imposing name from the London hotel where they held their first meeting "to discuss matters of mutual interest and concern."[91] No doubt judging that those on the receiving end of obscenity prosecutions would make faithful members, DLAS routinely asked publishers or distributors in legal trouble to join the society.[92] Many of these people were clients of Geoffrey Robertson or became his clients after approaching the society for help. DLAS was there for Arabella Melville when she was prosecuted in Leicester for selling copies of her magazine *Libertine* at her shop in the city center.[93] Melville was an anarchist with a doctorate in psychology. She stood for "the right for everyone to express his/her sexuality in any way he/she chooses, without guilt or anxiety, the only limit being that nothing should be inflicted on another without total informed unpressured consent."[94] Melville pledged her support to DLAS, and Robertson and John Mortimer successfully defended her on obscenity charges in Leicester Crown Court.[95] Hanau received money from DLAS for his legal battles and, when his fortunes turned, was pressured to donate to the society. He wanted to join the executive, but the rest of the committee balked.[96] One defendant whom DLAS failed to enlist was Julius Reiter. Twenty years after his conviction and prison sentence, Hank Janson's former publisher had followed demand from spicy novellas to photographic magazines. He was being prosecuted under the Post Office Act for distributing *Club International*.[97]

For several years after the *Oz* trial, DLAS monitored police action against underground papers and radical bookstores around Britain— another confiscation of *The Little Red School-Book* here, a prosecution of *IT* there. Given the political overtones of the seizures of *The Little Red School-Book*, Levy suggested they open a file on police intimidation. A lot of the legal liaison work was with small traders like the husband-and-wife team who ran a sex shop in Bexley and lost 45,000 leaflets in a police raid.[98] DLAS also worked with the burgeoning gay press. Gay porn and magazines with contact ads were vulnerable to charges of conspiracy to corrupt public morals, which, as we have seen, offered police lawyers and the DPP a way round the public-good defense in the Obscene Publications Act.[99] Anthony Grey, the DLAS treasurer, was also secretary of the Sexual Law Reform Society. Both determined and cautious, he had played a central part in the long struggle to turn Wolfenden's recommendations into law.[100]

There was no comparable link between DLAS and the women's movement (which is not to say that there weren't women in the society's leadership group). The executive periodically considered steps it could take to engage with the women's movement, say by inviting Eva Figes or Jill Tweedie onto the committee.[101] How this would have played out? While women's liberation groups did not support censorship, they would not make common cause with men in the objectification business. Ruth Wallsgrove wrote in *Spare Rib* in 1977 that she didn't want to choose between Mary Whitehouse and the publishers of a pornographic magazine. That was a choice "between two equally unacceptable alternatives—between censoring all mention of sex through vaguely worded laws that will be applied by men, and allowing pornography to invade my life at an ever increasing rate, on Radio One and in packets of bubblegum, and even in the radical press." Rather than seeking new laws, women should take direct action, picketing cinemas and talking to local newsagents, "and force men to re-examine their own attitudes to sex and women implicit in their consumption of porn."[102] In a paper written for the 1978 London Revolutionary Feminist Conference, Maria Coulias, Siva German, Sheila Jeffreys, Sandra McNeill, and Jan Winterlake entertained the idea of laws against pornography akin to the Race Relations Act's provision against hate speech—"incitement to sexual hatred"—but elsewhere stressed they wanted no part of state repression. They too put more store in direct action, including vandalizing billboards and newsstands. They recognized that it could be difficult "for those of us who were reared in the 'Sexual revolution' of the sixties to work out a clear perspective on porn. Most of us will have gone through the process of convincing ourselves that sex was not 'dirty' . . . and that porn, since it was about sex, was not revolting." Women needed to move past "the ruling male ideology of the sexual revolution" and recognize the real cause of the disgust women felt in the presence of pornography: not puritanism but "the obvious humiliation and degradation of women in porn which each woman knows applies to her." Feminists had to "enlist the 'prudishness' of all our sisters in the struggle" against pornography.[103] On the whole the censorship game—strict laws versus permissive ones—was not one British feminists chose to play in the seventies.

As well as defending booksellers and publishers, DLAS tried, with uneven success, to operate on a political front (in the words of Tony Smythe, who represented the National Council for Civil Liberties on the

DLAS executive). They organized teach-ins and public lectures on London's South Bank. They lobbied MPs—Conservatives and Liberals as well as Labour—and they made a concerted effort to recruit influential people in the arts and the media.[104] The society's membership was never more than modest. As a 1977 strategy document spelled out, "The *target groups* that the Society wishes to influence" were:

1. Communicators, i.e. authors, journalists, broadcasters, artists, etc.
2. Legislators, civil servants and other elected representatives and public officials
3. Opinion formers
4. The general public[105]

DLAS's biggest effort on the political front was the 1973 campaign against the Cinematograph and Indecent Displays Bill. The society worked in concert with the NCCL, the British Federation of Film Societies, and other organizations opposed to the bill.[106] When the bill passed its second reading, Hamling got himself on the standing committee and set about trying to amend it.[107] This was the best chance the bill's opponents had— until Heath called the election and they won by default.

Ron Bailey, the liaison between DLAS, the NCCL and other groups, urged them not to get complacent and to keep cooperating and establish an anticensorship equivalent of the Festival of Light. DLAS and its partners were persuaded and the ad hoc committee against the Cinematograph and Indecent Displays Bill was formalized as the National Coordinating Campaign against Censorship. Bailey was given the (paid) job of building it into a vehicle for agitating about the larger issues of censorship, not just the "sectional interests" of, say, book publishers or the Kingsley Committee.[108] This territory was free for DLAS to claim, as the National Council for Civil Liberties paid little attention to free speech issues (it concentrated instead on police powers, the right to protest, and antiracism initiatives).[109] As it turned out, Bailey did little institution-building and soon moved on,[110] but DLAS stuck with his guiding idea: the enemies of censorship needed to promote a positive message rather than being "merely . . . 're-active' or 'defensive.'" Moreover, "Freedom of speech, choice, information, and discussion are fundamental to democracy and the continuance of a 'free society'. *Censorship is Undemocratic*, is one theme of our attack."[111] This chimed with what Ben Whitaker was hearing from members: that DLAS "'should not restrict itself to Smut' but should cover the whole area of censorship."[112] Heeding the message, DLAS began to pay attention to government secrecy, censorship in prisons, hospitals, and the armed forces, and libel law as a form of censorship.[113]

Moving into new territory confronted the DLAS leadership with censorship issues that struggles over obscenity had not prepared them for. The executive was divided about whether to condemn the *Camden Journal*'s refusal to carry an advertisement for the National Front. Robertson said that "as an advert was neither literature nor art it would be wise to leave the subject alone." They resolved to write to the Press Council "to say that while the DLAS in no way supported the views of the National Front we considered that the Press Council should condemn all attempts to censor."[114] Later statements on the hate speech section in the Race Relations Act similarly sought to have it both ways; an article on censorship and race that Cousins wrote for DLAS's struggling journal *Uncensored* tied itself up in knots.[115] DLAS's failure to build a movement comparable to the Festival of Light was partly a failure of organization, but it also reflected the absence of a free speech consciousness in Britain comparable to the cult of the First Amendment in the United States. It was almost unthinkable that DLAS would feel obliged to defend the National Front to the extent the American Civil Liberties Union defended neo-Nazis planning to march through Skokie, Illinois, at about the same time.[116] Certainly Britain's leading free speech activists had not had to think seriously about whether they would defend neo-Nazis until the National Front tried to advertise in the *Camden Journal* in 1976.[117]

Whitehouse against Gay News

Whitehouse, like many conservative insurgents after her, alternated between speaking for a silent majority and playing the persecuted iconoclast. The liberals who opposed her were portrayed as powerful forces capable of suppressing alternative views, censoring procensorship arguments.[118] Whitehouse saw the noisy minorities she battled—civil libertarians, gay activists, feminists—as elements of "what might generally be called the 'humanist lobby.'" The "secular humanists and the anticensorship lobby," she contended, were "often, of course, one and the same thing."[119] It was true that the president of the National Secular Society, David Tribe, was also an anticensorship activist,[120] but there were also plenty of Anglicans in the ranks of those who supported the relaxation of censorship. Whitehouse herself complained about this fact. And her enemies' alternative to traditional values was not a monolithic secular humanism but what John Calder began to call "pluralism." Whitehouse was quite right, however, to recognize alliances between anticensorship activists and gay-rights campaigners. (She might have added another of her bêtes noires, sex-education advocates: DLAS's Jane Cousins was the author of a controversial sex-education book published by the feminist press Virago).[121] That alliance was only strengthened by Whitehouse's attack on *Gay News*.

In *Whatever Happened to Sex?* Whitehouse described the Gay Liberation Movement as an insidious social menace. For her purposes, *Gay News* was a better target than pornographic magazines such as *Street Boy*.[122] The Campaign for Homosexual Equality credited *Gay News* with popularizing "a new public view of homosexuality as a different aspect of loving and sexuality."[123] *Gay News* did "a great deal towards breaking down the strong sense of isolation I knew as a young man and which I believe no person should have to feel today in any liberal society," one reader remarked. The personal columns "are of great benefit to those homosexuals who are elderly and those who are reluctant to enter 'gay' clubs and public houses."[124] Rivals and critics who disapproved of the paper's commercialism nevertheless came to its aid. As Jeffrey Weeks observed, "*Gay News* was an important symbol of the changes that had taken place. Its defense was an essential part of homosexual politics."[125]

Whitehouse commenced legal proceedings against *Gay News* and its editor, Denis Lemon, after the paper published James Kirkup's "The Love That Dares Speak Its Name." The poem, its title playing ostentatiously on Lord Alfred Douglas's description of homosexuality, has one of the Roman soldiers present at the Crucifixion imagining sex with the dead Jesus: "For the last time / I laid my lips around the tip / of that great cock, the instrument / of our salvation, our eternal joy." An accompanying drawing, which was not part of the complaint and was seldom referred to in court, depicted the centurion lifting the naked Christ down, with Christ's penis swaying towards the soldier's thigh and scabbard.[126]

The case was a private prosecution for blasphemous libel, that is, blasphemy in written form. The last such case had been as long ago as 1922, and the last authoritative statement of the law was made by Lord Chief Justice Coleridge in the 1883 trial of the atheist Charles Bradlaugh (also codefendant, with Annie Besant, in an important obscenity case about birth control literature).[127] In 1949 the future Lord Denning declared: "the offence of blasphemy is a dead letter."[128] The director of public prosecutions, Hetherington, had rejected Whitehouse's pleas to take action against *Gay News*. The church kept its distance too. The archbishops of

Canterbury and York rebuffed Whitehouse's requests for support.[129] Given the concerns about church and state in the Anglican leadership's response to the late sixties' legislation on homosexuality, abortion, and divorce, it would have been surprising if they had done otherwise.[130] Antony Grey of DLAS contacted the Church of England synod and reported that their reaction to the prosecution was one of "acute embarrassment."[131]

Indicting *Gay News* for blasphemous libel meant that the defense could not plead literary merit or other aspects of the public-good defense, so the jury did not hear from the theologians and literary critics both sides had lined up.[132] The judge, Alan King-Hamilton, ruled Lemon's intentions in publishing Kirkup's poem irrelevant. The *Gay News* trial thus unfolded as obscene libel trials used to: the prosecution proved publication, and the jury decided, on the basis of the publication itself, whether it broke the law in its offensiveness. In Lemon's case, the jurors found Kirkup's poem blasphemous by a majority of ten to one. King-Hamilton fined the company £500 and gave Lemon a nine-month suspended sentence.

Lemon appealed all the way to the judicial committee of the House of Lords. The point of law at issue was whether the publisher's intention should be taken into account in blasphemy cases. This proved a difficult question because there had been no substantial judicial discussion of the offense for nearly a century, and the criminal law had changed a lot in that time. Was it right, as one law lord put it, that blasphemous libel "should be treated as having been immune from those significant changes in the general concept of mens rea in criminal law that have occurred in the last 100 years"?[133] Two of the judges concluded that an intention to outrage Christians was an essential part of the offense; the other three held that evidence about Lemon's motivation was irrelevant. The convictions therefore stood, and the offense of blasphemous libel retained its immunity to twentieth-century conceptions of criminal intent.

At least in theory. Lord Devlin's contention that if juries disagreed with particular laws they would refuse to convict does seem to apply to blasphemy and related offenses. Or, if the defendant cut a sympathetic figure, the jury might decide the prosecution was excessive and authoritarian. This was one of the lessons of a sedition case in 1947 against a newspaper editor who had published an anti-Semitic editorial. The editor, James Caunt, was speedily acquitted. The moral the director of public prosecutions took from the case was that newspaper editors not tied to fascist groups were the wrong kind of defendant in sedition trials.[134] In contrast, Dennis Lemon and *Gay News* were the right kind of defendants in a blasphemy trial in the seventies. Monty Python was not. *Monty Python's Life of Brian* was made in the wake of the *Gay News* appeal, and there were understandable concerns about its vulnerability to a blasphemy prosecution. They sought legal advice from Richard Du Cann, one of Gerald Gardiner's juniors in the *Lady Chatterley* trial. He recommended cuts, but the Monty Python troupe was able to reassure the British Board of Film Censors and themselves, after getting a second opinion from John Mortimer. Mortimer noted that sex played little part in the film's offensiveness, and, more importantly, that Monty Python "approached the status of a world-wide comedy cult." As Robert Hewison observed, "the Pythons' popularity and position as licensed jesters gave them better protection than a minority group like homosexuals."[135]

Gay News survived. A vigorous fundraising campaign by the paper and its allies, including DLAS, more than covered the legal bills.[136] Individuals and hastily convened organizations showed solidarity and defiance by circulating copies or Kirkup's poem or reciting it in public.[137] The former editor of *The Freethinker* was so incensed that he sent copies of Kirkup's poem to thirteen people, including Whitehouse and Longford. He was then charged under the Post Office Act with sending an indecent item through the mails. DLAS helped him out with £50 and Michael Rubinstein represented him.[138] Lemon petitioned the European Commission of Human Rights to rule on whether the law under which he had been convicted was compatible with the European Convention on Human Rights. Eventually, in 1982, the commission held that common-law blasphemy's restriction of freedom of expression was justified by the countervailing need to protect other citizens' religious feelings, provided the restrictions were not disproportionate.[139] In the decades to come there would be further challenges to the United Kingdom's blasphemy laws, including one that reached Strasbourg. The spectacular cases after the seventies involved sexualized affronts to religion, as *Gay News* had, rather than prosecutions under the Obscene Publications Act.[140]

Trouble in Film Censorship

Over John Trevelyan's tenure as secretary of the British Board of Film Censors from 1958 to 1971, the board loosened the constraints on what could be seen at a high street cinema. This change was gradual and did not arouse public controversy. Within months of Trevelyan's retirement, trouble erupted on multiple fronts. Trevelyan's successor Stephen Murphy raised the ire of Whitehouse, Longford, and the Festival of Light.[141] Murphy lasted only four years as chief. No doubt some of the conflict was down to differences in style, and the fact that Murphy, who had come from commercial television, did not have Trevelyan's years of close interaction with filmmakers and distributors.[142] But it was not all Murphy's fault. Two of the controversies of Murphy's early months at the BBFC involved films passed on Trevelyan's watch, Ken Russell's *The Devils* and Sam Peckinpah's *Straw Dogs*. Stanley Kubrick's *A Clockwork Orange* came up for classification after Trevelyan left. Murphy approved it, prompting adverse press comment and letter-writing campaigns. Kubrick's film was drafted into debates about violence and its causes. The situation in Northern Ireland inflected discussions in the United Kingdom, though Vietnam, other postcolonial wars, and the events of 1968 made the subject a preoccupation in many parts of the world. UNESCO convened a symposium on violence and the media.[143] In defense of Murphy it was said that many more films had been banned and cut in his first six months in the job than in Trevelyan's last six months.[144] It was also the case that the newspapers, alert to the way Whitehouse and Longford had affected the climate of opinion, were talking up prospective censorship battles as films that had excited discussion in Cannes or New York were submitted for classification in Britain.[145]

Murphy also inherited a problem of Trevelyan's making. From the late sixties the BBFC had to deal with a new generation of sex education films. This was, understandably, a controversial genre, and one of these films, Martin Cole's *Growing Up*, was a totem for many critics of the permissive society.[146] (Cole originally asked Jean Straker to shoot *Growing Up*, but he declined.)[147] Trevelyan was uncomfortable with making national policy on sex education films. He was undoubtedly trying to avoid conflict, but he was probably also mindful that these films would be shown in schools, and local education authorities exercised a lot of control over how sex education was taught.[148] Trevelyan would hold off on classifying particular films and invite local councils to decide whether to license them in their catchments; after observing councils' decisions, the board might then make its own classification. This policy alerted councils to their dormant powers of censorship. For a long time, most councils had been content to delegate film censorship to the BBFC, although its ratings were only recommendations. Once Trevelyan had encouraged councils to resume exercising their powers in the case of sex education films, it was not surprising that they should do so with regard to other films once the BBFC became embroiled in controversy and once local branches of the Festival of Light began lobbying their councilors.[149] The re-emergence of the "local option" gave the

Festival of Light the opportunity to engage in guerrilla warfare rather than contend with a national system.

The Greater London Council (GLC) already ran its own film censorship operation for the 234 licensed cinemas in its jurisdiction.[150] When the GLC was established in 1965, it acknowledged that "censorship infringes one of the most fundamental human liberties, freedom to communicate ideas to others." The founding members of the council resolved that its film censorship powers "should be restricted to preventing the kinds of harm which the law seeks to prevent in its provisions relating to the printed and spoken word."[151] The GLC regulations therefore stipulated that no film be exhibited that was likely to incite crime, disorder, or racial animosity or would "if taken as a whole . . . tend to deprave and corrupt persons who are likely to see it."[152] By adopting the language of the Obscene Publications Act, the GLC denied itself the broader censoring power wielded by the BBFC.[153] The GLC passed Laurence Merrick's documentary *Manson* in 1972 after the BBFC refused it a certificate on the grounds that "its almost subversive nature, its attitude towards the casual use of violence, and its portrayal of the use of drugs made it a dangerous film to show to young people."[154] The GLC regularly licensed films featuring partial nudity and simulated sex as naughty treats for Londoners and commercial travelers.[155] The "public displays" associated with such films were nevertheless strictly controlled, under a GLC policy instituted the year the Cinematograph and Indecent Displays Bill was introduced to Parliament.[156] The GLC had to approve the text and images used in all front-of-house posters and advertising.[157] Exhibitors of more explicit sex films did not submit them for classification and tended to bypass even the film clubs that the Cinematograph and Indecent Displays Bill targeted. These "blue films" were shown in private, unlicensed cinemas. Touts would bring clients to a doorman who would take their money and let them into a makeshift cinema in a cellar or other cramped space.[158] A lot of these movies were on 8mm film unsuitable for projection onto large screens.[159]

The parallel BBFC and GLC Film Viewing Board censorship regimes suited the BBFC as it dealt with products of the European avant-garde. James Ferman, the assimilated American who replaced Murphy, was pleased that Walerian Borowczyk's *The Beast* had been referred to the GLC, "since it presented us with interesting and unusual problems." The BBFC's reviewers recognized Borowczyk's artistic ambition, though they had their doubts about whether "the main story he has devised to contain the original dream sequence" was realized satisfactorily. Ferman added quickly, however, that "in a free society" a film should not have to "justify its exhibition through artistic excellence." In the end the BBFC and the distributor could not agree on cuts. Ferman apologized "for being so unsure of its wide acceptability" and told the GLC he thought that a local London certificate was "the appropriate way to handle the film at this stage," because "the film is probably suitable only to London and a few of the other metropolitan centres."[160] The GLC granted *The Beast* an "X-London" certificate.[161] Pier Paolo Pasolini's *Salò* was not so lucky: both the BBFC and the Greater London Council declined to certify it.[162]

Enid Wistrich took over the Film Viewing Board in April 1973 when Labour regained control of the GLC. On the application for GLC committee roles she put Planning and Transport first and Arts and Recreation second. She did not realize there was a film censorship committee until she saw it on the form. To her surprise, that was what she was offered. Asking why, she was told that they needed a woman "because the anti-pornography campaigners are always saying 'Would you take your wife to see this film?'"[163] Griffith-Jones's question lived on, though here the hypothetical wife may have been a moral standard rather than someone to be protected. Wistrich began to think about local government censorship. The sky had not fallen when the lord chamberlain stopped vetting plays, she reflected. Wistrich decided to take the job and see if she could abolish it. She wanted to get the Home Office to reform the law by applying the Obscene Publications Act to cinemas as it now did to theaters. The GLC's unilateral disarmament would likely force the Home Office to step in.[164] There was also a good chance that other local authorities would follow London's lead.[165] They had done so in the twenties when London's endorsement of the BBFC made the national film censorship system viable in the first place.

Wistrich's discussion paper of November 1974 proposing an end to film censorship by the GLC set off a round of pamphleteering from religious bodies, Whitehouse, and the Festival of Light. It drew her into a long and heated correspondence with David Holbrook. Other correspondents urged her to stand her ground. One man who described himself as "very, very English"—was he implying that she was not?—and "a Tory, in fact a True Blue Tory" wrote that he was sure she would understand "how very much it hurts me to have to appeal to you a Socialist . . . to fight for an aspect of freedom."[166] Conservative men on the council told Wistrich "with many a confident nudge and wink" that they agreed with her, and then became evasive when they had to take a public stand. Labour left-wingers struck her as uncertain what side to come down on; Labour Catholics, older members, and, she noticed, many of the East Enders, were in favor of censorship; the teachers supported abolition.[167] The question was put to a vote in January of 1975. Mary Whitehouse watched from the gallery, and Festival of Light demonstrators prayed outside London County Hall in the rain.[168] Wistrich's motion was defeated 50 to 44. She had said she would resign as chairman of the Film Viewing Board if her motion did not pass, and she was true to her word. Wistrich soon became a leading figure in DLAS. Whitehouse welcomed the prospect of a new chairman "more in touch with what the ordinary person thinks."[169] At first it looked as if Wistrich's successor would be her deputy Ken Livingstone, of whom Whitehouse would not have approved, but as it turned out another Labour councilor, Philip Bassett, was selected.[170] While Bassett was chairman, the Film Viewing Board passed *The Texas Chainsaw Massacre*, which became a notorious example of cinematic violence. Wistrich's defeat pleased Whitehouse, but it also meant that a censorship regime more permissive than the BBFC's prevailed in the capital.

The GLC system was legally vulnerable. The gap between indecency, which was covered by the Vagrancy Acts and sundry common-law offenses, and deprave-and-corrupt obscenity could give rise to a situation where a cinema was convicted on a charge of showing an indecent exhibition for showing a film that the GLC had approved. The legal academic Graham Zellick foresaw this in 1971, and it was precisely what happened a few years later with *More about the Language of Love*.[171] This was a Swedish sex-education film in which a panel discussion was spliced with scenes of people having sex. *Monthly Film Bulletin* described one of these scenes as genuinely moving and the rest blighted by "clichés borrowed from the soft-core industry."[172] The minutes of the Film Viewing Board's discussion are fragmentary: "Treated shame of impotence well"; "Commune situation bad"; "Doc[umentar]y film well done but people who wd. Need it won't go to such a film at pub[lic] cin[ema]"; "C[oul]d. B[oar]d. cut lesbian sequence"; "Final scene—woman touching penis beyond any limit." One member worried the board "wd. Get 'clobbered'" if they approved it.[173] They approved it and got clobbered by Raymond Blackburn.

Blackburn saw *More about the Language of Love* at the Jacey Cinema on Charing Cross Road. He went back a second time accompanied by Lord Longford.[174] Blackburn then complained to Sir Robert Mark, the Metropolitan Police commissioner brought in to rebuild after the Dirty Squad disaster and other corruption scandals of the early seventies.[175] With the DPP's backing, the police seized the print and the cinema company was charged with the common-law offense of showing an indecent exhibition.[176] At the trial the judge asked the jury to base its verdict on what they thought was "the minimum standard of public decency which a reasonably tolerant person living in a plural society would accept and adopt in central London today."[177] This was a liberal direction by the standards of the Old Bailey and one that echoed the assumption among the film censors that what was unsuitable for Preston might be all right in London. The jury made its judgment about standards in pluralist London and returned a guilty verdict. The defendants received a modest fine.

Members of the Film Viewing Board began to worry that they could be charged personally with aiding and abetting if they passed a film that was later found indecent. Blackburn had threatened as much two years earlier over the film version of *Oh! Calcutta!*[178] The GLC's solicitor told them this was unlikely but could not rule it out.[179] The council suspended its censorship operations to review its procedures. The director general and the council solicitor recommended adding the phrase "a grossly indecent performance thereby outraging the standards of public decency" to the grounds on which a film could be denied classification.[180] Blackburn wrote demanding they make such a change, but did not give them much time before issuing a writ for prohibition to get a court to compel the council to change its policies.[181] The first judge who heard him, Lord Chief Justice Widgery, held that the GLC's rules supplemented rather than contradicted the common law, and dismissed the application. Blackburn took the matter to the Court of Appeal. "Mr. Raymond Blackburn comes before us once again," Lord Denning began. Denning found that the GLC was exceeding its powers in applying the more stringent "deprave and corrupt" test to films. He went on, "It is wrong for a licensing authority to give their consent to that which is unlawful"—that is, which was in breach of the common law regarding indecent exhibitions.[182] The two other judges agreed that the GLC had exceeded its powers, and they endorsed Denning's proposal that, rather than make an order of prohibition immediately, they give the GLC time to put its house in order. Lord Justice Bridge added that he (unlike Denning) felt no enthusiasm for the result. "The one proposition which I imagine nearly everybody would assent to," he remarked, "is that the law in its present state is so full of anomalies and operates so uncertainly and unevenly that some rationalization is urgently needed."[183] Lord Justice Stephenson hoped "that this case may lead to early legislation to improve and clarify the law, which in this notoriously difficult and controversial field of human activity by common consent works badly."[184]

The council duly changed its rules governing film censorship to reflect the common-law standard of indecency instead of the statutory test of obscenity. They also resolved to ask the Home Office to remove local bodies' censorship powers and responsibilities.[185] After the Conservative landslide in the 1977 GLC election, film censorship was handled by a Public Services and Safety Committee, and its chairman and vice-chairman declared their intention to clamp down on sex films and "clean up" Soho.[186] Ken Livingstone's reign, under which the GLC became a byword for wild leftism, was still a few years into the future. In the meantime, central government included a provision in the Criminal Law Act 1977 that made film subject to the Obscene Publications Act.[187] The legislation explicitly ruled out prosecutions of film distributors and cinemas for common-law public morals offenses.[188]

Towards the Williams Committee

Magazine distributors as well as cinema companies had reason to worry. The appeal in *Director of Public Prosecutions v. Jordan* put an end to the therapeutic defense.[189] This line of defense amounted to using expert witnesses to make a policy argument about pornography rather than assess the redeeming features of particular publications, so it is not a surprise that the courts eventually put a stop to it. Around the same time, in late 1976, the Metropolitan Police made a renewed effort to crack down on the sale of pornographic magazines following a two-year arms race toward greater explicitness. The pace-setter was David Sullivan, whose portfolio of magazines included one named *Whitehouse*.[190] The Greater Manchester Police also put a lot of resources into suppressing pornographic magazines. Retailers were unsettled about the escalation of police action. The Kingsley Committee incorporated as a trade organization, the British Adult Publications Association Limited (BAPAL), and committed to self-censorship.[191] David Offenbach, the solicitor to the new body, described the structure as "a censoring committee rather along the lines of the British Board of Film Censors."[192] They introduced a code: no photographs of actual sexual contact, no erect penises, and so on.[193] Brian Moore, a BAPAL board member and magazine distributor, declared the code a success: "Up to May 1977 the contents of magazines were becoming 'stronger' at an alarming rate. The guidelines had stopped that trend and in some cases reversed it; as an example, photographs of girls inserting various objects in their vaginas had now disappeared from the magazines."[194] In 1978, the head of the reconstructed Obscene Publications Squad—Daphne Skillern, the second woman to reach the rank of commander in the Metropolitan Police—assured the public that the really worrying pornography was imported from continental Europe. "British magazines," she said, "were much straighter."[195]

In more ways than one. A publisher of gay male pornography remarked several years later that on "the old Kingsley Committee . . . we (Q Centaur Ltd) were a lone voice, eventually thrust out, so that such Guide Lines as we now have were drawn up by persons of a heterosexual nature, and they of course do not automatically relate to homosexuals' viewpoints very sympathetically."[196] Others in the business described BAPAL as "a highly effective cartel, through which the interests of the big publishers could effectively squeeze out competition by denying non-members or small publishers an outlet for their publications."[197] With help from DLAS, Arabella Melville explored the possibility of taking the pornographers' trade association to the Restrictive Practices Tribunal.[198] The fact that the pornographers were now also censors complicated relationships with their anticensorship comrades. BAPAL offered Antony Grey the post of general secretary, but he declined, telling his colleagues at DLAS that his conscience wouldn't let him. David Offenbach reportedly felt uncomfortable being their solicitor, but he didn't quit.[199] The biggest prize was John Trevelyan, who agreed to oversee the censorship operation.[200] Raymond Blackburn denounced him as "a paid front man for the pornographers."[201]

That the publishers of *Men Only* and *Whitehouse* had taken the law against them into their own hands was further confirmation that, as Lord Justices Bridge and Stephenson said, nearly everyone could agree that the law of obscenity worked badly. As the person with ultimate responsibility for prosecutions, the attorney general, Samuel Silkin, had to contend with the multiplying difficulties of the law in this area. He pressed the home secretary, Merlyn Rees, for a comprehensive review as a basis for new legislation. As Silkin recognized, being home secretary Rees was subject to political pressures that he was not. Rees hesitated but eventually said yes.[202] In mid-1977 the Home Office announced the appointment of a Committee on Obscenity and Film Censorship with the Cambridge philosophy professor Bernard Williams as its chair.

CHAPTER EIGHT

Philosophers and Pluralists

1977–1979

AFTER THE ARTS COUNCIL working party, which did not formally represent the Arts Council, and after Lord Longford's imitation of an official inquiry, which was imposing enough to convince people in high places to play along, there was, at last, a real "departmental committee" looking into censorship. Its purpose, Bernard Williams told the other members at their first meeting, was to recommend reforms and "to clarify for public debate the various issues involved in what was a complex and controversial area of public morality."[1] This clarification took place on the committee itself and out in the community, as people wrote in to express their opinions. Over 150 organizations and government bodies made formal submissions, and more than one thousand individuals wrote letters in response to advertisements the Williams Committee placed in daily and weekly newspapers. Some of these letters were short and scrappy, others rambled, and some were carefully composed essays. These letters were not a snapshot of popular thinking like an opinion poll, though they are broadly consistent with a Gallup survey in 1979. Gallup found that a large majority of British people believed sex did not belong in public but also found that, asked whether "the authorities should stop 'interfering' and allow people to decide what is fit for them to see and read," many more approved than disapproved of such intervention.[2] Rather than showing headline attitudes to censorship and pornography, the Williams Committee archive reveals people thinking their way through the changes brought about by "permissiveness," applying their understandings of morality and social conventions to the culture of seventies Britain.[3] Feminists wrote in to criticize a sexist culture at a level too fundamental for the committee's terms of reference to encompass. Gay rights groups appropriated liberal defenses of minority rights as they argued that "sexual minorities" needed art—and pornography—that reflected their identities. Individuals justified or opposed the sale of pornography on the basis of John Stuart Mill's harm principle. Others extrapolated from neighborly conventions to arrive at a version of the Wolfenden principle: people should be free to read what they wanted in the privacy of their own homes, but others should not have to be confronted with it in newsagents' shops. The Williams Committee was the occasion for the most far-reaching exploration of censorship in British history.

The Committee

The Committee on Obscenity and Film Censorship was not Bernard Williams's first time sitting as a moral philosopher on an inquiry where moral questions met public policy. When the Williams Committee began its work the chairman was still serving on the Royal Commission on Gambling. Besides Williams, the Committee on Obscenity and Film Censorship consisted of three lawyers, a psychiatrist, a bishop, a head teacher, a former chief constable, a film critic, a literary critic, a social worker, an industrial relations expert, and a journalist. There were ten men and three women.[4] The member who did the most to make the committee heed the views of the women's movement was Sheila Rothwell, the industrial relations academic who served on the still-new Equal Opportunities Commission.

Was this what Mary Whitehouse would have called another loaded committee? Her ally Ronald Butt wrote in his *Times* column that "if the views of some of its membership are anything to go by," the Williams Committee would probably produce "a flabby and 'progressive' document minimizing the gravity of these problems in false perspectives in the cool 'rationality' of committee prose."[5] Williams and the psychiatrist on the committee, Anthony Storr, were the two on the committee who had made some of their views about censorship and pornography public.[6] The year after the *Lady Chatterley's Lover* trial, Williams had addressed the Library Association on "Censorship and Reading." Though he welcomed the changes brought by the 1959 act, the law still "rested on a misconception about art and obscenity. . . . It required the courts to make a calculation which, from the nature of art and the concept of obscenity, was 'inconceivable.' He believed, however, that the issues were such that no good law could be framed." Books were banned "on the grounds that they do harm," but "we can in general have no notion of what harm they will do, to whom, or how."[7] Williams agreed to be a witness for Calder and Boyars in the *Last Exit* trial, and he made a donation to the appeal fund, though he did not follow some of the others into the Defence of Literature and the Arts Society.[8] The society asked Williams to speak at its annual general meeting in 1976 and he said no "on principle."[9] A year later, but before he was tapped to review the laws on obscenity, Williams was suggested as a possible "pro-censorship speaker to battle against John Mortimer" at a DLAS event.[10]

Storr too lent support to opponents of censorship but had his limits. He had been a defense witness in the *Fanny Hill* proceedings in 1964 and like Williams was one of the *Last Exit* witnesses who did not attract press coverage, but he reportedly refused to testify for the *Oz* editors.[11] The Arts Council working party sought his views. In his statement for the working party, Storr wrote: "In my view, disturbances of sexuality . . . have their origin in early childhood and are the result of the family environment to which the individual was exposed during his first five or six years. It is therefore highly unlikely that a book will have the effect of making somebody perverse who is not so already."[12] Antipornography campaigners took note and counted Storr among the enemy.[13]

On the other hand, none of the three lawyers on the committee was a noted civil libertarian. John Leonard was a prosecuting counsel at the Central Criminal Court. While the Williams Committee was sitting, he led for the Crown in the trial of two investigative journalists and their informant under the Official Secrets Act. In that case, Leonard went along with the security service's secret vetting of the jury pool.[14] He became an Old Bailey judge before the Williams Committee finished its work.[15] The law professor A.W.B. (Brian) Simpson was primarily a legal historian, publishing painstaking research on assumpsit before writing the garrulous books about bizarre Victorian cases that made him better known.[16] Ben Hooberman was a solicitor who did a lot of work for the Labour Party, though in trade union cases rather than anything like obscenity or libel. The committee's chairman also belonged to the Labour Party: when his ex-wife Shirley Williams defected with Roy Jenkins and others to found the Social Democratic Party in 1981, he followed them out of Labour. So did the journalist on the Williams Committee, Polly Toynbee of the *Guardian*, which perhaps shows the extent of the committee's alignment with the Labour government that appointed it.

Neither of the critics on the committee had form as campaigners against censorship. The Home Office chose David Robinson, film reviewer for *The Times*, when it could have chosen the *Evening Standard*'s

Alexander Walker, who had a record of agitation for laxer film censorship.[17] John Weightman, a professor of French, made his name as a book reviewer for the *Observer* and *Encounter*, but in other ways stood at an angle to the critical establishment. He was educated at what is now the University of Newcastle and taught at Westfield, one of the smaller constituent colleges of the University of London.

This was a various collection of people. All the same, they arrived at a consensus that was not simply a show. Individual committee members made only peripheral emendations to the draft report Williams wrote.[18] Simpson recalled that the committee did not hold a sustained discussion about possible recommendations until the end of its first year. Instead, informal conversations took place in breaks between interviews with experts and interested parties. According to Simpson, elements of agreement began to emerge in these discussions over lunch and coffee.[19] The committee's minutes bear out Simpson's recollection. As the committee began to work out its position during a weekend retreat in Hastings in July 1978, the range of options turned out to be narrow and the discussions quite uncontentious.[20] The eventual recommendations have a functional precision and liberal character that make it easy to see them as the working out of the chairman's premises, but they also followed the tendencies of the submissions and interviews.

The Williams Committee at Work

The committee embarked on a program of self-education. The most time-consuming part was learning how film censorship worked. James Ferman of the British Board of Film Censors attended many of the early meetings to explain the board's processes. Ferman showed the committee films that had been denied classification. He screened before and after versions of scenes that his staff asked to be modified. Ferman also gave talks about the board's approach to sex and violence and shared quirks of policy like the board's practice of cutting fights with nunchakus out of martial arts movies "to prevent a fashion for a new weapon."[21] (Bruce Lee fans wrote en masse to the Williams Committee to protest the censorship of their genre. They were encouraged to write by an editorial in *Kung Fu* magazine, the new venture of the former *Oz* editor Felix Dennis.)[22] Staff from the DPP's office spent a morning showing the committee films that cinema clubs had been prosecuted for showing, including child pornography.[23] Although it annoyed the committee members when morals campaigners described primetime television as pornographic, they also felt bound "to say to many people who express liberal sentiments about the principle of adult freedom to choose that we were totally unprepared for the sadistic material that some film makers are prepared to produce."[24]

The Williams Committee accepted that cinema's immediacy meant that there was a strong case for "some form of pre-release control." Any form of classification entailed censorship, "since the distributor would bargain for a particular grade of certificate and would be forced to make cuts to conform to the category."[25] The committee agreed that the commercialism and popular reach of film made it inappropriate to treat it like the theater, as the cinema owners' trade body wanted (that is, abolishing pre-censorship and leaving it to the courts, now that cinema was covered by the Obscene Publications Act).[26] Unlike the cinema owners, the film distributors wanted to keep the status quo. Many of those who were critical of the BBFC objected to it for governance reasons: they would have preferred a statutory body, or they were unhappy with local councils' place in the existing arrangements. Of course, some of the committee's witnesses disapproved of the BBFC's substantive decisions. The Nationwide Festival of Light accused the board of sitting by while violence and sex dragged cinema down to "almost inconceivable depths."[27] The Williams Committee was more inclined to think that Ferman and his staff set too much store in their cautious censorship: "we found a slight air of unreality in the Board's tendency to try to limit, by requiring minute cuts, the quantity of the potentially disturbing or offensive, as if the third glimpse of a bloodied face or the third twitch of the buttocks changed the quality of what had already been allowed twice."[28] The committee was also unimpressed by decisions made on ideological grounds, such as denying a certificate to *Manson*. Ferman told the Williams Committee he believed that "material should be prohibited if it could cause harm . . . to the fabric of society: it was the maintenance of certain standards which enabled societies to exist and thrive."[29] This was Devlin's contention in *The Enforcement of Morals* and one that many pressure groups made to the Williams Committee. Though no doubt sincere, Ferman's embrace of the role of moral guardian also helped his politicking. Ferman was working hard to rebuild the BBFC's reputation after the controversies of Murphy's tenure. Ferman's performances before the Williams Committee were among other things an effort to ensure his job did not disappear.

With cinema, the important questions and answers were "constitutional," about whether a statutory body or an industry body should be responsible, rather than about censorship itself. Print proved much more challenging. Here too, the committee had to educate itself and make decisions about what types of evidence it needed. For general fact-finding, the committee had its secretary, Jon Davey, a civil servant from the Home Office. For more demanding questions, the committee had access to the Home Office's Statistical Department and the newer Home Office Research Unit. The latter was a team of analysts that commanded respect in academia and was beginning to gain a reputation among politicians for liberal or progressive bias.[30] Both the Statistical Department and the Research Unit warned the committee of the methodological difficulties of surveying public attitudes to pornography. Simpson thought they should commission a survey anyway, lest the committee be accused of ignoring public opinion. Others made the point that the committee was eliciting submissions through newspaper advertisements and direct invitations to interested organizations. In any case, public opinion was subject to change, and it was important not to give the impression that public opinion was the only proper basis for reform. They decided against an attitude survey but did commission research on the circulation and readership of pornographic magazines.[31]

Then there was the "central question" of what effect pornography had on people.[32] This question was central because if pornography did not demonstrably cause harm it was harder to justify restricting it. The committee knew that research on the subject to date had yielded "contradictory and inconclusive results," and that it was unlikely that any new research they commissioned would produce unambiguous findings.[33] They resolved to rely on expert commentary on the existing research. Most of the psychiatrists they interviewed and requested submissions from tended towards Storr's opinion that it was difficult to establish any link between exposure to pornography and perversion or other psychopathology.[34] Maurice Yaffé updated the literature review he prepared for the *Longford Report* and found that the research was still inconclusive.[35] Hans Eysenck told them that the Danish evidence was mixed.[36] However, the committee did seek the Home Office Research Unit's assistance with a specific task in this area: a rigorous assessment of the claims of Dr. John Court.

Court was a British psychologist working at Flinders University in Australia. He posited a correlation between the availability of pornography and a rise in the incidence of reported sexual offenses. This was the opposite of the therapeutic argument that defense barristers ran until the House of Lords put a stop to it in *Director of Public Prosecutions v. Jordan* (1977). (Outside courtrooms, pornographers still asserted that their product provided an outlet that reduced levels of sexual offending.)[37]

Visiting Britain in 1976, Court volunteered his services to the prosecution in an obscene publications case concerning Scandinavian magazines at Snaresbrook Crown Court. His testimony made him a hero to antipornography campaigners.[38] Whitehouse implored the Williams Committee to interview him.[39] Williams said that "in view of the importance attached by the anti-pornography lobby to the work of Dr John Court," it would be necessary to discuss his work.[40] Simpson wanted an evaluation of the criminal statistics Court used, which the Home Office Research Unit duly provided.[41] The assessment of the data in the committee's report was damning. Sexual offenses in England and Wales had not risen as steeply as crime generally. Court had no meaningful evidence that pornography became more freely available after 1964, when legislation amending the 1959 Obscene Publications Act was passed, only a *Times* column by Ronald Butt. The Williams Committee concluded Court's argument could not "even survive as a plausible hypothesis."[42]

The committee invited a selection of those who had made written submissions to give oral evidence. Williams said the witnesses would fall into two categories: those the committee invited for "political" reasons, and those from whom it expected to learn something.[43] Most pressure groups fell into the former category. In its interviews with the police, the DPP, Customs, and the Post Office, the committee sought to gather information and probed the agencies to see what alternatives to the status quo they would be willing to accept. The committee was impressed by the submission from David Tudor Price, the senior treasury counsel, and agreed to use it as a starting point for questioning witnesses involved in the enforcement of the law.[44] Tudor Price argued that Britain still needed laws dealing with obscenity, but that the *Hicklin* test as modified by the 1959 act was unworkable. The existing laws should be scrapped and replaced by a new law that "would be more concerned with the prevention of or suppression of objectionable material as a nuisance to society rather than with the punishment of offenders. This approach would involve what in some Countries is called 'decriminalization.'"[45]

Tudor Price's contention that the existing law did not work was echoed by most witnesses who had a role in enforcing it, though not all of them. James Anderton, chief constable of Manchester, did not think the laws had failed. Forthright about his moral beliefs, Anderton said that "pornography and commercialised vice were an intolerable blot on any society which claimed to be civilised."[46] Anderton had established an obscene publications squad that systematically raided newsagents and their suppliers, including the biggest chain of all. Manchester police raided W. H.

Smith's Salford depot in October of 1977. After that the chain withdrew pornographic magazines from its outlets. "Many respectable corner-shop newsagents have stopped displaying 'soft-porn' magazines following visits and raids by the police," Anderton wrote in his submission to the Williams Committee.[47] Anderton's achievement in Manchester raised the possibility that the purported failure of the existing law was really a cover for other police forces' lack of interest in enforcing it. Richard Du Cann had an explanation. Speaking to the Williams Committee on behalf of the Criminal Bar Association, Du Cann attributed Manchester's conviction rate to "confining proceedings to the magistrates court." Magistrates sat alone, without juries, and imposed lesser penalties. "Local magistrates represented a very narrow section of the community," Du Cann said, "and a more representative view of what society regarded as obscene would be obtained from a jury, whose members had probably had some experience of pornography."[48] It went unsaid that juries skewed towards men, and that defense barristers did their best to ensure that.[49]

A delegation from the Metropolitan Police, who worked on nearly all the obscenity proceedings the DPP brought before juries at the Central Criminal Court, came before the Williams Committee prepared to describe "the operational difficulties they faced in applying a largely incomprehensible and sometimes practically unenforceable law." They would have preferred a single statute dealing with all forms of obscenity and, more controversially, proposed a single statutory body to oversee it. They commended the model of New Zealand's Obscene Publications Tribunal.[50] The police recognized that a tribunal would "raise the spectre of censorship," but they remarked that it was only realistic "to accept that restriction by court decision was already a form of censorship." Unsatisfactory as the "deprave and corrupt" test was, any new form of words "would still be subject to a subjective interpretation and the same uncertainty would be encountered as at present" (the same conclusion the Herbert Committee came to in the fifties). A tribunal would be able to apply consistent standards. "It would, in effect, take over one of the jury's functions—a function which juries had been singularly unsuccessful in performing—of deciding what was obscene."[51]

The Williams Committee thought that a New Zealand-style censorship board would be so utterly unacceptable in Britain that there was no point giving thought to the practicalities, which themselves were formidable.[52] Williams himself stressed that precensorship of print would be politically impossible in Britain. Other committee members worried that a tribunal would look like the lord chamberlain in a new guise and keep censorship perpetually in public discussion.[53] The committee made a counterproposal: a licensing system that could confine pornography to certain shops. The police delegation replied that this arrangement would "lift a burden from their shoulders," but it would require Parliament and public opinion "to accept that there should be no censorship for adults."[54] The police evidently had their doubts that people would accept this.

The DPP's representatives were not quite as eager as the Metropolitan Police to have the burden of obscenity prosecutions lifted from their shoulders, but they agreed that no alternative test for obscenity would be satisfactory—substituting "indecent" for "obscene" would not work—and they agreed that jury trials produced contradictory results. The DPP's department lent qualified support to "the 'nuisance' approach": controlling the worst pornography, but leaving the rest alone provided it was sold only to adults. There would still need to be restrictions on public display.[55] Here the DPP, like the Metropolitan Police, edged towards David Tudor Price's position and the point where the Williams Committee ended up.

Representatives of other interested bodies also proved willing to entertain the idea of treating pornography as a nuisance rather than continuing to treat it as criminal. At least, they saw merit in this approach when the difficulties of reforming the existing system were brought home to them. In its report, the Williams Committee remarked, "In many of our witnesses, from the Law Society to the Catholic Social Welfare Commission and from the Greater London Council to the Free Church Federal Council, we were struck by their readiness to agree with one another that the right way to deal with a lot of explicit sexual material at least, was to confine it to those who wanted it and prevent its offending everyone else."[56] Politicians from both major parties agreed; in an article in *The Times*, Norman St John-Stevas suggested shifting the law by placing it on the basis of public nuisance.[57] "Decriminalization" was not the first choice of, say, the Catholic Social Welfare Commission, but with millions of men buying pornography at their local newsagents' and the existing law intractable, it looked like a realistic solution.[58]

Harm and Freedom

The Williams Committee made three main recommendations: to regulate pornography and indecent displays as nuisances, to repeal obscenity laws dealing with the written word, and to establish a new body to deal with film censorship. One of the many idiosyncrasies of the British Board of Film Censors was that it was not in fact a board. The examiners reported to the secretary, and the secretary reported to the usually silent president. There was no appeal mechanism apart from asking local councils to assign their own ratings to a film. The Williams Committee decided that the anomalies of the BBFC's position meant that it could not attain the legitimacy it needed. They recommended abolishing local authorities' censorship powers and replacing the BBFC with a statutory agency. The staff of the proposed Board of Film Examiners would operate in much the same way as the BBFC staff, but their decisions would be overseen by a real board representing the film industry, local government, and "relevant expertise."[59] As Mary Warnock, another philosopher and regular on official committees, pointed out, the new body would be similar to the Independent Broadcasting Authority that oversaw commercial television.[60]

Concerning pornography, the only material the committee recommended prohibiting was material that depicted—or indeed was the outcome or record of—unlawful acts: rape, torture, the exploitation of children. Everything else should be restricted rather than prohibited: that is, sold and promoted in such a way that potentially offensive material did not obtrude onto children and onto adults who weren't looking for it. Banning only material that involved illegal acts would relieve officials of some of the line-drawing difficulties that had always plagued censorship in Britain. The terms "obscene," "indecent," and "deprave and corrupt" had become "useless" and should be abandoned.[61] The committee's test for restricting material was whether its "*unrestricted availability is offensive to reasonable people*," rather than whether the material was offensive as such.[62] This test was one BAPAL and the retailers' and distributors' trade bodies were happy with, and most anticensorship organizations came round to curbs on public displays.[63] DLAS's submission, written by Enid Wistrich, Anthony Grey, and Francis Bennion, accepted the need for restrictions on public displays because it explicitly grounded the freedom to look at indecent material on "the consent principle": "To be suddenly confronted with obscenity on a street hoarding or in a newsagent's shop is to experience it whether or not one consents to do so." "Freedom after all has two sides," the society submitted: "my right to do what I want and your right not to have me do to you what you do not want."[64]

These recommendations applied only to pictorial pornography. The committee noted that, in practice, works consisting entirely of text caused less offense than images. There were "basic psychological reasons" for this, which also justified the censorship of film as a medium of powerful immediacy. No one was harmed in the production of prose, and it did not cause immediate offense the way an explicit photograph on display in a shop did. It was certainly possible for prose to offend, but that possibility had to be weighed against the fact that the written word was, alongside speech, "the principal medium for the advocacy of opinions."[65] The committee concluded that publications consisting entirely of text should be neither restricted nor prohibited.[66] Though the Metropolitan Police and the DPP had already given up on prose, this was still a bold declaration. On a practical level, it would extricate the law from another of the empty or confusing formulations that entangled it. Restricting access to pictorial matter on the grounds of offensiveness, but not prohibiting it, and letting prose works circulate no matter what, meant that there was no need for a public-good test, which the Williams Committee found misconceived— not just in the form it took in the 1959 act, but generally. A public-good test assumed accepted authority, which was not available for new or avant-garde works or noncanonical art forms. It also required courts to weigh unrealistic causal claims—the harm a work could do versus the public good it might do.[67]

As Williams acknowledged, much of the evidence the committee received explicitly stated or took it for granted that no conduct should be outlawed "unless it can be shown to harm someone."[68] This principle, articulated most influentially by John Stuart Mill, was sufficiently simple and encompassing to function as a maxim, a one-sentence credo like the Golden Rule. In the report's chapter on "Law, Morality and the Freedom of Expression," Williams wrote, the shortest argument for the harm condition "is simply that there is a presumption in favour of individual freedom."[69] (With this chapter of the report it is appropriate to treat Williams as the author rather than a rapporteur summarizing collective opinion. Sending a draft of the chapter to the rest of the committee, Williams acknowledged "that this chapter covers ground which the Committee has not really discussed thoroughly.")[70] Mill regarded freedom of expression as a special and fundamental freedom, and many of the witnesses before the committee clearly shared this view, Williams observed. He accepted Mill's premise that (as Williams put it) since "human beings have no infallible source of knowledge about human nature . . . and do not know in advance what arrangements or forms of life may make people happy or enable them to be . . . original, tolerant, uncowed individuals," it was important to keep debate open.[71] Progress often originated in minority beliefs.[72] The next step in Mill's reasoning, that truth could only emerge from the competition of a free market of ideas, was less convincing. Against the idea that the truth will prevail under laissez-faire could be set Gresham's Law, the idea that bad coin drives out good, which was periodically cited in mid-century discussions of mass culture.[73] There was a more fundamental objection to the marketplace model. A longstanding critic of utilitarianism, Williams was unwilling to locate the value of free expression "solely in its consequences, such that it turns out on the whole to be more efficient to have it rather than not."[74] Williams followed up this lethal piece of philosopher demotic—eleven single-syllable words in a row—with a three-part declaration: "There is a right to free expression, a presumption in favour of it, and weighty considerations in terms of harms have to be advanced by those who seek to curtail it."[75]

Williams's reasoning had a special relevance in the case of obscenity law because (he contended) the pornography that caused most of the trouble was not a vehicle for ideas. It was a product in a lucrative marketplace, but not a marketplace of ideas. Williams described photographic pornography as "vacant and inexpressive" and stressed "the total emptiness of almost all the material we are concerned with."[76] This was one of the few points where the report did not acknowledge and critique alternative views. The US Supreme Court, in a 1969 case that the Williams Committee did not mention in its brief discussion of First Amendment jurisprudence, accepted that "the line between the transmission of ideas and mere entertainment is much too elusive . . . to draw," and it was irrelevant if pornographic movies lacked any identifiable "ideological content."[77] All the same, even the most brazen anticensorship witnesses quoting John Stuart Mill to the Williams Committee did not try to argue that the pictorials in *Club International* or *Men Only* were contributions to "free critical discussion." BAPAL's diligently footnoted submission quoted the introduction to *On Liberty*, not the relevant bit in the chapter on freedom of expression: "The only freedom which deserves the name, is that of pursuing our own good in our own way, so long as we do not attempt to deprive others of theirs, or impede their efforts to obtain it. . . . Mankind are greater gainers by suffering each other to live as seems good to themselves, than by compelling each to live as seems good to the rest."[78]

But if, for Bernard Williams and the pornographers' ghostwriter, it was the principle of freedom, not the specific content of the material, that counted, for others who quoted Mill the content spoke directly to the issue of minority rights. Protecting minorities was one of Mill's main justifications for freedom of the press in chapter two of *On Liberty*. Of course it was minorities of one kind or another who were usually on the receiving end of pressure to conform. The Scottish Homosexual Rights Group, which previously called itself the Scottish Minorities Group, appealed explicitly to *On Liberty* in declaring that "people should be free to fashion their lives as they judge best, so long as they do not harm others in the exercise of that freedom."[79] They told the Williams Committee that there was in Britain "too great a readiness to identify democracy with the enforcement of majority opinion on anything whatsoever. . . . There is a richer conception of democracy which, while allowing for majority opinion to prevail where the means to common purposes have to be decided, leaves individuals otherwise free to live according to their consciences; and we doubt whether the enforcement of morality—even the morality of the majority—is compatible with this conception of democracy." To be free, gay men and women "must be accorded *equality* with heterosexual people: must, that is, be accorded equal opportunities to discover and express their sexuality . . . to fashion their lives in accordance with their sexuality as they judge best." Harking back to the landmark obscenity trial in which the word "equal" had been so important, they wrote: "Whatever degree of explicitness is permissible in the description of what transpired between Lady Chatterley and Mellors must also be permissible in the description of what could have transpired between Mellors and Sir Clifford."[80] Even in "the relatively open society which exists in this country today we find many homosexual people who have never encountered a picture of human life which recognizes the possibility of significant human relationships on a homosexual foundation. Deprived of that possibility, such people cannot rightly be said to have made an informed choice of the stunted and desperate way of life which is so often theirs"— they had, in effect, been denied the chance to exercise responsibility. An informal and personal footnote gave an example of the converse: "Some of us in the Scottish Homosexual Rights Group recall with gratitude how our mental horizons were enlarged, our imaginative grasp of what was possible extended, by the film *Sunday Bloody Sunday*, in which a homosexual relationship was treated simply as a way of life, in no way inferior to a heterosexual one."[81]

Nalgay, the gay-rights caucus of a public servants' union, echoed these contentions: "As far back as the OZ trial it was made clear that contact advertisements involving homosexuals were, in the eyes of the law, per se more obscene than those involving heterosexuals." They argued that "those who do not conform with the heterosexual norm find little in the way of models from the traditional sources, such as the family, through which to grow towards a mature sexuality. For many gays books and films provide the only source of models from which to draw in the building of a positive identity as a gay adult."[82] Questions of identity were not much in evidence in discussions of civil liberties in Britain before the seventies. In asserting the importance of "public depiction" for "sexual minorities"—the term Jim Anderson of *Oz* preferred to "perverts"—gay-rights groups were wresting a British liberal tradition away from the private sphere.[83]

The most influential statement of liberal values in the mid-twentieth century was Wolfenden's:

> There must remain a realm of private morality and immorality which is, in brief and crude terms, not the law's business. To say this is not to condone or encourage private immorality. On the contrary, to empha-sise the personal and private nature of moral or immoral conduct is to emphasise the personal and private responsibility of the individual for his own actions, and that is a responsibility which a mature agent can properly be expected to carry for himself without the threat of punish-ment from the law. . . . We accordingly recommend that homosexual behaviour between consenting adults in private should no longer be a criminal offence.[84]

This was a charter for sexual liberty (as long as it remained private: it should be remembered that prostitution was also in Wolfenden's remit, and the committee proposed ways of pushing prostitution off the streets).[85] It presupposed, and legitimated, a respectable and private homosexuality.[86] It did not endorse a change in the public culture. With its imperative to come out, Gay Liberation did the opposite. In the incipient theorizing on identity in gay-rights groups' submissions to the Williams Committee, the liberal premium on individual autonomy was decoupled from Wolfenden's emphasis on private space and yoked to assertions that representations of "minority" sexualities belonged in the public domain.

The Wolfenden Principle and Neighborly Liberalism

Versions of the Wolfenden formula—regulate conduct in public, condone what consenting adults do in private—recur so regularly in the letters to the Williams Committee as to indicate that it encapsulated a widely shared principle. The letters from members of the public dwelt on a subject that was not front and center in the more formal submissions from interest groups: the visibility of pornography in shops. "The thing which I really feel strongly about is the proliferation of sex magazines which are on open display in newsagents," one woman wrote.[87] "I was searching in a local newsagents, on a very low shelf, for school materials—pencils, rulers, etc.," wrote another, "and picked up a magazine with a photograph of oral sex on the cover."[88] Women complained over and over of the embarrassment of confronting sexually explicit images, photographs of women in "unnatural poses," when they went to buy gardening magazines; or the sight of men leafing through explicit magazines; or seeing boys stare at the covers while they bought sweets.[89] Men worried about their sons growing up with all this sexual imagery.[90] One man who organized a monthly whip-round to buy magazines to share with his workmates at a Merseyside shipyard wrote to say that pornography should be confined to designated shops.[91] People of both sexes were uncomfortable seeing nudity and sex everywhere, but, of course, it was women who found it most oppressive to see photographs of other women arrayed before customers in newsagents' and corner shops.[92] "'Porn' is by & large a male oriented occupation, & the embarrassment to women of *all* ages is understandably because the nudes are *female*," M. D. Wood of Kendal in Cumbria wrote.

In a long letter, Wood described "the solo campaign of an ordinary housewife & mother (I left school at 15) to solve the problem of what many acknowledge to be indecent displays seen without choice by the general public in shops or outside cinemas." Wood wrote to her MP and the Home Office. She corresponded with the National Federation of Retail Newsagents. She asked female shop assistants how they felt about the magazines on display. One told her she had got used to them. But is that how it should be? Yes, a "very young mum" in the shop chimed in. "'That's all right for you & me' I said 'But how about your Granny & my Auntie. Poor dears, they curl up & die when they see this stuff.'" Another young woman agreed with Wood, telling her: "I hate these mags: that's *me* on the cover. How *dare* anyone display me like that."

Wood also conducted gotcha interviews with local police:

> "Why can't they be out of sight & available on request," I innocently asked our young village bobby, & his odd reply was "You can't stop people buying them." "I'm not trying to" I snapped "but if they have the right to buy, where's my right not to be offended by the display?"[93]

This idea of public indecency as a trade-off between different people's freedoms, a claim that mimicked the structure of the harm principle, was one also used by others who wrote to the Williams Committee.[94]

Wood said she differed from Mary Whitehouse in being uninterested in the magazines' contents. She simply wanted them sealed to stop children leafing through the pages, and she wanted nudes off the covers: "Vintage cars or Swiss scenery would settle *all* arguments as to what was indecent. You've heard them:—'It all depends what you mean' etc—Joadlike. And— 'What's indecent in Harrow isn't indecent in Hull.'" Cyril Joad was the celebrity philosopher of an earlier generation. His catchphrase, when asked about X, was "It all depends what you mean by X." It was a reference that fitted with Wood's self-presentation as a restless autodidact, mixing outrage with comedy, speaking the language of countervailing rights. Wood was prickly about professors, teachers, and clergymen; she wanted the Williams Committee to consult "the general public" rather than "some out of touch & insensitive individuals in the corridors of power." There was a class inflection to Wood's "general public": please, she wrote, don't ignore people who have no printed letterhead or typewriter. "The people who experience the greatest offence are the 'plebs'—who don't order by phone & pay by cheque." Wood's husband, "a committed Christian," told her she was wasting her time with her campaign: "You ought to know by now that NOBODY will do ANYTHING about ANYTHING." Her father, an atheist, had a different if not necessarily more encouraging take: "In a democracy you're assured of a hearing—nothing more."⁹⁵

Wood focused on public space, implicitly accepting men's entitlement to buy pornographic magazines but not overtly endorsing it. Others did endorse it, some explicitly invoking Wolfenden. A man who owned a storage business told the Williams Committee: "I believe the basic answer is à la Wolfenden. The sale or exhibition of material, films or stage production[s] likely to offend should be only inside premises clearly marked that such material or exhibitions are there . . . those who may be offended should use their democratic right not to enter and protect others' democratic right to see, hear and enjoy should they so wish."⁹⁶ Another man pointed to the Street Offences Act, which implemented Wolfenden's recommendations on solicitation, and said that the same thinking should apply to bookshops. He used some of Wolfenden's language to sum up the principle: "The law should not concern itself with what individuals wish to read or see in private. It should however protect individuals from having brought to their notice sexual manifestations which offend or disgust them."⁹⁷ A married couple from Hertford wrote to say that people should be free to use pornography, but others shouldn't have to encounter it involuntarily in newsagents or at cinemas. They likened pornography to smoking or drinking, seeing it, as the Williams Committee ultimately did, as a nuisance to be regulated.⁹⁸ A vicar from Essex, who hastened to say he was not a "trendy priest," nor "particularly liberal," said, "Whilst not in favour of pornography (chiefly because of the harm that it does to those who participate in it, especially children: this revolts me) I do feel that adults should be allowed to decide for themselves what book or magazines they wish to read in their own homes."⁹⁹

This popular Wolfendenism was articulated powerfully by a London woman, Sarah Hutchinson:

> I'm sure I'm speaking for an enormous number of ordinary people when I say that I feel the emphasis of the "guardians of public morality" has often been wrong. We are not concerned with the inches of pubic hair that may be shown in a strip club . . . nor with the sexual acrobatics that are performed on cinema screens in private houses and clubs. That sort of thing doesn't affect most people nor impinge on their lives, so long as it is kept "between consenting adults in private." What worries me much more is the sort of pornography with which we are all bombarded in our daily lives, and which we simply can't get away from. I can't send my young daughter out to buy a newspaper without her being offered pictures of nude women for sale, between the sweets and the tobacco. The morning paper has nudes on every page. Advertisements in magazines, on the underground, on hoardings, on television, show women's bodies for sale. . . . What I object to is not the nudity, it's the relationship implicit in these pictures of commodity, object for consumption.

Unlike people like Whitehouse or James Anderton, who had no truck with the women's movement, Hutchinson could make an argument about the commodification of women's bodies without having to tie it to a theory of the sacredness of sex and marriage. Her concern for her daughter was not simply, or not even, about children's innocence, but about "What kind of sense of herself" her daughter was going to grow up with "when this is the image that society gives her of womanhood." Like the gay-rights groups, Hutchinson saw in the images supplied by popular culture a stock of role models, for good or for ill. And, like the Hertford couple, she saw an analogy with passive smoking: "Please, less legal persecution but more strict licensing, so that nudity & pornography are available to those who want them but not forced upon those who do not (like smokers and non-smokers areas)."[100]

A lot of letter writers were, like Hutchinson, concerned to shield children. Yet "adult" was more than the opposite of "child": for many people who insisted on their right to choose what they read or watched, as long as it did not offend others or harm the vulnerable, "adult" implied the entitlements of citizenship. A man from Poole responding to the advertisement in the *Daily Mail* revived the old association between education and citizenship. Everyone in the country now had to spend at least ten years in school: "How can anyone, then try and justify or even trying [*sic*]to decide what such an educated adult (16) should see, and read." It was not right that an adult population could elect a government with power over nuclear weapons and yet "not have free choice of films or books."[101] The manager of a cinema in Cheshire who was prosecuted for showing *Salò* said: "As an adult aged 53 I would like to decide what plays or films I watch or what books I read. I do not wish to hand over this power of decision making to any individual or groups of individuals."[102] Alison de Reybekill, a "working woman and householder, in my late twenties," decried Whitehouse and other "guardians of public morals"—she too used the phrase—as "pseudo-parents standing over us dictating how we should enjoy ourselves."[103] De Reybekill detected another kind of paternalism in Whitehouse and company: the guardians of public morals fostered "a welfare-state style dependence in both men and women on 'those who know best' to think, choose, *and* govern for us." It would be better if those moralists devoted their energy to "helping men realise that women are real human beings too, and capable of at least as much potential for growth as independent selfdirecting people as they are." With its conception of women as classical liberal subjects, backed up by the claim of householder status, de Reybekill's letter suggests something like the affinity between permissiveness and neoliberalism that some of Thatcherism's early boosters argued for—though, perhaps reflecting the dynamics of a "decade of dealignment," she was also a *Guardian* reader.[104]

De Reybekill counted herself among a "growing percentage of women who believe that there is enough official dabbling in people's private lives and interests." Other correspondents too complained about meddling in private affairs, both by the state and by campaigners like Whitehouse. "There are far too many busy-bodies in this country trying to stop others from doing this, that, and the other," a man from North London wrote to say.[105] A man from Aylesbury said he didn't want to live in a police state. He was an ex-serviceman and should be able to read what he wanted. He said religion had a lot to answer for—burning witches, for instance—and that Mary Whitehouse would, if she could, burn people "who of there [*sic*] own freedom read & see sex films."[106] Some of these correspondents sound like the "True Blue Tory" who wrote to Enid Wistrich to congratulate her for fighting for freedom. A man from Hull, doubtful that the Williams Committee would heed anyone other than "Mrs Whitehouse and company," said that "freedom of choice . . . is very important in this depressing age what with censors, tax, prices unions etc it is fast becoming a police state not like England before the war when all this still went on and nothing was said."[107] Like de Reybekill's letter, this one put Whitehouse in company she was not used to keeping.

That morals campaigners did not in fact represent majority opinion was a common theme in the letters the Williams Committee received. A public librarian in Peterborough reported on a discussion that had taken place in the library. A club of about forty people aged between fifty and seventy met there and they spent a session talking about changing standards in literature. The librarian asked whether they thought he or his staff should vet books. Most of them said no, quite emphatically. "This liberal attitude even surprised me for if any age group would be concerned about present publishing surely this was it." He added, "From reports in the press of evidence given to the committee it seems to me that there is a danger that many ordinary people as opposed to well organised Pressure groups may be misrepresented. The views expressed by organisations claiming to speak for the 'silent majority' seem to contradict the views held by this community group."[108]

"This liberal attitude" did not mean approval of pornography. Nor was it necessarily an affirmation of "live and let live."[109] It reflected the individualism of English culture. As the historian Jon Lawrence has argued, this individualism pervaded the working-class neighborhoods popularly imagined to be close-knit and mutualist, as well as the detached living arrangements of the middle classes.[110] Even in the crowded streets of a "traditional" working-class community, the anthropologist Raymond Firth detected a "fierce assertive separateness" in the ways ordinary people conducted their affairs. Firth observed that the need to share space and facilities "tends to divide and individualise households as much as bring them together." His informants frequently declared: "We keep ourselves to ourselves, and then we can't get into trouble."[111] This was a common maxim in urban Britain. Keeping yourselves to yourselves was a way of carving out some autonomy in cramped conditions.[112] Working-class people embraced the new suburban housing estates built after the Second World War not because they were seduced by fantasies of middle-class domesticity but because they "wanted the chance to withdraw from *forced* sociability—to socialize instead on their own terms, with the family and friends of their choosing." Lawrence's research converges on Deborah Cohen's argument about changing conceptions of privacy among the middle classes in the late twentieth century: across British society, "the determination to protect domestic privacy mutated into a more powerful assertion of the right to live as one wished, in public as well as private."[113]

Expansive assertions of the right to live as one wished, and not hide, sound strongly in the gay-rights groups' submissions to the Williams Committee, as well as in the declarations of adult status by people who refused to answer to busybodies or state censorship. Yet a belief in private space as the site of freedom persisted. We can see it in the metaphors, which draw much of their power from being flatly practical descriptions of social arrangements, of things happening "behind closed doors" or "in the privacy of their own home." The working-class culture of "assertive separateness" and middle-class domesticity alike created zones of relative impunity. (For instance, violence against women was much less likely to meet with a vigilante response if it took place within the home than out in the street.)[114] Some of the people who wrote to the Williams Committee saying that they were opposed to censorship or criminal penalties provided that sexual heterodoxy was confined to private spaces and pornography was not on public display came to this conclusion by extrapolating from commonplace distinctions about behavior in the home and behavior in public. A woman who read the *Daily Mail* wrote: "Dozens of my generation (I am 33) have a great time behind their closed bedroom doors and enjoy a dirty joke (typical British hypocrisy) but we're still painfully embarrassed at going into a local High St newsagent with Gran and the children for comics & 'build your own Royal Family' type mags to be confronted with the display on the top shelf."[115] Letter after letter articulated this opposition between home or bedroom and street or shop, private and public, freedom and restraint. The Wolfenden principle mapped onto the neighborly liberalism of everyday life.

Feminism before the Williams Committee

Those active in the women's liberation movement were less likely to believe that public and private could be distinguished neatly, or that pornography really could be confined to specialist shops, kept under the counter, or concealed by pictures of the Alps. There was a continuity, some of the Williams Committee's correspondents suggested, between pornographic magazines, topless women on page three of the *Sun*, and suggestive pictures of women in advertisements for products as sexless as Colman's mustard.[116] Sheila Rothwell pushed the rest of the committee to heed "feminist arguments," and passed on material from WIRES, the Women's Information and Referral Service.[117] The Williams Committee received few submissions from the women's movement in response to its early advertisements, when most submissions came in, and at the beginning of 1979, when the committee's conclusions were already firming up, the secretariat appealed for more statements of feminist opinion. One woman who responded said that feminists may have become disillusioned with official channels and so had not written to the Williams Committee.[118] Nevertheless, she and others now wrote in.

The letters from women's liberation groups and individuals explicitly identifying with the movement tended not to fit into the "nuisance" approach to pornography. For practically all the Williams Committee's feminist correspondents, pornography was anything but "vacant and inexpressive": it was a powerful expression of a cultural assumptions. A Norfolk women's group submitted that pornography was a symptom of a sexist society, reflecting assumptions that women existed for men's pleasure and convenience and that violence and inequality were the nature of sexual encounters.[119] Cambridge Women's Liberation also used the language of symptoms: "Pornography is the symptom of a depersonalised society. It is a crude and debased form of erotica which is intended to titillate the viewer by humiliating the object." Catering largely to middle-aged heterosexual men, it "reflects the bias of society towards middle-aged heterosexual males." Capitalism was based on a system of hierarchies, and pornography was "one of the means of keeping people in their places"—men as well as women. Though their focus was obviously on women, a handful of submissions suggested that men too had something to gain by dismantling pornographic culture. A woman identifying herself as a lesbian feminist argued that pornography represented and perpetuated set roles for men and women, and she suggested that one of the insights of the women's liberation movement was that playing out these scripts restricted human development: "Pornography dictates strict rules for sex that separate people not only from each other but also from their selves."[120]

Laura Fulcher, a *Spare Rib* reader, combined these ideas about objectification, depersonalization, and gender roles. Pornography encouraged men to think of all women as available sex objects, she told the Williams Committee. The magazines always presented women "as objects and not real people. They exist only in so far as they relate to men's sexual needs."[121] A telling detail was found in boilerplate descriptions of the models' hobbies: travel, meeting people, tennis, or horse riding. "If they want to appear adventurous they may enjoy parachuting (Most pilots are men). . . . The main seller is passivity."[122] Although "hard porn" was consumed by a minority, it was the implicit anchor point of a sexualized mass culture:

> If hard porn wasn't around then page 3 of the Sun wouldn't exist. Page 3
> is accepted because it *isn't* a picture of someone sucking a cock. But it
> is the Sun that contains the real subversive image because it seems so

innocuous. Millions of *families* read that paper and see the picture. They see a woman as a[n] object of desire and nothing more. Objects of desire can be raped and killed and assaulted on the street because they are not real people, but just a projection of an individual's desires. (or what he is taught to desire).[123]

AFFIRM, the Alliance for Fair Images and Representation in the Media, said: "Although pornography plays a considerable role in establishing and reinforcing the way women are perceived and degraded, we won't spend energy in this area," of more importance was "the media that deal with other than clear-cut pornography," which had gradually been infiltrated by "violent and degrading images of women."[124]

Given the Advertising Standards Authority's lack of remit to do anything about the sexualization of advertising, AFFIRM supported some measures of censorship. Other feminist groups did not, their condemnation of pornography notwithstanding.[125] The Nottingham feminist collective SCUM 2—the name was presumably an allusion to Valerie Solanas's *SCUM Manifesto*—distanced itself from advocates of censorship on the ground that restrictive moralism and crude commercialism were part of the same complex. The Nottingham women were nevertheless open to what they described as more imaginative ways of discouraging the publication of degrading material, such as a porn tax; and, while there was censorship, fifty per cent of the censors should be women and censorship boards should include "'sexual minority groups' such as lesbians."[126] The Norfolk group worried that new legislation against pornography would also cover "things that are trying to question or change society's view of women and sex." They could imagine publications that were very explicit but showed sex between equal partners. Such challenges to assumptions of female subservience would be shocking to many people.[127]

Williams's first draft evidently did not register many of the ideas put forward by the women's liberation groups. After reading it, Sheila Rothwell sent Jon Davey a list of "'Feminist' Points," asking for the women's liberation arguments to be given more attention. She supplied some sentences explaining how the women's movement's diagnosis of the problem differed from Whitehouse's. Rothwell's additions were incorporated into the one paragraph of the report that really addressed feminist thinking.[128] As the Williams Committee was charged with reviewing obscenity law, pervasive and significant problems that could not be addressed by changes to legal controls were largely outside the terms of reference. The Williams Report's treatment of submissions from the women's movement reflected a broader pattern. The witnesses who had the most impact on the committee's recommendations were those involved in the administration of the law, who provided technical and practical advice. The broader concepts incorporated came from lawyers generalizing from practice—Tudor Price's "nuisance" approach—and from the committee itself, or from the chairman. Witnesses with fundamental critiques of the system but no viable detailed proposals got a hearing, and sometimes a critique, but little more.

"A Pluralistic Society"

"What became clear to us in the course of our discussions . . . ," the committee reported, "was that many of our witnesses had in mind a class of material which included much that could not remotely be dealt with under the kind of laws we were appointed to review." This judgment applied not only to feminists concerned with sexist advertising but also to much of what morals campaigners told the Williams Committee. Often, Williams wrote, "the arguments that were put to us about damage to culture, morality and social values were not primarily directed to the effects of pornography at all."[129] The fact that Mary Whitehouse's principal concern was television—"which in this country is hardly ever pornographic"—showed that her struggle was really with "the far wider aspects of media influence on the quality of life."[130] The mismatch between the committee's terms of reference and the cultural critique of the teacher turned antipornography campaigner David Holbrook was both poignant and absurd, even allowing for the determined understatement of civil service minutes. Weightman, who led the questioning, pushed Holbrook repeatedly:

> It was put to Mr Holbrook that his diagnosis of a cultural sickness and collapse associated with images of hate might not be very closely connected with pornography and still less with the laws on obscenity. Mr Holbrook said that culture was an essential need of man's existence which gave meaning to life . . .
>
> Questioned again about the extent to which the Obscene Publications Acts could ever deal with the commercialisation and trivialisation of culture which was at the basis of his argument, Mr Holbrook said that he was concerned about the denial of individuality inherent in pornographic material and its obsession with the desecration of human personality.[131]

There was another way in which Holbrook and Whitehouse, or Lord Longford and his colleagues in the Parliamentary Child and Family

Protection Group, were speaking outside the Williams Committee's parameters.[132] They all took it for granted that society depended on common moral values, as Devlin had argued in *The Enforcement of Morals*.[133] Returning to this issue in the report, Williams argued that Devlin exaggerated the level of moral consensus a society needed to hold together: "Certainly society requires some degree of moral consensus, but moral opinion can, and does, change without the disintegration of society. One thing that can happen is that the society moves to a new consensus; another is that it supports, in some particular area, a real degree of variety and pluralism."[134] Williams acknowledged a "yearning for a morally more homogeneous society" that took many forms, on both the left and the right. There were many people who would prefer—"or believe that they would prefer," he added archly—"a society less pluralistic than modern capitalist societies, and embodying a stronger moral consensus."[135] The link between sexual morality and capitalist society was one that many witnesses drew. James Anderton and the leaders of the Festival of Light objected to pornography as commercialized vice; Whitehouse described pornography as "the dirtiest face of capitalism," but, staunch Cold Warrior that she was, could not press the charge further.[136]

The word "pluralism" meant a lot of different things. Williams seems to have used the word simply to mean a diversity of values, rather than as a specifically philosophical term. John Calder had invoked pluralism on behalf of *Inside Linda Lovelace*: "We live in a pluralistic society where there are different acceptable codes of conduct and different ways of facing life."[137] The judge in the *More about the Language of Love* trial directed the jury to adopt the standard of "a reasonably tolerant person living in a plural society."[138] In Britain the term had often been used in political thought to describe either a third way between individualism and collectivism or a corporatist juggle of interest groups.[139] From the late sixties, "pluralism" was also used in the context of immigration and race, referring to policies and attitudes that would later be called multiculturalism.[140] In submissions to the Williams Committee, the multicultural sense of "pluralism" sometimes meshed with pluralism as moral diversity. A pluralist outlook thus protected more than one kind of minority. DLAS submitted that Christianity was "no longer . . . part of the law of England" and that "those responsible for formulating and administering the laws in our ethically pluralist and multi-racial society need to be careful not to use them to enforce the dogmas of a particular religion or denomination."[141] The National Campaign for the Reform of the Obscene Publications Acts supplied statistics on the proportion of the British population that did not "participate in any public religious activity" and added that there were over one million Muslims in Britain and that "pornography is not mentioned in the Koran and it is allowed in some Islamic countries (e.g. Malaysia and Lebanon)."[142] One man pushed the association between cultural diversity and sexual mores further: "Britain is becoming more & more cosmopolitan, esp London & large cities. Therefore a variation of tastes e.g. Natural sex, Gay sex, Lesbian child & other is more or less inevitable. Being a democratic state, we all need laws to govern us, but we all have different tastes, sexually & socially."[143] (The untroubled reference to sex with children was characteristic of a lot of seventies discussions of changing sexual norms.)[144] These submissions drew a connection between ethnic diversity and moral pluralism even though the pressure groups advancing these claims were made up primarily of atheists, agnostics, or Christians who had grown up in Britain. Perhaps ethnic diversity was a sort of rhetorical conscript in these arguments about changing mores; perhaps people who supported the passing of a conformist and repressive Britain really did think that everything was connected, that change in one sphere compelled change in another. That British culture was now "multi-racial and pluralist: that is to say, people adhere to different views of the nature and purpose of life" would also be cited as a reason to deregulate broadcasting.[145]

The Endgame

Appointed by a Labour government, the Williams Committee would report to its Conservative successor. Margaret Thatcher's election victory in May of 1979 put the committee under pressure in its final months. Morals campaigners welcomed the advent of a sympathetic government, which gave parliamentary time to a new private member's bill dealing with indecent displays.[146] Williams realized that fresh legislation could overtake the committee's findings and insisted on delivering the report before the debate on the bill's second reading.[147]

The government apparently decided to set the report aside even before it was written. In June, when the committee had settled on its recommendations and Williams was drafting the report, the minister of state at the Home Office answered a parliamentary question about the government's intentions: it would consider the report "and the reactions of interested people" and then consider what action, if any, was required. Interested parties duly sent their protests to the Home Office, which then undertook to hold formal consultations—including meetings with organizations that had already made submissions to the Williams Committee. The National Viewers' and Listeners' Association paid for John Court to fly back to Britain to rebut the Williams Report's charges.[148] After the round of consultation, the government announced that it had no plans to act on the Williams Report. The home secretary, William Whitelaw, would not have to defend liberalizing measures to the Conservative party rank and file.[149]

Meanwhile, the government granted safe passage to the Indecent Displays (Control) Bill, which Whitelaw acknowledged was actually much less stringent than the regime proposed by the Williams Report.[150] The Williams Report could be shelved, but it read the realities facing censorship on the eve of the eighties more accurately than any of the morals campaigners who thought their time had come. The scale of the pornography market meant that most police forces outside Manchester did treat it as a nuisance to be managed rather than a scourge that they could defeat. Police and prosecutors left sexually explicit prose alone. Private members' bills to amend the Obscene Publications Act with a new definition "which does not confuse juries and is John Mortimer proof" foundered because their solutions were as unfeasible or ineffective as the Williams Committee had said they were.[151]

Conclusion

CONTROVERSIES ABOUT CENSORSHIP roll on, but of late controversies about *obscenity* have not been so close to the storm center of social change as they were through the seventies. During the Thatcher years, critics of sex, violence, and blasphemy in popular culture and the arts had some victories, but not the counterrevolution they hoped for. After one setback, Mary Whitehouse complained to the prime minister: "This was precisely the kind of 'permissive society' Home Office response which we have come to recognise over the years and which we had hoped so much would have changed under your leadership."[1] It usually fell to the Home Office to explain that a new proposal to replace the Obscene Publications Act was impractical or unrealistic.[2] Though sympathetic, Thatcher was alert to the limitations of the censorship measures proposed to her. As a former barrister, she was wary of laws that could not be enforced effectively and consistently. She had seen the old laws against homosexuality that way and voted for the Sexual Offences Act in 1967 for that reason.[3]

In 1984 Thatcher received a delegation led by the Tory backbencher Lord Nugent to discuss a proposal to revise the law of obscenity. Nugent was accompanied by Ray Johnston of the Festival of Light, now renamed CARE (Christian Action Research and Education), and John Finnis, a legal philosopher in the Catholic natural law tradition.[4] This was an unusual alliance, given the evangelical character of the Festival of Light. Finnis had helped Nugent draft a bill amending the Obscene Publications Act.[5] Thatcher expressed reservations about its definition of obscenity, at which point her home secretary drew her attention to the Williams Committee's use of offensiveness as a guiding concept. Thatcher thought the idea had some merit and sent them away to revise the bill, which did not progress much further. Two years later, under renewed pressure from Whitehouse,

Thatcher turned to her "unofficial legal advisor," Alan King-Hamilton.[6] King-Hamilton had been the judge in the *Gay News* trial. Now retired from the bench, he was involved in Whitehouse's campaigns.[7] Believing, like many witnesses before the Williams Committee, that the existing law was unworkable, King-Hamilton drafted some proposals, but again, the definition of "obscenity" proved intractable.[8] The Obscene Publications Act of 1959 remains in force; the *Hicklin* phrase "deprave and corrupt" is still there.

During the debate on another hopeless bill to amend the Obscene Publications Act by itemizing forbidden types of scenes and poses, the Labour MP Clare Short made an exasperated speech to a near-empty House of Commons. She followed it up with a private member's bill of her own to ban photographs of topless women in newspapers. The main target was page three in the *Sun*, which was a strong supporter of Thatcher. Page three had been "central to the paper's brand identity" since the midseventies, and the *Sun* responded with a barrage of character assassination.[9] Short received so many letters of support, echoing those the Williams Committee received about pornography in public spaces, from such a range of women that she later published an anthology of them. She introduced her bill several times, and while it never became law, it rallied efforts outside Parliament to put pressure on newsagents. The campaign also publicized the links between pornography and sexual violence, as documented in hearings in Minneapolis as the city debated an ordinance against pornography drafted by Catharine MacKinnon and Andrea Dworkin, and which British feminists followed with interest.[10] Short worked with the National Union of Students, the Townswomen's Guild, and CARE. The latter had continued to lobby newsagents, and this joint campaign of the late eighties left many small retailers feeling defensive. Short and her allies went after W. H. Smith especially: its outlets could set the tone for the rest of the industry, and, as a wholesaler, it distributed most of the magazines sold in independent shops. Short secured a meeting with W. H. Smith's chairman, who said Smith's would reconsider their policy if the campaign could produce research proving the link between pornography and sexual violence. The activist groups did not have the resources to commission such research, so that was the end of the line with Smith's. Short pressed on with her campaign nevertheless.[11]

Short's organization was called Campaign against Pornography. It came in for criticism from other feminists who objected to its cooperation with Conservatives and its failure to consider where lesbian and gay pornography fitted in.[12] The name of a smaller competitor, the Campaign against Pornography and Censorship (CPC), signaled a refusal to see censorship as the answer to the problem of pornography. In practice, though, CPC found it difficult to do without the word "censorship." Catherine Itzin of CPC characterized pornography as a limitation on women's freedom, noted that society placed limits on the "freedom" to rape or incite racial hatred, and wound up saying: "So, in fact, we do want to censor pornography, but not with state intervention; we want the public to be able to do it." CPC proposed "civil rights legislation" that "would enable any woman . . . to sue a manufacturer or distributor of pornography on various grounds."[13] CPC was influenced by American feminist arguments about pornography as a form of violence in itself, and the civil remedy it proposed was based on MacKinnon and Dworkin's antipornography ordinance (which was overturned on First Amendment grounds).[14] English variations on MacKinnon and Dworkin's remedies made little headway, leaving a wide gap between the law, which addressed itself to the harms caused by voluntary or involuntary exposure to pornography, and a growing body of feminist thought exploring the harms pornography inflicted on women at large.[15] CPC folded in 1992; Itzin went to work for the Department of Health and exerted a profound influence on public policy concerning sexual violence.[16]

New media proved more amenable to restriction, as had been the case much earlier with cinema and broadcasting. Videocassettes, with their promise of privatizing the experience of watching pornographic movies, were the main problem—cable television was subject to the Obscene Publications Act, unlike BBC and ITV broadcasts. (In the small-world way of officialdom and censorship alike, the first director-general of the Cable Authority was Jon Davey, the secretary to the Williams Committee.)[17] Newspapers began agitating against "video nasties." This cute term referred sometimes to pornographic videos, sometimes to over-the-top horror movies like *Evil Dead*, and sometimes to an imagined hybrid of the two.[18] The campaign rapidly gained support, Whitehouse came on board, and the Conservatives included a pledge to deal with violent and obscene videos in their 1983 election manifesto. After the Thatcher government was re-elected, it again adopted the tactic of a private member's bill that the government would support. The Video Recordings Bill was sponsored by Graham Bright, one of a handful of Conservative candidates in marginal seats whom Whitehouse had stumped for.[19] Bright conferred with Whitehouse while drafting his bill, but when she saw the finished product she was not satisfied. Whitehouse wanted a ban on pornographic videos and Bright wanted a classification system. A ban would only drive the trade onto the black market, he insisted. The home secretary, Leon Brittan, also wanted a classification scheme, and Thatcher seems to have accepted that this was the only viable option.[20] The obvious solution was to enlist the BBFC rather than set up a new agency. This was unacceptable to Whitehouse, given the BBFC's record. She wanted a new classifying body with community representatives (which was what the Williams Committee had recommended in place of the BBFC).[21] The prime minister too was suspicious of the BBFC: in the Thatcherite imagination, cultural institutions from the BBC and the Church of England downwards were enemies within.[22] Brittan promised measures to improve the BBFC's accountability.[23] The BBFC, which changed its name to the British Board of Film Classification the same year, formally became an arm of the state for the first time in its history. James Ferman stayed in his job until 1999, weathering many more controversies along the way.[24]

One of those controversies concerned Martin Scorsese's *The Last Temptation of Christ* (1988). Scorsese's film, which features a dream sequence in which Jesus is tempted by the fantasy of an ordinary life married to Mary Magdalene, caused an uproar in Britain as elsewhere.[25] There was a rash of threatened and actual blasphemy cases involving artworks in the eighties. All of them involved sexually explicit representations of religious figures, as *Gay News* had. Sexualized challenges to religion in an increasingly secular public culture overtook "vacant and inexpressive" obscenity. The law of blasphemous libel had been the subject of intermittent deliberation in the decade since Whitehouse—and King-Hamilton—brought the offense back to life. The Law Commission recommended abolishing the common-law offense without replacing it, though two of the commissioners appended a note of dissent arguing that common-law blasphemy be replaced with a statutory offense covering insults to all religions.[26] The archbishop of Canterbury appointed a working party, which, like the dissenting law commissioners, recommended "a new offence which protects all religious believers."[27] As a matter of criminal law, it was the Home Office's responsibility, and the home secretary (Douglas Hurd by this point) decided the issue was not worth the time and effort.[28] A civil servant summed up the thinking: "This area is highly controversial and there is little prospect of obtaining a consensus. . . . there is no indication of any major gap in the law or that the present law, however imperfect, is causing serious practical problems."[29]

This was in March of 1988, only months before the storm over Salman Rushdie's novel *The Satanic Verses* broke. Demonstrations and book burnings took place in British cities with large Muslim populations. After Iran's

Ayatollah Khomeini issued a fatwa, Rushdie went into hiding with a security detail. The spectacle of Muslims protesting against blasphemy spurred some secularists to call for the abolition of the common-law offense and some MPs to introduce bills extending the law to religions other than Christianity.[30] The government resolved to block all these bills and rejected calls from Muslim groups to modify the law of blasphemy. Hurd gave a speech at Birmingham Central Mosque urging Muslims to integrate and explaining that integration involved respect for the rule of law and freedom of speech, even as he remained committed to maintaining a law that criminalized verbal and visual attacks on Christianity.[31] In a letter to Muslim community leaders, the Home Office minister John Patten said that extending blasphemy law to other religions would lead to conflict between people of different faiths. Muslims should be free to worship without interference, he said; the implicit quid pro quo was not imposing their values on others. "Modern Britain has plenty of room for diversity and variety. But . . . it is to the benefit of all, including the minorities themselves, that they should be part of the mainstream of British life."[32]

Even as Patten made this declaration a case about *The Satanic Verses* was pending. Abdul Choudhury, acting on behalf of a Muslim group formed to protest Rushdie's novel, attempted to bring a private prosecution for blasphemous libel.[33] The chief magistrate at Bow Street refused to issue summonses for the defendants, Rushdie and his publisher Viking Penguin. Choudhury then sought judicial review of the magistrate's decision so that the prosecution could go ahead. Choudhury's barrister, the Bangladeshi community leader Ali Mohammed Azhar, gathered together stray remarks from past cases, especially biblical references in judgments, to make the argument that blasphemous libel encompassed Islam and Judaism, but the three Queen's Bench Division judges had no doubt that these arguments were wrong. The only doubt was whether the law's protection extended beyond the Church of England and its doctrines to other Protestant denominations and Catholicism. The judges also dismissed Azhar's arguments based on the European Convention on Human Rights.[34] Choudhury applied to Strasbourg, but the European Commission of Human Rights declined to take up his case.

Another blasphemy case of the same time, though not one involving the crime of blasphemous libel, got further. At issue was another eroticization of the Crucifixion. Nigel Wingrove's short film *Visions of Ecstasy* included a pietà in which a naked Saint Teresa of Avila (nuns again) sits astride Christ's body and kisses his wounds. Wingrove wanted to release *Visions of Ecstasy* on videocassette and submitted it to the BBFC for classification. The board sought legal advice, which warned that a jury in a blasphemy trial about *Visions of Ecstasy* would likely convict. The board refused a certificate. An outright rejection was the only option as cutting that scene would have removed half the film.[35] Wingrove appealed to the Video Appeals Committee, which upheld the original decision.[36] Wingrove then took the case to Strasbourg, with Geoffrey Robertson as his counsel. They asked the European Commission of Human Rights to consider whether the common law of blasphemy was compatible with the European Convention on Human Rights.[37] As when Dennis Lemon applied to the European Commission of Human Rights, the government resolved to mount a vigorous defense of the UK's blasphemy laws in Strasbourg: if it did not, the attorney general warned, "we would effectively be conceding that the present blasphemy law could not be maintained," thus committing the government to reform.[38] The freedom of expression guaranteed in Article 10 of the European Convention is subject to restrictions "necessary in a democratic society." In assessing what counts as a necessary restriction on a right or freedom, the court applies a "margin of appreciation"—in effect, an allowance for the national legal traditions of the different countries that allow access to the European Court of Human Rights.[39] In Wingrove's case, which it finally heard in 1996, the court held that the British authorities acted within their margin of appreciation.[40]

However, the fact that the English law of blasphemy was compatible with the European Convention on Human Rights in 1996 did not mean it always would be. Rather, the Strasbourg court suggested in Wingrove's case, "there is as yet not sufficient common ground in the legal and social orders of the Member States of the Council of Europe to conclude that a system whereby a State can impose restrictions on the propagation of material on the basis that it is blasphemous is, in itself, unnecessary in a democratic society."[41] It was possible that the court's position on blasphemy would evolve as opinion in contracting states did. Indeed, participants in the 2006 House of Lords debate over a measure to include religion in Britain's laws against hate speech assumed that the common law of blasphemy was by this time incompatible with the rights and freedoms in the European Convention.[42] Strasbourg's coercive power is negligible: the European Convention on Human Rights works more through talk, as officeholders in the contracting states work to legitimate their systems and actions.[43] Blasphemous libel was finally abolished in 2008 after a backbench MP successfully moved an amendment to an omnibus bill. The trigger was another failed private prosecution followed by judicial review proceedings. A fundamentalist organization, Christian Voice, had objected to the BBC screening *Jerry Springer: The Opera*, in which biblical figures were depicted as guests fighting on a trashy talk show.[44]

By this time the rights and freedoms in the European Convention had been incorporated into domestic British law through the Human Rights Act 1998, one of the Blair government's constitutional reforms. These freedoms were hedged, in the Human Rights Act just as in the European Convention, by exceptions for national security, public safety, the protection of morals, and so on. As British petitioners to Strasbourg found over the years, those qualifications permitted extensive restrictions on civil liberties. Yet the Human Rights Act has meant that civil liberties considerations have been wired into the routines of statutory interpretation and legal reasoning.[45] (It has also made the culture of human rights a touchstone for those unhappy with a pluralist Britain, but that's another story.) Even when human rights are worked around, the normative basis of state action has shifted appreciably.

Another sea change of the nineties was, of course, the advent of the Internet. Even with slow dialup connections, the pornographic future was clearly visible. What was the point, James Ferman wondered in his valedictory report, "of cutting a gang-rape scene in a British version of a film if that film is accessible down a telephone line from outside British territorial waters?"[46] Ferman was alluding to the sixties pirate radio stations that broadcast from ships or abandoned fortifications just beyond the territorial limits of the BBC's monopoly: fittingly, piratical Internet entrepreneurs looked to repurpose some of those installations as microstates beyond the reach of government surveillance and intellectual property law.[47] Most of the steps taken by the state and Internet service providers since the late nineties to restrict access to online pornography have been intended to shield children. The number of prosecutions each year under the Obscene Publications Act, which now applies to online material, has dwindled to single digits.[48] The current Crown Prosecution Service guidelines are close to what the Williams Committee recommended. Authorities are advised not to prosecute under the Obscene Publications Act if the material does not involve "serious harm" to the participants and "is not otherwise inextricably linked with other criminality," if it is not directed primarily at under-eighteens, and if the activity photographed is fully and freely consensual.[49]

It is, in addition, an offense under the Criminal Justice and Immigration Act 2008 to possess "extreme pornographic images," that is, photographs showing actual or apparent rape, sexual interference with a human corpse, sex acts with animals, and sexual acts which result or are likely to result in serious injury.[50] This corresponds to the Williams Committee's unacceptable "outer margin" of images manifesting sexual violation. The ban on extreme pornography became law as a result of a campaign by the family of Jane Longhurst. Her murderer asphyxiated her; he had a history of viewing online pornography showing asphyxiation, rape, and necrophilia. In keeping with the law of unanticipated consequences that often applies in this area, the great majority of prosecutions under this section concern images of bestiality.[51]

The prohibition on extreme pornography involves possession of images, whereas the Obscene Publications Act, like common-law obscene libel before it, is concerned with publishers, wholesalers, and retailers. The statute most often used against child pornography also targets possession, though that was not the intention of its authors. The Protection of Children Act 1978 was a private member's bill that the beleaguered Callaghan Labour government chose not to resist. It was promoted by Whitehouse and the tabloids and inspired by similar legislation in the United States, though there was no evidence of an increase in the production of child pornography in Britain and police and the DPP were not asking for additional powers to deal with existing child pornography.[52] On its face, the Protection of Children Act applies only to producers of child pornography. However, in the early 2000s, courts ruled that downloading child pornography from a website or knowingly opening pornographic material sent as an email attachment amounted to "making" an image as defined by the act.[53] There were very few prosecutions until the courts refitted the act for the Internet age and its boom in child pornography. By the mid-2010s there were over three thousand prosecutions under the Protection of Children Act each year.[54] The Protection of Children Act has a simple "indecency" test, and courts do not have to consider the context of the images in question, so it does not have the complications the Obscene Publications Act has. As the legal scholar Jacob Rowbottom observes, this shift from the publisher or vendor, the traditional defendant in obscenity proceedings, to the viewer, helps account for the increase in convictions—there are more consumers than producers. The shift from the broad-based Obscene Publications Act to laws targeting a narrower range of material explains the apparent paradox that "the law has in some respects become more liberal, as content that was once illegal is now freely available, yet at the same has become much stricter and criminalising more people than ever."[55]

The legal position now is very different from what it was at the end of the twentieth century, but the conditions that have given rise to it bear a strong resemblance to those of earlier times. For all the difference the Law Commission and human rights have made, law reform still depends on government ministers. Home secretaries and others still have little to gain politically, and plenty to lose, from tidying up the law of obscenity. The legislative changes that have occurred have tended to be reactive, even precipitate. The ban on extreme pornography was the result of a highly charged campaign, as the horror comics act of the fifties and the child pornography legislation of the seventies were. The tipping point for abolishing blasphemous libel was a troublesome private prosecution, just as the provision curbing conspiracy to corrupt public morals was a response to Raymond Blackburn's efforts against *More about the Language of Love*. The ability of private citizens to initiate criminal proceedings and (since the early seventies) opportunities for judicial review of administrative action account for some of the peculiarities of English obscenity law. In both 2008 and 1977, the legislation was an omnibus criminal bill; on both occasions, it was a common-law crime that was extinguished.

The career of "conspiracy to corrupt public morals" in the sixties and seventies bears comparison with recent developments in another way too. The courts' recognition of conspiracy to corrupt public morals in the early sixties extended the reach of obscenity law, to the surprise of reformers who thought that the Obscene Publications Act of 1959 would supplant the common law; in the twenty-first century, the judicial decision that downloading an image amounts to making an image has transformed the Protection of Children Act from a symbolic gesture into the most important piece of obscenity law. Right from its beginning in *R v. Curll*, English obscenity law has owed much to judges' capacity to create what are in effect new offenses through extrapolation. In the nineteenth century, as A.W.B. Simpson remarked in a book on a subject far removed from obscenity and film censorship, "it was more or less a constitutional convention that criminal law was a matter for the judges, not for governments or parliament."[56] That remained the default position long into the twentieth century.

There was nothing like a constitutional convention concerning freedom of expression, even though the freedom of the press was part of the folklore of Britain as a free country.[57] In Britain, at least up to the 1960s, freedom of the press effectively meant freedom of political comment. The press was supposed to hold governments to account—more by critical commentary than by investigation. This rationale for freedom of the press also indicated its limits: the law offered little protection for utterances that were not directly linked to matters of public controversy. The apparent hypocrisy of judges and politicians holding forth on freedom of the press while remaining sanguine about the many restrictions on it makes more sense when we recognize that the political meeting and the leader column of a newspaper were the classic sites of freedom of speech in Britain.[58] Challenging or changing the law often meant redrawing the line between "opinion" or "comment" and abuse. The Society of Labour Lawyers used a similar metaphor as they pressed their case for criminalizing racist propaganda: only publications that went "beyond the borders of comment" would be affected.[59] Once the new law was on the books, white supremacist groups set about learning how to recalibrate their rhetoric so as to bring it back over the line into "normal political debate."[60]

The Society of Authors' campaign in the fifties for a new Obscene Publications Act adjusted the categories of protected and unprotected speech in a different way. The 1959 act established literature as a privileged form of expression analogous to political comment. It wasn't a recognition of a modernist conception of art as autonomous and autotelic, as a body of scholarship influenced by Pierre Bourdieu has suggested.[61] The argument for "literary freedom" even had the same structure as the case for open political debate: as the vigorous exchange of opinions sharpened policy, so did artistic freedom allow novelists to explore the human condition. Approaching literature in this way made the literary merit branch of the public-good defense closer to the 1959 act's safeguards for "other objects of general concern" than even Gerald Gardiner realized when he advised the Herbert Committee. The clergymen he examined as witnesses in the *Lady Chatterley's Lover* trial the following year treated Lawrence as a moral thinker and the novel as documentation of his thought. So did literary critics who could have said much more about the formal qualities of the novel. The novelist spoke to contemporary social issues, and social workers took the stand to comment on the novel. As fiction with an overt ethical vision—and a third-person narrator to articulate it—*Lady Chatterley's Lover* could be treated as a kind of manifesto, an artistic contribution to public debate on objects of general concern. At the time of the *Last Exit to Brooklyn* trial, Ian Hamilton observed that the law obliged defendants "to plead . . . that their books really belonged to, and had a useful role to play within, the court's scheme of morality." Defense lawyers also had to bring the offending books within the courts' scheme of *literature*—judges' and

juries' assumptions about what good books were and did. In their conformity to the courts' literary scheme as much as to their moral scheme, the
style of defense pioneered by Gardiner and extended by John Mortimer
and Geoffrey Robertson was, in Hamilton's word, "utilitarian."[62]

Recognizing literature as a category that warranted protection meant
accepting the censorship of pulp fiction or pinup magazines. For some on
the Herbert Committee, and the later Arts Council working party, "literary
freedom" really was what mattered; for others, it was more of a pragmatic
compromise in a society where freedom of expression could not be universal. Michael Rubinstein carefully followed Mr. Justice Stable's description
of literature as writing with a message as he prepared Penguin's defense
of *Lady Chatterley's Lover*, but at the Freedom of Vision teach-in six years
later Rubinstein spoke unabashedly of grown-ups deciding for themselves.
Freedom was not just a privilege of adulthood, it was a condition of maturity.[63] Rubinstein joined the Defence of Literature and the Arts Society,
which welcomed the pornographers into the free-speech tent, and there
he was in 1977 advising *Libertine*'s Arabella Melville about her options
for resisting the monopoly power of the porn barons. Over the sixties and
seventies, other established critics of censorship began to defend a more
encompassing conception of free speech, one in which freedom of expression was valuable in itself, not only as a means of protecting art or foster-
ing enlightenment. When Bernard Williams assessed the arguments of
anticensorship advocates, he explicitly rejected "utilitarian" justifications
of freedom of expression.[64]

The sexual revolution and contemporaneous changes in manners and
ideas about the good life were far from universally accepted, but they could
be tolerated on the basis that people should be free to live their own lives
as long as their conduct did not impinge upon others. Mill's harm principle, put into popular circulation again by the debate on the Wolfenden
Report, and Wolfenden's own declaration that what consenting adults did
in private was not the law's business, recurred in the letters people sent to
the Williams Committee. These liberal precepts corresponded with popular conventions about privacy and autonomy, conventions suggested by
vernacular phrases such as "in the privacy of their own homes," "behind
closed doors," "keep ourselves to ourselves," and "like grown-ups." If the
Williams Report appeared to Mary Whitehouse to be another liberal document whose ostentatious rationality belied its estrangement from what
real people thought, the Williams Committee's archive reveals a vernacular liberalism that was resistant to Whitehouse's claims to represent public
opinion.[65]

The decline of deference and conformity was a decline in forms of authority independent of the market. The unwritten rules of variable obscenity that associated responsible reading with the franchise in the nineteenth century entailed judgments about the mass market in print as well as about working-class readers. In 1857 Lord Campbell intervened to regulate "periodical papers . . . sold to any person who asked for them, and in any numbers"; Lord Chief Justice Cockburn noted that the pamphlet in the *Hicklin* case was "sold at the corners of streets, and in all directions." The mass market was a form of sociability corresponding to an emerging democracy. Early and mid-twentieth-century critics perceived a nexus between democracy and mass-market commodities or art forms, such as cigarettes and movies.[66] It was the mass market, not commerce as such, that was at issue. The small presses that printed D. H. Lawrence and James Hanley on hand-made paper were producing exquisite consumer goods, and even Sir Archibald Bodkin accepted that limited editions were in a different class from books distributed "through the trade in the ordinary course of business." A Customs official in 1957 wrote that even "the most aggravated indecency" could be allowed into the country if it was destined to be "carefully kept from the common eye." "Such works are not merchandise," he wrote, "but the prizes of the private collector."[67] It was the social judgments, not the attendant economic judgments, that attracted anger and derision. The social judgments were discredited from the left in the *Lady Chatterley's Lover* trial; the increasing power of market values, especially after Thatcher's election triumph, left less space for those on the right to critique a form of immorality that was highly commercial.

It is some time now since obscenity law was a magnet for wide-ranging discussions about society and culture.[68] None of the Article 10 cases from the United Kingdom to reach the European Court of Human Rights since the nineties has involved obscenity or blasphemy.[69] Over the past two decades the freedom of expression issues engaged by pornography have not seemed as pressing or, perhaps, as complex, as surveillance and counterterrorism measures, media ownership, net neutrality, social media companies' content-moderation practices, the conduct of other tech giants, corporate and government use of personal information, freedom of information, hackers wanting to set classified information free, lack of protection for investigative journalists and their sources (or insufficient constraints on intrusive journalists, depending on the context), restrictions on political protest, no-platforming in universities, and "fake news." Questions of sexuality and gender remain the law's business, but not so much the criminal law's business. The social mission of public morals measures has contracted as deference and conformity have declined and as rights and freedoms have been recognized more formally. Censorship is always significant, but it no longer signifies as much as it did between Lord Campbell's Act and the Williams Report, when England's conjuncture of literacy and inequality persistently turned censorship questions into citizenship questions.

ACKNOWLEDGMENTS

BETWEEN THEM the Australian Research Council and the University of Sydney made this book possible. A Queen Elizabeth II Fellowship and a Discovery Projects grant from the ARC provided funding for research trips and time to write. The University of Sydney has supported me with paid sabbaticals and by employing colleagues like Nick Eckstein, Sheila Fitzpatrick, Mark McKenna, Penny Russell, Shane White, and Andrew Fitzmaurice (who has since moved to Queen Mary University of London). I owe special debts to Shane and Andrew. Shane has read practically everything I've written since he hired me sixteen years ago. It's hard to accept that he'll be retired by the time this appears in print. As I started this book, Andrew was working on one of his own that also spanned law, culture, and politics. He became interested in the sort of "low" intellectual history I had done, and I learned from his creative revision of the history of political thought. I brought Andrew down to my level and he lifted me up to his.

Adrienne Stone and Duncan Ivison brought their immense learning and perceptiveness to bear on the chapter on the Williams Committee and the conclusion at a workshop under the auspices of the Sydney Social Sciences and Humanities Advanced Research Centre. I really appreciate Adrienne's generosity to a stranger in a different discipline and wish I'd been able to host her at SSSHARC rather than running the workshop over Zoom. Duncan also supported this research in its early stages when he was my head of school. Leigh Ann Wheeler showed me how important consumer rights were to British arguments against (and for) censorship. Sean Pryor read chapter two and helped me understand the publishing history of modernism better. Alana Harris and Lawrence Black each read several chapters and taught me new things about the post-1945 period. Warwick Anderson, Barbara Caine, Marco Duranti, John Gagné, Julia Horne, Matt Houlbrook, Miranda Johnson, Lara Kriegel, Kirsten McKenzie, Peter Mandler, Dirk Moses, Guy Ortolano, Susan Pedersen, Stephen Robertson, Emily Rutherford, Robert Schneider, Glenda Sluga, Philip Waller, and James Vernon read and markedly improved earlier versions of different parts of the book. My interpretation of what I've called "neighborly liberalism" owes a lot to conversations with Jon Lawrence and Deborah Cohen as well as their published work. Stefan Collini and Natasha Wheatley helped me think about the scope of the book and what key parts of it needed to do. Emma Wallhead generously shared her knowledge of the women's liberation movement. Robert Aldrich, Emma Barron, Alison Bashford, Nick Enfield, Tobias Harper, Iain McCalman, Peter McDonald, Ross McKibbin, Nicole Moore, Robert Scoble, Marc Stears, and Alan Travis answered queries and gave valuable advice. Peter Allender did research for me in the Penguin archive at the University of Bristol, Emma Grant and Jennie Taylor retrieved documents from repositories in London, and Laura Merrell found and copied documents in the Lilly Library at Indiana University. The peerless Rhiannon Davis provided research assistance, proofread, and did the index.

Ben Tate has been a sympathetic and astute editor. Pamela Marquez copyedited the manuscript with precision and grace. The two anonymous readers helped me tighten up the book in some places and broaden it out in others. Thanks too to Kathleen Cioffi, Josh Drake, Brigitta van Rheinberg, and everyone else at Princeton University Press who has worked on the book out of my line of sight. It has been a privilege to be a Princeton author.

Quotations from *Lady Chatterley's Lover* by D. H. Lawrence are reproduced by permission of Paper Lion Ltd, The Estate of Frieda Lawrence Ravagli and Cambridge University Press. © Cambridge University Press 1993. I am grateful to Katy Loffman of Paper Lion for arranging permission to quote from the novel.

I am grateful, too, to all the archive and library staff who have helped with the research. This is the first book of mine that was substantially researched in the National Archives at Kew. The place doesn't lend itself to sentimentality, but it has been the hub of multiple research trips that were also family trips. Those London summers were special times with my beloved Sarah, Rose, and Tessa, and I thank them for all our travels together.

ABBREVIATIONS

BL	British Library
BODLEIAN	Bodleian Library, Oxford
BRISTOL	University of Bristol Library
COFC	Committee on Obscenity and Film Censorship (the Williams Committee)
CUL	Cambridge University Library
DLAS	Defence of Literature and the Arts Society
HC Deb.	*House of Commons Debates*
HL Deb.	*House of Lords Debates*
HRC	Harry Ransom Humanities Research Center, University of Texas at Austin
INDIANA	Lilly Library, Indiana University
LMA	London Metropolitan Archives
LSE	London School of Economics
ODNB	*Oxford Dictionary of National Biography*
OED	*Oxford English Dictionary*
READING	University of Reading Library
TNA	The National Archives, Kew
ULL	University of London Library, Senate House
V&A	Victoria and Albert Museum

Introduction

1. H. Montgomery Hyde, ed., *The Lady Chatterley's Lover Trial (Regina v. Penguin Books Limited)* (London: The Bodley Head, 1990), 17, 62; C. H. Rolph, ed., *The Trial of Lady Chatterley: Regina v. Penguin Books Limited: The Transcript of the Trial* (Harmondsworth: Penguin, 1961), 17. For examples of Griffith-Jones at his most fearsome, see Ludovic Kennedy, *The Trial of Stephen Ward* (London: Victor Gollancz, 1964), 24, 168–69, 181, 209.

2. Selina Todd, "Domestic Service and Class Relations in Britain 1900–1950," *Past and Present*, no. 203 (2009): 181–204, 188; TNA, DPP 2/3077, part 1, "Thursday 20 October 1960 at 10.30 a.m. in Court 1."

3. Applications for press and visitor passes for the trial are preserved in TNA, CRIM 8/29.

4. Sybille Bedford, "The Trial of Lady Chatterley's Lover," in Bedford, *As It Was: Pleasures, Landscapes, and Justice* (London: Sinclair-Stevenson, 1990), 127–170, here 133. On the Scopes trial, see Edward J. Larson, *Summer for the Gods: The Scopes Trial and America's Continuing Debate over Science and Religion* (New York: Basic Books, 1997).

5. Hyde, *Lady Chatterley's Lover Trial*, 57, 285–286.

6. Robin Denniston to Martin Jarrett-Kerr, September 9, 1960, quoted in Mark Roodhouse, "Lady Chatterley and the Monk: Anglican Radicals and the Lady Chatterley Trial of 1960," *Journal of Ecclesiastical History* 59, no. 3 (2008): 475–500, 486.

7. Ian Hunter, David Saunders, and Dugald Williamson, *On Pornography: Literature, Sexuality and Obscenity Law* (Basingstoke: Macmillan, 1993), 10, 73.

8. Walter Montagu Gattie, "What English People Read," *Fortnightly Review*, n.s., 46 (September 1889): 320–21.

9. Hyde, *Lady Chatterley's Lover Trial*, 268. The guinea—a pound plus a shilling, or twenty-one shillings—was used for denominating professionals' fees and the cost of artworks and some luxury goods. It was a notional unit of currency: after the early nineteenth century there were no guinea coins or bills. Here is how Thomas Hardy describes the transaction in which a sailor "buys" Michael Henchard's wife for five guineas in *The Mayor of Casterbridge*: "The sailor hesitated a moment, looked anew at the woman, came in, unfolded five crisp pieces of paper, and threw them down upon the table-cloth. They were Bank-of-England notes for five pounds. Upon the face of this he clinked down the shillings severally—one, two, three, four, five."

10. There is a body of scholarship that explains this bargain in terms of an overlap between modernist ideas about the autonomy of art and Pierre Bourdieu's concept of the literary field. For ways in, see Loren Glass, "The Ends of Obscenity," *American Literary History* 21, no. 4 (2009): 869–76. *Pace* Anton Kirchofer, I am not persuaded that this approach works for the British case, because of the literary traditionalism of the principal advocates for reform in the 1950s and, more fundamentally, because the

place of the market in British thinking about art and culture does not fit with Bourdieu's schema. Kirchofer, "The Making of the 1959 Obscene Publications Act: Trials and Debates on Literary Obscenity in Britain before the Case of Lady Chatterley," in *Literary Trials: Exceptio Artis and Theories of Literature in Court*, ed. Ralf Grüttemeier (New York: Bloomsbury Academic, 2016), 49–68. Compare Christopher Hilliard, *To Exercise Our Talents: The Democratization of Writing in Britain* (Cambridge, MA: Harvard University Press, 2006), 287–90; Hilliard, *English as a Vocation: The "Scrutiny" Movement* (Oxford: Oxford University Press, 2012), chaps. 1–2; and, more obliquely, Stefan Collini, *The Nostalgic Imagination: History in English Criticism* (Oxford: Oxford University Press, 2019).

11. Deborah Cohen, *Family Secrets: Living with Shame from the Victorians to the Present Day* (London: Viking, 2013); Jon Lawrence, *Me, Me, Me? The Search for Community in Post-war England* (Oxford: Oxford University Press, 2019).

12. *Report of the Committee on Obscenity and Film Censorship*, Cmnd. 7772 (London: HMSO, 1972), paragraphs 5.9–5.10.

13. TNA, HO 265/2, British Adult Publications Association Limited, submission to COFC, June, 1978; HO 265/8, Scottish Homosexual Rights Group, submission to COFC, n.d. [1977 or 1978].

14. On punk ideas of "self-rule," see Matthew Worley, *No Future: Punk, Politics and British Youth Culture, 1976–1984* (Cambridge: Cambridge University Press, 2017), 174–75.

15. For a long time libel was a crime as well as a tort. Only in the nineteenth century did civil suits for damages surpass criminal prosecutions for libel, and the latter remained available for the worst attacks on a person's honor, which often meant an allegation of homosexuality. J. R. Spencer, "Criminal Libel—A Skeleton in the Cupboard," *Criminal Law Review* (1977): 383–94, 464–474; Christopher Hilliard, *The Littlehampton Libels: A Miscarriage of Justice and a Mystery about Words in 1920s England* (Oxford: Oxford University Press, 2017), 49–52.

16. Lord Diplock in Whitehouse v. Lemon [1979] AC 617, 633–34; Rex v. Keach (1665) 6 St Tr 701; R v. Taylor (1676) 1 Ventris 293. Though see Elliott Visconsi, "The Invention of Criminal Blasphemy: Rex v. Taylor (1676)," *Representations*, no. 103 (Summer 2008): 30–52.

17. Lynn Hunt, ed., *The Invention of Pornography: Obscenity and the Origins of Modernity, 1500–1800* (New York, 1993); Lynn Hunt, *The Family Romance of the French Revolution* (Berkeley and Los Angeles: University of California Press, 1992), chap. 4; Iain McCalman, *Radical Underworld: Prophets, Revolutionaries, and Pornographers in London, 1795–1840* (Cambridge: Cambridge University Press, 1988).

18. *The Humble Representation of Edmund Curll, Bookseller and Citizen of London, Concerning Five Books, Complained of to the Secretary of State* (n.p., [1725]), 7. See also David Saunders, "Copyright, Obscenity and Literary History," *ELH* 57, no. 2 (1990): 431–44, 436–37. *Venus in the Cloister* is reprinted in its entirety in Bradford K. Mudge, ed., *When Flesh Becomes Word: An Anthology of Early Eighteenth-Century Libertine Literature* (New York: Oxford University Press, 2004), 145–232.

19. Dominus Rex v. Curl [*sic*] (1727) 2 Strange 788 at 789, 790–91.

20. Colin Manchester, "A History of the Crime of Obscene Libel," *Journal of Legal History* 12, no. 1 (1991): 36–57, 40; A. A. Hanham, "Page, Sir Francis (1660/61?–1741),"

ODNB; Edward Foss, *The Judges of England: With Sketches of Their Lives, and Miscellaneous Notices Connected with the Courts at Westminster, from the Conquest to the Present Time*, vol. 8 (London: John Murray, 1864), 143–146.

21. *R v. Curl*, 792.

22. *R v. Curl*, 792.

23. William Blackstone, *Commentaries on the Laws of England*, 9th ed., 4 vols. (1783; repr., New York: Garland, 1978), 4:151–52 (italics in original). For subsequent criticisms of these assumptions, see Gregory Conti, "What's Not in *On Liberty*: The Pacific Theory of Freedom of Discussion in the Early Nineteenth Century," *Journal of British Studies* 55, no. 1 (2016): 57–75, 61–62.

24. David M. Rabban, *Free Speech in Its Forgotten Years* (Cambridge: Cambridge University Press, 1997), esp. 2, 14, 15, and chap. 3; Patterson v. Colorado, 205 U.S. 454, at 462 (1907); Leigh Ann Wheeler, *Against Obscenity: Reform and the Politics of Womanhood in America, 1873–1935* (Baltimore: Johns Hopkins University Press, 2004), 55–56.

25. William Pember Reeves, *State Experiments in Australia and New Zealand*, 2 vols. (London: Grant Richards, 1902); Stuart Macintyre, *A Colonial Liberalism: The Lost World of Three Victorian Visionaries* (Melbourne: Oxford University Press Australia, 1991); Nicole Moore, *The Censor's Library* (St Lucia, Queensland: University of Queensland Press, 2012); Paul Christoffel, *Censored: A Short History of Censorship in New Zealand* (Wellington: Department of Internal Affairs, 1989). The Irish Free State set up a censorship agency as part of its project of Catholicizing cultural independence. Senia Pašeta, "Censorship and its Critics in the Irish Free State, 1922–1932," *Past and Present*, no. 181 (2003): 193–218; Michael Adams, *Censorship: The Irish Experience* (Dublin: Scepter Books, 1968), chaps. 1–3.

26. Steve Nicholson, *The Censorship of British Drama, 1900–1968*, 4 vols. (Exeter: University of Exeter Press, 2003–15); David Thomas, David Carlton, and Anne Etienne, *Theatre Censorship: From Walpole to Wilson* (Oxford: Oxford University Press, 2007); Neville March Hunnings, *Film Censors and the Law* (London: George Allen and Unwin, 1967); Guy Phelps, *Film Censorship* (London: Victor Gollancz, 1975); James C. Robertson, *The Hidden Cinema: British Film Censorship in Action, 1913–1975* (London: Routledge, 1993).

27. John Trevelyan, *What the Censor Saw* (London: Michael Joseph, 1973), 207–11.

28. Robert Darnton, *Censors at Work: How States Shaped Literature* (New York: W. W. Norton, 2014), part 3; Peter D. McDonald, *The Literature Police: Apartheid Censorship and Its Cultural Consequences* (Oxford: Oxford University Press, 2009).

29. Christopher Hilliard, "Modernism and the Common Writer," *Historical Journal* 48, no. 3 (2005): 769–787, 770–72, 783–84. See also Stefan Collini, *Absent Minds: Intellectuals in Britain* (Oxford: Oxford University Press, 2006), chap. 5; and compare Jonathan Wild, "'A Strongly Felt Need': Wilfred Whitten/John O'London and the Rise of the New Reading Public," in *Middlebrow Literary Cultures: The Battle of the Brows, 1920–1960*, ed. Erica Brown and Mary Grover (Basingstoke: Palgrave Macmillan, 2012), 98–111.

30. See the list of rueful comments on the job by successive home secretaries in Paul Rock, *The Official History of Criminal Justice in England and Wales*, vol. 1, *The "Liberal Hour"* (London: Routledge, 2019), 35.

31. Lawrence Black, *Redefining British Politics: Culture, Consumerism and Participation, 1954–70* (Basingstoke: Palgrave Macmillan, 2010), chap. 5.

32. Deana Heath and Lisa Z. Sigel make the point that stringing together all the showy censorship trials is not enough: the "unspectacular" routines of law enforcement must be examined too. Deana Heath, "Obscenity, Censorship, and Modernity," in *A Companion to the History of the Book*, ed. Simon Eliot and Jonathan Rose (Malden, MA: Blackwell, 2007), 508–19, 509; Lisa Z. Sigel, "Censorship in Inter-War Britain: Obscenity, Spectacle, and the Workings of the Liberal State," *Journal of Social History* 45, no. 1 (2011): 61–83, 62. Heath and Sigel are not attacking a straw man: for a recent study that focuses solely on the big trials (and has no archival research), see Elisabeth Ladenson, *Dirt for Art's Sake: Books on Trial from "Madame Bovary" to "Lolita"* (Ithaca: Cornell University Press, 2007). That said, the big cases do matter, and there is still a lot we don't know about them.

33. See Peter Mandler, "The Problem with Cultural History," *Cultural and Social History* 1 (2004): 94–117, 115.

34. For the nineteenth century, see especially Lisa Z. Sigel, *Governing Pleasures: Pornography and Social Change in England, 1815–1914* (New Brunswick, NJ: Rutgers University Press, 2002). And, for the twentieth, Alan Travis, *Bound and Gagged: A Secret History of Obscenity in Britain* (London: Profile Books, 2000). Both as a historian and as the *Guardian*'s home affairs editor, Travis secured the early declassification of many sensitive files from the 1970s and 1980s that are discussed in the later chapters of this book. The following older works are still very useful: Alec Craig, *The Banned Books of England* (London: George Allen and Unwin, 1937); Craig, *Above All Liberties* (London: George Allen and Unwin, 1942); Craig, *Suppressed Books: A History of the Conception of Literary Obscenity* (1962; repr., Cleveland: World Publishing, 1963); H. Montgomery Hyde, *A History of Pornography* (London: Heinemann, 1964).

35. Sedition and hate speech are discussed in chapters 5 and 6 and blasphemy in chapter 7 and the Conclusion.

36. David Vincent, *The Culture of Secrecy: Britain, 1832–1998* (Oxford: Clarendon Press, 1999); K. D. Ewing and C. A. Gearty, *The Struggle for Civil Liberties: Political Freedom and the Rule of Law in Britain, 1914–1945* (Oxford: Oxford University Press, 2000); Martin Cloonan, *Banned! Censorship of Popular Music in Britain, 1967–92* (Aldershot: Arena, 1996).

37. Ewing and Gearty, *Struggle for Civil Liberties*, 65–69; Deian Hopkin, "Domestic Censorship in the First World War," *Journal of Contemporary History* 5, no. 4 (1970): 151–69; Ian McLaine, *Ministry of Morale: Home Front Morale and the Ministry of Information in World War II* (London: George Allen and Unwin, 1979).

38. The Obscene Publications Acts of 1857 and 1959 did not extend to Scotland or Northern Ireland. The Scottish legal system is substantially different from that of England and Wales (and Ireland before 1922 and Northern Ireland thereafter). In Scotland, prosecutors still had to secure a conviction before they could get an obscene publication destroyed. Private prosecutions were very rare in Scotland, whereas they were quite common in England. A number of important obscenity and blasphemy trials in England originated in private prosecutions. In Scotland public prosecutions were overseen by the Lord Advocate; the DPP was responsible only for England and

Wales. Similarly, it was the Scottish Office, not the Home Office, that was responsible for policy on the criminal law in Scotland. However, despite these legal and administrative differences, the consolidation of the publishing industry in London by the early twentieth century—Edinburgh no longer being the publishing center it once was—meant that decisions about whether a book was likely to be legally safe or not were made in London, according to advice about English law. There is scarcely any reference to Wales in this book. London's dominance of publishing and distribution meant that notable cases were most likely to arise there, and no Welsh police force appears to have gone its own way to the extent that it attracted national attention, as the Greater Manchester Police did in the 1970s.

39. The quotation comes from the back cover of C. H. Rolph, *Trial of Lady Chatterley.*

Chapter One. Obscenity, Literacy, and the Franchise, 1857–1918

1. David Vincent, *Literacy and Popular Culture: England, 1750–1914* (Cambridge: Cambridge University Press, 1989), 3–4; Raymond Williams, *The Long Revolution* (London: Chatto and Windus, 1961), 166; Richard D. Altick, *The English Common Reader: A Social History of the Mass Reading Public, 1800–1900* (1957; repr., Columbus: Ohio State University Press, 1998), 171–72.

2. Andrew Lees, *Cities Perceived: Urban Society in European and American Thought, 1820–1940* (Manchester: Manchester University Press, 1985), chap. 2; V.A.C. Gattrell, "The Decline of Theft and Violence in Victorian and Edwardian England," in *Crime and the Law: The Social History of Crime in Western Europe since 1500*, ed. V.A.C. Gattrell, Bruce Lenman, and Geoffrey Parker (London: Europa Publications, 1980), 238–337, here 272–73.

3. Wilkie Collins, "The Unknown Public," *Household Words*, no. 439 (21 August 1858): 217–24.

4. Christopher Hilliard, "Popular Reading and Social Investigation in Britain, 1850s–1940s," *Historical Journal* 57, no. 1 (2014): 247–71, 248–60; Mark Hampton, *Visions of the Press in Britain, 1850–1950* (Urbana: University of Illinois Press, 2004), chaps. 2–3.

5. Colin Manchester, "Lord Campbell's Act: England's First Obscenity Statute," *Journal of Legal History* 9, no. 2 (1988): 223–41, 224.

6. John Pollock, *Wilberforce* (London: Constable, 1977), 59–66; also 163–65, on the prosecution for seditious and blasphemous libel of the printer of a cheap edition of Thomas Paine's *The Age of Reason* in 1797/1798.

7. See M.J.D. Roberts, "The Society for the Suppression of Vice and Its Early Critics, 1802–1812," *Historical Journal* 26, no. 1 (1983): 159–76, *contra* Michael Mason, *The Making of Victorian Sexual Attitudes* (Oxford: Oxford University Press, 1994), 69–72.

8. Roberts, "Society for the Suppression of Vice," esp. 174.

9. Manchester, "Lord Campbell's Act," 225.

10. *Report from Select Committee on Metropolis Police Offices; with the Minutes of Evidence, Appendix, and Index: Parliament Session: 1837–38*, House of Lords

Papers, vol. 29, paper no. 373, p. 135. See also Henry Prichard, letter to Lord Campbell, quoted in *HL Deb.*, vol. 146 (July 13, 1857), col. 1356: "The truth is, that the trade is so lucrative that the dealers can well afford the risk of an occasional imprisonment. While their stocks are safe, their families can carry on their trade till their term of imprisonment expires, when they return to their old practices with increased experience of the modes by which the operation of the law may be eluded."

11. *Report from Select Committee on Metropolis Police Offices*, 134; William Cornish, J. Stuart Anderson, Ray Cocks, Michael Lobban, Patrick Polden, and Keith Smith, *The Oxford History of the Laws of England*, vol. 13, *1820–1914: Fields of Development* (Oxford: Oxford University Press, 2010), 365.

12. Gareth H. Jones and Vivienne Jones, "Campbell, John, first Baron Campbell of St Andrews," *ODNB*.

13. Bristow, *Vice and Vigilance*, 46.

14. Iain McCalman, "Unrespectable Radicalism: Infidels and Pornography in Early Nineteenth-Century London," *Past and Present*, no. 104 (August 1984): 74–110, 76–77.

15. Patricia Hollis, *The Pauper Press: A Study in Working-Class Radicalism of the 1830s* (Oxford: Oxford University Press, 1970), 127, 128, 200–201, 314.

16. McCalman, "Unrespectable Radicalism," 76.

17. Manchester, "Lord Campbell's Act," 226–27; Natalie Pryor, "The 1857 Obscene Publications Act: Debate, Definition and Dissemination, 1857–1868" (MPhil thesis, University of Southampton, 2014), 34.

18. David Vincent, *I Hope I Don't Intrude: Privacy and Its Dilemmas in Nineteenth-Century Britain* (Oxford: Oxford University Press, 2015), chap. 7, esp. p. 181.

19. Manchester, "Lord Campbell's Act," 226; Lynda Nead, *Victorian Babylon: People, Streets and Images in Nineteenth-Century London* (New Haven: Yale University Press, 2000), 189–91.

20. Nead, *Victorian Babylon*, 199; Iain McCalman, *Radical Underworld: Prophets, Revolutionaries, and Pornographers in London, 1795–1840* (Cambridge: Cambridge University Press, 1988), 221.

21. *HL Deb.*, vol. 145, 11 May 1857, cols. 102–3.

22. M.J.D. Roberts, "Morals, Art and the Law: The Passing of the Obscene Publications Act, 1857," *Victorian Studies* 28, no. 4 (1985): 609–29, 610–11, 618, 621–22.

23. Obscene Publications Act, 1857, 20 & 21 Vict., c. 83, s. 1.

24. Manchester, "Lord Campbell's Act," 227; Edward J. Bristow, *Vice and Vigilance: Purity Movements in Britain since 1700* (Dublin: Gill and Macmillan, 1977), 47; Betting Act, 1853, 16 & 17 Vict, c. 119, s. 11. See also Mark Clapson, *A Bit of a Flutter: Popular Gambling and English Society, c. 1823–1961* (Manchester: Manchester University Press, 1992), 23–24.

25. Bristow, *Vice and Vigilance*, 46–47.

26. A.W.B. Simpson, *Cannibalism and the Common Law: The Story of the Tragic Last Voyage of the Mignonette and the Strange Legal Proceedings to Which It Gave Rise* (Chicago: University of Chicago Press, 1984), 244.

27. Lindsay Farmer, "Reconstructing the English Codification Debate: The Criminal Law Commissioners, 1833–45," *Law and History Review* 18, no. 2 (2000): 397–426, with comments by Michael Lobban and Markus Dirk Dubber and a rejoinder by Farmer (427–44); Elizabeth Kolsky, "Codification and the Rule of Colonial

Difference: Criminal Procedure in British India," *Law and History Review* 23, no. 3 (2005): 631–83.

28. Cornish et al., *Fields of Development*, 367.

29. *The Confessional Unmasked: Showing the Depravity of the Romish Priesthood, the Iniquity of the Confessional and the Questions Put to Females in Confession*, 55th ed. (London: Protestant Electoral Union [1867]), 59.

30. McCalman, *Radical Underworld*, 221.

31. R v. Hicklin, 3 Queen's Bench (1867–68): 360 at 362.

32. G.I.T. Machin, "The Maynooth Grant, the Dissenters and Disestablishment, 1845–1847," *English Historical Review* 82, no. 322 (January 1967): 61–85.

33. Dominic Janes, "The Confessional Unmasked: Religious Merchandise and Obscenity in Victorian England," *Victorian Literature and Culture*, 41 (2013): 677–90, 679.

34. Roger Swift, "Anti-Catholicism and Irish Disturbances: Public Order in Mid-Victorian Wolverhampton," *Midland History* 9, no. 1 (1984): 87–108, 89; Jon Lawrence, "Popular Politics and the Limitations of Party: Wolverhampton, 1867–1900," in *Currents of Radicalism: Popular Radicalism, Organised Labour and Party Politics in Britain, 1850–1914*, ed. Eugenio F. Biagini and Alastair J. Reid (Cambridge: Cambridge University Press, 1991), 65–85, 70.

35. Swift, "Anti-Catholicism and Irish Disturbances," 94–98; Walter L. Arnstein, "The Murphy Riots: A Victorian Dilemma," *Victorian Studies* 19, no. 1 (1975): 51–71, 55.

36. Swift, "Anti-Catholicism and Irish Disturbances," 98.

37. *R v. Hicklin*, 360 at 362–63.

38. Obscene Publications Act, 1857, c. 83, s. 1.

39. John Stuart Mill, *On Liberty* (1859), in Mill, *Three Essays*, ed. Richard Wollheim (Oxford: Oxford University Press, 1975), chap. 2.

40. Gregory Conti, "What's Not in *On Liberty*: The Pacific Theory of Freedom of Discussion in the Early Nineteenth Century," *Journal of British Studies* 55, no. 1 (2016): 57–75.

41. The case was heard by the Court of Queen's Bench "in banc," with three judges, including the chief. In the mid-nineteenth century, before the modern appellate structure was in place, the Court of Queen's Bench sitting in banc would usually provide a definitive ruling on a point of law—in this case, whether a worthwhile purpose excused an obscene publication, or what the mens rea of "obscene libel" was—which the recorder had in effect asked for. This undermines Katherine Mullin's argument that the judges "probably intended to use obscenity legislation as a convenient tool to manage an acute and extraordinary instance of the effects of unregulated reading," that is, the Murphy riots, without consideration of the longer-term implications (495). Mullin does not discuss the exchanges between the judges and counsel, which bring out the importance of the questions of principle. Katherine Mullin, "Unmasking *The Confessional Unmasked*: The 1868 Hicklin Test and the Toleration of Obscenity," *ELH* 85, no. 2 (2018): 471–99, quotation from 495. Compare Peter D. McDonald, "Old Phrases and Great Obscenities: The Strange Afterlife of Two Victorian Anxieties," *Journal of Victorian Culture* 13, no. 2 (2007): 294–302, 295–99.

42. The full name of the case was *The Queen, on the Prosecution of Henry Scott, Appellant, v. Benjamin Hicklin and Another, Justices of Wolverhampton, Respondents.*

43. Stephen K. Roberts, *Radical Politicians and Poets in Early Victorian Britain: The Voices of Six Chartist Leaders* (Lewiston, NY: Edwin Mellen Press, 1993), chap. 6; Laurel Brake and Marysa Demoor, eds., *Dictionary of Nineteenth-century Journalism in Great Britain and Ireland* (Ghent and London: Academia Press and the British Library, 2009), 336; Joseph Foster, *Men-at-the-Bar: A Biographical Hand-List of the Members of the Various Inns of Court, Including Her Majesty's Judges, etc.*, 2nd ed. (London: The Author, 1885), 262. On Oastler see E. P. Thompson, *The Making of the English Working Class* (1963; repr., London: Penguin, 1980), 366–84.

44. *R v. Hicklin*, 360 at 363.

45. *R v. Hicklin*, 360 at 365, 366, 367.

46. C.E.A. Bedwell and M. C. Curthoys, "Hill, Alexander Staveley (1825–1905)," *ODNB*; Foster, *Men-at-the-Bar*, 218.

47. *R v. Hicklin*, 360 at 368.

48. Criminal Evidence Act, 1898, 61 & 62 Vict., c. 36.

49. *R v. Dixon* (King's Bench, 1814), 3 M. & S. 11 at 15.

50. *R v. Hicklin*, 360 at 375.

51. *R v. Hicklin*, 360 at 370.

52. *R v. Hicklin*, 360 at 371.

53. Ian Hunter, David Saunders, and Dugald Williamson, *On Pornography: Literature, Sexuality and Obscenity Law* (Basingstoke: Macmillan, 1993), 66–73; Deana Heath, *Purifying Empire: Obscenity and the Politics of Moral Regulation in Britain, India and Australia* (New York: Cambridge University Press, 2010), 51–52.

54. Cornish et al., *Fields of Development*, 370.

55. See, e.g., Thomas Starkie, *A Treatise on the Law of Slander and Libel: And Incidentally of Malicious Prosecutions*, 2nd ed. (2 vols., London: J. and W. T. Clarke, 1830), 1:xxvi, cxiv. Note also Sir Philip Yorke's use of the verb "tends" in *R v. Curl*, quoted above, p. 5.

56. Cornish et al., *Fields of Development*, 368.

57. *R v. Hicklin*, 360 at 365.

58. *R v. Hicklin*, 360 at 371.

59. *R v. Hicklin*, 360 at 372.

60. Lucy Bland, *Banishing the Beast: Feminism, Sex, and Morality* (1995; repr., London: Tauris Parke, 2001), 192.

61. Catherine Hall, Keith McClelland, and Jane Rendall, *Defining the Victorian Nation: Class, Race, Gender and the Reform Act of 1867* (Cambridge: Cambridge University Press, 2000); Anna Clark, "Gender, Class, and the Nation: Franchise Reform in England, 1832–1928," in *Re-Reading the Constitution: New Narratives in the Political History of England's Long Nineteenth Century*, ed. James Vernon (Cambridge: Cambridge University Press, 1996), 230–53; Jennifer Pitts, *A Turn to Empire: The Rise of Imperial Liberalism in Britain and France* (Princeton: Princeton University Press, 2005), 249.

62. Ben Griffin, *The Politics of Gender in Victorian Britain: Masculinity, Political Culture and the Struggle for Women's Rights* (Cambridge: Cambridge University Press, 2012), 205–6, 208, 213. The quotation is from Lord Elcho, reported in *The Times*, April 20, 1866.

63. Robert Saunders, "The Politics of Reform and the Making of the Second Reform Act, 1848–1867," *Historical Journal* 50, no. 3 (2007): 571–91, 578.

64. On Victorian understandings of "character," see Stefan Collini, *Public Moralists: Political Thought and Intellectual Life in Britain, 1850–1930* (Oxford: Oxford University Press, 1991).

65. Saunders, "Politics of Reform," 578; Griffin, *Politics of Gender*, 204–5.

66. Griffin, *Politics of Gender*, 205, quoting *The Times*, March 13, 1866.

67. Robert Saunders, *Democracy and the Vote in British Politics, 1848–1867: The Making of the Second Reform Act* (Farnham: Ashgate, 2011), 8–9, 21.

68. Saunders, "Politics of Reform," 582; Robert Lowe, *Speeches and Letters on Reform* (London: Robert John Bush, 1867), 12–13, 51–52.

69. *HC Deb.*, vol. 157, March 19, 1860, col. 886 (W. F. Campbell).

70. Richard Shannon, *Gladstone: God and Politics* (London: Continuum, 2007), 197, 198; F. B. Smith, *The Making of the Second Reform Bill* (Melbourne: Melbourne University Press, 1966), 111–20.

71. Saunders, "Politics of Reform," 584.

72. Saunders, "Politics of Reform," 585, 586, 587, 578.

73. Saunders, *Democracy and the Vote*, 243–50.

74. Saunders, "Politics of Reform," 589–91; Saunders, *Democracy and the Vote*, 252–57.

75. Saunders, *Democracy and the Vote*, 19.

76. Hall, McClelland, and Rendall, *Defining the Victorian Nation*, 93.

77. *HC Deb.*, vol. 186, March 26, 1867, cols. 636–37.

78. Hall, McClelland, and Rendall, *Defining the Victorian Nation*, 93–94.

79. On the masculinity of character, see Hall, McClelland, and Rendall, *Defining the Victorian Nation*, chap. 2; Clark, "Gender, Class, and the Nation"; Stefan Collini, "Political Theory and the 'Science of Society' in Victorian Britain," *Historical Journal* 23 (1980): 203–31, 217. See also Joan Wallach Scott, "On Language, Gender, and Working-Class History," in *Gender and the Politics of History* (New York: Columbia University Press, 1988), 54–67, 62–63.

80. A. O. Rutson, "Opportunities and Shortcomings of Government in England," in George C. Brodrick et al., *Essays on Reform* (London, 1867), 290; *HL Deb.*, vol. 188, July 23, 1867, col. 1981.

81. Wendy Donner, *The Liberal Self: John Stuart Mill's Moral and Political Philosophy* (Ithaca: Cornell University Press, 1991), 199.

82. John Stuart Mill, *Considerations on Representative Government* (1861) in Mill, *Three Essays*, 276, 278 (chap. 8).

83. *HC Deb.*, vol. 199, February 17, 1870, cols. 438–98; February 24, 1870, cols. 765–66; February 25, 1870, cols. 801–2; February 28, 1870, col. 884; March 14, 1870, cols. 1873–74, 1919–53; March 15, 1870, cols. 1963–2068; vol. 200, March 18, 1870, cols. 213–303; vol. 201, May 27, 1870, cols. 1496–98; May 31, 1870, cols. 1702–3; vol. 202, June 16, 1870, cols. 266–300; June 21, 1870, cols. 626–76; June 24, 1870, cols. 895–949; June 27, 1870, cols. 998–99, 1006–51.

84. *HC Deb.*, vol. 188, July 15, 1867, cols. 1548, 1549. Lowe's statement is sometimes quoted to suggest that Victorian elites saw education and the vote as inseparable. For instance, Alec Ellis, *Educating Our Masters: Influence on the Growth of Literacy in Victorian Working Class Children* (Aldershot: Gower, 1985), vi; Keith Evans, *The Development and Structure of the English Educational System* (London: University of London Press, 1975), 29.

85. See Eugen Weber, *Peasants into Frenchmen: The Modernization of Rural France, 1870–1914* (Stanford: Stanford University Press, 1976), chap. 18; Judith Surkis, *Sexing the Citizen: Morality and Masculinity in France, 1870–1920* (Ithaca: Cornell University Press, 2006), chap. 1.

86. Eugenio F. Biagini, *Liberty, Retrenchment, and Reform: Popular Liberalism in the Age of Gladstone, 1860–1880* (Cambridge: Cambridge University Press, 1992), 192–217; J. P. Parry, *Democracy and Religion: Gladstone and the Liberal Party, 1867–1875* (Cambridge: Cambridge University Press, 1986), 295–97, 301–6, 329–32; Jonathan Parry, *The Rise and Fall of Liberal Government in Victorian Britain* (New Haven: Yale University Press, 1993), 237–38, 262–65; Stephen Koss, *Nonconformity in Modern British Politics* (London: Batsford, 1975), 23–26; Robert F. Horton, "The Doomed Board Schools," *Fortnightly Review*, n.s., 60 (July 1896): 110–22; John Clifford, "Primary Education and the State," *Contemporary Review* 69 (March 1896): 441–56; A. M. Fairbairn, "The Policy of the Education Bill," *Contemporary Review* 69 (May 1896): 761–74; W. B. Ripon [i.e. William Boyd Carpenter, bishop of Ripon], "The Efficiency of Voluntary Schools," *Fortnightly Review*, n.s., 61 (January 1897): 117–24.

87. F. Seebohm, "On National Compulsory Education," *Fortnightly Review*, n.s., 8 (July 1870): 101–13; F. Seebohm, "The Education Difficulty," *Contemporary Review* 19 (February 1872): 281–300, especially 282–83; Clifford, "Primary Education and the State," 442–43; John Clifford, "The Destruction of the Board School," *Contemporary Review* 66 (November 1894): 641; E. Lyulph Stanley, "The New Education Bill," *Contemporary Review* 69 (May 1896): 760.

88. Walter Montagu Gattie, "What English People Read," *Fortnightly Review*, n.s., 46 (September 1889): 320–21; E. Lynn Linton, "Literature: Then and Now," *Fortnightly Review*, n.s., 67 (April 1890): 527. See also Charles Whibley, "The Education Difficulty," *Blackwood's Magazine* 165 (March 1899): 503.

89. *HL Deb.*, vol. 188, July 22, 1867, col. 1824; see also col. 1850.

90. Leigh, "What Do the Masses Read?" 176, 177 (order of quotations rearranged).

91. Walter Besant, "The Amusements of the People," *Contemporary Review* 45 (March 1884): 343–44; [B. G. Johns], "The Literature of the Streets," *Edinburgh Review* 165 (January 1887): 60–61; Gattie, "What English People Read," 308.

92. Geo. R. Humphery, "The Reading of the Working Classes," *Nineteenth Century* 33 (April 1893): 690–701, 692.

93. Andrew Lang and "X, a Working Man," "The Reading Public," *Cornhill Magazine*, n.s., 11 (December 1901): 79; James Haslam, *The Press and the People: An Estimate of Reading in Working-class Districts: Reprinted from the "Manchester City News"* (Manchester: Manchester City News, 1906); Francis Hitchman, "The Penny Press," *MacMillan's Magazine* 43 (1881): 385; Gattie, "What English People Read," 308.

94. Humphery, "Reading of the Working Classes," 692, 694. See also Johns, "Literature of the Streets," 65.

95. "A Censorship of Morals," *St James's Gazette*, 1 November 1888, 3; Stephen Koss, *The Rise and Fall of the Political Press in Britain*, 2 vols. (London: Hamish Hamilton, 1981–84), 1:233–34.

96. Katherine Mullin, "Pernicious Literature: Vigilance in the Age of Zola (1886–1899)," in *Prudes on the Prowl: Fiction and Obscenity in England, 1850 to the Present Day*, ed. David Bradshaw and Rachel Potter (Oxford: Oxford University Press, 2013), 30–51, 38.

97. The bishop of Bedford, moving a resolution at a meeting in St James's Hall that led to the formation of the National Vigilance Association, August 21, 1885. William Alexander Coote and A. Baker, eds., *A Romance of Philanthropy: Being a Record of Some of the Principal Incidents Connected with the Exceptionally Successful Thirty Years' Work of the National Vigilance Association* (London: National Vigilance Association, 1916), 6.

98. Roberts, *Making English Morals*, 230; Bland, *Banishing the Beast*, 99–105, 120–23.

99. Bristow, *Vice and Vigilance*, 202.

100. For Coote's personal story, see Coote and Baker, *Romance of Philanthropy*, 20–24.

101. Judith R. Walkowitz, *City of Dreadful Delight: Narratives of Sexual Danger in Late-Victorian London* (Chicago: University of Chicago Press, 1992), chaps. 3–4.

102. Coote and Baker, *Romance of Philanthropy*, 1–25; M.J.D. Roberts, *Making English Morals: Voluntary Association and Moral Reform in England, 1787–1886* (Cambridge: Cambridge University Press, 2004), 267–71.

103. *HC Deb.*, vol. 325, May 8, 1888, cols. 1708, 1711. See also Anthony Cummins, "Émile Zola's Cheap English Dress: The Vizetelly Translations, Late-Victorian Print Culture, and the Crisis of Literary Value," *Review of English Studies*, n.s., 60 (2009): 108–32, 119.

104. Samuel Smith, *My Life-Work* (London: Hodder and Stoughton, 1902), 477.

105. *HC Deb.*, vol. 325, May 8, 1888, col. 1715.

106. *HC Deb.*, vol. 325, May 8, 1888, col. 1708; Mullin, "Pernicious Literature," 33–35.

107. Bristow, *Vice and Vigilance*, 207; Ernest Alfred Vizetelly, *Emile Zola, Novelist and Reformer: An Account of His Life and Work* (London: John Lane, 1904), 265–66, 268, 270, 276–77.

108. Martin Hewitt, *The Dawn of the Cheap Press in Victorian Britain: The End of the "Taxes on Knowledge," 1849–1869* (London: Bloomsbury Academic, 2014), 77.

109. Henry Vizetelly, *Glances Back through Seventy Years: Autobiographical and Other Reminiscences*, vol. 2 (London: Kegan Paul, Trench, Trubner, 1893), 432.

110. Mullin, "Pernicious Literature," 35.

111. See McCalman, *Radical Underworld*, 235, 237, and, more broadly, 204–31.

112. Cummins, "Émile Zola's Cheap English Dress," 120; Ernest Vizetelly, *Emile Zola*, 278–79; also 255–56.

113. "Elle saisit à pleine main le membre du taureau, qu'elle redressa. Et lui quand il se sentit au bord, ramassé dans sa force, il pénétra d'un seul tour de reins, à fond." Emile Zola, *La Terre* (1887; repr., Paris: Charpentier, 1895), 10.

114. Mullin, "Pernicious Literature," 34. On the more explicit material available at the time see Lisa Z. Sigel, *Governing Pleasures: Pornography and Social Change in England, 1815–1914* (New Brunswick, NJ: Rutgers University Press, 2002), 94–95.

115. Mullin, "Pernicious Literature," 34.

116. Quoted in Cummins, "Émile Zola's Cheap English Dress," 115.

117. Humphery, "Reading of the Working Classes," 692.

118. Lise Shapiro Sanders, *Consuming Fantasies: Labor, Leisure, and the London Shopgirl, 1880–1920* (Columbus: Ohio State University Press, 2006).

119. Jonathan Wild, *The Rise of the Office Clerk in Literary Culture, 1880–1939* (Basingstoke: Palgrave Macmillan, 2006).

120. TNA, HO 144/A46657/41, H. Cuffe, memorandum of November 2, 1888, quoted in Bristow, *Vice and Vigilance*, 207–8; Cummins, "Émile Zola's Cheap English Dress," 124; see also 123.

121. Cummins, "Émile Zola's Cheap English Dress," 124, 110, 123; Roberts, "Morals, Art and the Law," 628.

122. Not everyone saw it this way. "If the English versions are offensive to the law," a writer for the Liverpool Mercury remarked, "it is hard to understand why the far more revolting French versions are allowed to circulate." *Pernicious Literature: Debate in the House of Commons: Trial and Conviction for Sale of Zola's Novels: With Opinions of the Press* (London: National Vigilance Association, 1889), 22.

123. Emily Crawford, "Emile Zola," *Contemporary Review* 55 (January 1889): 94–113; Janet E. Hogarth, "Literary Degenerates," *Fortnightly Review*, n.s., 57 (April 1895): 587; Robert Lee Wolff, *Sensational Victorian: The Life and Fiction of Mary Elizabeth Braddon* (New York: Garland, 1979), 317–20.

124. Cummins, "Émile Zola's Cheap English Dress," 128–29.

125. Dane Kennedy, *The Highly Civilized Man: Richard Burton and the Victorian World* (Cambridge, MA: Harvard University Press, 2005), 327 n. 33.

126. Kennedy, *Highly Civilized Man*, 218–26 (quotations from 226).

127. Coote and A. Baker, *Romance of Philanthropy*, 110; Bristow, *Vice and Vigilance*, 208–9.

128. *HC Deb.*, vol. 325, May 8, 1888, col. 1714.

129. Paul Johnson, "Class Law in Victorian England," *Past and Present*, no. 141 (November 1993): 168. I owe the parallel between Johnson's article and the history of obscenity law to Jon Lawrence, "Paternalism, Class, and the British Path to Modernity," in *The Peculiarities of Liberal Modernity in Imperial Britain*, ed. Simon Gunn and James Vernon (Berkeley: University of California Press, 2011), 147–64, 155–56.

130. John Frederick Archbold, *The Justice of the Peace, and Parish Officer: With the Practice of Country Attorneys in Criminal Cases: Comprising the Whole of the Law Respecting Indictable and Summary Offences, Commitments, Convictions, Orders, &c.*, 7th ed. James Paterson, 3 vols. (London: Shaw, 1875–78), 2:983–84; Samuel Stone, *The Justices' Manual, or, Guide to the Ordinary Duties of a Justice of the Peace: With Table of Cases, Appendix of Forms, and Table of Punishments*, 26th ed. George B. Kennett (London: Shaw, 1891), 645–46; *The Metropolitan Police Guide: Being a Compendium of the Law Affecting the Metropolitan Police*, 6th ed. James R. Roberts (London: HMSO, 1916), 1274; C. E. Howard Vincent, *Vincent's Police Code and General Manual of the Criminal Law*, 16th ed., rev. by the Commissioner of Police of the Metropolis (London: Butterworth, 1924), 145, 168; Charles Pilley, *Law for Journalists* (London: Pitman, 1924), 67–68.

131. Guinevere L. Griest, *Mudie's Circulating Library and the Victorian Novel* (Newton Abbot: David and Charles, 1970); J. A. Sutherland, *Victorian Novelists and Publishers* (London: Athlone Press, 1976); Alexis Weedon, *Victorian Publishing: The Economics of Book Production for a Mass Market, 1836–1916* (Aldershot: Ashgate, 2003); Simon Eliot, *Some Patterns and Trends in British Publishing* (London: Bibliographical Society, 1994).

132. So were the editors of periodicals that serialized novels before their publication in volume, but periodicals were not an oligopoly like the libraries.

133. Peter Keating, *The Haunted Study: A Social History of the English Novel, 1875–1914* (1989; repr., London: Fontana Press, 1991), 251–52.

134. George Moore, *Literature at Nurse, or, Circulating Morals* (London: Vizetelly and Co., 1885), 3–4.

135. Each grade of annual subscription fee at a circulating library corresponded to a certain number of volumes rather than titles. Philip Waller, *Writers, Readers, and Reputations: Literary Life in Britain, 1870–1918* (Oxford: Oxford University Press, 2006), 33.

136. George Moore, "A New Censorship of Literature," *Pall Mall Gazette*, 10 December 1884, 1–2, in George Moore, *Literature at Nurse, or, Circulating Morals: A Polemic on Victorian Censorship*, ed. Pierre Coustillas (Hassocks: Harvester Press, 1976), 27–32, 32.

137. Keating, *Haunted Study*, 257–60.

138. Keating, *Haunted Study*, 261–63.

139. Keating, *Haunted Study*, 275–79.

140. BL, Add 56871, Society of Authors Archive, ff. 70–82, "Library Censorship and Library Circulation" (1913); Waller, *Writers, Readers, and Reputations*, 58; Joseph McAleer, *Popular Reading and Publishing in Britain 1914–1950* (Oxford: Clarendon Press, 1992), 49; Arnold Bennett, *Books and Persons: Being Comments on a Past Epoch, 1908–1911* (London: Chatto and Windus, 1917), 88–89.

141. BL, Add 56871, Society of Authors Archive, ff. 70–82, "Library Censorship and Library Circulation" (1913).

142. Waller, *Writers, Readers, and Reputations*, 982.

143. Waller, *Writers, Readers, and Reputations*, 981–82.

144. BL, Add 56871, Society of Authors Archive, ff. 72–73, Mr Marshall, of W. H. Smith, notes for the Society of Authors (1913).

145. Waller, *Writers, Readers, and Reputations*, 982.

146. LSE/Women's Library, National Vigilance Association Papers, GB/106/4/NVA/S.88/F, W. A. Buckley-Evans to Col. G. Thompson, January 8, 1923.

147. Keating, *Haunted Study*, 272.

148. John Worthen, *D. H. Lawrence: The Life of an Outsider* (London: Allen Lane, 2005), 163–64.

149. Sir William Byles, December 1, 1915; offprint from Hansard in TNA, HO 45/13944.

150. "'The Rainbow': Destruction of a Novel Ordered," *The Times*, December 15, 1915. Methuen did not contest the order. Nicola Wilson says that the publishers received a small fine. In fact they had to pay ten guineas in costs. They were not charged with or convicted of any offense. Wilson, "Circulating Morals (1900–1915)," in Bradshaw and Potter, *Prudes on the Prowl*, 52–70, 69–70.

151. Worthen, *D. H. Lawrence*, 164.

152. Kyle S. Crichton, "An Interview with Lawrence," in *D. H. Lawrence: Interviews and Recollections*, ed. Norman Page, vol. 2 (London: Macmillan Press, 1981), 215–21, 218.

153. "I think there ought to be some system of private publication and private circulation," Lawrence told a correspondent in 1917; "I disbelieve utterly in the public, in humanity, in the mass." Andrew Nash, "D. H. Lawrence and the Publication of *Look! We Have Come Through!*" *Library* 12, no. 2 (June 2011): 142–63.

154. See Lawrence Rainey, *Institutions of Modernism: Literary Elites and Public Culture* (New Haven: Yale University Press, 1998), chaps. 2–3; Mark S. Morrisson, *The Public Face of Modernism: Little Magazines, Audiences, and Reception, 1905–1920* (Madison: University of Wisconsin Press, 2001); and compare Lise Jaillant, *Cheap Modernism: Expanding Markets, Publishers' Series, and the Avant-Garde* (Edinburgh: Edinburgh University Press, 2017).

155. Clive Bell, *On British Freedom* (London: Chatto and Windus, 1923), 12; Rachel Potter, "Censorship and Sovereignty (1916–1929)," in Bradshaw and Potter, *Prudes on the Prowl*, 71–89, 79–82.

Chapter Two. The Censorship versus the Moderns, 1918–1945

1. Jon Lawrence, "Forging a Peaceable Kingdom: War, Violence, and Fear of Brutalization in Post–First World War Britain," *Journal of Modern History* 75 (2003): 557–89.

2. Ross McKibbin, *Classes and Cultures: England, 1918–1951* (Oxford: Oxford University Press, 1998), 50–59.

3. Adrian Bingham, *Gender, Modernity, and the Popular Press in Inter-War Britain* (Oxford: Oxford University Press, 2004), 7, *contra* Billie Melman, *Women and the Popular Imagination in the Twenties: Flappers and Nymphs* (Basingstoke: Macmillan, 1988); Lucy Bland, *Modern Women on Trial: Sexual Transgression in the Age of the Flapper* (Manchester: Manchester University Press, 2013); Matt Houlbrook, "'A Pin to See the Peepshow': Culture, Fiction and Selfhood in Edith Thompson's Letters, 1921–1922," *Past and Present*, no. 207 (2010): 215–49.

4. HRC, Ottoline Morrell papers, 8/3, Henry Yorke (Henry Green) to Ottoline Morrell, February 25, 1933, describing James Hanley's early publications.

5. Philip Williamson and Edward Baldwin, eds., *Baldwin Papers: A Conservative Statesman, 1908–1947* (Cambridge: Cambridge University Press, 2004), 40.

6. The biographical information in this paragraph comes from F.M.L. Thompson, "Hicks, William Joynson- [nicknamed Jix], first Viscount Brentford (1865–1932)," *ODNB*. See also Huw F. Clayton, "'A Frisky, Tiresome Colt'? Sir William Joynson-Hicks, the Home Office and the 'Roaring Twenties', 1924–1929" (PhD diss., University of Wales, Aberystwyth, 2008), chap. 2. The classic trashing of Joynson-Hicks is Ronald Blythe, "The Salutary Tale of Jix," in *The Age of Illusion: England in the Twenties and Thirties, 1914–40* (1963; repr., Harmondsworth: Penguin, 1964), 24–54.

7. James J. Nott, "'The Plague Spots of London': William Joynson-Hicks, the Conservative Party and the Campaign against London's Nightclubs, 1924–29," in *Cultures, Classes and Politics: Essays on British History for Ross McKibbin*, ed. Clare V. Griffiths, James J. Nott, and William Whyte (Oxford: Oxford University Press, 2011), 227–46, 228–29; Jon Lawrence, "Class and Gender in the Making of Urban Toryism, 1880–1914," *English Historical Review* 108 (July 1993): 638–41. See also H. Montgomery Hyde, *A History of Pornography* (London: Heinemann, 1964), 177.

8. Philip Williamson, *Stanley Baldwin: Conservative Leadership and National Values* (Cambridge: Cambridge University Press, 1999), 227.

9. Nott, "Plague-Spots," 241–46; Ross McKibbin, "Class and Conventional Wisdom: The Conservative Party and the 'Public' in Interwar Britain," in McKibbin, *The*

Ideologies of Class: Social Relations in Britain, 1880–1950 (Oxford: Clarendon Press, 1990), 259–93, 281.

10. Viscount Brentford, *Do We Need a Censor?* (London: Faber and Faber, 1929), 20, 23–24.

11. John W. Wheeler-Bennett, *John Anderson: Viscount Waverley* (London: Macmillan, 1962), chaps. 3, 5, 6, 7 and pp. 102–8.

12. Wheeler-Bennett, *John Anderson*, 85.

13. Sir Chartres Biron, *Without Prejudice: Impressions of Life and Law* (London: Faber and Faber, 1936), 121.

14. Robert Jackson, *Case for the Prosecution: A Biography of Sir Archibald Bodkin, Director of Public Prosecutions, 1920–1930* (London: Arthur Barker, 1962), 168–69.

15. Frank Newsam, *The Home Office* (London: George Allen and Unwin, 1954), 134.

16. Keith Wilson, "Gwynne, Howell Arthur (1865–1950)," *ODNB.*

17. Stephen Koss, *The Rise and Fall of the Political Press in Britain*, 2 vols. (London: Hamish Hamilton, 1981–84), 2:437; Derek Sayer, "British Reaction to the Amritsar Massacre, 1919–1920," *Past and Present*, no. 131 (May 1991): 130–64, 157–58; Wilson, "Gwynne, Howell Arthur"; David Cesarani, "The Anti-Jewish Career of Sir William Joynson-Hicks, Cabinet Minister," *Journal of Contemporary History* 24, no. 3 (1989): 466.

18. Philip Gibbs, *The Hope of Europe* (London: William Heinemann, 1921), 74–75; Lawrence, "Forging a Peaceable Kingdom," 588.

19. Lawrence, "Forging a Peaceable Kingdom," 558 and n.

20. Koss, *Political Press*, 2:431, 435–36, 443; Williamson, *Stanley Baldwin*, 80.

21. Koss, *Political Press*, 2:453–455. See also Kingsley Martin, *The British Public and the General Strike* (London: Hogarth Press, 1926), 65.

22. Christopher Hilliard, "Modernism and the Common Writer," *Historical Journal* 48, no. 3 (September 2005): 769–87.

23. Quoted in Houlbrook, "Pin to See the Peepshow," 217.

24. TNA, HO 144/20071, Blackwell to Secretary, Customs and Excise, January 10, 1923.

25. TNA, HO 144/20071, Bodkin to [Sir John Anderson], December 29, 1922.

26. TNA, HO 144/20071, Harris, notes in minutes pages, January 1, 1923.

27. Postal Archives, POST 23/9/27, Sir Ernley Blackwell to Secretary, General Post Office, January 23, 1923.

28. Alan Travis, *Bound and Gagged: A Secret History of Obscenity in Britain* (London: Profile Books, 2000), 26.

29. Postal Archives, POST 23/9/27, M. W. Browning to GPO Parcels Department, February 17, 1932; G. B. McAlpine to R. W. Hatswell, February 26, 1932; R. Richardson to Assistant Controller, March 24, 1933.

30. There are copies of the warrants and mailing lists of postmasters to notify in Postal Archives, POST 23/9/27.

31. Alistair McCleery, "A Hero's Homecoming: *Ulysses* in Britain, 1922–37," *Publishing History* 46 (January 1999): 67–93, 72–75; Ian MacKillop, *F. R. Leavis: A Life in Criticism* (New York: St. Martin's Press, 1995), 88–91.

32. TNA, HO 144/20071, Anderson, note on minutes page, n.d. (July 1926).

33. TNA, HO 144/20071, Bodkin to A. C. Seward, July 31, 1926.

34. TNA, HO 144/20071, Seward to Bodkin, August 5, 1926. In the early 1930s, several other literary critics and one psychologist successfully asked permission to import a copy for scholarly uses. Postal Archives, POST 23/9/27, unsigned copy of Home Office letter to Desmond MacCarthy, January 31, 1934; E. Haigh to Secretary, Board of Customs and Excise, January 3, 1933; G. B. McAlpine to R. W. Hatswell, December 5, 1930.

35. TNA, DPP 1/92, [A. H. Bodkin], "Re 'Sleeveless Errand': Rex v. Eric Honeywood Partridge: Brief to Apply for Order of Destruction," n.d. [February 1929].

36. TNA, DPP 1/92, Bodkin to Anderson, February 19, 1929 (copy).

37. TNA, DPP 1/92, [Bodkin] to George T. Knight, Chief Constable of Hertfordshire, February 20, 1929 (copy); DPP 1/92, [Bodkin] to C. E. Gower, Chief Constable of Monmouth, February 21, 1929; Bodkin, "Re 'Sleeveless Errand,'" February 1929. The printers were required by the Newspapers, Printers and Reading Rooms Repeal Act 1869 to keep such a list for three months.

38. TNA, DPP 1/92, Bodkin, "Re 'Sleeveless Errand,'" February 1929.

39. See also TNA, DPP 1/92, "Re Eric Honeywood Partridge (trading as the Scholartis Press): Index to Police Reports, Statements, etc.," n.d. [February or March 1929].

40. TNA, DPP 1/92, Bodkin, "Re 'Sleeveless Errand,'" February 1929.

41. TNA, DPP 1/92, Bodkin, "Re 'Sleeveless Errand,'" February 1929.

42. "Seized Novel Condemned," *The Times*, March 5, 1929.

43. TNA, MEPO 3/383; G. R. Nicholls to Assistant Chief Constable, December 12, 1929; N. L. Bicknell to H. M. Howgrave-Graham, December 4, 1929; "T. B." to Bicknell, n.d.; Bernard Causton and G. Gordon Young, *Keeping It Dark, or, the Censor's Handbook* (London: Mandrake Press, [1930]), 53 n.

44. See Christopher Hilliard, "'Is It a Book That You Would Even Wish Your Wife or Your Servants to Read?' Obscenity Law and the Politics of Reading in Modern England," *American Historical Review* 118, no. 3 (2013): 653–78, 667–68.

45. TNA, MEPO 3/932, minutes pages, note 24, April 14, 1935; note 7, September 21, 1934.

46. TNA, MEPO 3/932, minutes pages, note 7, September 21, 1934.

47. TNA, MEPO 3/932, minutes pages, note 24, April 14, 1935. For Wontners, see Stefan Petrow, *Policing Morals: The Metropolitan Police and the Home Office, 1870–1914* (Oxford: Oxford University Press, 1994), 39.

48. Here I am referring to stipendiary magistrates, paid judges with a legal background. In the 1920s the word magistrate was still sometimes used to refer to a lay justice of the peace sitting on a police court bench.

49. Biron, *Without Prejudice*, 302–4 (quotation from 303).

50. Laura Doan, *Fashioning Sapphism: The Origins of a Modern English Lesbian Culture* (New York: Columbia University Press, 2001), chap. 1; TNA, DPP 1/88, Rubinstein, Nash to Director of Public Prosecutions, October 19, 1928.

51. "A Book That Must Be Suppressed," *Sunday Express*, August 19, 1928.

52. David Bradshaw, "James Douglas: The Sanitary Inspector of Literature," in *Prudes on the Prowl: Fiction and Obscenity in England, 1850 to the Present Day*, ed. David Bradshaw and Rachel Potter (Oxford: Oxford University Press, 2013), 90–110. For Douglas's teasing, see Doan, *Fashioning Sapphism*, 17–18.

53. Nicola Wilson, "Circulating Morals (1900–1915)," in Bradshaw and Potter, *Prudes on the Prowl*, 52–70, 69; Bradshaw, "James Douglas," 108.

54. Michael Baker, *Our Three Selves: The Life of Radclyffe Hall* (London: Hamish Hamilton, 1985), 223–24.

55. Michael S. Howard, *Jonathan Cape, Publisher: Herbert Jonathan Cape, G. Wren Howard* (London: Jonathan Cape, 1971), 103–4.

56. Hall was incensed: Howard, *Jonathan Cape*, 104; Diana Souhami, *The Trials of Radclyffe Hall* (London: Weidenfeld and Nicolson, 1998), 179.

57. TNA, HO 144/22547, Jonathan Cape to Sir William Joynson-Hicks, August 20, 1928; "Publisher's Letter," *Daily Express*, August 20, 1928.

58. "Publisher's Letter," *Daily Express*, August 20, 1928.

59. Souhami, *Trials of Radclyffe Hall*, 167–68, 173.

60. For book prices see Q. D. Leavis, *Fiction and the Reading Public* (London: Chatto and Windus, 1932), 12.

61. Howard, *Jonathan Cape*, 103. On the category of "middlebrow," see Erica Brown and Mary Grover, eds., *Middlebrow Literary Cultures: The Battle of the Brows, 1920–1960* (Basingstoke: Palgrave Macmillan, 2012).

62. Howard, *Jonathan Cape*, part 1, chap. 6.

63. Travis, *Bound and Gagged*, 52.

64. TNA, HO 144/22547, Sir Guy Stephenson to Sir John Anderson, August 21, 1928.

65. Newman Flower, ed., *The Journals of Arnold Bennett*, 3 vols. (London: Cassell, 1930–33), 3:271, entry for August 24, 1928 (emphasis in original).

66. TNA, HO 144/22547, Joynson-Hicks, note of August 22, 1928 on Stephenson's opinion addressed to Anderson, August 21, 1928.

67. Cape's biographer (and successor at his firm) describes his action as an attempt to make sure Hall's moral purpose in writing the book would not be thwarted. Howard, *Jonathan Cape*, 106. Howard does not say how much Holroyd-Reece paid Cape for the rights. It seems unlikely that *The Well of Loneliness* was a money-spinner for Cape the way T. E. Lawrence's *Revolt in the Desert* and Kathleen Mayo's *Mother India* had been the previous year, when the firm's net profit rose from the usual £2000 to almost £28,000, which attracted the attention of the Inland Revenue. Howard, *Jonathan Cape*, 94, 95. Still, Howard does not provide comparable figures for 1928 or 1929 (part 1, chaps. 7–9).

68. Travis, *Bound and Gagged*, 55–57.

69. TNA, HO 144/22547, Sir Francis Floud to Winston Churchill, October 9, 1928.

70. Travis, *Bound and Gagged*, 61.

71. Travis, *Bound and Gagged*, 60–63.

72. Souhami, *Trials of Radclyffe Hall*, 194–98.

73. Virginia Woolf to Vita Sackville-West, August 20, 1928, in *The Letters of Virginia Woolf*, vol. 3, *1923–1928*, ed. Nigel Nicolson and Joanne Trautmann (New York: Harcourt Brace Jovanovich, 1977), 520.

74. King's College Archive Centre, Cambridge, E. M. Forster papers, 18/235, Radclyffe Hall to E. M. Forster, August 27, 1928 and August 31, 1928.

75. Howard, *Jonathan Cape*, 108.

76. On MacCarthy's standing see John Gross, *The Rise and Fall of the Man of Letters: Aspects of English Literary Life since 1800* (London: Weidenfeld and Nicolson, 1969), 244.

77. Alec Craig, *The Banned Books of England* (London: George Allen and Unwin, 1937), 37–38.

78. Craig, *Banned Books*, 39.

79. "Novel Condemned as Obscene," *The Times*, November 17, 1928.

80. Matthew Grimley, *Citizenship, Community, and the Church of England: Liberal Anglican Theories of the State Between the Wars* (Oxford: Oxford University Press, 2004), 144, 147; R.F.V. Heuston, *Lives of the Lord Chancellors, 1885–1940* (Oxford: Clarendon Press, 1987), 582–84, 586.

81. "Condemned Novel," *The Times*, December 15, 1928.

82. TNA, HO 144/22547, Bodkin to Anderson, December 14, 1928. "In view of the discreditable action, as I regard it, of Mr Jonathan Cape," Bodkin added, "it would appear undesirable to accept any undertaking in the future to withdraw objectionable books from circulation."

83. Doan, *Fashioning Sapphism*, 193 (italics in original).

84. See C. H. Rolph, *Books in the Dock* (London: André Deutsch, 1969), 80. Testimony from doctors and other experts was sometimes permitted in cases involving sexology or books purporting to be anatomical works: ULL, Alec Craig Papers, MS1091, box 2, file 4, "Summary Report of Police Proceedings Regarding 'An Introduction to the Study of the Physiology & Bio-Chemistry of the Sexual Impulse among Adults in Mental & Bodily Health': A study by Edward Charles, published by Boriswood Limited, publishers, of 15a, Harrington Road, London, S.W.7," typescript, n.d.; TNA, CRIM 1/60/4, Bow Street Police Court, R. v. Harry Sidney Nicholls and Alice Maud Taylor, deposition of Thomas Bond, Consulting Surgeon at Westminster Hospital, February 6, 1900. The book in the latter case was entitled *Kalygynomia, or, The Laws of Female Beauty*. There is a description of it in Peter Fryer, *Private Case— Public Scandal: Secrets of the British Museum Revealed* (London: Secker and Warburg, 1966), 59.

85. See chapter 3. The same point had been said in connection with Lawrence and *The Rainbow*. BL, Society of Authors Archive, Add 56985, ff. 330–32, G. H. Thring, "Instructions to Settle Draft Bill re Libel," October 1924. In subsequent discussions, however, *The Well of Loneliness* was treated as the exemplary case.

86. For detail see Christopher Hilliard, "The Literary Underground of 1920s London," *Social History* 33, no. 2 (2008): 164–82; David Goodway, "Charles Lahr: Anarchist, Bookseller, Publisher," *London Magazine*, n.s., 17, no. 2 (July 1977): 46–55.

87. For example, Jack Lindsay, *Fanfrolico and After* (1962), in *Life Rarely Tells: An Autobiography in Three Volumes* (Ringwood, Victoria: Penguin, 1982), 684, 689–90, 754.

88. John Worthen, *D. H. Lawrence: The Life of an Outsider* (London: Allen Lane, 2005), 399.

89. Celia Marshik, *British Modernism and Censorship* (Cambridge: Cambridge University Press, 2006), esp. 14–15.

90. Worthen, *D. H. Lawrence*, 354; Rachel Potter, *Obscene Modernism: Literary Censorship and Experiment, 1900–1940* (Oxford: Oxford University Press, 2013), 121–22.

91. D. H. Lawrence, *Lady Chatterley's Lover* (Florence: Privately Printed, 1928).

92. Craig Munro, "Lady Chatterley in London: The Secret Third Edition," in *D. H. Lawrence's "Lady": A New Look at "Lady Chatterley's Lover,"* ed. Michael Squires and Dennis Jackson (Athens: University of Georgia Press, 1985), 222–35; Craig Munro,

Inky Stephensen: Wild Man of Letters (1984; repr., St Lucia: University of Queensland Press, 1992), 82; Jay A. Gertzman, *A Descriptive Bibliography of "Lady Chatterley's Lover," with Essays toward a Publishing History of the Novel* (New York: Greenwood Press, 1989), 30–31, 57.

93. Worthen, *D. H. Lawrence*, 384, 388.

94. Munro, *Inky Stephensen*, 82.

95. TNA, HO 144/20642, Bodkin to Anderson, September 6, 1929; HO 144/20642, R. L. Bicknell to W. O. Colyer, October 7, 1929; Gertzman, *Descriptive Bibliography*, 16.

96. TNA, HO 144/20642, Bodkin to Anderson, September 6, 1929.

97. On fine printing and book collecting in the interwar period, see Oliver Simon, *Printer and Playground: An Autobiography* (London: Faber and Faber [1956]), chap. 2; Francis Meynell, *My Lives* (London: The Bodley Head, 1971), chaps. 9, 11; D. L. LeMahieu, *A Culture for Democracy: Mass Communication and the Cultivated Mind in Britain between the Wars* (Oxford: Clarendon Press, 1988), 160.

98. State Library of New South Wales, Sydney, Stephensen Papers, MLMSS 1284, box 25, "Mandrake Press—Points for Defence," n.d.

99. Worthen, *D. H. Lawrence*, 398; see also Munro, *Inky Stephensen*, 85–86; Munro, "Lady Chatterley in London," 226.

100. This paragraph is based on Neville March Hunnings, *Film Censors and the Law* (London: George Allen and Unwin, 1967), 51–89, 100–105, 133–37.

101. On Scotland's divergence from English local government's response to the 1909 act, see Julia Bohlmann, "A Licence Not to Censor: The Cinematograph Act 1909 in Scotland," *Journal of British Cinema and Television* 15, no. 4 (2018): 491–512.

102. London County Council v. Bermondsey Bioscope Co Ltd [1911] 1 KB 445.

103. R. M. Morris, "Harris, Sir Sidney West (1876–1962)," *ODNB*.

104. The court of King's Bench gave its blessing to this arrangement in Mills v. London County Council [1925] 1 KB 213.

105. Hunnings, *Film Censors and the Law*, 51–79, 133–37; Mike Hally, "Local Authorities and Film Censorship: A Historical Account of the Naughty Pictures Committees in Sale and Manchester," *Entertainment and Sports Law Journal* 11, no. 1 (2013): 1–20.

106. David Thomas, David Carlton, and Anne Etienne, *Theatre Censorship: From Walpole to Wilson* (Oxford: Oxford University Press, 2007), 94–95, 98, 108.

107. Dorothy Knowles, *The Censor, the Drama, and the Film, 1900–1934* (London: George Allen and Unwin, 1934), 58–59, 117.

108. Guy Phelps, *Film Censorship* (London: Victor Gollancz, 1975), 32–34.

109. Trevelyan, *What the Censor Saw*, 40–43.

110. Phelps, *Film Censorship*, 35.

111. Hunnings, *Film Censors and the Law*, 137–38.

112. Nicholas Pronay, "The Political Censorship of Films in Britain between the Wars," in *Propaganda, Politics and Film, 1918–45*, ed. Nicholas Pronay and D. W. Spring (London: Macmillan Press, 1982), 98–125, 105.

113. Pronay, "Political Censorship of Films," 122.

114. McKibbin, "Class and Conventional Wisdom"; Alison Light, *Forever England: Femininity, Literature and Conservatism between the Wars* (London: Routledge, 1991), esp. chap. 3.

115. McKibbin, *Classes and Cultures*, 431.

116. Hunnings, *Film Censors and the Law*, 97–99; Knowles, *The Censor, the Drama, and the Film*, 192.

117. Paddy Scannell, "Broadcasting and the Politics of Unemployment, 1930–1935," *Media, Culture and Society* 2 (1980): 15–28; Paddy Scannell and David Cardiff, *A Social History of British Broadcasting*, vol. 1, *1922–1939: Serving the Nation* (Oxford: Basil Blackwell, 1991).

118. McKibbin, *Classes and Cultures*, 459–68; see also 96–98.

119. League of Nations, *Records of the International Conference for the Suppression of the Circulation of and Traffic in Obscene Publications Held at Geneva from August 31st to September 12th, 1923*, C. 734 M. 299 (Geneva: League of Nations, 1923), 5, 36; TNA, HO 144/22547, notes in minutes page, 527705/64, February-March 1929; HO 144/22547, A. Crapper to Director, Investigations Branch, Attorney-General's Department, Canberra, 21 December 1928.

120. See above, p. 67.

121. *Correspondence Respecting the International Conferences on Obscene Publications and the "White Slave Traffic," Held in Paris, April and May, 1910*, Cd 6547 (London: HMSO, 1912).

122. LSE/Women's Library, NVA Papers, GB/106/4/NVA/S.88/E. See also Julia Laite, "Between Scylla and Charybdis: Women's Migrant Labour and Discourses of Sexual Trafficking in the West," *International Review of Social History* 62, no. 1 (2017): 37–65, 57–58.

123. LSE/Women's Library, NVA Papers, GB/106/4/NVA/S.88/3, unsigned copy of letter from Sempkins to Fraulein Pfleiderer, July 27, 1933.

124. LSE/Women's Library, NVA Papers, GB/106/4/NVA/S.88/5.

125. "Woman's Defence of a Book: 'Ignorance Leads to Divorce Court': Magistrate's View of Verses," *Daily Telegraph*, October 17, 1935; "Defence of a Book: Evidence for Publishers," *The Times*, October 17, 1935; Alec Craig, "The Sexual Impulse Prosecution," *Plan*, November 1935, 17–20, 18, copy in ULL, Alec Craig Papers, MS1091/2/4. On Charles's book see Hera Cook, *The Long Sexual Revolution: English Women, Sex, and Contraception, 1800–1975* (Oxford: Oxford University Press, 2004), 212–15.

126. "Books on Sex Matters: Magistrate and Police Action," *The Times*, March 13, 1935; TNA, MEPO 3/932, F. Sharpe to A. Askew, October 11, 1934, July 18, 1935.

127. See the planning documents in LSE/Women's Library, GB/106/4NVA/S.88/T; and, for the suspicion, GB106/4/NVA/S.88/B, Sempkins to S. Cohen, October 9, 1928; Cohen to Sempkins, October 10, 1928.

128. Allison Lorna Elizabeth Wee, "Trials and Eros: The British Home Office v. Indecent Publications, 1857–1932" (PhD diss., University of Minnesota, 2004), 195.

129. Wee, "Trials and Eros," 213, 215.

130. TNA, HO 45/24939, H. Houston, note on minutes page, 595957/20, July 28, 1932; Wee, "Trials and Eros," 232, 235.

131. Compare Wee, "Trials and Eros," 195.

132. TNA, HO 144/22547, S. W. Harris to Secretary, GPO, July 3, 1929 (copy).

133. TNA, HO 144/14042, Clynes to bishop of London, March 24, 1930; Wee, "Trials and Eros," 224–25.

134. F. D. Barry, revised by Mark Pottle, "Atkinson, Sir Edward Hale Tindal (1878–1957)," *ODNB*.

135. For examples, see the documents reproduced in Wee, "Trials and Eros," 230–31, 236.

136. TNA, HO 45/24939, Atkinson to Under-Secretary of State, April 14, 1932.

137. Edward Tindal Atkinson, *Obscene Literature in Law and Practice* (London: Christophers, [1937]), 10–11.

138. James Fitzjames Stephen, *A Digest of the Criminal Law (Crimes and Punishments)*, 4th ed. (London: Macmillan, 1887), 105, article 172. Stephen's submission was a rejoinder to the *Hicklin* decision (note his reference to religion), and especially to its dismissal of questions of intent and justification.

139. United States v. One Book Called "Ulysses," 5 F. Supp. 182 at 183 (Southern District of New York, 1933).

140. Geoffrey Faber to Donald Somervell, January 5, 1934; Somervell to T. S. Eliot, January 6, 1934, and editorial notes, in *The Letters of T. S. Eliot*, vol. 7, *1934–1935*, ed. Valerie Eliot and John Haffenden (London: Faber and Faber, 2017), 9–12.

141. TNO, HO 144/20071, J. F. Henderson, notes in minutes page, 186428/60, October 7, 1936.

142. TNO, HO 144/20071, J. F. Henderson, minute, 186428/61, November 6, 1936.

143. Postal Archives, POST 23/9/27, J.D.R. Pimlott to Director General, GPO, November 12, 1936.

144. TNA, HO 144/22547, R. R. Scott to the Chief Constable, April 7, 1937 (printed circular).

145. Meic Stephens, "Hanley, James (1901–1985)," *ODNB*; John Fordham, *James Hanley: Modernism and the Working Class* (Cardiff: University of Wales Press, 2002); Ken Worpole, *Dockers and Detectives*, 2nd ed. (Nottingham: Five Leaves Publications, 2008), 108–14.

146. ULL, Sir Louis Sterling Library, SLV/36/6, T. E. Shaw [T. E. Lawrence] to Hanley, August 2, 1931 (copy).

147. J. W. Lambert and Michael Ratcliffe, *The Bodley Head, 1887–1987* (London: The Bodley Head, 1987), 272–73.

148. Lambert and Ratcliffe, *Bodley Head*, p. 243. The reader was the novelist Ethel Mannin.

149. Anthony Burgess, "Introduction" to James Hanley, *Boy* (1931; repr., London: Penguin, 1992), ix–x; HRC, Walpole papers, Hanley to Walpole, November 15 [1931].

150. James Armstrong, "The Publication, Prosecution, and Re-publication of James Hanley's *Boy* (1931)," *Library*, 6th ser., 19, no. 4 (1997): 351–62, 352–54.

151. HRC, Hanley Papers, Misc. (file on the prosecution of Boriswood), Neville Isitt to Boriswood, January 22, 1935.

152. Christopher Hilliard, "The Twopenny Library: The Book Trade, Working-Class Readers, and 'Middlebrow' Novels in Britain, 1930–42," *Twentieth Century British History* 25, no. 2 (June 2014): 199–220.

153. Armstrong, "James Hanley's *Boy*," 355; HRC, James Hanley papers, Misc., "Summary—Report of the Police Proceedings against the Directors and the Firm of Boriswood Limited in Regard to the Book Entitled 'Boy' Written by James Hanley," n.d.

154. HRC, Hanley Papers, Misc, C. J. Greenwood to National Libraries, November 29, 1934.

155. HRC, Hanley Papers, Misc, Neville Isitt to The National Library, December 3, 1934.

156. HRC, Hanley Papers, Misc, Isitt to Boriswood, January 22, 1935.

157. HRC, Hanley Papers, Misc, Field, Roscoe to [Boriswood], February 11, 1935; Hanley Papers, Misc, "Report of the Police Proceedings." Field, Roscoe were the Society of Authors' solicitors. The other lawyer who advised them was the barrister Neville Laski.

158. HRC, Hanley Papers, Misc, "Report of the Police Proceedings."

159. Armstrong, "James Hanley's *Boy*," 358. Jack Kahane of Obelisk got into this line of work when he bought the rights to *The Sleeveless Errand*. Neil Pearson, *Obelisk: A History of Jack Kahane and the Obelisk Press* (Liverpool: Liverpool University Press, 2007), 63–67.

160. Forster, "Liberty in England," 62, 65, 66.

161. Forster, "Liberty in England," 66.

162. P. N. Furbank, *E. M. Forster: A Life*, 2 vols. (New York: Harcourt Brace Jovanovich, 1977–78), 2:231–32; Chris Moores, *Civil Liberties and Human Rights in Twentieth-Century Britain* (Cambridge: Cambridge University Press, 2017), chap. 1. Forster played an important role in the Society of Authors campaign to reform libel law in the late 1930s and 1940s: Christopher Hilliard, "Authors and Artemus Jones: Libel Reform in England, 1910–1952," *Literature and History*, forthcoming.

Chapter Three. Protecting Literature, Suppressing Pulp, 1945–1959

1. *Staffs Employed in Government Departments: Statement Showing the Civil Staffs Employed in Government Departments on 1st October, 1945, Compiled from Returns Furnished to the Treasury*, Cmd. 6718 (London: HMSO, 1945), 75.

2. A. W. Brian Simpson, *In the Highest Degree Odious: Detention Without Trial in Wartime Britain* (Oxford: Clarendon Press, 1993), chaps. 5–19.

3. Gisela C. Lebzelter, *Political Anti-Semitism in England, 1918–1939* (London: Macmillan, 1978), 68–70; Thomas Linehan, *British Fascism, 1918–39: Parties, Ideology and Culture* (Manchester: Manchester University Press, 2000), 71–79; TNA, CRIM 1/864; "Attack on Jews: Articles in Fascist Paper: Seditious Libel Charge," *The Times*, August 15, 1936; "Attack on Jews: Alleged Libellous Articles," *The Times*, September 19, 1936.

4. On *Miss Callaghan Comes to Grief*: Elisabeth Ladenson, "After Jix (1930–1945)," in *Prudes on the Prowl: Fiction and Obscenity in England, 1850 to the Present Day*, ed. David Bradshaw and Rachel Potter (Oxford: Oxford University Press, 2013), 111–37, 135–36; TNA, CRIM 1/1409, R v. Jarrolds Ltd and René Raymond, Central Criminal Court, May 13, 1942, indictment, plea, deposition, list of exhibits. For the popularity of *No Orchids for Miss Blandish*, see University of Sussex, Mass-Observation Archive, TC 20/7/A, anon, "Reading in the Forces," n.d.; Joseph McAleer, *Popular Reading and Publishing in Britain 1914–1950* (Oxford: Clarendon Press, 1992), 92.

5. *HC Deb.*, vol. 567, March 29, 1957, col. 1570. On the trial, see Chris Waters, "Disorders of the Mind, Disorders of the Body Social: Peter Wildeblood and the Making of the Modern Homosexual," in *Moments of Modernity: Reconstructing Britain, 1945–1964*, ed. Becky Conekin, Frank Mort, and Chris Waters (London: Rivers Oram, 1999), 134–51; Peter Wildeblood, *Against the Law* (1955; repr., Harmondsworth: Penguin, 1957).

6. The back cover of C. H. Rolph, ed., *The Trial of Lady Chatterley: Regina v. Penguin Books Limited* (Harmondsworth: Penguin, 1961), described the trial as "probably the most thorough and expensive seminar on Lawrence's work ever given."

7. Norman St John-Stevas, *Obscenity and the Law* (London: Secker and Warburg, 1956), 111; Jeffrey Weeks, *Sex, Politics and Society: The Regulation of Sexuality since 1800*, 3rd ed. (Abingdon: Routledge, 2012), 307; John Springhall, *Youth, Popular Culture and Moral Panics: Penny Gaffs to Gangsta-Rap, 1830–1996* (New York: St. Martin's Press, 1998), 173; John Campbell, *Roy Jenkins: A Well-Rounded Life* (London: Jonathan Cape, 2014), 182.

8. Prosecution of Offences Regulations 1946 (S.I. 1946 No. 1467 [L. 17]), reg. 1; *Minutes of Evidence Taken before the Select Committee on the Obscene Publications Bill: And Appendices: In Session 1956–57* (London: HMSO, 1958), qq. 177–78, 180–83. Compare s. 1(c) of the Prosecution of Offences Regulations: Regulations Respecting the Director of Public Prosecutions, 1886. After 1946, the attorney general still had the power to direct the director of public prosecutions to commence proceedings.

9. TNA, HO 45/25212, "Regulations under the Prosecution of Offences Acts 1879 to 1908: Memorandum by the Director of Public Prosecutions" (1945); Mathew to Sir Oscar Dowson, May 3, 1945.

10. TNA, HO 45/25212, S. H. Burley, untitled memorandum, February 21, 1946.

11. J.Ll.J. Edwards, *The Law Officers of the Crown: A Study of the Offices of Attorney-General and Solicitor-General of England with an Account of the Office of the Director of Public Prosecutions of England* (London: Sweet and Maxwell, 1964); Hartley Shawcross, *Life Sentence: The Memoirs of Lord Shawcross* (London: Constable, 1995), 66–77.

12. R.F.V Heuston, *Lives of the Lord Chancellors, 1885–1940* (Oxford: Clarendon Press, 1987).

13. Edwards, *Law Officers*, 309–11 and chap. 15 generally.

14. Edwards, *Law Officers*, chap. 11.

15. TNA, HO 45/25212, Ede, annotation of February 27, 1946 on Sir Alexander Maxwell to Ede, February 26, 1946; Maxwell, note on minutes page, February 27, 1946; L. S. Brass to Mathew, March 2, 1946.

16. As we will see in the next chapter, Mathew made the decision to launch the most significant obscenity case of the twentieth century, the *Lady Chatterley's Lover* trial, without informing the Home Office.

17. TNA, HO 302/4, "House of Commons: Select Committee on Obscene Publications Bill: Brief for Sir Frank Newsam on His Appearance before the Committee on Monday, 20th May, at 5 p.m." There is a copy of the 1954 list in TNA, DPP 6/59. The document had a blank cover and chiefs of police were instructed to keep its existence confidential, lest the list of titles that had previously been condemned be confused with a censor's index of forbidden books. The distinction was a legitimate one for those versed in the technicalities of British obscenity regulation, but, unsurprisingly, those outside the system did not always see the difference.

18. TNA, HO 302/1, notes on minutes pages, August 5 and August 10, 1954; HO 302/1, J.H.W., notes of a meeting on August 25, 1954 between Sir Theobald Mathew and Sir Frank Newsam, with Philip Allen and J.H.W also present, August 27, 1954; HO 302/1, Mathew to Philip Allen, October 20, 1954; HO 302/1, untitled, undated

typescript list of authors, titles, and details of destruction orders against them; HO 302/1, "Extract from the Minutes of the 67th meeting of the Central Conference of Chief Constables—Held at the Home Office on 10th November, 1954."

19. TNA, HO 302/4, "House of Commons: Select Committee on Obscene Publications Bill: Memorandum Submitted on Behalf of the Home Secretary" (1957), appendix B. A working party of civil servants from different departments remarked in passing that one reason for the increase in enforcement activity in the second half of the 1940s was the way the 1946 regulations obliged chief constables to inform the DPP of any "cases of obscene or indecent libels, exhibitions or publications, in which it appears to the chief officer of police that there is a prima facie case for prosecution." In cases of obscene publications, this requirement was tantamount to a stipulation that the DPP be informed of every application for a destruction order, as the Obscene Publications Act 1857 prescribed that warrants and destruction orders should be granted only for materials that the bench thought would also justify an indictment for prosecution for obscene libel at common law. The fact that the Scottish pattern was similar to that in England and Wales suggests that the 1946 regulations, which did not apply in Scotland, did not make much difference. Prosecution of Offences Regulations 1946, reg. 2(d); TNA, HO 302/13, "Working Party on the Law of Obscenity: Draft Report (Final Revise)."

20. A similar pattern can be observed in the enforcement of laws against homosexual activity: Matt Houlbrook, *Queer London: Perils and Pleasures in the Sexual Metropolis, 1918-1957* (Chicago: University of Chicago Press, 2005), 34.

21. The classic account is George Orwell, "The Art of Donald McGill" (1941), in *The Collected Essays, Journalism and Letters of George Orwell*, ed. Sonia Orwell and Ian Angus, 4 vols. (Boston: Nonpareil Books, 2000), 2:155–65, esp. 155.

22. John K. Walton, *The British Seaside: Holidays and Resorts in the Twentieth Century* (Manchester: Manchester University Press, 2000), 61–62.

23. TNA, HO 302/13, "Report of the Working Party on the Law on Obscenity," November 1955.

24. Harry Cocks, "'The Social Picture of Our Own Times': Reading Obscene Magazines in Mid- Twentieth-Century Britain," *Twentieth Century British History* 27, no. 2 (2016): 171–94, 175.

25. TNA, CUST 49/4712, "House of Commons: Select Committee on Obscene Publications Bill: Memorandum of Evidence by the Home Office," draft typescript, May 14, 1957.

26. "Order to Destroy 108,000 Books," *The Times*, October 12, 1954, 4.

27. Cocks, "Reading Obscene Magazines," 192. See also Kingsley Amis, "The 'Cheesecake' Periodicals," *Author* 66, no. 2 (Winter 1955): 28–30.

28. On mail order see Cocks, "Reading Obscene Magazines," 188–92; Lisa Z. Sigel, *Making Modern Love: Sexual Narratives and Identities in Interwar Britain* (Philadelphia: Temple University Press, 2012), 24–25. Charles Haynes, father and son, ran a mail order business selling explicit photographs, pornographic books and magazines, birth-control guides, and (probably spiced-up versions of) the *Decameron* from circa 1890 to circa 1940. The Metropolitan Police file on them (TNA, MEPO 3/2459) is a large one. Lisa Z. Sigel describes Charles and Co's operations in "Censorship in Interwar Britain: Obscenity, Spectacle, and the Workings of the Liberal State," *Journal of Social History* 45 (2011): 61–83.

29. TNA, CUST 49/4712, M. G. Whittome to B. Rose, April 26, 1957.

30. TNA, CUST 49/4712, "House of Commons: Select Committee on Obscene Publications Bill: Memorandum of Evidence by the Commissioners of Customs and Excise," May 1957.

31. TNA, CUST 49/4712, "Importation of Indecent or Obscene Books and Other Articles," n.d. [1957].

32. TNA, CUST 49/4712, "Obscene Publications Bill: Customs Objections to Clause 4," appendix A, "List of obscene matter seized 1956."

33. Maurice Girodias, "Introduction" to *The Olympia Reader: Selections from the Traveller's Companion Series* ed. Maurice Girodias (New York: Grove Press, 1965), 11–29, 18–23; H. Montgomery Hyde, A History of *Pornography* (London: Heinemann, 1964), 203.

34. TNA, CUST 49/4712, "House of Commons: Select Committee on Obscene Publications Bill: Memorandum of Evidence by the Home Office," draft typescript, May 14, 1957; *Minutes of Evidence*, q. 25.

35. Helen Wickstead, "Soho Typescripts: Handmade Obscene Books in Postwar London Bookshops," *Porn Studies* 7, no. 2 (2020): 187–211.

36. TNA, CUST 49/4712, F. Thornton to Ministère de l'Intérieure, September 3, 1953 and December 1, 1953 (copies).

37. TNA, CUST 49/4712, H. W. Stotesbury to Directeur des Services de Police Judiciaire, Ministère de l'Intérieure, October 15, 1956.

38. Girodias, "Introduction" to *Olympia Reader*, 24–26; Hyde, *History of Pornography*, 202.

39. "The Orphan" is reproduced in its entirety in Martin Barker, *A Haunt of Fears: The Strange History of the British Horror Comics Campaign* (London: Pluto, 1984), 98–105.

40. For the British context see especially Selina Todd and Hilary Young, "Baby-Boomers to 'Beanstalkers': Making the Modern Teenager in Post-War Britain," *Cultural and Social History* 9 (2012): 451–67; Abigail Wills, "Delinquency, Masculinity and Citizenship in England, 1950–1970," *Past and Present*, no. 187 (May 2005): 157–85; Mathew Thomson, *Lost Freedom: The Landscape of the Child and the Post-War British Settlement* (Oxford: Oxford University Press, 2013).

41. UNESCO Digital Library, UNESCO/MC/31, United Nations Educational, Scientific and Cultural Organization, "Expert Meeting on the Creation of an International Body to Study the Influence of Mass Media on Children: Final Report," 28 November 1956; Philippe Bauchard, *The Child Audience: A Report on Press, Film and Radio for Children* (Paris: UNESCO, 1953), 30; TNA, PREM 11/858, R. J. Guppy to P. G. Oates, March 4, 1954.

42. Paul Christoffel, *Censored: A Short History of Censorship in New Zealand* (Wellington: Department of Internal Affairs, 1989), 20–23; Nicole Moore, *The Censor's Library* (St Lucia, Queensland: University of Queensland Press, 2012), 211–16.

43. "Code of the Comics Magazine of Association of America, Inc.," October 26, 1954; Comics Magazine Association of America, press release, December 28, 1954, copies of both in TNA, FO 371/114437.

44. *HC Deb.*, vol. 539, March 28, 1955, col. 51.

45. Fredric Wertham, *The Seduction of the Innocent* (London: Museum Press, 1955); Bart Beaty, *Fredric Wertham and the Critique of Mass Culture* (Jackson: University Press of Mississsippi, 2005).

46. Barker, *Haunt of Fears*, 25.

47. Christopher Hilliard, *English as a Vocation: The "Scrutiny" Movement* (Oxford: Oxford University Press, 2012), chaps. 2, 4, 6.

48. Edward Blishen, *Roaring Boys: A Schoolmaster's Agony* (1955; repr., Bath: Chivers, 1974); Laura Tisdall, "Inside the 'Blackboard Jungle': Male Teachers and Male Pupils at English Secondary Modern Schools in Fact and Fiction, 1950 to 1959," *Cultural and Social History* 12, no. 4 (2015): 489–507, 499.

49. "Restricting Sale of 'Horror Comics,'" *The Times*, November 13, 1954, 4; TNA, PREM 11/858, "'Horror Comics': Memorandum by the Secretary of State for the Home Department, the Secretary of State for Scotland and the Minister of Education," November 25, 1954, C. (54) 359.

50. TNA, PREM 11/858, Jock Colville to Bracken, March 6, 1954; Colville to Churchill, March 16, 1954; Colville to R. J. Guppy, March 19, 1954.

51. TNA, C. (54) 372, "'Horror Comics': Memorandum by the Attorney-General," December 1, 1954, copy in TNA, PREM 11/858.

52. TNA, FO 371/114437, Burley to M. A. Wenner, February 19, 1955; FO 371/114437, Wenner, note in minutes pages, AU1672/4, February 23, 1955.

53. Children and Young Persons (Harmful Publications) Act, 1955, 3 & 4 Eliz. 2, c. 28, ss. 2, 3, 4.

54. Barker, *Haunt of Fears*, 8; Bauchard, *Child Audience*, 30; TNA, PREM 11/858, "American Type Comics," c. March 1954.

55. *Report of the Committee on Obscenity and Film Censorship*, Cmnd. 7772 (London: HMSO, 1979), appendix 1, paras. 25, 42.

56. TNA, HO 302/13, "Report of the Working Party on the Law on Obscenity," November 1955.

57. Norman A. Lazenby, "The New British Pulps," *Writer*, 3rd ser., 7, no. 3 (March 1951): 21. Lazenby's own success as a pulp writer, which allowed him to give up his day job in the late 1940s, is documented in the papers of the Newcastle Writers' Club, of which he was a member. Tyne and Wear Archives Service, SX88/1/2, Newcastle Writers' Club minutes, November 7, 1950. On the "popular writing" movement, see Christopher Hilliard, *To Exercise Our Talents: The Democratization of Writing in Britain* (Cambridge, MA: Harvard University Press, 2006), chaps. 1–3, 8.

58. Steve Holland, *The Trials of Hank Janson* (Tolworth: Telos, 2004), chap. 3.

59. George Orwell, "Raffles and Miss Blandish" (1944), in Orwell, *Collected Essays*, 3: 223, 224.

60. TNA, DPP 2/2301, R. v. Carter and Reiter, Central Criminal Court, January 14, 1945, transcript of summing up, verdict, and sentencing, p. 30.

61. Holland, *Trials of Hank Janson*, 115.

62. TNA, DPP 2/2301, "Statement of Reginald Alfred Baldwin," November 25, 1953; "Statement of Hugh Watson," November 25, 1953.

63. Holland, *Trials of Hank Janson*, 133–35.

64. Holland, *Trials of Hank Janson*, 128.

65. TNA, DPP 2/2301, R. v. Carter and Reiter, Central Criminal Court, January 14, 1945, transcript of summing up, verdict, and sentencing, p. 24.

66. TNA, DPP 2/2301, "The Queen against Reginald Herbert Carter, Arc Press Ltd. New Fiction Press Ltd Julius Reiter and Gaywood Press Ltd.: Observations to Counsel: Mr. Maxwell Turner," n.d.

67. Dodson was the recorder of London, hence Sir Gerald rather than Mr. Justice.

68. *Both Sides of the Circle: The Autobiography of Christmas Humphreys* (London: George Allen and Unwin, 1978).

69. TNA, DPP 2/2301, R v. Carter and Reiter, Central Criminal Court, January 14, 1954, transcript of summing up, verdict, and sentencing, pp. 28–29.

70. Roger Davidson and Gayle Davis, *The Sexual State: Sexuality and Scottish Governance, 1950–80* (Edinburgh: Edinburgh University Press, 2012), 219; R v. Reiter and Others [1954] 2 QB 16 at 19, 21.

71. *R v. Reiter and Others*, 16 at 20–21, quoting Gellatly v. Laird 1953 SC(J) 26. Cockburn had made the same point about comparisons in *R v. Hicklin*, 3 Queen's Bench (1867–68): 360 at 371.

72. TNA, HO 302/13, "Report of the Working Party on the Law on Obscenity," November 1955.

73. *Minutes of Evidence*, q. 174.

74. Stevas, *Obscenity and the Law*, 111.

75. David Bradshaw, "American Beastliness, the Great Purge and its Aftermath (1946–1959)," in Bradshaw and Potter, *Prudes on the Prowl*, 138–58, 138, 147–49.

76. Weeks, *Sex, Politics and Society*, 307.

77. Springhall, *Youth, Popular Culture and Moral Panics*, 173. See also Stevas, *Obscenity and the Law*, 111, and the exchange between Mark Bonham Carter and the former Labour home secretary James Chuter Ede, *HC Deb.*, vol. 597, December 16, 1958, cols. 1027–29.

78. Houlbrook, *Queer London*, 34–35. See also Brian Lewis, *Wolfenden's Witnesses: Homosexuality in Postwar Britain* (Basingstoke: Palgrave Macmillan, 2016), 5.

79. LSE, Rolph Papers, 2/3/11, C. H. Rolph, "Books and the Censorship: An Account of the Origin and Operation of the Obscene Publications Acts 1959 to 1964," May 1968; Rolph, *Trial of Lady Chatterley*, 2–3.

80. TNA, HO 302/13, "Report of the Working Party on the Law on Obscenity," November 1955; HO 302/13, "Working Party on the Law of Obscenity," minutes of first meeting, February 17, 1955; *Minutes of Evidence*, qq. 167–68, 170–71, 174, 179.

81. TNA, HO 302/1, Mathew to Newsam, n.d. (August 1954). At the time Deutsch was trading as Allen Wingate.

82. *Minutes of Evidence*, q. 174.

83. TNA, HO 302/1, Mathew to Newsam, n.d. (August 1954).

84. *The Philanderer* was first published in New York by Simon and Schuster in 1952 as *The Tightrope*. Another book with that title had been published in Britain not long before, so it was given a new title.

85. TNA, CRIM 1/2439, [Warburg?] to Lieper, April 23, 1952.

86. R v. Secker Warburg Ltd and Others 2 [1954] All ER 683. Most of Stable's summing up was reproduced in a report, probably by Hewitt, in the Society of Authors' magazine: "The Test of Obscenity: Regina v. Martin Secker and Warburg, Fredric John Warburg and the Camelot Press Limited," *Author*, 65, no. 1 (Autumn 1954): 1–5, 1. All quotations from Stable in this paragraph come appear in the report in the *Author*.

87. *Minutes of Evidence*, 109. Bodkin had proposed this test to himself when he read *The Sleeveless Errand*: "Imagine a daughter in a respectable English household

reading" it. TNA, DPP 1/92, "Re 'Sleeveless Errand': Rex v. Eric Honeywood Partridge: Brief to Apply for Order of Destruction," n.d. (c. March 1929).

88. James Fitzjames Stephen, *A Digest of the Criminal Law (Crimes and Punishments)*, 4th ed. (London: Macmillan, 1887), 349, "Note XI (to Article 172)." The link between Stable's summing up and Stephen's *Digest* is noted in Bodleian, Roy Jenkins Papers, MS Jenkins 92, Hewitt, "Memorandum on the Progress of the Obscene Publications Bill," January 1, 1959.

89. Norman St John-Stevas, "The Obscene Publications Bill, 1955," *Author* 65, no. 3 (spring 1955): 54–56, 54.

90. "The Test of Obscenity," *Author* 65, no. 2 (winter 1954), 23–24, 23.

91. *Minutes of Evidence*, qq. 830–831.

92. Victor Bonham-Carter, *Authors by Profession*, vol. 2, *From the Copyright Act 1911 until the End of 1981* (London: The Bodley Head and the Society of Authors, 1984), 115. The account here is based on Roy Jenkins's papers in the Bodleian Library, Oxford, as well as Cabinet documents and parliamentary debates. For a perceptive account based on published sources, see Anton Kirchofer, "The Making of the 1959 Obscene Publications Act: Trials and Debates on Literary Obscenity in Britain before the Case of Lady Chatterley," in Ralf Grüttemeier, ed., *Literary Trials: Exceptio Artis and Theories of Literature in Court* (New York: Bloomsbury Academic, 2016), 49–68.

93. The active campaigners on the left were Roy Jenkins, then a Gaitskellite Labour MP, and C. R. Hewitt of the *New Statesman*. The Conservatives included Tony Lambton, Hugh Fraser, and Norman St John-Stevas (who did not become an MP until the 1960s). A. P. Herbert had been an independent MP, but his sympathies and cultural allegiances were Tory.

94. Alec Craig, *The Banned Books of England* (London: George Allen and Unwin, 1937); Craig, *Above All Liberties* (London: George Allen and Unwin, 1942); Craig, *Suppressed Books: A History of the Conception of Literary Obscenity* (1962; repr., Cleveland: World Publishing, 1963); ULL, Alec Craig Papers, MS1091.

95. By the mid-1950s *The Times* had published between 500 and 1000 of his letters. Reginald Pound, *A. P. Herbert: A Biography* (London: Michael Joseph, 1976), 91–92.

96. Alana Harris, "'Pope Norman', Griffin's Report and Roman Catholic Reactions to Homosexual Law Reform in England and Wales, 1954–1971," in *New Approaches in History and Theology to Same-Sex Love and Desire*, ed. Mark D. Chapman and Dominic Janes (Cham: Springer, 2018), 93–116.

97. "Obscenity in Literature," *Author* 65, no. 3 (spring 1955), 49–50, 50.

98. A. P. Herbert, *I Object: Letter to the Electors of East Harrow: With Some Proposals for the Reform of the Machinery of Government* (London: The Bodley Head, 1959). The committee began work as the horror comics campaign was gathering momentum. Herbert wrote to the home secretary, Lloyd George, to raise the issue of obscene publications urgently before horror comics used up all the legislative oxygen. In February 1955, as the government introduced its Children and Young Persons (Harmful Publications) Bill, Herbert wrote to *The Times* urging that this single-issue bill be replaced with a more comprehensive one providing protection for literature alongside powers to crack down on horror comics. Opposition MPs made similar

arguments to no avail. TNA, HO 302/12, A. P. Herbert to Gwilym Lloyd George, December 2, 1954; *The Times*, February 21, 1955; "Obscenity in Literature," *Author* 65, no. 4 (Summer 1955), 77–79, 78.

99. TNA HO 302/13, [Stevas], "Legal Note," n.d.; Norman St John-Stevas, "The Obscene Publications Bill, 1955," *Author*, 65, no. 3 (spring 1955), 54–56.

100. Stephen, *Digest*, 105, article 172.

101. TNA, HO 302/13, "Obscene Publications (Consolidation) Bill," typescript (1955).

102. Bodleian, MS Jenkins 92, "Expert Evidence," anonymous, undated handwritten notes addressed to "Roy."

103. TNA HO 302/13, [Stevas], "Legal Note," n.d.; Stevas, "Obscene Publications Bill, 1955,", 55

104. This claim is based on a comparison of the figures in TNA, CUST 49/4712, "House of Commons: Select Committee on Obscene Publications Bill: Memorandum of Evidence by the Home Office," draft typescript, May 14, 1957, with those in Bodleian, MS Jenkins 92, "Summary of Indecent Publication Prosecutions undertaken by the Director of Public Prosecutions for the Period 1946 to 1956," n.d. (despite its title the latter document covers applications for destruction orders as well as prosecutions for obscene libel).

105. *HC Deb.*, vol. 538, March 15, 1955, cols. 1127–1130.

106. TNA, HO 302/12, A. W. Peterson, note in minutes pages, January 25, 1955.

107. TNA, HO 302/13, Newsam to Sir Charles Cunningham, November 1, 1954; Bodleian, MS Jenkins 92, "Obscene Publications Bill (Chronology)," undated typescript; Bodleian, MS Jenkins 92, A. P. Herbert to Gwilym Lloyd George, December 7, 1954. Newsam began assembling the civil service working party even before the Herbert Committee was formed.

108. TNA, HO 302/12, Sir Austin Strutt, note in minutes pages, January 3, 1955.

109. TNA, HO 302/13, H. Stotesbury, "Obscene Publications Bill: Note for S. of S's Use at Legislation Committee, Tuesday, November 22nd" (1955).

110. TNA, HO 302/3, Stotesbury, note in minutes pages, November 30, 1955; "Obscene Publications Bill: Brief for Sir Hugh Lucas-Tooth on the Motion for the Second Reading, November 25th"; HO 302/3, "Cabinet: Extract from Minutes of a Meeting of the Legislation Committee Held on 6th March, 1956"; Stotesbury, "Note for Legislation Committee Tuesday, 6th March, 1956: Item—Obscene Publications Bill," March 3, 1956; *HC Deb.*, vol. 546, November 25, 1955, cols. 1891–92.

111. *HC Deb.*, vol. 560, November 21, 1956, col. 1754.

112. There was even the danger that Lambton's bill would get a second reading despite government opposition, and the government would be embarrassed as it had recently been when a private member's bill to abolish capital punishment made it this far.

113. TNA, HO 302/3, Strutt, "Obscene Publications Bill," n.d. (March 1957).

114. TNA, HO 302/3, Newsam, "Obscene Publications Bill," March 26, 1957.

115. TNA, HO 302/3, fragment of briefing for home secretary for Legislation Committee, anonymous but with emendations in Newsam's hand, n.d. (probably March 26, 1957); Butler to David [Renton], March 28, 1957; Newsam to Butler, March 27, 1957.

116. Butler's view, Newsam guessed, was that "if the Legislative Cttee think that the Bill should be opposed, (as distinct from point out difficulties,) the A.G. should undertake the job of opposing it!" TNA, HO 302/3, Newsam, handwritten postscript, March 26, 1957, on Newsam, "Obscene Publications Bill," March 26, 1957.

117. TNA, HO 302/3, Newsam to Butler, March 27, 1957, and Butler's undated note on the same letter.

118. *HC Deb.*, vol. 567, March 29, 1957, cols. 1578–1581; "The Obscene Publications Bill," *Author* 67, no. 4 (Summer 1957): 71.

119. *Report from the Select Committee on Obscene Publications*, HC 123-I (London: HMSO, 1958), minutes, 12 December 1957, esp. q. 58.

120. *Minutes of Evidence*, q. 781.

121. *Report from the Select Committee*, proceedings, xvi–xvii, and paras. 2, 20. See also *HC Deb.*, vol. 597, December 16, 1958, cols. 1026–27.

122. TNA, CAB 134/1972, Cabinet: Home Affairs Committee, minutes of meeting on November 21, 1958. Manningham-Buller was not a member of the committee, but as attorney general he was supposed to have a say on matters of law reform. The minutes summarize points from the ensuing discussion without specifying who made them, but the objection to requiring the DPP or attorney general's fiat was one that Manningham-Buller had made in his submission to the select committee.

123. "Memorandum by the Attorney General," para. 3, in *Report from the Select Committee*. See also Edwards, *Law Officers*, 237 n.

124. TNA, LCO 72/258, Lord Rodger of Earlsferry to Kenneth Clarke, June 3, 1992.

125. TNA, CAB 134/1972, Cabinet: Home Affairs Committee, minutes of meeting on November 21, 1958.

126. R. A. Butler, *The Art of the Possible: The Memoirs of Lord Butler* (1971; repr., Harmondsworth: Penguin, 1973), 234.

127. "Obscene Publications," *Author* 69, no. 2 (Winter 1958): 36–37, 37.

128. TNA, HO 302/21, Kilmuir to Manningham-Buller, December 5, 1958.

129. TNA, HO 302/21, Manningham-Buller to Kilmuir, December 2, 1958.

130. There is a mordant analysis of Manningham-Buller's character in Patrick Devlin, *Easing the Passing: The Trial of Dr John Bodkin Adams* (London: Bodley Head, 1985).

131. TNA, CUST 49/4712, anonymous handwritten note on Stevas's "Legal Note," n.d.

132. TNA, CAB 129/95/50, "Obscene Publications Bill: Memorandum by the Lord Chancellor," December 15, 1958.

133. Herbert, *I Object*, 5.

134. Pound, *A. P. Herbert*, 256.

135. *HC Deb.*, vol. 597, December 16, 1958, col. 1026. Jenkins too could not resist alluding to Herbert's stunt: "Perhaps we should not inquire too closely as to why there has, apparently, been a rather sudden change of heart on the part of the Government." *HC Deb.*, vol. 597, December 16, 1958, col. 1005.

136. Pound, *A. P. Herbert*, 257.

137. Bodleian, MS Jenkins 92, Jenkins to [Herbert Committee members], January 14, 1959.

138. Roy Jenkins, *A Life at the Centre* (London: Macmillan, 1991), 122.

139. Bodleian, MS Jenkins 92, Hewitt, "Memorandum on the Progress of the Obscene Publications Bill," January 1, 1959; MS Jenkins 92, Hewitt, "Obscene Publications Bill," February 25, 1959. Gardiner represented the publishers Heinemann in one of the 1954 obscenity prosecutions. TNA, CRIM 1/2496, R v. Baxter and Others.

140. Bodleian, MS Jenkins 92, Butler to Jenkins, January 27, 1959.

141. *HC Deb.*, vol. 597, December 16, 1958, col. 1002; "Memorandum Submitted on Behalf of the Secretary of State for the Home Department," *Minutes of Evidence*, May 20, 1957, 3. In his speech in Parliament, Butler used some of the same phrases as the working party's report.

142. *HC Deb.*, vol. 597, December 16, 1958, col. 1002.

143. Bodleian, MS Jenkins 92, Hewitt, "Memorandum on the Progress of the Obscene Publications Bill," January 1, 1959.

144. Bodleian, MS Jenkins 92, Hewitt, "Memorandum on the Progress of the Obscene Publications Bill," January 1, 1959.

145. Bodleian, MS Jenkins 92, Jenkins to [Herbert Committee], January 14, 1959.

146. Bodleian, MS Jenkins 92, Gardiner to Hewitt, January 26, 1959.

147. Bodleian, MS Jenkins 92, Jenkins to [Herbert Committee], January 14, 1959.

148. Bodleian, MS Jenkins 92, Hewitt, "Herbert Committee: Government 'Draft Clauses' Discussed with Home Office Advisers," February 6, 1959. The Herbert Committee representatives appear to have agreed with H. W. Stotesbury of the Home Office that the expert testimony provision could serve as a substitute for an author's right to be heard at the trial of their publisher.

149. Bodleian, MS Jenkins 92, G. P. Renton to Jenkins, February 6, 1959. David Renton, the Home Office minister who would have represented the government, was bogged down in another standing committee dealing with the Street Offences Bill, which implemented the Wolfenden Committee's recommendations about prostitution. G. P. Renton (no relation) was Butler's private secretary.

150. Jenkins, *Life at the Centre*, 123.

151. Jenkins, *Life at the Centre*, 123.

152. Bodleian, MS Jenkins 92, Hewitt, "Herbert Committee: Government 'Draft Clauses' Discussed with Home Office Advisers," February 6, 1959; *HC Deb.*, vol. 604, April 24, 1959, col. 804; Bodleian, MS Jenkins 92, Herbert, "Expert Evidence—Note on the Solicitor-General's Remarks Variously Reported in the Papers This Morning (March 19, 1959)." *Halsbury's Laws of England* provided support for Manningham-Buller's view, as someone on the Herbert Committee knew. Bodleian, MS Jenkins 92, "Expert Evidence," anon., handwritten notes addressed to Roy Jenkins.

153. Bodleian, MS Jenkins 92, Butler to Jenkins, April 16, 1959.

154. Jenkins, *Life at the Centre*, 124.

155. Jenkins, *Life at the Centre*, 124.

156. Trinity College Archives, Cambridge, R. A. Butler Papers, RAB G34/99, Jenkins to Butler, August 9, 1959.

157. Stephen, *Digest*, 105, article 172; Obscene Publications Act, 1959, 7 & 8 Eliz 2, c. 66, s. 4(1) (italics added).

158. *HC Deb.*, vol. 604, April 24, 1959, col. 857. The MP was Sir Kenneth Pickthorn, former president of Corpus Christi College, Cambridge.

159. TNA, LO 2/146, G. E. Dudman to Manningham-Buller, December 17, 1958; Bodleian, MS Jenkins 92, "Note by the Director of Public Prosecutions as to the Prosecutions of the Distributors of Vols. I and II of Lolita," n.d.

160. Bodleian, MS Jenkins 92, Gerald Barry to Denys Kilham Roberts, January 10, 1959. Hewitt received a copy of this letter as well: LSE, Rolph Papers, 2/3/9. Barry did not spell out his reasons, but it is not difficult to see how Weidenfeld and Nicolson's publication of *Lolita* could cause trouble. If the book appeared and the police and the DPP took no action, that would give the impression that the law posed no threat to literature; and if the book were the subject of legal proceedings, and people who had not read it were only aware of the plot, it might appear that the "reputable publishers" were not so reputable after all. See the remarks of Sir Godfrey Nicholson and Charles Doughty in the Commons debate of 16 December 1958: *HC Deb.*, vol. 597, December 16, 1958, cols. 1007–8.

161. TNA, LO 2/146, Manningham-Butler to Robert Jenkins, January 1960, day not specified.

162. TNA, LO 2/146, Dudman, "Lolita," October 27, 1959.

163. TNA, LO 2/146, Dudman, "Note," November 11, 1959, summarizing meeting of November 2, 1959.

Chapter Four. The Lady Chatterley's Lover *Trial, 1960*

1. References to the trial proceedings are to H. Montgomery Hyde, ed., *The Lady Chatterley's Lover Trial (Regina v. Penguin Books Limited)* (London: The Bodley Head, 1990); and C. H. Rolph, ed., *The Trial of Lady Chatterley: Regina v. Penguin Books Limited: The Transcript of the Trial* (Harmondsworth: Penguin, 1961). There is also a copy of the partial transcript produced by the stenographers George Walpole Ltd in TNA, DPP 2/3077, part 4. Both the Hyde and Rolph volumes are selective. Hyde is more comprehensive, but Rolph includes some exchanges that Hyde does not. Hyde's edition uses the official transcripts. The Rolph volume is probably based on the partial transcripts produced by the Press Association. There is one point in this chapter, concerning Richard Hoggart's testimony, where a discrepancy between the two versions is material; I have followed Rolph, whose version is corroborated by Sybille Bedford's account for *Esquire* (and was seared in Hoggart's memory).

2. Peter Mandler, *The English National Character: The History of an Idea from Edmund Burke to Tony Blair* (New Haven: Yale University Press, 2006), 216–17.

3. "Notes on Contributors," in Gerald Gardiner and Andrew Martin, eds., *Law Reform Now* (London: Victor Gollancz, 1964), vii.

4. On Gardiner's part in the foundation of the Society of Labour Lawyers, see Nick Blake and Harry Rajak, *Wigs and Workers: A History of the Haldane Society of Socialist Lawyers, 1930–1980* (London: Haldane Society of Socialist Lawyers, [1980]), 33–35.

5. Stefan Collini, "Critical Minds: Raymond Williams and Richard Hoggart," in *English Pasts: Essays in History and Culture* (Oxford: Oxford University Press, 1999), 210–30, 227; Stephen Brooke, "Gender and Working Class Identity in Britain during the 1950s," *Journal of Social History* 34, no. 4 (2001): 773–95.

6. Stefan Collini, *The Nostalgic Imagination: History in English Criticism* (Oxford: Oxford University Press, 2019); Guy Ortolano, *The Two Cultures*

Controversy: Science, Literature and Cultural Politics in Postwar Britain (Cambridge: Cambridge University Press, 2009); Perry Anderson, "Components of the National Culture," *New Left Review* 50 (July–August 1968), 84–85.

7. Christopher Hilliard, *English as a Vocation: The "Scrutiny" Movement* (Oxford: Oxford University Press, 2012), chaps. 2, 4, 5. Leavis himself declined a request to testify for Penguin because he was unwilling to defend *Lady Chatterley's Lover* as a great work of literature—he thought it didactic and a failure by Lawrence's own artistic criteria—or as essential to a proper understanding of the novelist's other works. Leavis was not in favor of censorship, and had made a target of himself by teaching *Ulysses* before the import ban was lifted. But he had a history of refusing to choose between two imperfect options, no matter the stakes, and he abstained again. F. R. Leavis, "The Orthodoxy of Enlightenment," in Leavis, *Anna Karenina and Other Essays* (London: Chatto and Windus, 1967), 235–41; Leavis, "'Under Which King, Bezonian?'" *Scrutiny* 1, no. 3 (December 1932): 205–14.

8. Richard Hoggart, *The Uses of Literacy: Aspects of Working-Class Life, with Special References to Publications and Entertainments* (London: Chatto and Windus, 1957).

9. Raymond Williams, *Culture and Society, 1780–1950* (London: Chatto and Windus, 1958).

10. Bristol, Penguin Archive, A520, Dieter Pevsner to Eunice Frost, April 21, 1959. I have corrected a typo in the quoted passage ("developemtn").

11. Wolf Lepenies, *Between Literature and Science: The Rise of Sociology*, trans. R. J. Hollingdale (1985; English trans. Cambridge: Cambridge University Press, 1988), chap. 6; Peter Mandler, "Good Reading for the Million: The 'Paperback Revolution' and the Co-Production of Academic Knowledge in Mid Twentieth-Century Britain and America," *Past and Present*, no. 244 (August 2019): 235–69, 265.

12. D. H. Lawrence, *Lady Chatterley's Lover* (1928), in *Lady Chatterley's Lover; A Propos of Lady Chatterley's Lover*, ed. Michael Squires (Cambridge: Cambridge University Press, 1993), 152 (all quotations from the novel are from this edition); F. R. Leavis, "D. H. Lawrence" (1932) in Leavis, *For Continuity* (Cambridge: Minority Press, 1933), 111–48, 135–38.

13. D. H. Lawrence, "A Propos of Lady Chatterley's Lover" (1930) in *Lady Chatterley's Lover; A Propos of Lady Chatterley's Lover*, ed. Squires, 313–14.

14. On Penguin see Mandler, "Good Reading"; Rick Rylance, "Reading with a Mission: The Public Sphere of Penguin Books," *Critical Quarterly* 47, no. 4 (2005): 48–66; Nicholas Joicey, "A Paperback Guide to Progress: Penguin Books 1935–c. 1951," *Twentieth Century British History* 4, no. 1 (1993): 25–56; Jeremy Lewis, *Penguin Special: The Life and Times of Allen Lane* (London: Penguin, 2005), chaps. 5–6; Richard Hornsey, "'The Penguins Are Coming': Brand Mascots and Utopian Mass Consumption in Interwar Britain," *Journal of British Studies* 57, no. 4 (2018): 812–39; Richard Williams, *The First Thousand Penguins: Penguin Main Series 1–1000: A Bibliographic Checklist with a Guide to Their Value* (Scunthorpe: Dragonby Press, 1987).

15. Lewis, *Penguin Special*, 315–16, 319–20; Rolph, *Trial of Lady Chatterley*, 85 (testimony of W. E. Williams); Grove Press, Inc. v. Christenberry, 175 F. Supp. 488 (Southern District of New York, 1959).

16. Allen Lane was involved in The Bodley Head's first steps to publishing *Ulysses*: "The Ban on 'Ulysses,'" *Evening Standard*, January 20, 1934. John Lane of The Bodley

Head was Allen's uncle. Allen struck out on his own and founded Penguin in 1935. Penguin did not have a record of taking chances on avant-garde or controversial books for the simple reason that most of its list consisted of paperback reprints of novels first published by other firms. Its only originals were non-fiction.

17. The average print run for a Penguin was between 40,000 and 50,000. Penguin had recently printed 200,000 copies of John Braine's *Room at the Top*, a topical angry-young-man novel, and 250,000 of Nicholas Monserrat's *The Cruel Sea*, which had eluded the Isle of Man's crackdown on obscenity despite a scene comparable to those in Hank Janson. Rolph, *Trial of Lady Chatterley*, 87–88 (testimony of W. E. Williams).

18. Lewis, *Penguin Special*, 320.

19. TNA, DPP 2/3077, part 1, Sir Austin Strutt to Sir Theobald Mathew, June 17, 1960.

20. Alistair McCleery, "Lady Chatterley's Lover Re-covered," *Publishing History* 59 (2006): 61–84, 71.

21. TNA, DPP 2/3077, part 1, F. G. Markin to DPP, March 25, 1960.

22. TNA, HO 265/70, *Censorship in the Arts: The Full Text of the Freedom of Vision Teach-in, Held at Hampstead Old Town Hall, October 2nd 1966 from 3 p.m. till 10 p.m.* (London: Academy of Visual Arts, n.d.), 40.

23. TNA, DPP 2/3077, part 1, Crump to F. G. Markin, March 25, 1960.

24. TNA, DPP 2/3077, part 1, "The Queen against Penguin Books Limited: Re Lady Chatterley's Lover," undated typescript.

25. TNA, DPP 2/3077, part 1, "The Queen against Penguin Books Limited: Re Lady Chatterley's Lover," undated typescript.

26. TNA, DPP 2/3077, part 1, Mervyn Griffith-Jones, "Re 'Lady Chatterley's Lover': Opinion," July 27, 1960. Presumably out of habit, Griffith-Jones referred to "obscene libel" rather than the new Obscene Publications Act.

27. TNA, DPP 2/3077, part 1, George Dudman, "Lady Chatterley's Lover," c. December 6, 1960.

28. TNA, DPP 2/3077, part 1, Manningham-Buller to Mathew, August 20, 1960.

29. TNA, LO 2/148, "Lady Chatterley's Lover," note attached to letter from Dudman to A. R. Isserlis, December 6, 1960.

30. TNA, DPP 2/3077, part 1, Jack Simon to Mathew, August 25, 1960.

31. Dudman wrote, "This is balls" beside the line "It would not be proper to discuss the reasons for the Director's decision." Next to the sentence "The Director's action has enabled a High Court ruling to be obtained on the interpretation of the new law, in particular on the admissibility of expert evidence," Dudman wrote, "This is balls too." TNA, LO 2/148, "History of the recent legislation," n.d., with "A.G. P.S." written in the top right-hand corner, and annotations in Dudman's distinctive hand.

32. TNA, DPP 2/3077, part 1, Mathew to Strutt, August 17, 1960; TNA, LO 2/148, George Dudman, "Lady Chatterley's Lover," c. December 6, 1960 (sent with a cover letter to A. R. Isserlis, December 6, 1960).

33. "The Test of Obscenity: Regina v. Martin Secker and Warburg, Fredric John Warburg and the Camelot Press Limited," *Author* 65, no. 1 (Autumn 1954): 1–5, 2.

34. TNA, HO 302/21, Manningham-Buller to Kilmuir, December 2, 1958.

35. TNA, LO 2/148, George Dudman, "Lady Chatterley's Lover," c. December 6, 1960 (sent with a cover letter to A. R. Isserlis, December 6, 1960).

36. TNA, DPP 2/3077, part 1, Mathew to Lane, March 28, 1961. Lane had sent Mathew a copy of C. H. Rolph's edition of the trial transcript. "How very nice of you," Mathew replied. "I still think privately that the only great message to be gleaned from Lady Chatterley is that duration is more important than frequency."

37. D. H. Lawrence, *Lady Chatterley's Lover* (Hamburg: Odyssey Press, 1933). On Holroyd-Reece's determination to publish *Lady Chatterley's Lover* and Lawrence's unpublished manuscripts in the early 1930s, see Lise Jaillant, *Cheap Modernism: Expanding Markets, Publishers' Series, and the Avant-Garde* (Edinburgh: Edinburgh University Press, 2017), 111.

38. TNA, DPP 2/3077, part 1, statement by the accused, Bow Street Magistrates' Court, September 8, 1960.

39. "Lady Chatterley," *Observer*, September 18, 1960; TNA, DPP 2/3077, part 1, "Complete Extractions from Who's Who Concerning Persons Mentioned Below," n.d.

40. TNA, DPP 2/3077, part 1, Mathew to Helen Gardner, August 23, 1960; Mathew to N. G. Annan, August 23, 1960; Gardner to Mathew, August 24, 1960; Annan to Mathew, August 24, 1960.

41. TNA, DPP 2/3077, part 1, "The Queen against Penguin Books Limited: Case to Advise," n.d.

42. TNA, DPP 2/3077, part 1, "Extract from The Spectator, October 1, 1932" (typed extract from David Cecil's review of *D. H. Lawrence's Letters*, edited by Aldous Huxley; and a typed copy of "Obscene Writing" by Cecil). There is a story, which is difficult to verify, that Eliot hung around the Old Bailey during the *Lady Chatterley's Lover* trial so that if the prosecution quoted *After Strange Gods* he could appear for the defense and disown his comments. Peter Ackroyd, *T. S. Eliot* (London: Hamish Hamilton, 1984), 331.

43. Graham Hough, *The Dark Sun: A Study of D. H. Lawrence* (London: Duckworth, 1956).

44. Hough, *Dark Sun*, 161; underlined in the copy in TNA, DPP 2/3077, part 1.

45. Hough, *Dark Sun*, 161–62; underlined in copy in TNA, DPP 2/3077, part 1.

46. TNA, DPP 2/3077, part 1, "The Queen against Penguin Books Limited: Note to Counsel," n.d.

47. Bristol, Penguin Archive, DM1679/9, Michael B. Rubinstein, "Regina v. Penguin Books Limited: re: Lady Chatterley's Lover: Draft Brief on hearing of the trial at the Old Bailey: Mr Gerald Gardiner Q.C.," October 7, 1960, 1; handwritten emendation made October 11, 1960 or later.

48. Diana Souhami, *The Trials of Radclyffe Hall* (London: Weidenfeld and Nicolson, 1998), 194–98.

49. Bristol, Penguin Archive, DM1679/9, Rubinstein, "Draft Brief," 13; Bodleian, MS Jenkins 92, OPA box, "Expert Evidence," anonymous, undated handwritten notes addressed to "Roy."

50. Bodleian, MS Jenkins 92, Gardiner to C. R. Hewitt, January 26, 1959.

51. R v. Secker Warburg, Ltd. and Others 2 [1954] All ER 683 at 685, 688; Bristol, Penguin Archive, DM1679/9, Rubinstein, "Draft Brief," 7–8. The DPP's staff remarked that Lawrence's reference in *A Propos of Lady Chatterley's Lover* to "a proper reverence for sex seems to find some echo in Stable J's judgment in the case of the 'Philanderer.'" TNA, DPP 2/3077, part 1, "Some Extracts from 'A propos of Lady Chatterley's Lover,'" n.d.

52. For literature's "message," see *R v. Secker Warburg*, 683 at 688, quoted by Rubinstein: Bristol, Penguin Archive, DM1679/9, Rubinstein, "Draft Brief," 7.

53. On this popular theory of literature, see Christopher Hilliard, *To Exercise Our Talents: The Democratization of Writing in Britain* (Cambridge, MA: Harvard University Press, 2006), chap. 3.

54. Bristol, Penguin Archive, DM1679/9, Rubinstein, "Draft Brief," 1.

55. Brian Way, "Sex and Language: Obscene Words in D. H. Lawrence and Henry Miller," *New Left Review* no. 27 (September–October 1964): 72 (italics in original). For the sorts of problems that indirect modes of narration can give rise to in obscenity trials, see Dominick LaCapra, *"Madame Bovary" on Trial* (Ithaca: Cornell University Press, 1982).

56. Obscene Publications Act, 1959, 7 & 8 Eliz 2, c. 66, s. 4(1).

57. Sam Brewitt-Taylor, *Christian Radicalism in the Church of England and the Invention of the British Sixties, 1957–1970: The Hope of a World Transformed* (Oxford: Oxford University Press, 2018), 182–85.

58. Hyde, *Lady Chatterley's Lover Trial*, 127–28.

59. Mark Roodhouse, "Lady Chatterley and the Monk: Anglican Radicals and the Lady Chatterley Trial of 1960," *Journal of Ecclesiastical History* 59, no. 3 (2008): 475–500, 481. DPP officials came across Jarrett-Kerr's *D. H. Lawrence and Human Existence* in the course of their research, but they copied only Eliot's two-page foreword, which revised his own earlier assessment in the course of commending Jarrett-Kerr's. TNA, DPP 2/3077, part 1, "Copy: Foreword by T. S. Eliot to 'D. H. Lawrence and Human Existence' by Father William Tiverton," n.d.

60. Roodhouse, "Lady Chatterley and the Monk," 479.

61. Roodhouse, "Lady Chatterley and the Monk," 490.

62. Matthew Grimley, "Law, Morality and Secularisation: The Church of England and the Wolfenden Report, 1954–1967," *Journal of Ecclesiastical History*, 60, no. 4 (2009): 725–41, 730–31.

63. Hyde, *Lady Chatterley's Lover Trial*, 129 (the Rev Prebendary Alfred Stephan Hopkinson).

64. Bristol, Penguin Archive, DM1679/9, Rubinstein, "Draft Brief," 10.

65. Hyde, *Lady Chatterley's Lover Trial*, 164–66, 192 (Hemmings); Rolph, *Trial of Lady Chatterley*, 107–8 (Jones); Bristol, Penguin Archive, DM1679/9, Rubinstein, "Draft Brief," 13 (Jones).

66. Someone on the DPP staff commented: "It is interesting to notice that Lawrence himself was bitterly opposed to 'sex education' for children." TNA, DPP 2/3077, part 1, "Notes on Mr. Gardiner's Opening Address," n.d. (October 1960).

67. See the account of Gardiner's defense of the *Daily Mirror* columnist and professional grump William Connor in the libel suit brought by the pianist Liberace in 1959 in H. Montgomery Hyde, *Their Good Names: Twelve Cases of Libel and Slander with Some Introductory Reflections on the Law* (London: Hamish Hamilton, 1970), chap. 12.

68. Though in cross-examination the prosecution asked other witnesses, especially Graham Hough, to comment on the quality of the writing in particular passages.

69. Hyde, *Lady Chatterley's Lover Trial*, 205.

70. Hyde, *Lady Chatterley's Lover Trial*, 206.

71. Raymond Williams, *Keywords: A Vocabulary of Culture and Society* (London: Fontana, 1976).

72. Roger Dataller, *The Plain Man and the Novel* (London: Thomas Nelson, 1940); Storm Jameson, *The Georgian Novel and Mr Robinson* (London: Heinemann, 1929).

73. Hyde, *Lady Chatterley's Lover Trial*, 137.

74. Hyde, *Lady Chatterley's Lover Trial*, 148.

75. Bedford, "Trial of Lady Chatterley's Lover," 162; Richard Hoggart, *An Imagined Life: Life and Times, Volume III, 1959–91* (1992; repr., Oxford: Oxford University Press, 1993), 55–56; Rolph, *Trial of Lady Chatterley*, 100. The version used by Hyde does not name Hoggart's institution but renders the sentence: "You are not addressing the university at the moment" (Hyde, *Lady Chatterley's Lover Trial*, 149). I think the court stenographer on whom Hyde relies misheard Griffith-Jones.

76. Hyde, *Lady Chatterley's Lover Trial*, 150–54.

77. D. H. Lawrence, *The First Lady Chatterley* (New York: Dial Press, 1944), v; copy in TNA, DPP 2/3077, part 3. This copy was Exhibit 6 at the trial.

78. Hyde, *Lady Chatterley's Lover Trial*, 102.

79. Lawrence, *Lady Chatterley's Lover*, 283.

80. Hyde, *Lady Chatterley's Lover Trial*, 103; Hough, *Dark Sun*, 161.

81. Katherine Anne Porter, "A Wreath for the Gamekeeper," *Encounter*, January 1960, 69–77.

82. Hyde, *Lady Chatterley's Lover Trial*, 96–98.

83. Hyde, *Lady Chatterley's Lover Trial*, 281.

84. Lawrence, *Lady Chatterley's Lover*, 246.

85. Hyde, *Lady Chatterley's Lover Trial*, 294–96.

86. Geoffrey Robertson, "The Trial of Lady Chatterley's Lover," *Guardian*, October 22, 2010; Sue Rabbitt Roff, "How Huge Gamble by Lady Chatterley Lawyers Changed Obscenity Law Forever," *Conversation*, November 21, 2017; Simon Hoggart, *A Long Lunch: My Stories and I'm Sticking to Them* (London: John Murray, 2010), 13.

87. The exhibit is in TNA, DPP 2/3077, part 4.

88. Of course it could have saved Griffith-Jones himself from embarrassment, but he showed no compunction earlier in the trial about quoting offensive words.

89. The law was changed in 1964 to give the defense the final speech. See Patrick Devlin, *Easing the Passing: The Trial of Dr John Bodkin Adams* (London: Bodley Head, 1985), 160.

90. Hyde, *Lady Chatterley's Lover Trial*, 295.

91. Hyde, *Lady Chatterley's Lover Trial*, 291–92.

92. Gardiner fastidiously confirmed each witness's degrees, appointments, and war service before moving on to questions about *Lady Chatterley's Lover*.

93. The issue lurked in the margins of the debates on the various Obscene Publications Bills in the 1950s. Roy Jenkins commented that it was hard to justify "say[ing] that a book is pornographic if it is sold for 5s. but quite all right if it is sold for 65s. (*HC Deb.*, vol. 597, December 16, 1958, col. 1009). Another MP thought it "an extraordinary doctrine that a book may be an obscene publication in one shop and a fine example of literature in another." (*HC Deb.*, vol. 597, December 16, 1958, col. 1038 [Ronald Bell, MP for Buckinghamshire, South]).

94. Advising Penguin executives in August 1960, when it was not yet clear that the DPP would charge Penguin rather than seek a destruction order, Richard Du Cann said that he expected the preliminary hearing would play out in this way: "The [police] witnesses would appear before the Metropolitan Magistrate and/or the Chairman of London Sessions whose tendency will be to say firstly 'Let this book in and you let anything in' and secondly 'At 3/6d. a copy this would be likely to fall into the hands of 15-year olds' etc." Bristol, Penguin Archive, DM 1679/9, "Notes of Conference with Mr Richard Du Cann . . . on Friday 12th August 1960 attended by Sir William Williams and Miss E. Frost of Penguin Books Limited and Mr Michael Rubinstein." Du Cann and Jeremy Hutchinson were Gardiner's juniors in the trial, though at the time of this conference Rubinstein was planning to instruct John Streeter, who had acted for him in obscenity cases before, as lead counsel. Bristol, Penguin Archive, DM 1679/9, Rubinstein to Schmoller, n.d.

95. *Popular Culture and Personal Responsibility: A Conference of Those Engaged in Education . . . Verbatim Report* (London, [1960]), 51. Even King thought he was opposed to censorship! If *Lolita* was priced at 25 shillings, it cost more than seven times as much as the Penguin *Lady Chatterley's Lover*. John Sutherland says that *Lolita* in fact cost twenty-two shillings and sixpence, about six and a half times as much as the Penguin *Lady Chatterley's Lover*. Sutherland, *Reading the Decades: Fifty Years of the Nation's Bestselling Books* (London: BBC, 2002), 49.

96. TNA, DPP 2/3077, part 1, "The Queen against Penguin Books Limited: Case to Advise," n.d.

97. Hyde, *Lady Chatterley's Lover Trial*, 57. The figure of £5 strained plausibility: what edition of a 300-page book would cost 28 times more than the paperback?

98. Hyde, *Lady Chatterley's Lover Trial*, 61, 282, 286.

99. Hyde, *Lady Chatterley's Lover Trial*, 285–86.

100. Roodhouse, "Lady Chatterley and the Monk," 487. "Roaring boys" is an allusion to Edward Blishen's novel based on his experience teaching tearaways in a north London secondary modern school. See above, p. 70. On Leslie Paul see Jonathan Rose, *The Intellectual Life of the British Working Classes* (New Haven: Yale University Press, 2001), 453–55.

101. Hyde, *Lady Chatterley's Lover Trial*, 303.

102. Bristol, Penguin Archive, DM1679/9, Rubinstein, "Draft Brief," 12–13.

103. I have not traced this case.

104. Hyde, *Lady Chatterley's Lover Trial*, 268; Rolph, *Trial of Lady Chatterley*, 195. In Hyde, the word "relationships" occurs in the singular the first two times. In the quoted passage I have changed it to the plural, as it appears in Rolph, and as it appears in Hyde the third time the word is used.

105. Hyde, *Lady Chatterley's Lover Trial*, 268.

106. John Baxendale, "'You and I—All of Us Ordinary People': Renegotiating 'Britishness' in Wartime," in *"Millions like Us"? British Culture in the Second World War*, ed. Nick Hayes and Jeff Hill (Liverpool: Liverpool University Press, 1999), 295–322; Alison Light, *Forever England: Femininity, Literature, and Conservatism between the Wars* (London: Routledge, 1991), esp. 154; Sonya O. Rose, *Which People's War? National Identity and Citizenship in Britain, 1939–1945* (Oxford: Oxford University Press, 2003), chap. 5; Hilliard, *To Exercise Our Talents*, chaps. 6–7. I think the 1940s quality of Gardiner's rhetoric is consistent with Peter Mandler's observation

of "a mid-century moment . . . in which affluence and education . . . and existential searching and widening horizons triggered by world war . . . spread to mass audiences and were catered to by an anti-fascist and democratic ethos in key sections of the intellectual and cultural elite, including the progressives and adult-educators in charge at Penguin." Mandler, "Good Reading," 265–66.

107. Leigh Ann Wheeler, *How Sex Became a Civil Liberty* (New York: Oxford University Press, 2013), chap. 3.

108. Jon Lawrence, "Paternalism, Class, and the British Path to Modernity," in *The Peculiarities of Liberal Modernity in Imperial Britain* ed. Simon Gunn and James Vernon (Berkeley: University of California Press, 2011), 147–64, 156.

109. Rolph, *Trial of Lady Chatterley*, 248–50; Hyde, *Lady Chatterley's Lover Trial*, 332–33.

110. It sold a further 1.3 million copies in 1961. The novel sold in large volumes in the company's overseas markets, even in Canada where the Penguin competed with American editions. McCleery, "Lady Chatterley's Lover Re-covered," 73–79.

111. TNA, MEPO 2/10400, J. Kennedy to ACC, April 8, 1963.

112. LMA, Public Morality Council Archive, A/PMC/125, Parliamentary, Patrol and Propaganda Sub-committee minutes, May 22, 1963.

113. Only one of whom, Forster, appeared for Penguin in 1960. The others included Iris Murdoch, Samuel Beckett, Graham Greene, A. J. Ayer, and the journalists J. R. Ackerley, Kenneth Allsop, Malcolm Muggeridge, Melvin Lasky, and Karl Miller. TNA, DPP 2/3610, Lawford and Co. to Maurice Crump, March 11, 1963.

114. TNA, MEPO 2/10400, Mervyn Griffith-Jones, "Re: John Calder (Publishers) Limited: Opinion," April 2, 1963.

115. For a related argument, see Sean Matthews, "The Trial of Lady Chatterley's Lover: 'The Most Thorough and Expensive Seminar on Lawrence's Work Ever Given,'" in *New D. H. Lawrence*, ed. Howard J. Booth (Manchester: Manchester University Press, 2009), 169–91, 170. For a discussion of treatments of the trial as a gateway to the permissive society, see Nick Thomas, "'To-Night's Big Talking Point Is Still That Book': Popular Responses to the Lady Chatterley Trial," *Cultural and Social History* 10, no. 4 (2013): 619–34, 620.

116. Michael Bell, "F. R. Leavis," in *The Cambridge History of Literary Criticism*, vol. 7, *Modernism and the New Criticism*, ed. A. Walton Litz, Louis Menand, and Lawrence Rainey, (Cambridge: Cambridge University Press, 2000), 389–422, 392. See also Stefan Collini, *Absent Minds: Intellectuals in Britain* (Oxford: Oxford University Press, 2006), esp. chaps. 6, 7, 16–18 and p. 421.

Chapter Five. The Liberal Hour, 1961–1969

1. Jon Lawrence, "Paternalism, Class, and the British Path to Modernity," in *The Peculiarities of Liberal Modernity in Imperial Britain*, ed. Simon Gunn and James Vernon (Berkeley: University of California Press, 2011), 147–64, esp. 163.

2. Matthew Grimley, "Law, Morality and Secularisation: The Church of England and the Wolfenden Report, 1954–1967," *Journal of Ecclesiastical History* 60, no. 4 (2009): 725–41, 730–31; Mark Jarvis, *Conservative Governments, Morality and Social Change in Affluent Britain, 1957–64* (Manchester: Manchester University Press, 2005).

3. Philip Larkin, "Annus Mirabilis" (1967), in *Collected Poems*, ed. Anthony Thwaite (1988; repr., New York: Farrar, Straus, Giroux and The Marvell Press, 1989), 167.

4. Humphrey Carpenter, *That Was Satire That Was: Beyond the Fringe, The Establishment Club, Private Eye and That Was the Week That Was* (London: Victor Gollancz, 2000).

5. Mary Whitehouse, *Who Does She Think She Is?* (London: New English Library, 1971), chap. 5; *Mary Whitehouse, Quite Contrary: An Autobiography* (London: Sidgwick and Jackson, 1993), 12–13; Longford Committee Investigating Pornography, *Pornography: The Longford Report* (London: Coronet Books, 1972), 97 (hereafter *Longford Report*).

6. Jarvis, *Conservative Governments, Morality and Social Change*, 69, 95, 96.

7. On the death penalty, abortion, and homosexual acts, see Paul Rock's monumental volume, *The Official History of Criminal Justice in England and Wales*, vol. 1, *The "Liberal Hour"* (London: Routledge, 2019).

8. Jenkins, *A Life at the Centre*, 208–10.

9. In opposition, Wilson approached Gardiner about accepting a peerage so that he could become lord chancellor in a Labour government. There would be no going back to the bar after a term as lord chancellor, so Gardiner had a lot to lose if, as seemed likely, Labour was not in office for long, but he decided to accept: Muriel Box, *Rebel Advocate: A Biography of Gerald Gardiner* (London: Victor Gollancz, 1983), 141–44. As it turned out, Labour won the 1964 election by only three seats; Wilson called another election for March 1966 and secured a more robust majority.

10. Richard Thurlow, *Fascism in Britain: From Oswald Mosley's Blackshirts to the National Front* (London: I. B. Tauris, 1998), chap. 9, esp. p. 232; Neill Nugent, "Postwar Fascism?" in *British Fascism: Essays on the Radical Right in Interwar Britain*, ed. Kenneth Lunn and Richard C. Thurlow (London: Routledge, 1980), 213–15; Nigel Copsey, *Anti-Fascism in Britain* (Basingstoke: Palgrave-Macmillan, 1999), 105.

11. National Council for Civil Liberties, *Public Order* (London, n.d.), copy in TNA, HO 342/83; *HC Deb.*, vol. 680, July 9, 1963, cols. 1077–79.

12. *HC Deb.*, vol. 680, July 9, 1963, cols. 1059–60.

13. *HC Deb.*, vol. 680, July 9, 1963, col. 1063. The biographer Jean Overton Fuller made the same analogy discussing the topic in the correspondence columns of the *Daily Telegraph*: "Surely a test comparable to that employed in deciding whether the matter is obscene could be applied to utterances concerning race. It is above all the use of disgusting (sometimes literally obscene) epithets . . . which incite to hatred, and their suppression would not be equivalent to the suppression of free speech." *Daily Telegraph*, August 28, 1962.

14. TNA, HO 376/3, Andrew Martin and Cedric Thornberry, "Memorandum concerning the draft Bill prepared by the Committee on Racial Discrimination and Incitement of the Society of Labour Lawyers," July 7, 1964.

15. Keith Hindell, "The Genesis of the Race Relations Bill," *Political Quarterly* 36 (1965): 390–405; *Towards Tomorrow: The Autobiography of Fenner Brockway* (London, 1977), 224; TNA, HO 342/82, "Colour Discrimination," minutes of interdepartmental meeting held on January 28, 1960.

16. Erik Bleich, *Race Politics in Britain and France: Ideas and Policymaking Since the 1960s* (Cambridge: Cambridge University Press, 2003), 46–47; Kathleen Paul,

Whitewashing Britain: Race and Citizenship in the Postwar Era (Ithaca, NY: Cornell University Press, 1997), 175–77.

17. Richard P. Longaker, "The Race Relations Act of 1965: An Evaluation of the Incitement Provision," *Race* 11 (1969): 125–56, 131–32, 144; Gavin Schaffer, "Legislating against Hatred: Meaning and Motive in Section Six of the Race Relations Act of 1965," *Twentieth Century British History* 25 (2014): 251–75, 252, 275; E.J.B. Rose et al., *Colour and Citizenship: A Report on British Race Relations* (Oxford: Oxford University Press for the Institute of Race Relations, 1969), 688.

18. BL, Lord Chamberlain's Plays Correspondence, LR 1964/1, *A Patriot for Me*, "Royal Court Theatre: 'A Patriot for Me,'" anon. carbon copy on Lord Chamberlain's Office letterhead, 12 July 1965; David Thomas, David Carlton, and Anne Etienne, *Theatre Censorship: From Walpole to Wilson* (Oxford: Oxford University Press, 2007), 189–90.

19. Thomas, Carlton, and Etienne, *Theatre Censorship*, 185.

20. Thomas, Carlton, and Etienne, *Theatre Censorship*, 183–88, 191–92.

21. Thomas, Carlton, and Etienne, *Theatre Censorship*, 192.

22. Thomas, Carlton, and Etienne, *Theatre Censorship*, 194–95.

23. Joint Committee on Censorship of the Theatre, *Report: Together with the Proceedings of the Committee, Minutes of Evidence, Appendices and Index*, H.L. 255, H.C. 503 (London: HMSO, 1967), 7; see also ix.

24. Joint Committee on Censorship of the Theatre, *Report*, 163. See also Peter Lloyd, *Not for Publication* (London: Bow Group Publications, 1968).

25. Joint Committee on Censorship of the Theatre, *Report*, xix.

26. This paragraph derives from the excellent detailed account in Thomas, Carlton, and Etienne, *Theatre Censorship*, 198–224.

27. Television Act, 1954, 2 & 3 Eliz 2, c. 55, s. 3(1)(a); Carpenter, *That Was Satire That Was*, 227.

28. On "Mrs Wilson's Diary," see Carpenter, *That Was Satire That Was*, 291–92.

29. Richard Crossman, *The Diaries of a Cabinet Minister*, vol. 2 (London: Hamish Hamilton and Jonathan Cape, 1976), 442–43 (entry for July 26, 1967).

30. Buggery and gross indecency remained criminal offenses when the participants were male crew members on a UK merchant ship. Sexual Offences Act, 1967, c. 60, s. 2.

31. *Report of the Committee on Homosexual Offences and Prostitution*, Cmnd. 247 (London: HMSO, 1957), paras. 61, 62.

32. Patrick Devlin, *The Enforcement of Morals* (Oxford: Oxford University Press, 1965), 16, 22, 10.

33. Christopher Hilliard, "Words That Disturb the State: Hate Speech and the Lessons of Fascism in Britain, 1930s–1960s," *Journal of Modern History* 88, no. 4 (2016): 764–96, 770–71; Alana Harris, "'Pope Norman', Griffin's Report and Roman Catholic Reactions to Homosexual Law Reform in England and Wales, 1954–1971," in *New Approaches in History and Theology to Same-Sex Love and Desire*, ed. Mark D. Chapman and Dominic Janes (Cham: Springer, 2018), 93–116, 107.

34. H.L.A. Hart, "Immorality and Treason," *Listener*, July 30, 1959, 162–63.

35. John Stuart Mill, *On Liberty* (1859) in Mill, *Three Essays*, ed. Richard Wollheim (Oxford: Oxford University Press, 1975), 15.

36. The avowedly Utilitarian aspects of Hart's case tended to attract less popular attention—Hart believed that "the use of legal coercion by any society" could be justified "only for the sake of some countervailing good," and was open to some "paternalistic" measures such as controls on drugs and compulsory seatbelt use. H.L.A. Hart, *Law, Liberty, and Morality* (Stanford: Stanford University Press, 1963), 20; Nicola Lacey, *A Life of H.L.A. Hart: The Nightmare and the Noble Dream* (Oxford: Oxford University Press, 2004), 257–58.

37. Hart, "Immorality and Treason," 163.

38. Lacey, *Life of H.L.A. Hart*, 220–21; Stefan Collini, *Absent Minds: Intellectuals in Britain* (Oxford: Oxford University Press, 2006), 404–6. Sir John Wolfenden reviewed Hart's book in the *Spectator*. University of Reading Library, Wolfenden Papers, box 2.

39. Whitehouse, *Who Does She Think She Is?*, 25–26, 28; Ben Thompson, ed., *Ban This Filth! Letters from the Mary Whitehouse Archive* (London: Faber and Faber, 2012), 18–24; Callum G. Brown, *The Battle for Christian Britain: Sex, Humanists and Secularisation, 1945–1980* (Cambridge: Cambridge University Press, 2019), 170–73.

40. Mark Roodhouse, "Lady Chatterley and the Monk: Anglican Radicals and the Lady Chatterley Trial of 1960," *Journal of Ecclesiastical History* 59, no. 3 (2008): 475–500, 487; H. Montgomery Hyde, ed., *The Lady Chatterley's Lover Trial (Regina v. Penguin Books Limited)* (London: The Bodley Head, 1990), 285–86.

41. "A Senior Mistress" [Mary Whitehouse], "Tomorrow May Be Too Late" (1963), in Thompson, *Ban This Filth*, 25–27, 25.

42. Whitehouse, *Who Does She Think She Is?*, 145–49.

43. TNA, HO 256/719.

44. *Censorship in the Arts: The Full Text of the Freedom of Vision Teach-in, Held at Hampstead Old Town Hall, October 2nd 1966 from 3 p.m. till 10 p.m.* (London: Academy of Visual Arts, n.d.), 30 (copy in TNA, HO 265/70).

45. Thompson, *Ban This Filth*, 38.

46. Lawrence Black, *Redefining British Politics: Culture, Consumerism and Participation, 1954–70* (Basingstoke: Palgrave Macmillan, 2010), 118–19.

47. Thompson, *Ban This Filth*, 38, 69.

48. M. A. McCarthy and R. A. Moodie, "Parliament and Pornography: The 1978 Child Protection Act," *Parliamentary Affairs* 34, no. 1 (1981): 47–62, 50–51.

49. Thompson, *Ban This Filth*, 77–78; Whitehouse, *Who Does She Think She Is?*, 64.

50. Black, *Redefining British Politics*, 120–21. The Mothers' Union statement is partially reproduced in Thompson, *Ban This Filth*, 76.

51. Black, *Redefining British Politics*, 117–18, 119.

52. Black, *Redefining British Politics*, 115–16.

53. LMA, Public Morality Council Archive, A/PMC/125, Youth for Decency, "Newsletter," no. 2 (November 1963), typescript; "Young Vigilantes Declare War on the Morals-Benders," *Sunday Times*, April 7, 1963.

54. LMA, Public Morality Council Archive, A/PMC/125, executive committee minutes, March 13, 1963 and April 25, 1963.

55. The PMC remained an ecumenical body presided over by an Anglican bishop.

56. Maurice Crump, "Pornography as Big Business," in *Pornography and Public Morals*, ed. George Tomlinson (London: Public Morality Council, 1963), 21–6, 21–2;

Kenneth G. Greet, "Looking Ahead—The Search for a Constructive Solution," in Tomlinson, *Pornography and Public Morals*, 13–17, 16; Harry Cocks, "'The Social Picture of Our Own Times': Reading Obscene Magazines in Mid-Twentieth-Century Britain," *Twentieth Century British History* 27, no. 2 (2016): 171–94.

57. Whitehouse, *Who Does She Think She Is?*, 64.

58. Greet, "Looking Ahead," 15.

59. Greet, "Looking Ahead," 16–17.

60. Greet, "Looking Ahead," 16–17.

61. This was the Rev. Stephan Hopkinson, who had testified for the defense in the *Lady Chatterley's Lover* trial.

62. Brown, *Battle for Christian Britain*, 157–69, esp. 168–69 (quotation from 169).

63. *Censorship in the Arts*, 4, 5. The organizers knew that Crump had spoken at the PMC's (much larger) conference.

64. *Censorship in the Arts*, 2.

65. John Junor, rev. by M. C. Curthoys, "Gordon, John Rutherford (1890–1974)," *ODNB*; Adrian Bingham, *Family Newspapers? Sex, Private Life, and the British Popular Press 1918–1978* (Oxford: Oxford University Press, 2009), 115–16, 183.

66. Brian Boyd, *Vladimir Nabokov: The American Years* (Princeton: Princeton University Press, 1991), 295.

67. Leonora Merry, "Elizabeth Straker," *Guardian*, 3 February 2009.

68. Straker v. DPP [1963] 1 QB 926; Obscene Publications Act, 1964, c. 74, s. 2.

69. Ed Bates, *The Evolution of the European Convention on Human Rights: From Its Inception to the Creation of a Permanent Court of Human Rights* (Oxford: Oxford University Press, 2010), 185–88.

70. Convention for the Protection of Human Rights and Fundamental Freedoms (1950), article 10(1); *Censorship in the Arts*, 46.

71. Convention for the Protection of Human Rights and Fundamental Freedoms, article 10(2).

72. Marco Duranti, *The Conservative Human Rights Revolution: European Identity, Transnational Politics, and the Origins of the European Convention* (New York: Oxford University Press, 2017), chap. 4. Bates's thorough account does not bring to light any work done by the civil service in anticipation of changes after individual petition to Strasbourg was granted and suggests that many informed observers thought it would make little difference to the UK. Bates, *Evolution of the European Convention*, 185–91.

73. For instance, Norman Sheppard of TRACK: *Censorship in the Arts*, 51.

74. *Censorship in the Arts*, 22–23.

75. *Censorship in the Arts*, 48.

76. *Censorship in the Arts*, 24.

77. *Censorship in the Arts*, 25.

78. *Censorship in the Arts*, 27.

79. *Censorship in the Arts*, 33–34.

80. *Censorship in the Arts*, 35.

81. *Censorship in the Arts*, 41.

82. *Censorship in the Arts*, 40.

83. *Censorship in the Arts*, 57.

84. *Censorship in the Arts*, 36–37, 57.

85. *Censorship in the Arts*, 57.

86. Black, *Redefining British Politics*, 122, 129–30.

87. *Censorship in the Arts*, 30–31.

88. To be sure, speaking in Hampstead's Old Town Hall entailed fewer constraints than a brief for counsel in an obscenity case: but a prominent solicitor like Rubinstein never left the expectations of his profession in this office.

89. *Censorship in the Arts*, 11–13.

90. *Censorship in the Arts*, 44.

91. Paul Overy, "The Art of Detachment," *Listener*, September 29, 1966, 459.

92. TNA, HO 302/40, G.M.B. Owen to R. J. Guppy, October 13, 1966.

93. Overy, "Art of Detachment," 459; TNA, HO 302/40, K. P. Witney, untitled memo, January 9, 1967; HO 302/40, Guppy to Witney, October 7, 1966; J. A. Chilcott, "Note of a Meeting Held at 4.45 p.m. on Friday, 14th October, in Room 201 of the Home Office," October 18, 1966.

94. A parallel in Leeds was more disturbing. There the police had invoked the Vagrancy Act to raid a gallery that was exhibiting works by Stassinas Paraskos upstairs, away from public view, going against the express advice of the DPP. TNA, HO 302/40, K. P. Witney, untitled memo, January 9, 1967.

95. Patricia Hollis, *Jennie Lee: A Life* (Oxford: Oxford University Press, 1997), chaps. 9–12, and, for Goodman's appointment, 259.

96. John Trevelyan, *What the Censor Saw* (London: Michael Joseph, 1973), 211.

97. Brian Brivati, *Lord Goodman* (London: Richard Cohen Books, 1999), 33–36, 40–44, 64–67, 74–78, and chaps. 4, 6, 7 generally. The dinner at which Gerald Gardiner was sounded out about becoming lord chancellor was hosted by Goodman. Box, *Rebel Advocate*, 141.

98. TNA, HO 302/40, Lee to Jenkins, December 15, 1966.

99. TNA, HO 302/40, Jenkins to Lee, May 17, 1967.

100. TNA, HO 302/40, Jenkins to Lee, January 21, 1967; G.M.B. Owen, untitled memo, November 18, 1966; R. J. Guppy, "Proposals for amending the Vagrancy Acts 1824 and 1838 and the Obscene Publications Acts 1959 and 1964," January 17, 1967.

101. Angela Bartie and Eleanor Bell, *The International Writers' Conference Revisited: Edinburgh, 1962* (Glasgow: Cargo Publishing, 2012), 174–77.

102. Bartie and Bell, *International Writers' Conference*, 112–32, quotation from 121.

103. TNA, MEPO 2/10400, Mervyn Griffith-Jones, "Re: John Calder (Publishers) Limited: Opinion," April 2, 1963.

104. TNA, C. (54) 372, "'Horror Comics': Memorandum by the Attorney-General," December 1, 1954, copy in TNA, PREM 11/858.

105. Alastair McCleery, "Late News from the Provinces: The Trial of *Cain's Book*," in *The Scottish Sixties: Reading, Rebellion, Revolution?*, ed. Eleanor Bell and Linda Gunn (Amsterdam: Rodopi, 2013), 135–51, 146–47; John Calder (Publications) Ltd. v. Powell [1965] 1 QB 509.

106. TNA, DPP 2/4127, anonymous note in minutes pages, April 15, 1964.

107. TNA, DPP 2/4127, Michael Evelyn, note in minutes pages, January 13, 1966; DPP 2/4127, Crump to Skelhorn, April 14, 1966.

108. Among the indicators of mainstream literary approval were good reviews in the *Sunday Telegraph* and the *Spectator* and Westminster Public Library's decision to order copies.

109. TNA, DPP 2/4127, Crump to Skelhorn, April 14, 1966.

110. TNA, DPP 2/4127, note in minutes pages, April 28, 1966; TNA, HO 302/40, "Cabinet: Home Affairs Committee: Memorandum by the Secretary of State for the Home Department" (draft), February 13, 1967.

111. Jean Straker and his allies asked the DPP to suppress the proceedings on the grounds that they contravened the European Convention on Human Rights. TNA, DPP 2/4127, Straker to Crump, August 3, 1966; Straker to DPP, August 5, 1966; G. F. Westcott to DPP, August 1, 1966; P. W. Barker et al., undated, untitled petition.

112. "A Decent Reticence," *The Times*, November 3, 1960, 13.

113. The latter category included Robert Maxwell, then a Labour MP, and H. Montgomery Hyde, a barrister, sometime Ulster Unionist MP, and authority on Oscar Wilde and his circle. In these respects Hyde was a figure akin to Norman St John-Stevas, though Hyde was obviously less committed to the anticensorship cause. "Obscenity Prosecution by M.P.: U.S. Novel 'A Collection of Dirty Stories,'" *The Times*, October 28, 1966; "My Compassion Was Aroused, Woman Publisher Says," *The Times*, November 14, 1966, 9. On Hyde, see R. B. McDowell, "Hyde, Harford Montgomery [H. Montgomery Hyde] (1907–1989)," *ODNB*. The Herbert Committee knew him as an MP interested in obscenity reform, but he does not seem to have taken much part in their campaign. Bodleian, Roy Jenkins Papers, MS Jenkins 92, untitled memo listing "non-members of the Society [of Authors] . . . interested in the question of obscenity," n.d. (c. 1954). He testified in support of *Fanny Hill* in 1964: H. Montgomery Hyde, *A History of Pornography* (London: Heinemann, 1964), 219–22.

114. TNA, HO 302/40, "Cabinet: Home Affairs Committee: Memorandum by the Secretary of State for the Home Department" (draft), February 13, 1967.

115. V&A, Arts Council of Great Britain Papers, ACGB/59/1, box 3. "The Publishers Association: Obscene Publications Act: Memorandum" (originally October 1966; this version reissued with a postscript in May 1968). The magistrate in the *Last Exit* hearing was Leo Gradwell: "'Last Exit' Ruled to Be Obscene," *The Times*, December 12, 1966. The previous year, Gradwell ruled that the Royal Court "club" performances of Bond's *Saved* had broken the law. Steve Nicholson, *The Censorship of British Drama, 1900–1968*, vol. 4, *The Sixties* (Exeter: University of Exeter Press, 2015), 165. He was a Catholic who sometimes wrote on questions of sexual morality in the *Tablet*: Alana Harris, "'Pope Norman': Griffin's Report and Roman Catholic Reactions to Homosexual Law Reform in England and Wales, 1954–1971," in *New Approaches in History and Theology to Same-Sex Love and Desire*, ed. Mark D. Chapman and Dominic Janes (Cham: Springer, 2018), 93–116, 100.

116. TNA, HO 302/40, "Cabinet: Home Affairs Committee: Memorandum by the Secretary of State for the Home Department" (draft), February 13, 1967.

117. TNA, HO 302/40, J. Semken to R. F. Skemp, March 1, 1967.

118. TNA, DPP 2/4127, Douglas-Mann and Co. to DPP, December 21, 1966.

119. TNA, DPP 2/4127, [J. F. Claxton?], note in minutes pages, January 23, 1967.

120. TNA, DPP 2/4127, Douglas-Mann and Co to DPP, February 2, 1967; Bruce Douglas-Mann, letter to *The Times*, December 7, 1967, 9.

121. TNA, DPP 2/4127, Skelhorn to J. F. Claxton, January 4, 1967.

122. "I don't see that they can expect anything other than a prosecution once they say that they intend to continue publication." TNA, DPP 2/4127, [J. F. Claxton?], note in minutes pages, January 23, 1967.

123. TNA, DPP 2/4127, Sir Cyril Black to Sir Elwyn Jones, 26 January 1967.

124. "Enter the Experts for 'Last Exit': Publishers Marshall Their Forces," *The Times*, February 7, 1967, 10.

125. "New Case Expected over 'Last Exit,'" *The Times*, February 6, 1967, 9.

126. Ian Hamilton, "Cutting Candy Dead," *Listener*, September 12, 1968, 341.

127. A. Alvarez, "Last Exit," *Listener*, December 7, 1967, 740.

128. "When Jury Consider Whether Book Is Obscene," *The Times*, July 23, 1968, 16.

129. "'Last Exit' Appeal Succeeds," *The Times*, August 1, 1968, 10.

130. Brivati, *Lord Goodman*, 152–55. Jennie Lee suggested something similar after the raid on the Fraser gallery. TNA, HO 302/40, Lee to Jenkins, December 15, 1966.

131. V&A, ACGB/59/1, box 3, R. E. Barker to Goodman, January 16, 1968.

132. V&A, ACGB/59/1, box 3, Goodman to White, February 6, 1968; Goodman to Barker, February 6, 1968. Goodman must have assumed that the fact that he was also the solicitor for the appellant in an ongoing obscenity case would not discredit the undertaking.

133. V&A, ACGB/59/1, box 3, "Invited to 1968 Conference," typescript, June 3, 1969.

134. TNA, HO 302/29, Whitehouse to Callaghan, February 10, 1969; Whitehouse, *Who Does She Think She Is?*, 102–4.

135. Whitehouse wrote to the home secretary and to Jennie Lee challenging the working party's legitimacy as an Arts Council initiative, but to no avail. TNA, HO 302/29, N. W. Stuart (Lee's private secretary) to Whitehouse, April 22, 1969. Whitehouse declined an invitation to be interviewed on the ground that "My presence at one of your meetings could be interpreted as an acknowledgment of the validity of this particular investigation." V&A, ACGB/59/1, box 3, Mary Whitehouse to Eric W. White, January 16, 1969.

136. V&A, ACGB/59/1, box 3, EWW to Kathleen Raine, July 28, 1969.

137. Indiana, Calder and Boyars MSS, box 156, Free Art Legal Fund, leaflet, 1967. The "trustees" named on the front page included Frank Kermode and Reginald Davis-Poynter, both of whom were members of the Arts Council and both of whom also served on the working party.

138. TNA, HO 265/70, "Report by the Working Party Set up by a Conference on the Obscenity Laws Convened by the Chairman of the Arts Council of Great Britain," July 14, 1969.

139. V&A, ACGB/59/1, box 3, Jenkins, untitled notes, n.d.

140. Trevelyan, *What the Censor Saw*, chaps. 7–10, 15; James C. Robertson, *The Hidden Cinema: British Film Censorship in Action, 1913–1972* (London: Routledge, 1989), chap. 4; *The Obscenity Laws: A Report by the Working Party Set up by a Conference Convened by the Chairman of the Arts Council of Great Britain* (London: André Deutsch, 1969), 17–18 (hereafter *Report by the Working Party*).

141. V&A, ACGB/59/1, box 1, minutes of working party meeting, October 24, 1968.

142. Thomas, Carlton, and Etienne, *Theatre Censorship*, chap. 5; compare chap. 7.

143. V&A, ACGB/59/1, box 1, "The Arts Council of Great Britain: Working Party on Obscenity Laws," undated list of members of Sub-Committee A (to report on Abolition) and Sub-Committee LR (to report on Law Reform).

144. V&A, ACGB/59/1, box 1, minutes of Sub-Committee LR meetings, November 6, 1968, November 26, 1968.

145. LSE, Rolph Papers, 2/3/16, "Draft Report (prepared by Mr. Benn W. Levy)" (revised version of April 10, 1969).

146. V&A, ACGB/59/1, box 1, working party minutes, April 15, 1969.

147. V&A, ACGB/59/1, box 2, William Gaskill to White, April 30, 1969.

148. For Calder over *Cain's Book*: McCleery, "Late News," 146.

149. V&A, ACGB/59/1, box 2, John Mortimer to Montgomerie, June 2, 1969.

150. V&A, ACGB/59/1, box 2, "Whilst You Were Out" form with notes of Code Holland's call, April 23, 1969.

151. V&A, ACGB/59/1, box 2, Frank [Kermode] to Eric [White], April 29, 1969.

152. V&A, ACGB/59/1, box 2, Hewitt to Eric White, April 20, 1969 (emphasis in original); copy in LSE, C. H. Rolph Papers, 2/3/16; Rolph Papers, 2/3/16, Hewitt to Barber, April 20, 1969 (copy). Warburg told F. L. Jenkins at the Arts Council that Levy's paper was "lucid, witty and almost completely convincing. I am not sure it has not converted me." V&A, ACGB/59/1, box 2, Warburg to Jenkins, April 9, 1969.

153. LSE, Rolph Papers, 2/3/14, Hewitt to Barber, May 24, 1969.

154. *Report by the Working Party*, 13.

155. *Report by the Working Party*, 51, 52, 53.

156. *Report by the Working Party*, 15, 51–53; V&A, ACGB/59/1, box 3, Lewes to Montgomerie, January 15, 1969; LSE, Rolph Papers, 2/3/16, "Report on Discussion with Mr. C. H. Lewes on 16th December, 1968," with additional points added by Lewes on January 15, 1969.

157. *Report by the Working Party*, 15 n.

158. I have not seen him mentioned in any of the HO, LO, LCO, DPP, or CRIM files pertaining to obscenity proceedings or policy in the 1950s, 1960s, or 1970s.

159. V&A, ACGB/59/1, box 3, White to Goodman, May 23, 1968; Lewes to White, June 7, 1968; White to Goodman, June 12, 1968; Goodman to White, June 26, 1968.

160. *Report by the Working Party*, 23; Maurice R. Kay, "Depravity and Corruption for the Public Good," *Modern Law Review* 32, no. 2 (March 1969): 198–202, 201.

161. *Report by the Working Party*, 23–24.

162. *Report by the Working Party*, 24.

163. *Report by the Working Party*, 24, 27. The rationale for the horror comics legislation was that violence was something different from obscenity.

164. See also the initial appraisal of the psychiatrist who later testified for the prosecution against *Last Exit to Brooklyn*, "This section also describes Benzedrine taking, a habit that is causing considerable concern at the present time." TNA, DPP 2/4127, Wilfrid Warren to Maurice Crump, April 27, 1966.

165. *Report by the Working Party*, 19, 28–29.

166. *Report by the Working Party*, 14–15.

167. *Report by the Working Party*, 35–37, 39–41.

168. Black, *Redefining British Politics*, 133–34.

169. Antipornography campaigners agreed, of course. Lord Longford's committee remarked: "although we can all choose to avoid entering cinema premises, we cannot avoid the intrusion on our privacy of offensive front-of-house display." *Longford Report*, 275; also 82.

170. TNA, HO 302/30, draft of a letter to Hugh Willatt for Callaghan to sign, n.d.; M. A. Clayton, note in minutes pages, September 8, 1969; *HC Deb.*, vol. 787, July 24, 1969, cols. 2109–10. The government also blocked private members' bills on the subject. TNA, HO 302/30, "Background Note: Arts Council Working Party on Obscenity," n.d.; *HC Deb.*, vol. 780, March 25, 1969, col. 1292, answering a question from Ben Whitaker.

171. The Arts Council had it published commercially, by André Deutsch. Brivati, *Lord Goodman*, 156–57.

172. "Drop Censorship . . . Anything Goes," *Daily Express*, July 16, 1969.

173. A.W.B. Simpson, *Pornography and Politics: A Look back to the Williams Committee* (London: Waterlow Publishers, 1983), 29; TNA, HO 265/19, COFC minutes, June 30, 1978 (interview with Mary Whitehouse); *Longford Report*, 46–48; CUL, David Holbrook papers, MS Add. 9987, box 37, Holbrook to Margaret Allen, November 14, 1973; *HC Deb.*, vol. 711, May 3, 1965, cols. 957–58 (Sir Barnett Janner); TNA, HO 265/77, John Hanau to Jon Davey, September 25, 1977. Julius Streicher's periodical *Die Stürmer* was often cited as an example of the corrosive consequences of a lack of censorship. Streicher was convicted at Nuremburg and executed. Mervyn Griffith-Jones prosecuted.

174. "Mrs Whitehouse Sets the Obscene," *Guardian*, July 16, 1969; Black, *Redefining British Politics*, 134; Whitehouse, *Who Does She Think She Is?*, 105–9.

Chapter Six. Subversion from Underground, 1970–1971

1. References to the trial proceedings are to Tony Palmer, *The Trials of Oz* (London: Blond and Briggs, 1971) supplemented by the partial transcripts in TNA, J 82/1934–1936.

2. Jonathon Green, *Days in the Life: Voices from the English Underground, 1961–1971* (1988; repr., London: Heinemann, 1989), 337, 386; Palmer, *Trials of Oz*, 33; *Oz*, no. 9 (February 1968). See also Rosie Boycott, *A Nice Girl like Me: A Story of the Seventies* (London: Pan Books, 1984), 56.

3. *Oz*, no. 26 (February–March 1970): 46.

4. On the ads, see the cross-examination of Neville: Palmer, *Trials of Oz*, 93–94.

5. Green, *Days in the Life*, 393–95.

6. I would also guess that someone educated at Westminster School and Trinity College, Cambridge, had enough Latin to know what "cunnilingus" meant.

7. See especially the transcript excerpts in Palmer, *Trials of Oz*, 118, 131, 167.

8. Green, *Days in the Life*, 393.

9. The bill from Offenbach and Co. appended to Jim Anderson's legal aid claim of 5 August 1971 (in TNA, CRIM 1/5453/3) itemizes Robertson's work. Robertson, who became a prominent barrister, was not yet admitted to the bar in England.

10. Palmer, *Trials of Oz*, 235–36.

11. Peter Mandler, "Educating the Nation, I: Schools," *Transactions of the Royal Historical Society* 24 (2014): 5–28, 13–25.

12. Geoffrey Robertson, *The Justice Game* (London: Chatto and Windus, 1998), 23.

13. The remoteness of *Oz* from the experience of most of the people likely to be empanelled as jurors was probably one reason Neville called witnesses who could demonstrate expertise on emerging cultural forms, such as the DJ John Peel and the critic George Melly. Neither Peel nor Melly seems to have helped the defense case much, and they spent most of their time on the stand answering questions about sex and whether they were family men. Palmer, *Trials of Oz*, 95–98 (Melly), 159–63 (Peel).

14. For instance, in the examination of Edward de Bono. TNA, J 82/1935, *Oz* trial transcripts, transcript of tapes 59–64.

15. Compare John Sutherland's characterization of John Mortimer's defense of the *Oz* editors as an example of an "alliance between Hampstead and the counter-culture." Sutherland was explicitly using Hampstead as shorthand for "liberal intelligentsia," but it can serve as a token for the literary intelligentsia too. Mortimer himself, of course, was a writer and bohemian as well as a liberal lawyer. John Sutherland, *Offensive Literature: Decensorship in Britain, 1960-1982* (London: Junction Books, 1982), 3.

16. TNA, CRIM 1/5453/3, A.G.H. Robins, "Social Enquiry Report," August 3, 1971. In his application for legal aid, Dennis said his income from *Oz* ranged from £40 to £80 a month. TNA, CRIM 1/5453/2, Dennis, Legal Aid Statement of Means form, signed November 1, 1970.

17. See for instance the photographs chosen for content about drug use in *Oz*, no. 34 (April 1971): cover and pp. 31–32; but practically every issue contains evidence for this point. For criticism along these lines from within *Oz* several years later, see David Widgery, "Imprisoned by Chauvinism" (1973), in *Preserving Disorder: Selected Essays 1968-88* (London: Pluto Press, 1989), 104–9, 109.

18. Palmer, *Trials of Oz*, 92–3, 199.

19. *Fanny Hill* was also the subject of obscenity proceedings in Britain around the same time. The DPP sought a destruction order against a shop in the Tottenham Court Road that was selling *Fanny Hill* alongside magic tricks and novelties. Griffith-Jones led for the crown and did not call expert witnesses. Jeremy Hutchinson and Richard Du Cann, both of whom had been involved in Penguin's defense in the *Lady Chatterley's Lover* trial, acted for the retailer. They called seven experts to attest to the book's literary qualities and its value as a historical document. The chief magistrate granted the destruction order. H. Montgomery Hyde, *A History of Pornography* (London: Heinemann, 1964), 208–33.

20. *The Obscenity Laws: A Report by the Working Party Set up by a Conference Convened by the Chairman of the Arts Council of Great Britain* (London: André Deutsch, 1969), 17–18, 116–118; V&A, Arts Council of Great Britain Papers, ACGB/59/1, box 3, "Report on Discussion with Mr. H. Agerbal (Press Counsellor) and Mr. Knud Plougmann (assistant Press Attaché) at the Royal Danish Embassy in London," n.d. (April 1969); "Denmark's Legislation concerning Pornography," undated handout produced by the Danish Embassy in London; Frances Jenkins to John Montgomerie and Benn Levy, April 16, 1969.

21. On British pornography of this time, see Marcus Collins, "The Pornography of Permissiveness: Men's Sexuality and Women's Emancipation in Mid Twentieth-Century Britain," *History Workshop Journal*, no. 47 (Spring 1999): 99–120, 103–4; and, for pornography before the mid-1960s, Harry Cocks, "'The Social Picture of Our

Own Times': Reading Obscene Magazines in Mid-Twentieth-Century Britain," *Twentieth Century British History* 27, no. 2 (2016): 171–94; Simon Szreter and Kate Fisher, *Sex Before the Sexual Revolution: Intimate Life in England, 1918–1963* (Cambridge: Cambridge University Press, 2010), 106–7.

22. TNA, 302/49, Geoffrey de Deney, "Enforcement of the Obscenity and Indecency Legislation," n.d. (October 1972).

23. TNA, HO 265/1, C. James Anderton to Jon Davey, July 19, 1978; *Pornography: The Longford Report* (London: Coronet Books, 1972), 314–17.

24. Palmer, *Trials of Oz*, 92; Barry Miles, *London Calling: A Countercultural History of London since 1945* (London: Atlantic Books, 2010), 308; *Longford Report*, 315.

25. TNA, HO 302/49, Geoffrey de Deney, November 12, 1971; Alan Travis, *Bound and Gagged: A Secret History of Obscenity in Britain* (London: Profile Books, 2000), 209–13.

26. On police raids of *Oz* and *IT*, see Green, *Days in the Life*, 158; Miles, *London Calling*, chap. 16; TNA, HO 302/41, L. Alton, "Obscene Publications—International Times," March 30, 1967; "The Witch-Hunt of Oz," NCCL *Bulletin*, January 1971, [1]; TNA, CRIM 1/5453/2, Frederick Luff, statement, October 1, 1970.

27. Nigel Fountain, *Underground: The London Alternative Press, 1966–74* (London: Routledge, 1988), 25.

28. Angela Bartie and Eleanor Bell, *The International Writers' Conference Revisited: Edinburgh, 1962* (Glasgow: Cargo Publishing, 2012), esp. 37–38.

29. Fountain, *Underground*, chaps. 3–4; Miles, *London Calling*, chaps. 16, 24.

30. John Davis, "Community and the Labour Left in 1970s London," in *The Art of the Possible: Politics and Governance in Modern British History, 1885–1997: Essays in Memory of Duncan Tanner*, ed. Chris Williams and Andrew Edwards (Manchester: Manchester University Press, 2015), 207–23, 213; John Davis, "Rents and Race in 1960s London: New Light on Rachmanism," *Twentieth Century British History* 12, no. 1 (2001): 69–92; Ruth Glass, assisted by Harold Pollins, *London's Newcomers: The West Indian Migrants* (1960; repr., Cambridge, MA: Harvard University Press, 1961).

31. John Williams, *Michael X: A Life in Black and White* (London: Century, 2008).

32. Rowe started working at *Oz* on June 1, 1970. TNA, CRIM 1/5453/2, Ronald Kent, statement, November 1, 1970.

33. On the Sydney *Oz* and its context, see Stephen Alomes, *When London Calls: The Expatriation of Australian Creative Artists to Britain* (Cambridge: Cambridge University Press, 1999), 173–96.

34. *Oz* (Sydney), June 1963, July 1963, and January, June, and October 1965.

35. Nicole Moore, *The Censor's Library* (St Lucia: University of Queensland Press, 2012), 245–50; Peter Coleman, *Obscenity, Blasphemy, Sedition: Censorship in Australia* (Brisbane: Jacaranda Press, [1963]), 31–34.

36. "The Judgment of Mr. Locke," *Oz* (Sydney), no. 14 (October 1964): 9–12, 9.

37. Moore, *The Censor's Library*, 257–59.

38. TNA, DPP 2/4349, notes in minutes pages, February 17 and 21, 1967.

39. Green, *Days in the Life*, 146–47.

40. Green, *Days in the Life*, 147. *Oz* published a piece by Jerry Rubin that year: "Vote, Vote, Vote, for Whoever You Like," *Oz*, no. 11 (April 1968): 8–9.

41. Green, *Days in the Life*, 153.

42. TNA, DPP 2/4349. Enoch Powell complained to the Metropolitan Police about a cartoon that depicted him urinating over his shoes. TNA, DPP 2/4349, R. L. Tilley to Detective Superintendent, CID, New Scotland Yard, July 5, 1968.

43. TNA, DPP 2/4349, Derek Boone, "The London Oz," April 28, 1967.

44. See Harry Cocks, "Conspiracy to Corrupt Public Morals and the 'Unlawful' Status of Homosexuality in Britain after 1967," *Social History* 41, no. 3 (2016): 267–84.

45. Green, *Days in the Life*, 326–27; Knuller (Publishing, Printing and Promotions) Ltd. v. Director of Public Prosecutions [1972] AC 435.

46. Law Commission, *Report on Conspiracy and Criminal Law Reform*, Law Com. no. 76 (London: HMSO, 1976), para. 3.17.

47. Shaw v. Director of Public Prosecutions [1962] AC 220 at 268.

48. Patrick Devlin, *The Enforcement of Morals* (London: Oxford University Press, 1965), 87–91, quotation at 91.

49. Cocks, "Conspiracy," 274–75.

50. Law Commission, *Conspiracy and Criminal Law Reform*, para. 3.17.

51. TNA, DPP 2/4349, Frederick Luff to R. Clarke, June 8, 1970.

52. TNA, DPP 2/4349, Brian Leary, "The Queen against Richard Neville, James Anderson, Felix Dennis and Oz Publications Ink Limited: Advice," n.d.

53. TNA CRIM 1/5453/1, *Oz* subscription list seized by police, n.d.

54. TNA, DPP /4349, Hugh [?] M. Lumley to A/D Met, July 27, 1970.

55. TNA, DPP /4349, Hugh [?] M. Lumley to A/D Met, July 27, 1970.

56. Green, *Days in the Life*, 385.

57. Green, *Days in the Life*, 385–386; Charles Shaar Murray, "Lennon, Lenin, the Oz School Kids Issue and Me," *Word*, April 2011, 108–11.

58. TNA, CRIM 1/5453/2, Mick J. Davis to *Oz*, n.d. (mid-1970).

59. *Oz*, no. 28 (May 1970): 6–12.

60. "School Kids Oz?," *Oz*, no. 28 (May 1970): 4.

61. "Anne," "One Side of Freedom" in "I Wanna Be Free," *Oz*, no. 28 (May 1970): 14; Palmer, *Trials of Oz*, 46–47.

62. TNA, CRIM 1/5453/2, "Viv," untitled, undated MS article.

63. Robertson, *Justice Game*, 25.

64. On Schofield see James Hampshire and Jane Lewis, "'The Ravages of Permissiveness': Sex Education and the Permissive Society," *Twentieth Century British History* 15, no. 3 (2004): 290–321, 296–97; Jeffrey Weeks, *Coming Out: Homosexual Politics in Britain, from the Nineteenth Century to the Present* (London: Quartet Books, 1977), 157, 169, 177–78.

65. Robertson, *Justice Game*, 26, 27. Schofield was also on the executive of the National Council for Civil Liberties in the 1970s. Chris Moores, *Civil Liberties and Human Rights in Twentieth-Century Britain* (Cambridge: Cambridge University Press, 2017), 192 n.

66. TNA, CRIM 1/5453/2, "Viv," untitled, undated MS article.

67. TNA, DPP 2/4349, Brian Leary, "The Queen against Richard Neville, James Anderson, Felix Dennis and Oz Publications Ink Limited: Advice," n.d.

68. TNA, DPP /4349, Lumley to A/D Met, July 27, 1970.

69. His mother testified that she supported her son's actions and had read and discussed his contributions to *Oz* in draft.

70. Palmer, *Trials of Oz*, 70–71.

71. Palmer, *Trials of Oz*, 36–37.

72. Palmer, *Trials of Oz*, 73–77; Valerie Grove, *A Voyage round John Mortimer* (London: Viking, 2007), 250.

73. David Tribe, *Questions of Censorship* (London: George Allen and Unwin, 1973), 154, 327 n. 48; David Limond, "The UK Edition of *The Little Red Schoolbook*: A Paper Tiger Reflects," *Sex Education*, 12, no. 5 (2012): 523–34, 525.

74. Limond, "*Little Red Schoolbook*," 525.

75. Handyside in an interview with David Tribe: *Questions of Censorship*, 154.

76. Richard Handyside, "The Law in Action: The Little Red Schoolbook and the Police," *DLAS Newsletter*, February 1973, 6–10, 7.

77. He appealed to the London Sessions, which confirmed the verdict and sentence and imposed a further £1000 in costs for the appeal hearing. Tribe, *Questions of Censorship*, 165, 180.

78. Handyside, "Little Red Schoolbook and the Police," 10.

79. His counsel was Cedric Thornberry, an active member of the Society of Labour Lawyers who did a lot of work before the European Court of Human Rights but otherwise does not appear to have been very involved in censorship disputes.

80. Handyside v United Kingdom [1976] ECHR 5. On UK cases before the European Court of Human Rights, see above, pp. 180, 218–19. Article 10(2) reads: "The exercise of these freedoms, since it carries with it duties and responsibilities, may be subject to such formalities, conditions, restrictions or penalties as are prescribed by law and are necessary in a democratic society, in the interests of national security, territorial integrity or public safety, for the prevention of disorder or crime, for the protection of health or morals, for the protection of the reputation or rights of others, for preventing the disclosure of information received in confidence, or for maintaining the authority and impartiality of the judiciary."

81. Tribe, *Questions of Censorship*, 164–65; Limond, "*Little Red Schoolbook*," 525–26.

82. David Limond, "Risinghill and the Ecology of Fear," *Educational Review* 54, no. 2 (2002): 165–72, 166. It should be added that Duane was not a devotee of the comprehensive school model and streamed classes by academic ability.

83. Leila Berg, *Risinghill: Death of a Comprehensive School* (Harmondsworth: Penguin, 1968). On the silences and distortions of Berg's book, see Limond, "Risinghill."

84. Mathew Thomson, *Lost Freedom: The Landscape of the Child and the British Post-War Settlement* (Oxford: Oxford University Press, 2013), 200–203.

85. Alastair J. Reid, "The Dialectics of Liberation: The Old Left, the New Left and the Counter-Culture," in *Structures and Transformations in Modern British History*, ed. David Feldman and Jon Lawrence (Cambridge: Cambridge University Press, 2011), 261–80.

86. Thomson, *Lost Freedom*, 204–205.

87. C. B. Cox and A. E. Dyson, eds., *Fight for Education: A Black Paper* (London: Critical Quarterly Society, [1969]); C. B. Cox and A. E. Dyson, eds., *Black Paper Two: The Crisis in Education* (London: Critical Quarterly Society, [1969]); Brian Cox, *The Great Betrayal* (London: Chapmans, 1992), chaps. 7–9.

88. Palmer, *Trials of Oz*, 157–58.

89. TNA, J 82/1936, *Oz* trial transcripts, transcript of tape 95.

90. TNA, J 82/1936, *Oz* trial transcripts, transcript of tape 95.

91. Palmer, *Trials of Oz*, 156–57.

92. Palmer, *Trials of Oz*, 152–53.

93. "'Please Sir, May I Be Excused?' Schools Action Unit Miscarriage," *Oz*, no. 28 (May 1970): 13.

94. TNA, J 82/1936, *Oz* trial transcripts, transcript of tape 95.

95. TNA, DPP 2/4349, Marsha Rowe to Katherine Milburn, November 3, 1970.

96. Palmer, *Trials of Oz*, 137–38.

97. Palmer, *Trials of Oz*, 123–26. Michael Duane said the Rupert cartoon "challenges the whole idea that this kind of rubbishy sentimentality is suitable for children. It brings together this notion of Rupert, this horrible sentimental little bear, with the more realistic activities of a male human being . . . this can only be a good thing if it helps people to realise just how bad, how destructive in the long run such mush as Rupert is." TNA, J 82/1936, *Oz* trial transcripts, transcript of tape 95.

98. Mathew Thomson, *Psychological Subjects: Identity, Culture, and Health in Twentieth-Century Britain* (Oxford: Oxford University Press, 2006), 258.

99. Thomson, *Psychological Subjects*, 259–60.

100. Matthew Hilton, *Smoking in British Popular Culture, 1800–2000: Perfect Pleasures* (Manchester: Manchester University Press, 2000), 218.

101. Palmer, *Trials of Oz*, 147–48.

102. Palmer, *Trials of Oz*, 114 (Dennis), 102 (Anderson).

103. Palmer, *Trials of Oz*, 148.

104. TNA, 302/49, Geoffrey de Deney, "Enforcement of the Obscenity and Indecency Legislation," n.d. (October 1972); see also *Longford Report*, 201–02.

105. Palmer, *Trials of Oz*, 13.

106. Palmer, *Trials of Oz*, 200, 202.

107. Both had criticized Devlin's thesis: Ronald M. Dworkin, "Lord Devlin and the Enforcement of Morals," *Yale Law Journal* 75, no. 6 (1966): 986–1005, Devlin, *Enforcement of Morals*, viii, xiv (referring to Wollheim's critique in *Encounter*). Palmer claims that A. J. Ayer had been asked and said no. *Trials of Oz*, 73.

108. Palmer, *Trials of Oz*, 179. In fact "I Wanna Be Free" was two articles, Anne Townsend's and another by Roger Vartoukian on the same theme, like two essays written in response to the same question set in class.

109. Palmer, *Trials of Oz*, 180. This was a response to a question from counsel for the company, Oz Publications Ink Limited, which was also a defendant. The company's barrister did not take up much of the court's time.

110. Palmer, *Trials of Oz*, 180.

111. Palmer, *Trials of Oz*, 181.

112. Palmer, *Trials of Oz*, 167.

113. Palmer, *Trials of Oz*, 257; TNA, J 82/1932, "R. v. Neville and Others: 'Trial Diary,'" n.d.

114. Robertson, *Justice Game*, 23.

115. Palmer, *Trials of Oz*, 165; "Marty Feldman Asks Judge: 'Am I Waking You Up?'" *Daily Telegraph*, July 20, 1971.

116. Even Leary lost track of time and in a lull scribbled a note to Mortimer asking how long they had been going. TNA, CRIM 1/5453/1.

117. TNA, CRIM 1/5453/3, Offenbach and Co bill attached to Jim Anderson's legal aid claim, August 5, 1971; Stanley Cohen, *Folk Devils and Moral Panics: The Creation of the Mods and Rockers* (London: MacGibbon and Kee, 1972).

118. Green, *Days in the Life*, 389.

119. Green, *Days in the Life*, 389–91; Boycott, *Nice Girl*, 57.

120. By a majority of 10 to 1. Majority verdicts became permissible in 1967. One juror had been discharged during the trial because her daughter was giving birth.

121. Green, *Days in the Life*, 388.

122. Sutherland, *Offensive Literature*, 124. The tale grew in the telling. Neville, Dennis, and Anderson were not given "short back and sides" haircuts, but rather had their hair trimmed from shoulder length to level with their ears and only slightly less dishevelled. This was a style known in the prison system as "Home Office Length." "Oz Trio Get Jail Haircuts," *Daily Telegraph*, July 31, 1971.

123. TNA, CRIM 1/5453/3, A. W. Griffiths, medical reports on Neville (August 2, 1971), Dennis (August 3, 1971), and Anderson (August 3, 1971); A.G.H. Robins, "Social Enquiry Report," August 3, 1971.

124. "Outcry as Oz Editors are Jailed," *Daily Telegraph*, August 6, 1971; "Grave Disquiet among Some Lawyers," *The Times*, August 6, 1971. Argyle passed sentence just before the deadline set by the full bench of the high court when Mortimer applied to have the defendants released on bail. TNA, J 82/1932, D. R. Thompson, "Court of Appeal Criminal Division . . . Note for the Hon. Mr. Justice James," October 18, 1971.

125. Bruce Page, Tony Delano, John Pilger, Philip Knightley, Murray Sayle, Peter Porter, Clive James, letter to the editor, *The Times*, August 7, 1971. They gave Fleet Street as their address.

126. TNA, J 82/1932, Anthony Pruim (the company's accountant) to Offenbach and Co, August 2, 1971.

127. TNA, J 82/1932, R. v. Neville, Anderson, and Dennis, application for bail, Court of Appeal, Criminal Division, judgment of Mr Justice Griffiths, August 9, 1971. They provided two sureties: the publisher Deborah Rogers and Tony Palmer, a journalist who interpreted the underground to readers of the *Observer* and the *Spectator* and produced a quick book about the trial before the appeal was heard. TNA, J 82/1932, notices of application for bail (R3 Form 4), for Neville, Anderson, and Dennis, each dated July 29, 1971.

128. Tribe, *Questions of Censorship*, 152. The barrister was Jeremy Hutchinson, who assisted Gerald Gardiner in the *Lady Chatterley's Lover* trial.

129. TNA, J 82/1932, Regina v. Neville, Anderson, Dennis, and Oz Publications Ink Limited, Court of Appeal, Criminal Division (Lord Chief Justice Widgery, Mrs Justice James, and Mr Justice Bridge), "Judgment," November 5, 1971. See also *Longford Report*, 369.

130. TNA, J 82/1932, Regina v. Neville, Anderson, Dennis, and Oz Publications Ink Limited, Court of Appeal, Criminal Division (Lord Chief Justice Widgery, Mrs. Justice James, and Mr. Justice Bridge), "Judgment," November 5, 1971.

131. TNA, HO 265/37, David Tudor Price, submission to Committee on Obscenity and Film Censorship, October 21, 1977.

132. TNA, DPP 2/4349, Lynda Anderson to Director of Public Prosecutions, August 6, 1971 (emphasis in original).

133. TNA, HO 302/49, Sir Philip Allen to Waldron, August 6, 1971; Allen to Skelhorn, August 19, 1971. This file was released in the late 1990s on the application of Alan Travis. See his account in *Bound and Gagged*, 248–54.

134. TNA, HO 302/49, de Deney to Francis Graham-Harrison, October 23, 1972.

135. TNA, HO 302/49, de Deney, "Note for the Record," December 18, 1972; de Deney to Graham-Harrison, October 23, 1972.

136. TNA, HO 302/49, Waldron to Allen, March 1, 1972.

137. TNA, HO 302/49, Waldron to Allen, August 17, 1971; Graham-Harrison to Waddell, November 17, 1972.

138. On the decision not to initiate proceedings over *Oh! Calcutta!*, see Steve Nicholson, *The Censorship of British Drama, 1900–1968*, vol. 4, *The Sixties* (Exeter: Exeter University Press, 2015), 282–85.

139. TNA, HO 302/49, G. E. Fenwick to Commander [Wallace Virgo], August 11, 1971. Compare "NCCL Press Statement on 'Oz' Verdict," [National Council for Civil Liberties] *Bulletin*, August 1971, 1.

140. Luff left the Obscene Publications Squad in mid- to late 1970. TNA, CRIM 1/5453/2, Luff, deposition, September-October 1970.

141. Gordon Honeycombe and Adam Acworth, *Adam's Tale* (London: Hutchinson, 1974), 199–202.

142. Travis, *Bound and Gagged*, 201–02, 205, 215, 254.

Chapter Seven. Campaigners and Litigants, 1972–1977

1. TNA, HO 302/51, "A New Law of Obscenity? Discussion with Prof. Ronald Dworkin and Michael Havers, Q.C., M.P.," February 4, 1972.

2. Havers entered Parliament in 1970, becoming MP for Wimbledon when Sir Cyril Black retired. Havers acted for Black in the latter's application for a destruction order against *Last Exit to Brooklyn*: "Obscenity Prosecution by M.P.: U.S. Novel 'A Collection of Dirty Stories,'" *The Times*, October 28, 1966.

3. TNA, HO 302/50, Society of Conservative Lawyers, "The Pollution of the Mind: New Proposals to Control Public Indecency and Obscenity," n.d. (1971).

4. Paul Johnson, "Pakenham, Francis Aungier [Frank], first Baron Pakenham and seventh earl of Longford (1905–2001)," *ODNB*.

5. CUL, David Holbrook Papers, MS Add.9987/8/3, David Holbrook, "The Political Dangers of Cultural Debasement," typescript, 1972–1973; David Holbrook, ed., *The Case against Pornography* (London: Tom Stacey, 1972).

6. Savile had hosted Longford on *Speakeasy*, a radio program on which a studio audience of teenagers put questions to adult authorities. Avril Fox, "'Speakeasy,'" COSMO/DLAS Newsletter, no. 2, June 1971, no page numbers (copy in LSE, DLAS Papers). See also George Melly, *Revolt into Style: The Pop Arts* (1970; repr., New York, 1971), 249.

7. On *Spare Rib*, see "Interview with Marsha Rowe," *Palaver*, May 10, 2010, accessed December 16, 2019, https://afonsoduarte.tumblr.com/post/538575214/interview-with-marsha-rowe; Boycott, *Nice Girl*, 57–62; Nigel Fountain, *Underground: The London Alternative Press, 1966–74* (London: Routledge, 1988), 171–74.

8. Bonny Boston, "Crotchety?," *Spare Rib*, no. 5 (November 1972): 21.

9. TNA, HO 302/56, Allen to Francis Graham-Harrison and J. H. Waddell, November 24, 1971. Margaret Thatcher, the education secretary, was considering getting a school inspector to give evidence to the inquiry. The civil service head of her department contacted the Home Office to inquire how they were responding.

10. Among the press grandees giving interviews were the editors of the *Daily Mirror* and the *Sunday Mirror* and the chairman of the company that owned them, Hugh Cudlipp; Rupert Murdoch, owner of the *Sun* and the *News of the World*; Vere Harmsworth, owner of the *Daily Mail*; Sir Max Aitken, proprietor of the *Daily Express*; Lord Hartwell of the *Daily Telegraph*; David Astor of the *Observer*; William Rees-Mogg of *The Times*; and Harold Evans of the *Sunday Times*. *Pornography: The Longford Report* (London: Coronet Books, 1972), 321–22.

11. Barry Cox, John Shirley, and Martin Short, *The Fall of Scotland Yard* (Harmondsworth: Penguin, 1977), 183.

12. *Longford Report*, 15.

13. *Longford Report*, 120–27; V&A, Arts Council of Great Britain Papers, ACGB/59/1, box 3, Mogens Moe to Eric White, May 7, 1969.

14. *Longford Report*, 121, 125–26; *The Obscenity Laws: A Report by the Working Party Set up by a Conference Convened by the Chairman of the Arts Council of Great Britain* (London: André Deutsch, 1969), 25 n. (hereafter *Report by the Working Party*). The Arts Council working party's claim of 25 percent decline was confirmed by a press officer at the Danish embassy in London, according to the report.

15. The bookseller Thomas Joy, one of the quiet ones on the Arts Council working party, said that he had felt justified in recommending a five-year suspension of the obscenity laws in 1969, but the rising tide of pornography and permissiveness had made him reconsider. *Longford Report*, 202–4 (Montgomerie), 82–83 (Hewitt), 299–300 (Joy).

16. The *Longford Report* made much of A. P. Herbert's protest—in *The Times*, as ever—about *Oh! Calcutta!*: "My colleagues and I, in 1954, began a worthy struggle for reasonable liberty for honest writers. I am sorry to think that our efforts seem to have ended in a right to represent copulation, veraciously, on the public stage." *Longford Report*, 11 (the first page of the introduction), 17 (first page of chapter 1), 282–83; A. P. Herbert, "Indecency on the Stage: A Change in Law Needed," *The Times*, August 26, 1970.

17. Since, according to the 1959 act, being in the public good made an obscene publication legitimate but did not make it any less obscene, that is, depraving and corrupting of those likely in all the relevant circumstances to read it or see it. *Report by the Working Party*, 23; *Longford Report*, 369.

18. As a law lord remarked in 1972: "It can only have been the pressure of Parliamentary compromise which can have produced a test so difficult for the courts." Director of Public Prosecutions v. Whyte [1972] AC 849 at 861–62 (Lord Wilberforce). See also Peter D. McDonald, "Old Phrases and Great Obscenities: The Strange Afterlife of Two Victorian Anxieties," *Journal of Victorian Culture* 13, no. 2 (2007): 294–302, 299.

19. *Longford Report*, 369–70. They did not blame the judges for allowing it.

20. *Longford Report*, 371.

21. Like its Arts Council counterpart, it was published by a commercial press.

22. LSE, DLAS Papers, executive committee minutes, March 4, 1975. John Calder and Hans Eysenck were among the conference's sponsors.

23. Matthew Grimley, "Anglican Evangelicals and Anti-Permissiveness: The Nationwide Festival of Light, 1971–1983," in *Evangelicalism and the Church of England in the Twentieth Century: Reform, Resistance and Renewal*, ed. Andrew Atherstone and John Maiden (Woodbridge: Boydell Press, 2014), 183–205, 184–86.

24. Amy C. Whipple, "Speaking for Whom? The 1971 Festival of Light and the Search for the 'Silent Majority,'" *Contemporary British History*, 24, no. 3 (2010): 319–39, 322–24; Grimley, "Anglican Evangelicals and Anti-Permissiveness," 184–86.

25. Grimley, "Anglican Evangelicals and Anti-Permissiveness," 185; Andrew Atherstone, "The Keele Congress of 1967: A Paradigm Shift in Anglican Evangelical Attitudes," *Journal of Anglican Studies* 9, no. 2 (2011): 175–97. One of the plenary speakers at Keele was the evangelical, former missionary, and Islamic legal expert Sir Norman Anderson, who became vice-chairman of the Longford Committee. Atherstone, "Keele Congress," 181, 185–86.

26. Whipple, "Speaking for Whom?," 335.

27. TNA, HO 265/7, Nationwide Festival of Light, submission to COFC, January 1978.

28. Before he took the job with the Festival of Light, Johnston was a lecturer at the University of Newcastle Institute of Education, training university graduates for teaching careers.

29. Matthew Grimley, "Thatcherism, Morality and Religion," in *Making Thatcher's Britain*, ed. Ben Jackson and Robert Saunders (Cambridge: Cambridge University Press, 2012), 78–94, 85.

30. Guy Phelps, *Film Censorship* (London: Victor Gollancz, 1975), 66–67.

31. *HC Deb.*, vol. 872, May 3, 1974, col. 261W.

32. Colin Manchester, "Indecent Displays (Control) Act 1981," *Statute Law Review* 3, no. 1 (1982): 31–39. Thatcher was one of the government sponsors of the 1973 bill. Cinematograph and Indecent Displays Bill (HC), October 31, 1973.

33. TNA, HO 265/20, COFC minutes, January 24, 1979, oral evidence from *Forum*. There was an American precedent in Citizens for Decent Literature's Operation News-Stand at the end of the 1950s. H. Montgomery Hyde, *A History of Pornography* (London: Heinemann, 1964), 194.

34. *An Appeal to All Newsagents* (London: Nationwide Festival of Light, c. 1977), copy in TNA, HO 265/82; TNA, HO 265/82, Vivienne Chasmar to J. C. Davey, September 23, 1977. For a similar, earlier campaign by the NFOL, see *Longford Report*, 31.

35. Roger King, "The Middle Class in Revolt?," in *Respectable Rebels: Middle Class Campaigns in Britain in the 1970s*, ed. Roger King and Neill Nugent (London: Hodder and Stoughton, 1979), 1–22, 4. Compare Lawrence Black, *Redefining British Politics: Culture, Consumerism and Participation, 1954–70* (Basingstoke: Palgrave Macmillan, 2010), 108.

36. Attorney-General (on the relation of McWhirter) v. Independent Broadcasting Authority [1973] 1 All ER 689 at 699.

37. Lord Denning, *The Discipline of Law* (London: Butterworths, 1979), part 3.

38. Raymond Blackburn, *I Am an Alcoholic* (London: Allan Wingate, 1959), chaps. 4–10.

39. "Blackburn Sent to Prison for Two Years," *The Times*, January 28, 1955; "Raymond Blackburn," *The Times*, November 5, 1991.

40. "Turning-point in War on Porn," *Sunday Telegraph*, August 24, 1975; Robin Blackburn, "Obituary of Raymond Blackburn," *Guardian*, November 5, 1991.

41. R v. Commissioner of Police of the Metropolis ex parte Blackburn [1968] 2 QB 118; "Ex-MP Wants Police Ordered to Enforce Gaming Law," *The Times*, January 25, 1968. See also Raymond Blackburn, letter to the editor, *The Times*, May 26, 1989.

42. R v. Commissioner of Police of the Metropolis ex parte Blackburn [1973] QB 241; Cox, Shirley, and Short, *Fall of Scotland Yard*, 193.

43. Christopher Forsyth, "Lord Denning and Modern Administrative Law," *Denning Law Journal* 14, no. 1 (1999): 57–69, 60.

44. Lord Harris of High Cross, rev. by Marc Brodie, "McWhirter, (Alan) Ross, 1925–1975," *ODNB*.

45. LSE, DLAS Papers, J. C. Swaffield, "Exercise of the Council's Powers of Film Censorship for Adults," appendix B, November 28, 1974. The other representatives of the NFOL who met with the Greater London Council as it prepared this report were Steve Stevens and the Rev. Eddy Stride.

46. Morals campaigners were alerted to Warhol earlier, after controversies over the censorship of his films *Trash* and *Heat*. James C. Robertson, *The Hidden Cinema: British Film Censorship in Action, 1913–1975* (London: Routledge, 1993), 146; Enid Wistrich, *"I Don't Mind the Sex, It's the Violence": Film Censorship Explored* (London: Marion Boyars, 1978), 31.

47. *Attorney General (on the relation of McWhirter) v. Independent Broadcasting Authority*, 689 at 692–93.

48. Jeremy Potter, *Independent Television in Britain*, vol. 3, *Politics and Control, 1968–1980* (Basingstoke: Macmillan, 1989), 125.

49. The difference between the BBC's charter and the Television Act in this respect was described by one of the BBC's critics, Peregrine Worsthorne, as a secret weapon allowing it to exploit eroticism and compete unfairly: one of the arguments for breaking up the BBC, according to Worsthorne. *Longford Report*, 227. Later in the 1970s, Worsthorne was an active member of Norris McWhirter's National Association for Freedom. Neill Nugent, "Freedom Association," in King and Nugent, *Respectable Rebels*, 76–100, 91.

50. *Attorney General (on the relation of McWhirter) v. Independent Broadcasting Authority*, 689 at 694. On the issue of the attorney general's support, see Gouriet v. Union of Post Office Workers 8 [1978] AC 435; Peter Radan, "Law, Politics, and the Attorney-General: The Context and Impact of *Gouriet v Union of Post Office Workers*," *Macquarie Law Journal* 16 (2016): 105–26.

51. *Attorney General (on the relation of McWhirter) v. Independent Broadcasting Authority*, [1973] 1 All ER 689 at 696, 701–702.

52. Black, *Redefining British Politics*, 108.

53. On the Responsible Society and its membership, see Dallas Cliff, "Religion, Morality and the Middle Class," in King and Nugent, *Respectable Rebels*, 127–52, 129, 141–42.

54. Potter, *Independent Television*, 129–30.

55. Robertson, *Hidden Cinema*, 153–55.

56. "'Last Tango' Sex Obscene, Says Man, 70," *Daily Telegraph*, November 26, 1974.

57. "The Story behind Filmmaker Bernardo Bertolucci's Last Public Controversy," *Washington Post*, November 27, 2018. Shackleton said on another occasion that "the film was a record of obscenities practised by Marlon Brando and Maria Schneider and was not a fictional event." Phelps, *Film Censorship*, 61.

58. Blackburn issued writs against the president and secretary of the BBFC but soon withdrew them: Robertson, *Hidden Cinema*, 153. A complainant in Cornwall tried to bring charges under the Vagrancy Acts in February of 1974, but the magistrate dismissed the case. LSE, DLAS Papers, J. C. Swaffield, "Exercise of the Council's Powers of Film Censorship for Adults."

59. Geoff Robertson, "Film Censorship Merry-Go-Round," *New Statesman*, June 28, 1974, 912, 914; "Judge Throws 'Last Tango' Test Case Out," *Guardian*, November 28, 1974; Phelps, *Film Censorship*, 61.

60. Graham Zellick, "Films and the Law of Obscenity," *Criminal Law Review* (March 1971): 126–50, 131–32.

61. "'Last Tango' Case Is Thrown Out," *Daily Telegraph*, November 28, 1974.

62. Grimley, "Anglican Evangelicals and Anti-Permissiveness," 192–93. Ernest Wistrich was director of the European Movement, whose chairman was Lord Harlech, the president of the British Board of Film Censors, which was also suspect. Robert Saunders, *Yes to Europe! The 1975 Referendum and Seventies Britain* (Cambridge: Cambridge University Press, 2018), 101; *Report of the Committee on Obscenity and Film Censorship*, Cmnd. 7772 (London: HMSO, 1979) (hereafter "Williams Report"), para. 12.23.

63. Blackburn sued the attorney general in 1971, arguing that the government had no power to sign the Treaty of Rome because that would bind succeeding Parliaments. McWhirter argued that the British government's powers were vested in the Crown and could not be transferred by a treaty. In both cases the Court of Appeal declined to act. Lord Denning was willing to entertain the idea that the litigants had standing; the other judges "deprecate[d] litigation the purpose of which is to influence political decisions." Blackburn v. Attorney-General [1971] 2 All ER 1380 (quotation from Lord Justice Salmon at 1383).

64. Edward Shackleton, "The Inadequacy of the Law When Dealing with Obscene Films," *Daily Telegraph*, August 12, 1977, 9; Mark Vasey-Saunders, *The Scandal of Evangelicals and Homosexuality: English Evangelical Texts, 1960–2010* (2015; repr. Abingdon: Routledge, 2016), 77.

65. TNA, DPP 2/5459, R. Peskett, "Hugh Shadforth Watts, 'Field House', Honeysuckle Lane, High Salvington, Worthing," November 25, 1975. The DPP already had several files on Watts and AGAL: TNA, DPP 2/5459, note in minutes pages, August 5, 1974.

66. TNA, DPP 2/5459, O. R. Johnston to DPP, September 4, 1974, March 15, 1975, September 4, 1975.

67. Vaughan was also the distributor of Warhol's *Heat*. Wistrich, "I Don't Mind the Sex," 31.

68. TNA, HO 265/79, untitled press release (NFOL 64), c. 1975.

69. Phelps, *Film Censorship*, 63–64; LSE, DLAS Papers, J. C. Swaffield, "Exercise of the Council's Powers of Film Censorship for Adults," November 28, 1974; LSE, DLAS Papers, National Co-ordinating Committee against Censorship, minutes of meeting held February 14, 1975.

70. TNA, DPP 2/5459, Watts to K. M. Ham, December 6, 1975.

71. TNA, DPP 2/5459, [A. H. Gordon?], note in minutes pages, August 22, 1974 (order of quotations rearranged).

72. TNA, DPP 2/5459, Gordon, note in minutes pages, November 26, 1975; anon, note in minutes pages, n.d. (before November 26, 1975).

73. Mary Whitehouse, *Whatever Happened to Sex?* (Hove: Wayland Publishers, 1977), 143–44.

74. A Gallup poll in 1979 backed up this assessment: "Survey Shows Confused Attitudes to Porn," *Guardian*, March 7, 1979.

75. See the table in Whitehouse, *Whatever Happened to Sex?*, 143–44.

76. Ros Schwartz, "A Question of Allegiance?" in *Feminism and Censorship: The Current Debate*, ed. Gail Chester and Julienne Dickey (Bridport: Prism Press, 1988), 11–16, 11–12.

77. The novelist was Mervyn Jones, who had also appeared in the *Last Exit* and *Oz* trials.

78. Gavin Schaffer, "Till Death Us Do Part and the BBC: Racial Politics and the British Working Classes, 1965–75," *Journal of Contemporary History* 45, no. 2 (2010): 454–77, 460; Mary Whitehouse, *Who Does She Think She Is?* (London: New English Library, 1971), chap. 9.

79. TNA, DPP 2/5459, N. Richards, "R. v. Johannes Heinrich Hanau: Heinrich Hanau Publications Limited: Universal Tandem Publishing Coy. Ltd.," n.d.

80. Anna Coote and Lawrence Grant, eds., *Civil Liberty: The NCCL Guide* (Harmondsworth: Penguin, 1972).

81. TNA, DPP 2/5459, Hanau, untitled, undated statement.

82. TNA, DPP 2/5459, Calder, deposition, Bow Street Magistrates Court, February 5, 1975.

83. TNA, DPP 2/5459, note in minutes pages, n.d.

84. TNA, DPP 2/5459, Richards, "R. v. Johannes Heinrich Hanau," n.d. Compare the evidence of the Criminal Bar Association to the Williams Committee several years later: juries "would rather acquit than guess their way to a conviction." Williams Report, para. 2.9.

85. John Sutherland, *Offensive Literature: Decensorship in Britain, 1960–1982* (London: Junction Books, 1982), 135. The Metropolitan Police came to the same conclusion: TNA, HO 265/19, COFC minutes, April 21, 1978.

86. Indiana, Calder and Boyars MSS, box 156, Free Art Legal Fund, leaflet, 1967.

87. LSE, DLAS Papers, executive committee minutes, September 13, 1972.

88. Camilla Schofield and Ben Jones, "'Whatever Community Is, This Is Not It': Notting Hill and the Reconstruction of 'Race' in Britain after 1958," *Journal of British Studies* 58, no. 1 (2019): 142–73, 165.

89. LSE, DLAS Papers, "What DLAS Is All About / What DLAS Does," leaflet, c. 1977.

90. Indiana, Calder and Boyars MSS, box 156, John Calder to Gordon E. Moody, April 17, 1968; Calder to D. K. Cameron, April 24, 1968.

91. TNA, HO 265/2, *A Guide to B.A.P.A.L.: The British Adult Publications Association Limited* (n.p., n.d. [c. 1978]).

92. LSE, DLAS Papers, executive committee minutes, September 17, 1975 (concerning David Gold).

93. *Libertine* was billed as a combination of *Oz*, *Forum*, and *Suck*, the sex magazine edited by Jim Haynes, formerly of *IT* and a collaborator of Calder's in early 1960s Edinburgh. Sutherland, *Offensive Literature*, 160–61; "Sex Magazine Producers are Cleared," *Daily Telegraph*, February 12, 1977.

94. NCROPA (National Campaign for the Reform of the Obscene Publications Acts) Virtual Archive, Miscellaneous Documents, "From Libertine 15: Our Beliefs: This Is What Our Trial Is About" (c. 1977), accessed February 4, 2021, www.infotextmanuscripts.org/ncropa/ncropa-misc-arabella.jpg.

95. DLAS papers, executive committee minutes, September 17, 1975; Francis Bennion, "The Libertine Trial," *New Statesman*, February 18, 1977, 210–11.

96. LSE, DLAS Papers, executive committee minutes, September 14, 1977; TNA, HO 265/77, John Hanau to Jon Davey, September 25, 1977.

97. LSE, DLAS Papers, executive committee minutes, January 16, 1974.

98. These two "refused to pay protection money to anyone." LSE, DLAS Papers, executive committee minutes, September 11, 1973.

99. A spate of police action against the magazines *Him Exclusive* and *Gay Circle* in 1975 prompted adverse coverage in the *Guardian* and a speech by David Steel MP, the sponsor of the bill decriminalizing abortion in 1967, decrying a "new illiberalism." LSE, DLAS Papers, executive committee minutes, September 17, 1975.

100. Jeffrey Weeks, *Coming Out: Homosexual Politics in Britain, from the Nineteenth Century to the Present* (London: Quartet Books, 1977), chap. 15.

101. LSE, DLAS Papers, executive committee minutes, May 9, 1972, June 9, 1976.

102. Ruth Wallsgrove, "Pornography: Between the Devil and the True Blue Whitehouse," *Spare Rib*, no. 65 (December 1977): 44–46, 46.

103. LSE/Women's Library, Sally Alexander Papers, 7SAA/1, folder 8, Maria Coulias, Siva German, Sheila Jeffreys, Sandra McNeill, and Jan Winterlake, "Pornography," paper written for London Revolutionary Feminist Conference, February 1978. I am grateful to Emma Wallhead for showing me her copy of this document.

104. DLAS successfully courted the *Sunday Times* editor Harold Evans and Simon Jenkins, editor of the paper's Insights section. They cultivated Nicholas de Jongh of the *Guardian* as someone who could be briefed discreetly about Mary Whitehouse's activities. LSE, DLAS Papers, executive committee minutes, January 7, 1976. See also Geoffrey Robertson, *The Justice Game* (London: Chatto and Windus, 1998), 30.

105. LSE, DLAS Papers, "Defence of Literature and the Arts Society: An Outline Plan for Future Action," n.d. (c. 1977) (emphasis in original).

106. LSE, DLAS Papers, executive committee minutes, November 22, 1973; Martin Loney (NCCL) to "Dear Colleague," December 19, 1973; "Indecent Acts," one-page supplement to *Civil Liberty* 39, no. 7 (1973); LSE, DLAS Papers, British Federation of Film Societies, "The Case against the Cinematograph and Indecent Displays Bill," n.d. The Kingsley Committee donated £1000 to the joint campaign committee and pledged a further £500. LSE, DLAS Papers, executive committee minutes, December 19, 1973.

107. LSE, DLAS Papers, executive committee minutes, December 19, 1973.

108. LSE, DLAS Papers, Ron Bailey, report to the Ad Hoc Committee against the Cinematograph and Indecent Displays Bill, February 13, 1974.

109. See Chris Moores, *Civil Liberties and Human Rights in Twentieth-Century Britain* (Cambridge: Cambridge University Press, 2017), chaps. 3–4. The claim in the main text is mine rather than Moores', but his book provides support for it.

110. LSE, DLAS Papers, National Co-ordinating Committee against Censorship, minutes of meeting held July 24, 1974; LSE, DLAS Papers, Antony Grey to Kenneth Hale, February 5, 1975.

111. LSE, DLAS Papers, Bailey, "Discussion Paper for Discussion at Committee Meeting 5 March," March 3, 1974.

112. LSE, DLAS Papers, executive committee minutes, July 15, 1976; also December 13, 1976 (reports of AGM attendees saying that "they were glad DLAS had discussed non-pornographic censorship for once").

113. LSE, DLAS Papers, executive committee minutes, September 17, 1975.

114. LSE, DLAS Papers, executive committee minutes, July 15, 1976.

115. LSE, DLAS Papers, [Jane Cousins,] "Censorship and Race," n.d. (1977).

116. Philippa Strum, *When the Nazis Came to Skokie: Freedom for Speech We Hate* (Lawrence: University Press of Kansas, 1999).

117. See also Moores, *Civil Liberties*, 167–68, on the National Council for Civil Liberties and the National Front. However, compare the NCCL's relations with the Paedophile Information Exchange around the same time: Moores, *Civil Liberties*, 187–209.

118. Mary Whitehouse, *Whatever Happened to Sex?*, 20–21. David Holbrook was so convinced that he was being silenced by a press beholden to pornography that he began compiling an anthology of rejection letters to be entitled *The New Censorship in England*. CUL, David Holbrook Papers, MS Add.9987/8/3, Holbrook to Peter Elstob, January 23, 1977.

119. Whitehouse, *Whatever Happened to Sex?*, 56, 19; Whitehouse, *Who Does She Think She Is?*, 65.

120. For Tribe, see *Report by the Working Party*, 99–104; David Tribe, *Questions of Censorship* (London: George Allen and Unwin, 1973).

121. Jane Cousins, *Make It Happy: What Sex Is All About* (London: Virago, 1978); Catherine Riley, *The Virago Story: Assessing the Impact of a Feminist Publishing Phenomenon* (New York: Berghahn, 2018), 22.

122. Geoffrey Robertson defended *Street Boy* as well as *Gay News*.

123. TNA, HO 265/20, COFC minutes, September 1, 1978, oral evidence of the Campaign for Homosexual Equality (represented by Peter Ashman and Griffith Vaughan Williams). On the Campaign for Homosexual Equality, see Martha Robinson Rhodes, "Bisexuality, Multiple-Gender-Attraction, and Gay Liberation Politics in the 1970s," *Twentieth Century British History* 32, no. 1 (2021): 119–42.

124. TNA, HO 265/20, Julian Carter to Jon Davey, October 15, 1977.

125. Weeks, *Coming Out*, 222–23, 230.

126. This page of *Gay News* no. 96 is reproduced in Alan Travis, *Bound and Gagged: A Secret History of Obscenity in Britain* (London: Profile Books, 2000), 258.

127. Books that were the subject of obscenity prosecutions were often criticized for blasphemy as well (in fictional dialogue, for instance), but the publishers were not

charged with blasphemy. See George Ryley Scott, *"Into Whose Hands": An Examination of Obscene Libel in Its Legal, Sociological and Literary Aspects* (London: Gerald G. Swan, 1945), 101 n.

128. Alfred Denning, *Freedom under the Law* (London: Stevens and Sons, 1949), 46.

129. Robertson, *Justice Game*, 137–38.

130. Daniel S. Loss, "The Institutional Afterlife of Christian England," *Journal of Modern History* 89 (June 2017): 282–313, 304.

131. LSE, DLAS Papers, executive committee minutes, September 14, 1977.

132. The ornate phrasing of the indictment included the word obscene, and John Mortimer tried unsuccessfully to convince the judges in the High Court and the Court of Appeal that charges should have been laid under the Obscene Publications Act. TNA, DPP 2/6624, R. v. Gay News Limited, Court of Appeal judgment, March 17, 1978, p. 6.

133. Whitehouse v. Lemon [1979] AC 617, 636.

134. TNA, LCO 2/3347, Sir Frank Soskice to Sir Hartley Shawcross, November 25, 1947 (reporting the words of the DPP, Theobald Mathew); Hilliard, "Words That Disturb the State," 769–84.

135. Robert Hewison, *Monty Python: The Case Against* (London: Methuen, 1981), 68–69 (the Mortimer quotation is from a photograph of part of his opinion, reproduced on p. 68). For a very different interpretation of *The Life of Brian* and blasphemy law, see David Nash, *Blasphemy in the Christian World: A History* (Oxford: Oxford University Press, 2007), 211–16.

136. Robertson, *Justice Game*, 138; LSE, DLAS Papers, executive committee minutes, 9 June 1977, July 13, 1977.

137. TNA, DPP 2/6624, G. B. Ross-Cornes to Sir Tony Hetherington, July 7, 1978; TNA, DPP 2/6624, B. C. Reggiori to Robbins Olivey and Lake, July 19, 1978; "Group Reissues Blasphemy Case Poem," *The Times*, February 22, 1978; Leslie J. Moran, "Dangerous Words and Dead Letters: Encounters with Law and *The Love That Dares to Speak Its Name*," *Liverpool Law Review* 23 (2001): 153–65, 163.

138. LSE, DLAS Papers, executive committee minutes, July 13, 1978; TNA, DPP 2/6624, T. C. Hetherington to G. B. Ross-Cornes, September 28, 1977.

139. Gay News Ltd v. United Kingdom (1983) 5 EHRR 123; Russell Sandberg and Norman Doe, "The Strange Death of Blasphemy," *Modern Law Review* 71, no. 6 (2008): 971–86, 974–76.

140. See the Conclusion, pp. 217–20.

141. Phelps, *Film Censorship*, chap. 4; John Trevelyan, *What the Censor Saw* (London: Michael Joseph, 1973), chap. 15.

142. Trevelyan, *What the Censor Saw*, chap. 14.

143. Mary Burnet, *The Mass Media in a Violent World* (Paris: UNESCO, 1971).

144. Trevelyan, *What the Censor Saw*, 221.

145. Phelps, *Film Censorship*, 91–94.

146. David Limond, "'I Never Imagined That the Time Would Come': Martin Cole, the *Growing Up* Controversy and the Limits of School Sex Education in 1970s England," *History of Education* 37, no. 3 (2008): 409–29; James Hampshire and Jane Lewis, "'The Ravages of Permissiveness': Sex Education and the Permissive Society,"

Twentieth Century British History 15, no. 3 (2004): 290–321, 303–4; Whitehouse, *Who Does She Think She Is?*, 145–49.

147. Tribe, *Questions of Censorship*, 157.

148. See also Callum G. Brown, *The Battle for Christian Britain: Sex, Humanists and Secularisation, 1945–1980* (Cambridge: Cambridge University Press, 2019), 189–90. Trevelyan had been a local education director before joining the BBFC.

149. Phelps, *Film Censorship*, 69–72; LSE, DLAS Papers, executive committee minutes, September 9, 1974.

150. As of 1975: Wistrich, *"I Don't Mind the Sex,"* 19.

151. Quoted in LSE, DLAS Papers, Enid Wistrich, "Note (28.11.74) by Chairman, Film Viewing Board: The Future of Film Censorship for Adults."

152. LSE, DLAS Papers, J. C. Swaffield, "Exercise of the Council's Powers of Film Censorship for Adults," 28 November 1974; Enid Wistrich, "Note (28.11.74) by Chairman, Film Viewing Board: The Future of Film Censorship for Adults."

153. Neville March Hunnings, *Film Censors and the Law* (London: George Allen and Unwin, 1967), 13–14.

154. TNA, HO 265/19, COFC minutes, January 6, 1978, oral evidence of James Ferman. The decision was made while Stephen Murphy was secretary of the BBFC, but Ferman affirmed the decision later in the 1970s.

155. Wistrich, *"I Don't Mind the Sex,"* 26–27.

156. Wistrich, *"I Don't Mind the Sex,"* 52–53. The policy was Wistrich's innovation. In her book she doesn't make the connection with the Cinematograph and Indecent Displays Bill, however. Wistrich was against restrictions on films but accepted "the case for restricting obscene, violent and indecent material on public display." TNA, HO 265/5, Enid Wistrich, "Submission to the Committee on Obscenity and Film Censorship" on behalf of the Fabian Society, April 1978.

157. LMA, GLC/DG/EL/01/453, includes copies of draft promotional materials for *More about the Language of Love*, marked up by the council to show which parts were and were not approved; GLC/DG/EL/01/505, unsigned copy of letter sent on behalf of Director-General to Gwenan Williams, October 27, 1978.

158. Law Commission, *Report on Conspiracy and Criminal Law Reform*, Law Com. no. 76 (London: HMSO, 1976), paras. 3.34–3.36.

159. *Longford Report*, 277; TNA, HO 265/19, COFC minutes, February 17, 1978, oral evidence of Customs and Excise.

160. LMA, GLC/DG/EL/01/453, J. C. Ferman to Swaffield, July 10, 1978.

161. A decision that the Rev. Eddy Stride of the Festival of Light urged them to reconsider. LMA, GLC/DG/EL/01/453, Edgar George Stride, statement, September 26, 1978.

162. LMA, GLC/DG/EL/01/492 (1976–1977).

163. Wistrich, *"I Don't Mind the Sex,"* 13–14.

164. Enid Wistrich, letter to *The Times*, January 28, 1975.

165. "It is believed that, had the resolution referred to above been carried, some other local authorities in major urban centres would have taken steps to follow a similar course." Law Commission, *Conspiracy and Criminal Law Reform*, para. 3.44.

166. Wistrich, *"I Don't Mind the Sex,"* 64–69, quotation from 68 (ellipsis in original).

167. Wistrich, *"I Don't Mind the Sex,"* 69–70.

168. "Viewing Board Chairman Keeps Her Pledge to Resign," *The Times*, January 29, 1975.

169. Ray Johnston wrote of "the small coterie of atheistic Hampstead intellectuals who set the pace for the industry in the letter columns of the *Guardian* and on the Greater London Council Viewing Board." O. R. Johnston, "The Law of the Cinema," *Third Way*, September 22, 1977, 13–15, 14.

170. "Support for GLC Retention of Film Veto," *The Times*, January 30, 1975.

171. Graham Zellick, "Films and the Law of Obscenity," *Criminal Law Review* (March 1971): 126–50, 146–48; TNA HO 265/2, British Board of Film Censors, "Evidence to the Home Office Committee on Obscenity and Film Censorship," February 1979.

172. Gareth Jones, "Mera ur kärlekens språk (*More About the Language of Love*)," *Monthly Film Bulletin*, August 1974, 181.

173. LMA, GLC/DG/EL/01/453, [G. M. Tudge], "More about the Language of Love," handwritten notes, n.d.

174. "X-rated Sex Film Seized by Yard," *Sunday Times*, August 11, 1974.

175. "Summonses Taken out over Swedish Film," *The Times*, August 22, 1974; Cox, Shirley, and Short, *Fall of Scotland Yard*, chap. 3; David Woodland, *Crime and Corruption at the Yard* (Barnsley: Pen and Sword True Crime, 2015).

176. LMA, GLC/DG/EL/01/453, "Note by Vice-Chairman Film Viewing Board," n.d.; W. Tofts, "More about the Language of Love" (note on proceedings in Marlborough Street Magistrates Court), October 1, 1974. Blackburn was no doubt paying attention when Whitehouse took proceedings under the Vagrancy Acts against the cinema showing *Blow Out* (*La Grande Bouffe*), which also bore a GLC certificate. The magistrate told her the Vagrancy Acts "were not designed to prevent indecent exhibitions within the closed walls of the cinema," but suggested that *La Grande Bouffe* amounted to an indecent exhibition at common law—a hint for next time. Phelps, *Film Censorship*, 62, 65; LSE, DLAS Papers, J. C. Swaffield, "Exercise of the Council's Powers of Film Censorship for Adults."

177. LMA, GLC/DG/EL/01/453, "Film Censorship: 'More about the Language of Love': Summing up, Central Criminal Court 5 June 1975," appendix B of "Court Decision (5.6.75) re 'More about the Language of Love'; Council's Rules of Management," report by Director General and Solicitor and Parliamentary Officer, July 4, 1975.

178. "Action Threat If Film Is Shown," *Guardian*, January 5, 1973.

179. LMA, GLC/DG/EL/01/453, "Court Decision (5.6.75) re 'More about the Language of Love'; Council's Rules of Management," report by Director General and Solicitor and Parliamentary Officer, July 4, 1975.

180. LMA, GLC/DG/EL/01/453, "Court Decision (5.6.75) re 'More about the Language of Love'; Council's Rules of Management," report by Director General and Solicitor and Parliamentary Officer, July 4, 1975.

181. LMA, GLC/DG/EL/01/453, "Film Viewing Board—16.7.75: Amended Rules of Management."

182. *R v. GLC*, ex parte Blackburn [1976] 1 WLR, 550 at 558, 559–560.

183. *R v. GLC*, ex parte Blackburn, 550 at 567.

184. *R v. GLC*, ex parte Blackburn, 550 at 564.

185. LSE, DLAS Papers, executive committee minutes, June 9, 1976.

186. Bernard Brook-Partridge, letter to editor, *Daily Telegraph*, November 24, 1978; LMA, GLC/DG/EL/01/505, Brian Cassidy to Kenneth Baker, January 19, 1979; "GLC Declares War on Soho Film 'Porn Brokers,'" *Daily Telegraph*, October 1, 1977; "Cinema Clubs in Soho Pledge to Aid Clean-Up," *Daily Telegraph*, October 13, 1977; "Soho People 'Fear Sex Film Firm,'" *Daily Telegraph*, November 11, 1977; TNA, HO 265/21, COFC minutes, February 7, 1979.

187. Williams Report, paras. 4.36–37.

188. Criminal Law Act, 1977, c. 45, s. 53. In this the government had the backing of the Law Commission, though the commission went further and recommended the total abolition of conspiracy to corrupt public morals and related common-law crimes. Law Commission, *Conspiracy and Criminal Law Reform*, para. 3.17; and see the recommendations in paras. 3.149–3.153.

189. Director of Public Prosecutions v. Jordan [1977] AC 699 at 719, 723. Mortimer and Robertson acted for Margaret Jordan, a Swansea newsagent.

190. Williams Report, paras. 4.8, 4.19–4.20.

191. TNA, HO 265/2, *A Guide to B.A.P.A.L.: The British Adult Publications Association Limited* (n.p. [c. 1978]); HO 265/20, COFC minutes, September 1, 1978, oral evidence of the British Adult Publications Association Ltd.

192. LSE, DLAS Papers, executive committee minutes, July 13, 1977.

193. TNA, HO 265/2, *Guide to B.A.P.A.L.*

194. TNA, HO 265/20, COFC minutes, September 1, 1978, oral evidence of the British Adult Publications Association Ltd.

195. Sutherland, *Offensive Literature*, 172–74 (quotation from 174); TNA, HO 265/20, COFC minutes, November 3, 1978, oral evidence of the Metropolitan Police (Skillern was among those present); "Daphne Skillern," *Daily Telegraph*, November 7, 2012. Though see the testimony of the Federation of London Wholesale Newspaper Distributors and David Tudor Price to the Williams Committee: TNA, HO 265/21, COFC minutes, February 7, 1979.

196. TNA, HO 265/79, Alan Gloak to [Jon Davey], April 13, 1978.

197. Williams Report, para. 4.22.

198. LSE, DLAS Papers, executive committee minutes, July 13, 1977.

199. LSE, DLAS Papers, executive committee minutes, September 14, 1977.

200. TNA, HO 265/2, *Guide to B.A.P.A.L.*; Williams Report, 4.21–4.22.

201. TNA, HO 265/1, Raymond Blackburn, submission to COFC, January 26, 1978.

202. S. C. Silkin, "Foreword" to Simpson, *Pornography and Politics*, vii–xi, viii–ix.

Chapter Eight. Philosophers and Pluralists, 1977–1979

1. TNA, HO 265/19, COFC minutes, September 2, 1977.

2. "Survey Shows Confused Attitudes to Porn," *Guardian*, March 7, 1979.

3. See Bill Schwarz, *The White Man's World* (Oxford: Oxford University Press, 2011), 37–47, for a reading of another archive of letters as texts of simultaneous reflection on social change; and, on ordinary people engaging comparably with social scientific investigations, Jon Lawrence, *Me, Me, Me? The Search for Community in*

Post-war England (Oxford: Oxford University Press, 2019), esp. the comments on p. 6; Florence Sutcliffe-Braithwaite, *Class, Politics, and the Decline of Deference in England, 1968–2000* (Oxford: Oxford University Press, 2018).

4. There was one Black man (Vivian White, a social worker from Cardiff who was also secretary of the United Caribbean Association); the rest of the committee members were white. *Report of the Committee on Obscenity and Film Censorship*, Cmnd. 7772 (London: HMSO, 1979) (hereafter "Williams Report"), iv; A.W.B. Simpson, *Pornography and Politics: A Look back to the Williams Committee* (London: Waterlow Publishers, 1983), 2–3, 24.

5. Quoted in Gordon Hawkins and Franklin E. Zimring, *Pornography in a Free Society* (Cambridge: Cambridge University Press, 1998), 12.

6. Simpson, *Pornography and Politics*, 24.

7. "Banning of Books 'Can be Harmful,'" *Guardian*, September 23, 1961. C. R. Hewitt saw this report and kept a clipping: LSE, C. H. Rolph Papers, 2/3/9.

8. Indiana, Calder and Boyars MSS, box 156, Bernard Williams to John Calder, November 24, 1967.

9. LSE, DLAS Papers, executive committee minutes, September 30, 1976.

10. The other names floated were Lord Goodman and the political scientists Bernard Crick and Ralph Miliband. DLAS's press officer Jane Cousins said she didn't know enough about any of them "to know where they stand," "apart from B Williams." LSE, DLAS Papers, Jane Cousins to executive committee members, January 5, 1977.

11. TNA, LO 2/161, G. E. Dudman to Solicitor General, June 3, 1964; H. Montgomery Hyde, *A History of Pornography* (London: Heinemann, 1964), 227; John Sutherland, *Offensive Literature: Decensorship in Britain, 1960–1982* (London: Junction Books, 1982), 69, 118.

12. *The Obscenity Laws: A Report by the Working Party Set up by a Conference Convened by the Chairman of the Arts Council of Great Britain* (London: André Deutsch, 1969), 82–83.

13. Frederick Watts quoted this passage with contempt in the lead-up to the *Inside Linda Lovelace* trial. TNA, DPP 2/5459, Watts to T. Taylor, November 29, 1975. See also TNA, HO 265/84, J. M. Ray to Davey, December 12, 1977.

14. Geoffrey Robertson, *The Justice Game* (London: Chatto and Windus, 1998), chap. 5. The prosecution was ordered by the attorney general, Sam Silkin.

15. A decade later he destroyed his reputation with a lenient sentence for rape. James Morton, "Sir John Leonard," *Guardian*, August 26, 2002.

16. A.W.B. Simpson, *Cannibalism and the Common Law: The Story of the Tragic Last Voyage of the Mignonette and the Strange Legal Proceedings to Which It Gave Rise* (Chicago: University of Chicago Press, 1984); A.W.B. Simpson, *Leading Cases of the Common Law* (Oxford: Clarendon Press, 1996).

17. Alexander Walker, "Introduction" to Guy Phelps, *Film Censorship* (London: Victor Gollancz, 1975), 7–13; Phelps, *Film Censorship*, 96, 164; LSE, DLAS Papers, executive committee minutes, February 25, 1976.

18. TNA, HO 265/49.

19. Simpson, *Pornography and Politics*, 31.

20. TNA, HO 265/20, COFC minutes, July 14–15, 1978.

21. TNA, HO 265/19, COFC minutes, October 28, 1977.

22. TNA, HO 265/38, Mike Devereaux to [Davey], December 5, 1977.

23. TNA, HO 265/19, COFC minutes, May 5, 1978.

24. Williams Report, para. 12.8.

25. TNA, HO 265/20, COFC minutes, July 14–15, 1978.

26. Williams Report, para. 12.5.

27. Williams Report, para. 12.23.

28. Williams Report, para. 12.24.

29. TNA, HO 265/19, COFC minutes, May 19, 1978 (oral evidence of James Ferman). It was Stephen Murphy who refused *Manson* a certificate, but Ferman stood by the decision when the documentary was resubmitted to the board in the midseventies.

30. David Faulkner, *Servant of the Crown: A Civil Servant's Story of Criminal Justice and Public Service Reform* (Hook: Waterside Press, 2014), 74–75.

31. TNA, HO 265/19, COFC minutes, October 7, 1977.

32. TNA, HO 265/19, COFC minutes, September 2, 1977.

33. TNA, HO 265/19, COFC minutes, January 20, 1978.

34. TNA, HO 265/19, COFC minutes, June 30, 1978.

35. Williams Report, appendix 5. In the years since his service for Longford, Yaffé had appeared as a defense witness for Hanau and publishers and retailers of pornographic magazines. There is a list of expert witnesses in cases from *Lady Chatterley's Lover* onwards in TNA, HO 265/51, [Davey?], "Obscene Publications: Use of the Public Good Defence," n.d.

36. HO 265/20, COFC minutes, January 10, 1979.

37. TNA, HO 265/5, William Edwards (chief executive of Figcrest Ltd), submission to COFC, September 4, 1978.

38. *An Appeal to All Newsagents* (London: Nationwide Festival of Light, c. 1977), copy in TNA, HO 265/82.

39. She said that the anticensorship lobby in Britain and in Denmark were trying to discredit Court's expertise. TNA, HO 265/7, submission from the National Viewers' and Listeners' Association, n.d.

40. TNA, HO 265/19, COFC minutes, June 15, 1978; HO 265/51, Bernard Williams to committee members, July 17, 1979.

41. TNA, HO 265/19, COFC minutes, June 2, 1978; HO 265/4, John Court, submission to COFC, n.d.

42. Williams Report, 6.30–6.43, quotation from 6.42.

43. TNA, HO 265/19, COFC minutes, January 20, 1978. When Eysenck and a colleague brought out a book entitled *Sex, Violence and the Media*, the committee agreed unenthusiastically that this "made it almost unavoidable . . . to invite Professor Eysenck to give oral evidence." That in turn obliged them to invite "another psychologist who might be able to provide a balance to evidence from such a controversial figure as Professor Eysenck." They chose Sir Martin Roth as a counterweight to Eysenck. HO 265/20, COFC minutes, September 22, 1978; HO 265/20, COFC minutes, January 10, 1979.

44. Bernard Williams knew Tudor Price from the gambling royal commission. Royal Commission on Gambling, *Final Report*, 2 vols, Cmnd. 7200 (London: HMSO, 1978), 1:3.

45. TNA, HO 265/37, David Tudor Price, submission to COFC, October 21, 1977.

46. TNA, HO 265/19, COFC minutes, June 2, 1978; HO 265/1, "Pornography—A Personal View," text of an address by Anderton to the Manchester Club, February 24, 1978.

47. TNA, HO 265/1, Anderton, submission to COFC, July 19, 1978. The Greater Manchester Police energetically prosecuted retailers as well as distributors under the Obscene Publications Act. This was a different approach from that of the Metropolitan Police. Because London was where most of the magazine publishers were based, the police in the capital focused on them and the headquarters of the national distribution chains, leaving retailers alone unless complaints from the public warranted action. After failing to secure a conviction in an important case in 1977, the Metropolitan Police reconsidered this policy and decided to go after retailers too, bringing their approach into line with Manchester's. Williams Report, para. 4.24.

48. TNA, HO 265/20, COFC minutes, October 6, 1978. Simpson was unconvinced: *Pornography and Politics*, 80.

49. Whitehouse, *Whatever Happened to Sex?*, 143–44.

50. On which see Paul Christoffel, *Censored: A Short History of Censorship in New Zealand* (Wellington: Department of Internal Affairs, 1989), 24–26.

51. TNA, HO 265/19, COFC minutes, April 21, 1978.

52. Williams Report, para. 9.22.

53. TNA, HO 265/20, COFC minutes, January 24, 1979.

54. TNA, HO 265/19, COFC minutes, April 21, 1978.

55. TNA, HO 265/19, COFC minutes, April 21, 1978.

56. Williams Report, para. 9.2.

57. Williams Report, para. 9.3.

58. *Pornography: Evidence Submitted by the Catholic Social Welfare Commission to the Home Office Committee Appointed in September 1977* (Abingdon: Social Welfare Commission, 1978), 3, 7, 12–14.

59. Williams Report, paras. 13.4.34–40; see also para. 12.11.

60. Mary Warnock, "The Williams Report on Obscenity and Film Censorship," *Political Quarterly* 51, no. 3 (1980): 341–344, 343. Warnock was a member of the IBA.

61. Williams Report, para. 9.21, 13.4.2.

62. Williams Report, paras. 9.30–9.32 (emphasis in original). The proposed reforms went further than the DPP's representatives had been willing to go. The DPP would also have prohibited highly explicit images of sex acts that were not themselves illegal.

63. Williams Report, paras. 9.2, 9.4; TNA, HO 265/5, Fabian Society, submission to COFC, April 1978; HO 265/2, British Humanist Association, submission to COFC, n.d.; HO 265/4, Defence of Literature and the Arts Society, submission to COFC, March 1978.

64. TNA, HO 265/4, Defence of Literature and the Arts Society, submission to COFC, March 1978; LSE, DLAS Papers, executive committee minutes, September 14, 1977. Wistrich also wrote the Fabian Society's submission. Francis Bennion was a barrister and one of the leaders of Freedom under Law, an organization that had affinities with the McWhirter brothers' causes. Bennion initiated proceedings to block disruptive protests, especially by the antiapartheid movement.

65. Williams Report, para. 7.22.

66. Williams Report, para. 13.4.6.

67. Williams Report, para.8.19–8.24.

68. Williams Report, para. 5.1.

69. Williams Report, para. 5.7.

70. TNA, HO 265/51, Bernard Williams to committee members, July 17, 1979.

71. Williams Report, paras. 5.15, 5.21.

72. Williams Report, para. 5.20.

73. Williams Report, para. 5.19; Harry Hopkins, *The New Look: A Social History of the Forties and Fifties in Britain* (London: Secker and Warburg, 1963), 236; Christopher Hilliard, *English as a Vocation: The "Scrutiny" Movement* (Oxford: Oxford University Press, 2012), 173, 176.

74. Williams Report, para. 5.24; Bernard Williams, "A Critique of Utilitarianism," in J.J.C. Smart and Bernard Williams, *Utilitarianism: For and Against* (Cambridge: Cambridge University Press, 1973), 77–150.

75. Williams Report, para. 5.24.

76. Williams Report, paras. 5.16–5.19, 5.24.

77. Stanley v. Georgia, 394 U.S. 557 (1969), at 564–66 (Justice Marshall). The Williams Report noted that the Supreme Court had excluded hard-core pornography from the category of speech protected by the First Amendment, but "right to be let alone" arguments like that in *Stanley v. Georgia* were not just First Amendment arguments. The Williams Committee's informant was Frederick Schauer, an American law professor on sabbatical at Cambridge. Williams Report, para. 5.18; TNA, HO 265/19, COFC minutes, May 19, 1978; HO 265/79, Schauer to Davey, February 10, 1978.

78. TNA, HO 265/2, British Adult Publications Association Limited, submission to COFC, June 1978; John Stuart Mill, *On Liberty* (1859), in Mill, *Three Essays*, ed. Richard Wollheim (Oxford: Oxford University Press, 1975), 18.

79. On the Scottish Homosexual Rights Group, see Roger Davidson and Gayle Davis, *The Sexual State: Sexuality and Scottish Governance, 1950–80* (Edinburgh: Edinburgh University Press, 2012), chap. 1.

80. They went on: "If a chaste kiss between hero and heroine merits a 'U' certificate [for 'universal,' permitting unrestricted access], then so must a chaste kiss between heroine and heroine."

81. TNA, HO 265/8, "Submission by the Scottish Homosexual Rights Group (Formerly Scottish Minorities Group) to the Committee on Obscenity and Film Censorship," n.d. (1977 or 1978). For similar arguments, see HO 265/8, Campaign for Homosexual Equality, Westminster Group, submission to COFC, February 23, 1978. On the progress of *Sunday Bloody Sunday* through the BBFC process, see John Trevelyan, *What the Censor Saw* (London: Michael Joseph, 1973), 208–9.

82. TNA, HO 265/6, Nalgay, the Nalgo Gay Group, submission to COFC, February 1978. Nalgo was the National and Local Government Officers Association. On gay groups in professional organizations, see Jeffrey Weeks, *Coming Out: Homosexual Politics in Britain, from the Nineteenth Century to the Present* (London: Quartet Books, 1977), 217.

83. Tony Palmer, *The Trials of Oz* (London: Blond and Briggs, 1971), 102.

84. *Report of the Committee on Homosexual Offences and Prostitution*, Cmnd. 247 (London: HMSO, 1957), paras. 61–62.

85. For context, see Julia Laite, *Common Prostitutes and Ordinary Citizens: Commercial Sex in London, 1885–1960* (London: Palgrave Macmillan, 2012), chap. 10, esp. pp. 174, 177, 178, 180, 182.

86. Matt Houlbrook, *Queer London: Perils and Pleasures in the Sexual Metropolis, 1918–1957* (Chicago: University of Chicago Press, 2005), 255–63.

87. TNA, HO 265/74, Carolyn F. Outram to Davey, n.d.

88. TNA, HO 265/72, Patricia Ade to Davey, September 15, 1977.

89. TNA, HO 265/72, Hilary Simon to Davey, September 3, 1977; HO 265/72, Shirley Harris to Davey, 7 September 1977; HO 265/72, K. Reynolds to [Davey], October 3, 1977; HO 265/74, Mavis Giles to [Davey], October 5, 1977.

90. TNA, HO 265/89, Glenys E. Woods to [Davey], March 22, 1979; HO 265/72, P. A. Lynn to Davey, September 5, 1977.

91. TNA, HO 265/78, A. B. Warburton to Jon Davey, September 27, 1977.

92. TNA, HO 265/74, S. Dargan to Davey, October 6, 1977; HO 265/74, P. Gollop to Sir, October 6, 1977.

93. TNA, HO 265/72, M. D. Wood to [Davey], August 3, 1977.

94. "Every time freedom is given for the publisher to display more blatantly the pornographic, there is less freedom for me and my family to view every shop window in a given area." TNA, HO 265/74, Howard G. Robinson (Ebbw Vale) to COFC, September 27, 1977. Roy Jenkins, as home secretary, said that it was not possible to legislate what magazines people might buy, "but, by not legislating, he is forcing me to see this offensive stuff when I go in to buy my 'Amateur Gardening.'" TNA, HO 265/72, Marjorie H. Morton (Lasswade, Midlothian) to [Davey], September 15, 1977.

95. TNA, HO 265/72, M. D. Wood to [Davey], August 3, 1977 (emphasis in original).

96. TNA, HO 265/72, M.C.H. Harrison to Davey, September 9, 1977.

97. TNA, HO 265/72, M. R. Bonavia, "Submission to the Committee on Obscenity and Film Censorship," n.d.

98. TNA, HO 265/89, J. E. and A. M. Parsell to [Davey], March 24, 1979.

99. TNA, HO 265/88, Michael Burgess to Davey, August 11, 1978.

100. TNA, HO 265/72, Sarah Hutchinson to [Davey], n.d.

101. TNA, HO 265/74, I. Lowther to Sirs, September 23, 1977.

102. TNA, HO 265/72, Benedict Beresford to Sir, September 3, 1977.

103. TNA, HO 265/89, Alison de Reybekill to [Davey], March 17, 1979.

104. Samuel Brittan, *Capitalism and the Permissive Society* (1973), reprinted in Brittan, *A Restatement of Economic Liberalism* (Basingstoke: Macmillan, 1988), 1–209, esp. 4–5, 28–29, 33–34. On Brittan's role in building support for neoliberal ideas in the United Kingdom, see Daniel Stedman Jones, *Masters of the Universe: Hayek, Friedman, and the Birth of Neoliberal Politics* (2012; repr., Princeton: Princeton University Press, 2014), 161, 174, 207, 233. For "dealignment," see Bo Särlvik and Ivor Crewe, *Decade of Dealignment: The Conservative Victory of 1979 and Electoral Trends in the 1970s* (Cambridge: Cambridge University Press, 1983).

105. TNA, HO 265/72, I. Batchelor to Davey, November 11, 1977.

106. TNA, HO 265/74, Walter Withers to Mr Rees, n.d., received by Home Office on October 14, 1977.

107. TNA, HO 265/74, C. O. Smith to [Davey], September 1977 (day obscured).

108. TNA, HO 265/88, Alan T. Bates to Davey, November 22, 1978.

109. TNA, HO 265/72, B. B. Taylor to [Davey], September 7, 1977; HO 265/74, H. G. Webster to Davey, n.d; HO 265/74, D. M. White to [Davey], n.d.

110. Lawrence, *Me, Me, Me*, 2. See also Emily Robinson, Camilla Schofield, Florence Sutcliffe-Braithwaite, Natalie Thomlinson, "Telling Stories about Post-war Britain: Popular Individualism and the 'Crisis' of the 1970s," *Twentieth Century British History* 28, no. 2 (2017): 268–304, 278.

111. Raymond Firth and Judith Djamour, "Kinship in South Borough," in *Two Studies of Kinship in London*, ed. Raymond Firth (London: Athlone Press, 1956), 33–63, 34.

112. Lawrence, *Me, Me, Me*, chaps. 2, 3 and p. 5; Jon Lawrence, "Inventing the 'Traditional Working Class': A Re-Analysis of Interview Notes from Young and Willmott's Family and Kinship in East London," *Historical Journal* 59, no. 2 (2016): 567–93.

113. Lawrence, *Me, Me, Me*, 5; Deborah Cohen, *Family Secrets: Living with Shame from the Victorians to the Present Day* (London: Viking, 2013), esp. 235–36.

114. Joanna Bourke, *Working-Class Cultures in Britain, 1890–1960: Gender, Class and Ethnicity* (London: Routledge, 1994), 71–74; Ben Jones, *The Working Class in Mid-Twentieth-Century England: Community, Identity and Social Memory* (Manchester: Manchester University Press, 2012), 135.

115. TNA, HO 265/74, "Jane Johnson" to Davey, n.d. Compare Kate Fisher and Simon Szreter's conclusion from their oral history interviews on sexual codes before the 1960s: "Some of our respondents did not find themselves enjoying sex despite their 'inhibited' and private culture, but, rather, because of it." Simon Szreter and Kate Fisher, *Sex Before the Sexual Revolution: Intimate Life in England, 1918–1963* (Cambridge: Cambridge University Press, 2010), 387.

116. TNA, HO 265/89, Glenys E. Woods to [Davey], March 22, 1979; HO 265/88, Ann H. Griffiths to [Davey], December 9, 1978.

117. TNA, HO 265/51, Sheila Rothwell to Davey, November 6, 1978; HO 265/49, Rothwell to Davey, October 7, 1979.

118. TNA, HO 265/89, Laura Fulcher to [Davey], n.d.

119. TNA, HO 265/89, Avis Greenwell, Wendy Fulger, Jenny Dunton, and Christine Rainger to committee, March 13, 1979.

120. TNA, HO 265/89, Carolan Urquhart to Madam/Sir, March 16, 1979.

121. See also TNA, HO 265/89, Kathleen Jones to Davey, April 23, 1979.

122. For samples of models' profiles and professed opinions, see Marcus Collins, "The Pornography of Permissiveness: Men's Sexuality and Women's Emancipation in Mid Twentieth-Century Britain," *History Workshop Journal*, no. 47 (Spring 1999): 99–120, 110–15.

123. TNA, HO 265/89, Laura Fulcher to [Davey], n.d. (emphasis in original).

124. TNA, HO 265/1, Patricia Anne Lloyd, for AFFIRM, to Davey, n.d. (1979).

125. Williams Report, para. 6.64.

126. TNA, HO 265/89, Alex K. Smith, secretary, SCUM 2 Collective, to Davey, n.d.

127. TNA, HO 265/89, Avis Greenwell, Wendy Fulger, Jenny Dunton, and Christine Rainger to committee, March 13, 1979.

128. TNA, HO 265/49, Rothwell to Davey, October 7, 1979; Williams Report, para. 6.64 (para. 6.65 in the draft Rothwell was commenting on).

129. Williams Report, para. 6.78.

130. Williams Report, para. 6.78.

131. TNA, HO 265/19, COFC minutes, June 15, 1978; Williams Report, paras. 6.79–6.80.

132. TNA, HO 265/7, Parliamentary Child and Family Protection Group, submission to COFC, n.d.

133. See also TNA, HO 265/7, Nationwide Festival of Light, submission to COFC, January 1978.

134. Williams Report, para. 5.9.

135. Williams Report, para. 5.10.

136. TNA, HO 265/19, COFC minutes, June 30, 1978.

137. TNA, DPP 2/5459, Calder, deposition, Bow Street Magistrates Court, February 5, 1975.

138. LMA, GLC/DG/EL/01/453, "Film Censorship: 'More about the Language of Love': Summing up, Central Criminal Court 5 June 1975," appendix B of "Court Decision (5.6.75) re 'More about the Language of Love'; Council's Rules of Management," report by Director General and Solicitor and Parliamentary Officer, July 4, 1975.

139. Tim Rogan, *The Moral Economists: Self, Society and the Critique of Capitalism in Twentieth-Century Britain* (Princeton: Princeton University Press, 2018), 25–32; Marc Stears, *Progressives, Pluralists, and the Problems of the State: Ideologies of Reform in the United States and Britain, 1909–1926* (Oxford: Oxford University Press, 2002); Jan-Werner Müller, *Contesting Democracy: Political Ideas in Twentieth-Century Europe* (New Haven: Yale University Press, 2011), 50–54.

140. *OED*, s.v. "pluralism," n. 4; *Education for All: The Report of the Committee of Inquiry into the Education of Children from Ethnic Minority Groups*, Cmnd. 9453 (London: HMSO, 1985), para. 4.

141. TNA, HO 265/4, Defence of Literature and the Arts Society, submission to COFC, March 1978.

142. TNA, HO 265/6, National Campaign for the Reform of the Obscene Publications Acts, submission to COFC, April 1978.

143. TNA, HO 265/88, Robin Smythe to Davey, August 4, 1978.

144. Mathew Thomson, *Lost Freedom: The Landscape of the Child and the British Post-War Settlement* (Oxford: Oxford University Press, 2013), 168–79.

145. *Report of the Committee on the Future of Broadcasting*, Cmnd. 6753 (London: HMSO, 1977), para. 4.5. See also para. 9.31: "Those of us who feel that the time has come to divide BBC Radio and Television do so after deep thought. We act in accordance with the concept of pluralism which has been the *leit motiv* of all of us in this report." For connections between procensorship sentiment and opposition to the BBC's power, see *Longford Report*, 227; on broadcasting and ideas about competition, see Adrian Johns, *Death of a Pirate: British Radio and the Making of the Information Age* (New York: W. W. Norton, 2011).

146. Thatcher herself had been a sponsor of the 1973 Indecent Displays Bill.

147. TNA, HO 265/18, R. Creedon, "Note for the File," September 7, 1979.

148. Martin Durham, *Sex and Politics: The Family and Morality in the Thatcher Years* (Basingstoke: Macmillan, 1991), 80.

149. Simpson, *Pornography and Politics*, 47–50.

150. Simpson, *Pornography and Politics*, 50. Over the next few years this pattern was repeated. The government's "strategy" in this area, a civil servant wrote, was to act through private member's bills (much as Roy Jenkins did in the sixties, though the official did not draw that parallel). TNA, PREM 19/1792, "Obscene Publications Act," paper prepared by the Home Office and accompanying W. R. Fittall to P. A. Bearpark, September 26, 1986.

151. TNA, PREM 19/1792, Hartley Booth, "Meeting on Obscenity—4.30 pm, Wednesday 1 October 1986," notes for Thatcher. An example is the idea of basing an antipornography law on a list of the poses and sex acts that could not be shown: PREM 19/1792, "Brief for Prime Minister's Meeting with Lord Nugent to Discuss His Draft Bill to Reform the Obscene Publications Acts on Monday, 6 February at 11 A.M.," February 1984; Williams Report, paras. 9.23–24.

Conclusion

1. TNA, PREM 19/1792, Mary Whitehouse to Margaret Thatcher, July 21, 1986; also Michael Alison to Thatcher, December 15, 1983.

2. TNA, PREM 19/1792, "Obscenity: Present Law," Home Office briefing document, August 1986.

3. Matthew Grimley, "Thatcherism, Morality and Religion," in *Making Thatcher's Britain*, ed. Ben Jackson and Robert Saunders (Cambridge: Cambridge University Press, 2012), 78–94, 80.

4. TNA, PREM 19/1792, Timothy Flesher to Nigel Pantling, February 6, 1984; Nugent to Thatcher, December 12, 1983; John M. Finnis, "Reason and Passion: The Constitutional Dialectic of Free Speech and Obscenity," *University of Pennsylvania Law Review* 116 (1967–68): 222–43; John Finnis, *Natural Law and Natural Rights* (Oxford: Clarendon Press, 1980).

5. TNA, PREM 19/1792, Alison to Thatcher, December 15, 1983.

6. TNA, PREM 19/1792, "Obscene Publications Act," paper prepared by the Home Office and accompanying W. R. Fittall to P. A. Bearpark, September 26, 1986.

7. TNA, PREM 19/1792, Alan King-Hamilton to Thatcher, August 5, 1986. King-Hamilton was Jewish, like several others on whom Thatcher leaned as she thought through questions of public morality: Grimley, "Thatcherism, Morality and Religion," 85, 92.

8. TNA, PREM 19/1792, King-Hamilton to Thatcher, August 5, 1986.

9. Adrian Bingham, *Family Newspapers? Sex, Private Life, and the British Popular Press 1918–1978* (Oxford: Oxford University Press, 2009), 221.

10. The Minneapolis hearings are documented in Catharine A. MacKinnon and Andrea Dworkin, eds., *In Harm's Way: The Pornography Civil Rights Hearings* (Cambridge, MA: Harvard University Press, 1997), 39–268.

11. All quotations from Clare Short, "Introduction" to *Dear Clare: This Is What Women Feel about Page Three*, ed. Kiri Tunks and Diane Hutchinson (London: Hutchinson Radius, 1991).

12. Barbara Norden, "Campaign against Pornography," *Feminist Review*, no. 35 (Summer 1990): 1–8. On connections with conservatives, including Johnston and CARE, see Martin Durham, *Sex and Politics: The Family and Morality in the Thatcher Years* (Basingstoke: Macmillan, 1991), 97–98.

13. "Fighting Pornography: New Campaign Launched," *Spare Rib*, May 1989, 39–41, 39.

14. American Booksellers v. Hudnut 771 F 2d 323 (1985) (Seventh Circuit Court of Appeals) affirmed, 475 U.S. 1001 (1986) (United States Supreme Court). Itzin edited a volume that included contributions by MacKinnon and Dworkin. Catherine Itzin, ed., *Pornography: Women, Violence, and Civil Liberties* (Oxford: Oxford University Press, 1992).

15. See Katharine Gelber and Adrienne Stone, "Constitutions, Gender and Freedom of Expression: The Legal Regulation of Pornography," in *Constitutions and Gender*, ed. Helen Irving (Cheltenham: Edward Elgar, 2017), 463–81, esp. 468, 475–76.

16. Julie Bindel, "Catherine Itzin Obituary," *Guardian*, April 14, 2010.

17. For a detailed account of the origins of the video classification scheme, see Julian Petley, *Film and Video Censorship in Contemporary Britain* (Edinburgh: Edinburgh University Press, 2011), chaps. 1–3. For Davey, see Paul Bonner with Lesley Aston, *Independent Television in Britain*, vol. 6, *New Developments in Independent Television, 1981–92: Channel 4, TV-am, Cable and Satellite* (Basingstoke: Palgrave Macmillan, 2003), 406.

18. Durham, *Sex and Politics*, 84.

19. Durham, *Sex and Politics*, 86.

20. TNA, PREM 19/1792, Brittan to Whitehouse, October 10, 1983; Flesher to Thatcher, October 25, 1983.

21. TNA, PREM 19/1792, Whitehouse to Flesher, n.d. (October 1983).

22. The Thatcher government had also made a show of abolishing quangos. See Michael Cole, "Quangos: The Debate of the 1970s in Britain," *Contemporary British History* 19, no. 3 (2005): 321–52, 339–42.

23. TNA, PREM 19/1792, Brittan to Thatcher, January 19, 1984. The legislation, which was passed in 1984, included provision for appeals against classification decisions. Video Recordings Act, 1984, c. 39, s. 4(3). The lack of an appeals mechanism had been one of the Williams Committee's criticisms of the BBFC. After 1984 the BBFC's remit also included video games, though "computer games" would be more accurate for the early years. The games classified in the 1980s tended to be text-based adventure games.

24. Petley, *Film and Video Censorship*, chaps. 4, 7, 10; Alan Travis, *Bound and Gagged: A Secret History of Obscenity in Britain* (London: Profile Books, 2000), 281–86.

25. Travis, *Bound and Gagged*, 281; "The Last Temptation of Christ," accessed March 23, 2020, https://bbfc.co.uk/case-studies/last-temptation-christ.

26. It was not even certain that the common law applied to Christian denominations other than Anglicanism, except insofar as their tenets overlapped. Bowman v. Secular Society Limited [1917] AC 406; Russell Sandberg and Norman Doe, "The Strange Death of Blasphemy," *Modern Law Review* 71, no. 6 (2008): 971–86, 978.

27. TNA, LCO 72/258, Bishop of London's Group on Blasphemy, "Offences against Religion and Public Worship," c. January 1988.

28. TNA, LCO 72/258, N. Hodgson, "Law Commission Report No. 145: Offences against Religion and Public Worship," March 21, 1988.

29. TNA, LCO 72/258, R. E. Hawkes to Mr Sanderson, March 16, 1988.

30. *HC Deb.*, April 12, 1989, col. 908 (Tony Benn, calling for abolition, as he had after *Gay News*); TNA, LCO 72/258, Waddington to John Wakeham, July 6, 1989; Waddington to Howe, March 5, 1990; Howe to Waddington, March 9, 1990. Perhaps anticipating endless debate about what constituted a religion (cases about the Church of Scientology were already snaking through courts in several jurisdictions), the Conservative MP Harry Greenway introduced a bill itemizing the faiths covered—Christianity, Islam, Hinduism, Sikhism, Judaism, Buddhism. TNA, LCO 72/258, Waddington to Howe, March 20, 1990.

31. Rita Chin, *The Crisis of Multiculturalism in Europe: A History* (Princeton: Princeton University Press, 2017), 182.

32. "Minister Rules out Blasphemy Law for Islam," *Independent*, July 7, 1989. Ellipsis in original.

33. And seditious libel, on the grounds that *The Satanic Verses* stirred up ill-will between different classes of Her Majesty's subjects. This was the branch of seditious libel that had been used unsuccessfully against anti-Semites in the 1930s and 1940s, and which section 6 of the Race Relations Act 1965 supplanted (but did not repeal): Christopher Hilliard, "Words That Disturb the State: Hate Speech and the Lessons of Fascism in Britain, 1930s-1960s," *Journal of Modern History*, 88, no. 4 (December 2016): 764–96. The magistrate and the Divisional Court ignored this byway of sedition law and held that the action had to be directed at the state.

34. R v. Chief Metropolitan Stipendiary Magistrate, ex parte Choudhury [1991] 1 All ER 309 at 319; Robert McCorquodale, "Blasphemous Verses," *Cambridge Law Journal* 50, no. 1 (1991): 22–24.

35. "Visions of Ecstasy," accessed March 23, 2020, https://bbfc.co.uk/case-studies /visions-ecstasy.

36. Wingrove v. United Kingdom (1997) 24 EHRR 1.

37. TNA, LCO 72/258, Kenneth Clarke to Sir Nicholas Lyell, May 27, 1992.

38. TNA, LCO 72/258, Lyell to Clarke, June 4, 1992.

39. George Letsas, "Two Concepts of the Margin of Appreciation," *Oxford Journal of Legal Studies* 26 (2006): 705–32.

40. *Wingrove v. United Kingdom*, paras. 53–57. No anticensorship campaigner had a success on a par with Ross McWhirter's comrades, who secured a posthumous victory for him by suspending their aversion to European institutions and successfully persuading the Strasbourg court that the trade union closed shop was incompatible with the European Convention's guarantee of freedom of association. [Lord Harris of High Cross, rev. by Marc Brodie, "McWhirter, (Alan) Ross, 1925-1975," *ODNB*; Young, James and Webster v. United Kingdom [1981] ECHR 4.

41. *Wingrove v. United Kingdom*, para. 57.

42. Sandberg and Doe, "Strange Death of Blasphemy," esp. 981; House of Lords Select Committee on Religious Offences in England and Wales, *First Report*, vol. 1, HL 95-I, 2003, appendix 3, para. 12. See also Ian Hunter, "English Blasphemy," *Humanity* 4, no. 3 (2013): 403–28, 417–20; Elliott Visconsi, "The Invention of Criminal Blasphemy: Rex v. Taylor (1676)," *Representations*, no. 103 (Summer 2008): 30–52, 45–47.

43. For other manifestations of this principle, see Susan Pedersen, *The Guardians: The League of Nations and the Crisis of Empire* (Oxford: Oxford University

Press, 2015), 4; Stephen Lovell, "'Glasnost' in Practice: Public Speaking in the Era of Alexander II," *Past and Present*, no. 218 (February 2013): 127–58.

44. R (on the application of Stephen Green) v. City of Westminster Magistrates' Court and Others [2007] EWHC (Admin) 2785; Sandberg and Doe, "Strange Death of Blasphemy," 981–84.

45. An early example involving charges under the Obscene Publications Act is R v. Perrin [2002] EWCA Crim 747.

46. Quoted in Travis, *Bound and Gagged*, 289.

47. Adrian Johns, *Death of a Pirate: British Radio and the Making of the Information* Age (New York: W. W. Norton, 2011), 251–54.

48. Jacob Rowbottom, "The Transformation of Obscenity Law," *Information and Communications Technology Law* 27 (2018): 4–29, 27, table A2.

49. The CPS adds: "Non-consent for adults must be distinguished from consent to relinquish control." "Obscene Publications," revised January 2019, accessed March 25, 2020 https://www.cps.gov.uk/legal-guidance/obscene-publications. The Obscene Publications Act was amended in 1994 to cover electronic publication. Criminal Justice and Public Order Act, 1994, c. 33, s. 168(1), schedule 9, paragraph 3.

50. Criminal Justice and Immigration Act, 2008, c. 4, s. 63.

51. Clare McGlynn and Hannah Bows, "Possessing Extreme Pornography: Policing, Prosecutions and the Need for Reform," *Journal of Criminal Law* 83 (2019): 473–88, 481–82.

52. M. A. McCarthy and R. A. Moodie, "Parliament and Pornography: The 1978 Child Protection Act," *Parliamentary Affairs* 34, no. 1 (1981): 47–62, 53, 62.

53. Suzanne Ost, *Child Pornography and Sexual Grooming: Legal and Societal Responses* (Cambridge: Cambridge University Press, 2009), 55–56.

54. Rowbottom, "Transformation of Obscenity Law," 28, table A3.

55. Rowbottom, "Transformation of Obscenity Law," 24.

56. A.W.B. Slmpson, *Cannlbullsm und the Common Luw. The Stoiy uf the Tiugic Last Voyage of the Mignonette and the Strange Legal Proceedings to Which It Gave Rise* (Chicago: University of Chicago Press, 1984), 244.

57. Peter Mandler, *The English National Character: The History of an Idea from Edmund Burke to Tony Blair* (New Haven: Yale University Press, 2006), 83.

58. Hilliard, "Words That Disturb the State," 764–65, criticizing Lisa Z. Sigel, "Censorship in Inter-war Britain: Obscenity, Spectacle, and the Workings of the Liberal State," *Journal of Social History* 45 (2011): 61–83, 76.

59. TNA, HO 376/3, Andrew Martin and Cedric Thornberry, "Memorandum concerning the draft Bill prepared by the Committee on Racial Discrimination and Incitement of the Society of Labour Lawyers," July 7, 1964.

60. Richard P. Longaker, "The Race Relations Act of 1965: An Evaluation of the Incitement Provision," *Race* 11 (1969): 125–56, 144–45.

61. Pierre Bourdieu, *The Rules of Art: Genesis and Structure of the Literary Field*, trans. Susan Emanuel (Cambridge: Polity Press, 1996), part 1; Anton Kirchofer, "The Making of the 1959 Obscene Publications Act: Trials and Debates on Literary Obscenity in Britain before the Case of Lady Chatterley," in *Literary Trials: Exceptio Artis and Theories of Literature in Court*, ed. Ralf Grüttemeier (New York: Bloomsbury Academic, 2016), 49–68.

62. Ian Hamilton, "Cutting Candy Dead," *Listener*, September 12, 1968, 341.

63. *Censorship in the Arts: The Full Text of the Freedom of Vision Teach-in, Held at Hampstead Old Town Hall, October 2nd 1966 from 3 p.m. till 10 p.m.* (London: Academy of Visual Arts, n.d.), 11–13.

64. Williams Report, para. 5.24.

65. Jon Lawrence uses the phrase "vernacular liberalism" in "Labour and the Culture Wars of Modern Politics," *Political Quarterly* 91, no. 1 (January-March 2020): 31–34, which draws on his book *Me, Me, Me? The Search for Community in Post-war England* (Oxford: Oxford University Press, 2019). In an earlier article, I spoke instead of "vernacular libertarianism" (Hilliard, "Words That Disturb the State," 795–96). "Vernacular liberalism" seems more accurate given my argument in chapter 8 about the Wolfenden principle and neighborly conventions.

66. The classic statement is J. B. Priestley, *English Journey* (1934; repr., Harmondsworth: Penguin, 1977), 376. See also Christopher Hilliard, *To Exercise Our Talents: The Democratization of Writing in Britain* (Cambridge, MA: Harvard University Press, 2006), 287–90; D. L. LeMahieu, *A Culture for Democracy: Mass Communication and the Cultivated Mind in Britain between the Wars* (Oxford: Clarendon Press, 1988).

67. TNA, CUST 49/4712, "Importation of Indecent or Obscene Books and Other Articles," n.d. (1957).

68. Compare Rowbottom, "Transformation of Obscenity Law," 25.

69. The subjects of these cases were insufficient protection of a journalist's sources under electronic surveillance; television companies' bans on advertisements by animal rights' organizations; a tabloid's breach of a celebrity's privacy; a court order prohibiting media coverage of a trial; a court order to disclose a leaked document; a claimant's right to receive information from the government about the chemical weapons tests he participated in in the early 1960s; whether denial of the vote to a convicted criminal infringed their freedom of expression; the unavailability of legal aid in defamation suits; being denied permission to solicit signatures for a petition in a shopping mall. Given the time lag between the final decision of a UK court or tribunal and a hearing in Strasbourg, these cases reflect the impact of post-9/11 surveillance and the ferment over media ethics and investigative journalism that led to the Leveson inquiry of 2011/2012 rather than very recent developments. Joanna Dawson, "UK Cases at the European Court of Human Rights since 1975," House of Commons Library Briefing Paper no. CBP 8049, December 19, 2019; Lord Justice Leveson, *An Inquiry into the Culture, Practices and Ethics of the Press*, HC 780-I, 4 vols (London: The Stationery Office, 2012).

MANUSCRIPT SOURCES

Bodleian Library, Oxford
  H. A. Gwynne Papers
  Roy Jenkins Papers

British Library, London
  Lord Chamberlain's Plays Correspondence
  Society of Authors Archive

Cambridge University Library
  David Holbrook Papers

Harry Ransom Humanities Research Center, University of Texas at Austin
  James Hanley Papers
  Storm Jameson Papers
  Ottoline Morrell Papers
  Hugh Walpole Papers

Hull History Centre
  Liberty Archive

King's College Archive Centre, Cambridge
  E. M. Forster Papers

Lilly Library, Indiana University, Bloomington
  Calder and Boyars Papers

London Metropolitan Archives
  Greater London Council Papers
  Public Morality Council Papers

London School of Economics
  Defence of Literature and the Arts Society Papers
  C. H. Rolph Papers

London School of Economics/Women's Library
  Sally Alexander Papers
  National Vigilance Association Papers

The National Archives, London
  Cabinet (CAB)
  Central Criminal Court (CRIM)
  Customs and Excise (CUST)
  Director of Public Prosecutions (DPP)
  Foreign Office (FO)
  Home Office (HO)

Law Officers (LO)
Lord Chancellor's Office (LCO)
Metropolitan Police (MEPO)
Prime Minister's Office (PREM)
Supreme Court of Judicature (J)

Postal Archives, London
Royal Mail Archive (POST)

State Library of New South Wales, Sydney
P. R. Stephensen Papers

Trinity College Archives, Cambridge
R. A. Butler Papers

Tyne and Wear Archives Service, Newcastle
Newcastle Writers' Club Minutes

University of Bristol Library
Penguin Archive

University of London Library, Senate House
Alec Craig Papers
Charles Lahr Papers
Louis Sterling Library

University of Reading Library
John Wolfenden Papers

University of Sussex, Brighton
Mass-Observation Archive

Victoria and Albert Museum, London
Arts Council of Great Britain Papers

INDEX

Locators in italics refer to figures.

A NOTE ON THE TYPE

THIS BOOK has been composed in Miller, a Scotch Roman typeface designed by Matthew Carter and first released by Font Bureau in 1997. It resembles Monticello, the typeface developed for The Papers of Thomas Jefferson in the 1940s by C. H. Griffith and P. J. Conkwright and reinterpreted in digital form by Carter in 2003.

Pleasant Jefferson ("P. J.") Conkwright (1905–1986) was Typographer at Princeton University Press from 1939 to 1970. He was an acclaimed book designer and AIGA Medalist.

The ornament used throughout this book was designed by Pierre Simon Fournier (1712–1768) and was a favorite of Conkwright's, used in his design of the *Princeton University Library Chronicle*.